ALL THE IRON MEN

Welcome to Heaven Boys, We're Already Served our Time in Hell

A Novel of the Pacific War

by

Robert E. Wilhelm III

CONTENTS

BOOK I: *"ALOHA" MEANS GOODBYE*.....6

BOOK II: *INTO THE JAWS OF THE TIGER*.....113

BOOK III: *TYPHOON*.....265

BOOK IV: *ABOVE US, HELL*.....337

Dear Reader,

    Thank you for your purchase of this publication. Because of it, a donation has been made to the two Veterans charities noted on the back cover. Our Veterans are a National Treasure. Thank you for helping them and their families.

Copyright 1996

WGAW Reg # 1515594

QuarterDeck Entertainment LLC

www.quarterdeckent.com

DEDICATION

**TO MY PARENTS,
FOR GIVING ME LIFE, ALL YOUR LOVE, CARE & INSTRUCTION,**

**TO MY MOTHER,
FOR MY APPRECIATION & LOVE OF THE '40'S ERA AND THAT GREAT BIG BAND SOUND**

**TO MY FATHER,
HIMSELF A VETERAN U.S. NAVY SUBMARINER WHO SERVED IN DIESEL BOATS & WHO INTRODUCED ME TO THE SEA AND ALL ITS UNDERWATER WONDERMENT**

AND TO THE GREATEST GENERATION OF AMERICANS WHO EVER LIVED.

PEARL HARBOR, HAWAII:
JANUARY 1942

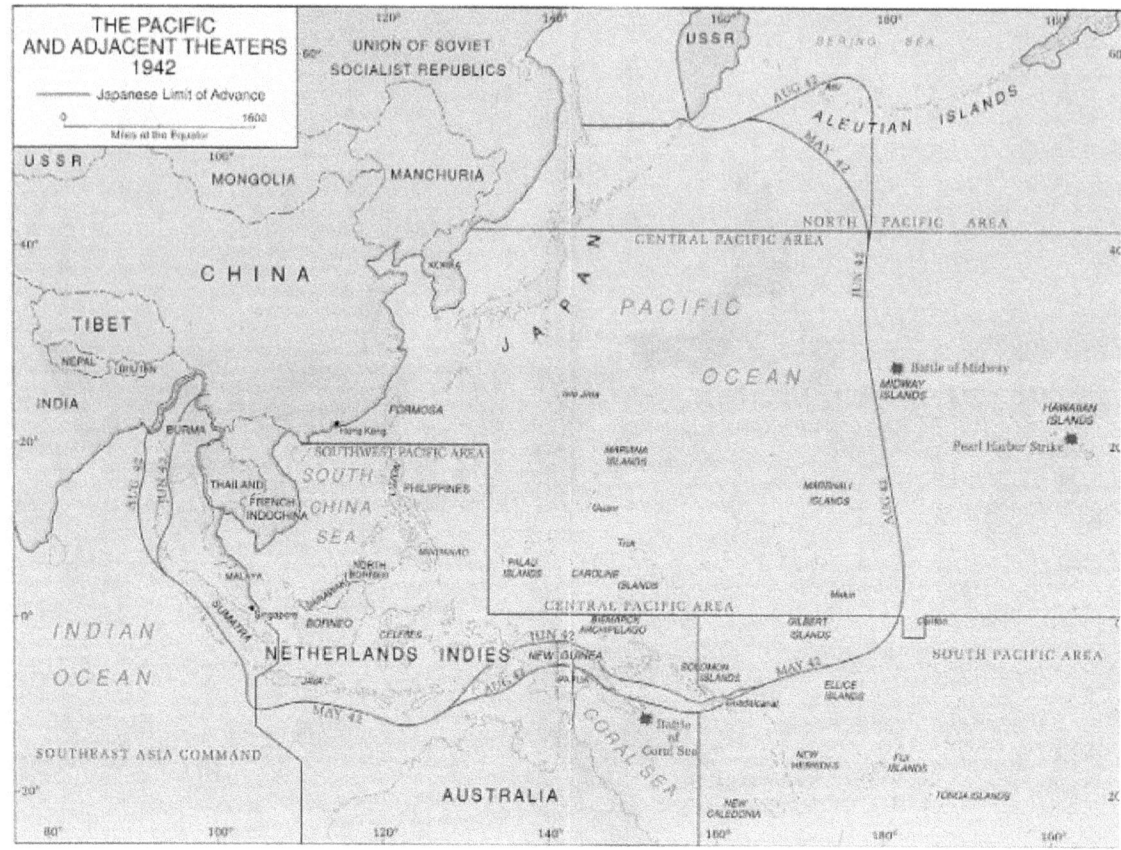

The Rising Sun of Imperial Japan is ascendant over the entire Pacific Ocean west of the Hawaiian Islands. The forces of the Empire of Japan are victorious at every turn. After inflicting a crushing defeat on the American Navy during the sneak attack on Pearl Harbor, following in quick succession are an enormously triumphant string of Japanese blitzkrieg campaigns; Wake Island is invaded and its garrison completely wiped out. In Hong Kong, the isolated British forces are not expected to hold out more than two months. In the Philippines, a disaster unrivaled in U.S. history looms for the beleaguered American and Filipino defenders. Cut-off from re-supply by the absolute Japanese supremacy of the waves, their future bodes little for them except hunger, disease, starvation, and death. Australia is isolated and is itself fighting for survival against the advancing Japanese might. The American West Coast is wide open for a Japanese invasion that is considered imminent. In the north Japanese Forces are massing to invade America proper: Attu and Kiska are soon to be under assault. With the bulk of the U.S. Pacific Fleet crippled by the surprise Japanese attack on December 7, there is but one small, unbroken - yet untested - reserve left; the U.S. Submarine Force, Pacific Fleet.

It is they who must hold the line and if necessary, sacrifice themselves to stem the exultant tide of the Rising Sun. With antiquated equipment and even greener crews, they are ordered out to strike the first blows at a country protected by the most fearsome naval force in recorded history.

They faced the impossible and unquestioningly sailed into the jaws of the tiger. For many never returned, and lie still and entombed in their iron coffins at the bottom of the sea. Linked forevermore by that common bond of men grasped together in a struggle to the death on raging seas, they forged a bond of iron that will transcend generations for all time.

It is for them, in memorial, that this book was written.

> There are no roses on a sailor's grave,
> No lilies on an ocean wave,
> The only tribute is the seagulls sweeps,
> and the tears that a sweetheart weeps.
> - GERMAN SONG

Author's Note:

Although a novel, this is not a work of fiction. The journey upon which you are about to embark is one of truth, only in the characters does fiction enter the equation. Each event that follows was actually experienced by an American Submarine Crew during the undersea war against Japan. Painstaking research has been undertaken to assure accuracy in all details, events, and equipment. No similarities between any persons - living or deceased - is intended. Any errors or misinterpretations which follow are solely the fault of the author.

Book I:

'Aloha' means 'Goodbye'...

Over forty hours now...over forty hours of relentless pounding under high explosive. Temperature here in after engine room an easy hundred and ten degrees. Men are becoming incoherent. Many beginning to rave. Must we continue to suffer like this? Oh Death, please come! Please release us from this blistering hell of heat and high explosive. There is no air anymore. Our mouths hang open as we attempt to suck what little remains into our tortured lungs. Our vision is blurred from searing, skull-splitting headaches. The Gunner's mate collapses beside me, his body convulsing into spasmodic vomiting. Through the semi-darkness I can no longer see his face - it's a blessing. Please God, just take us. Take us swiftly. Let this torture continue not one moment more. Let us be released from this scorching Hades...

A weak voice croaks behind me - someone's attempting to sing...

> The Minstrel Boy to the war has gone...
>
> In the ranks of death you'll find him,
>
> His father's sword he hath girded on..
>
> And his wild harp slung behind him...

The journey here began a hundred years ago, when I was a boy. I am that no longer, but a weak and crippled old man...

  *   *   *

The ocean breeze that wafts over Diamond Head is heavy with the taste of salt. The roar of the breakers crashing against the steep lava-rock cliffs seemingly echoes on into eternity. The sun throws its last flecks of light across the horizon, turning the crystal blue Pacific a deep shade of amber. The sounds of the night are there: insects chirp, wheeze, and click. A hundred species of tropical birds twitter and flutter about, and the palm fronds rustle gently and whisper their secrets in the wind. All blend peacefully with the lonely singsong notes of the omnipresent seagulls, forming their own collage of nature's music. Seabirds noisily flutter from one tidal pool to the next, pecking around for baitfish trapped inside the rocky tarns by the outgoing tide.

Beside me, the Skipper leans against the car. A 1936 white convertible Auburn Boattail Speedster, a car seemingly more suited to a Hollywood film star than an underpaid naval officer. Snare drum sized headlights protrude in front of the hood like gigantic eyes. Gleaming running boards accent each side from hood to trunk, like shoulders of stainless steel. A resplendent white leather interior and gleaming chromed exhaust pipes - three on each side - project from the long engine cowling. Spotless thick-band whitewall tires; the impeccably styled spare tire carrier; the fold-down, chrome-edged windscreen - a picture of extravagant splendor I've never seen the likes of before. The Skipper produces a gold cigarette case from his white dress jacket, opens it, and neatly withdraws a cigarette with long, masculine fingers.

"Nice out here, isn't it?"

Silently I nod. A loud rumble; grand breakers are swirling and smashing into the jagged cliffs below.

He chuckles a briefly. "With such beauty it's hard to believe there's a war on." He is still a moment, the cigarette momentarily forgotten in his left hand. "You heard Manila ran up the white flag this morning. Weren't able to hold out a month."

"Yes sir." Manila - capital of the Philippine Islands, finally succumbed to the ever-advancing Japanese. I watch as a flame shoots out of the top of his lighter and connects with the end of his cigarette. Even in the rapidly approaching darkness, the glow of the lighter flame illuminates the verdigris-tinged double golden dolphin insignia on his collar. The much coveted double dolphins; in gold for officers and silver for the enlisted men, denote a unique and very special cadre. Part of a small crack caste of men meticulously selected for the most perilous duty ever known to the seafarer. All volunteers to a man; submariner - the elite!

Lt. Comdr. John Tyreen shifts the cap back on his head and draws on his cigarette. His chiseled features accented by an unruly shock of blond hair, usually hidden underneath his cap, perpetually worn at a jaunty angle. He's now in command of the boat I'm to ship out on - the *USS Bullhead*. A boat that even in the youth of this war has already seen heavy action. The *Bullhead*'s previous commander was killed during the first patrol.

He's distracted and introspective. He's barely spoken all evening. When he does, his words come out in sharp, clipped phrases that shed little light on his innermost thoughts. He came himself to collect me once I received my orders today for the *Bullhead*. Introducing himself and explaining away his interest in coming personally as if it revealed some weakness. Even now, he stares quietly out over the vast rolling sea as if it held some deep, dark secret. Tomorrow dawns a new patrol. Is this the reason to his taciturn manner? My nerves get more brittle by the hour.

"Ever been to a *luau*?"

Having only been in Hawaii two days I haven't had time to do anything and respond as much.

"Well, let's get you an education then."

Five minutes later we're roaring down the coast road that runs from Diamond Head around Maunalua Bay towards Makapuu Point, as the Skipper informs me that our destination is off the coast road on Koko Head. He hunches forward out of the wind and lights another cigarette, then lets out a rebel yell as he slams the Speedster into high gear and taking the next curve with such force it slams me back into the white leather seat. A glance over at him shows a hunched figure with an evil grin; he's clearly enjoying himself. A kid with a new toy on Christmas morning. We take the next curve at breakneck speed and come roaring up behind a slower moving car. The Skipper curses and downshifts, the engine growling in protest and lurching me forward in the seat. The car in front of us is moving no faster than thirty-five or forty miles per hour.

Cursing, the Skipper slams the engine into high gear and whips the Speedster madly into the left lane. Snaking around a sharp curve, we're nearly blinded by the glaring headlights of a truck barely fifty yards away. Involuntarily I cry out as the Skipper whips the Speedster into the right lane in the nick of time - missing the truck by mere yards.

My stomach sits in my throat. There is a lighthearted chuckle beside me. "Something wrong?"

"That was close!" is all I can manage.

The Skipper shrugs it off. "Ensign, you're in 'the boats' now. As a submariner, you earn your pay by cheating death. You must get used to that."

"Sir." "The 'boats" - truly a submariner's term. Any other type of vessel in the Navy is referred to as a "ship." But a submarine is always a 'boat.'

Suddenly we're on a secondary road, which is really nothing more than a dirt track bordered by sugar cane fields on either side. We rumble along this farm track for what seems like an eternity until parked cars and jeeps loom up under the glare of our headlights. Figures moving about. In the air is the definite bass beat of drums. The Skipper pulls the car off to the side and kills the engine. "This is it." Grabbing his cap, he hops out of the car.

Drums, shouting, yelling, laughing - sounds like this *luau* is a real blowout.

"Every boat in the fleet must be here." The Skipper observes, stroll three steps ahead of me through the soft, white sand. We move past the parked vehicles, in which several figures lie sprawled in inebriated slumber. To the right, a group of petty officers shoot a game of craps on the hood of a jeep. To the left, a group of bluejackets sing "Anchors Aweigh" drunkenly and off-key. We pass close enough so that they hastily come to attention and salute. The Skipper returns it without so much as a glance in their direction. By the flickering light of the tiki lamps, a hundred or so bodies move around. The Skipper stops in mid stride in front of two officers, each with a young Hawaiian girl on each arm and a bottle of beer in each hand. One of them quickly recognizes the Skipper, drops his arm from around the girl's waist and tries to manage a salute while coming to attention, while still holding the beer in his left hand. His movements are sluggish and exaggerated.

"Captain Tyreen sir," the figure stammers, 'Good to see you!"

The Skipper nods. "All three of me. Our XO - Lt. Bainbridge, and our Engineering officer Schumacher. Gentlemen, meet our newest junior officer,' he says, gesturing at me, 'Ensign Alvin Watts - fresh from the States."

They stare at me with sort of a semi-scowl. Eyes narrowed and faces tight; you'd think I was the enemy. I come to attention with a salute that's never returned.

"Welcome aboard Ensign!" They reply, teetering from side to side. The Hawaiian girls giggle; they both appear to be sober. Both wear native Hawaiian clothes - grass skirts and skimpy cloth coverings over their breasts.

The Skipper glances around. "Good turnout."

The fellow pointed out to me as the XO clears his throat. "So far we've got the better part of three boats crews, *Wahoo, Skipjack, and* us."

"And Waldron and Pike?"

"They'll be along shortly sir,' the XO stammers through a belch, 'I took their duty report two hours ago; all provisions and torpedoes loaded aboard. The boat is clear for sea."

The Skipper snaps off a salute. "Very good Mr. Bainbridge." He turns to me, a wry smile on his face, "How 'bout some gasoline?"

On the beach now. The roar of the breaking surf mixes with the heavy beat of Hawaiian drums. A million ghosts and apparitions dance dreamily across the sand, cast there by the blazing tiki lamps and torches. There must be close to at least a hundred people here, some dancing - all drinking - some strolling near the surf with a Hawaiian girl or local nurse in tow. The Skipper exchanges a few words with one of the local Hawaiian men. A moment later I'm surrounded by three Hawaiian girls slipping floral *leis* around my neck, smiling and chattering incessantly

"*Aloha*" and other words in their native language I do not understand. The man to whom the Skipper was speaking approaches me - takes my hand -and starts pumping it up and down.

"*Aloha malihini, aloha malihini!*"

"Huh?"

The Skipper is beside me. "He says, 'welcome newcomer.'"

The man starts chattering away, still pumping my arm like a derrick. Then he takes my hand in both of his and looks straight into my eyes. The chuckling voice beside me is the Skipper.

"Sir, I don't understand."

"My Hawaiian isn't all that good, ' the Skipper advises, 'but he wants to know if you're going to go out and kill lots of Japs for him."

At the mention of the word "Japs", the man screws up his face and spits. "Japs!" Balls of saliva are smacking into the sand below him. "Japs....putuuooee! They bomb my home! You kill lots of Japs yes?"

"I'll try sir." He immediately launches into more Hawaiian chatter.

"He says it's time for you to have a drink and something to eat."

I return the smile. "Thank you -'

"*Mahalo-*" the Skipper corrects, "*Mahalo*' means 'thank you'." I repeat this, and the man seems enormously pleased. He laughs uproariously, slaps me on the shoulder with such force it almost knocks me off balance. The Skipper beckons, and leads me through a crowd toward a large hole dug in the sand filled with ice and beer. A smiling young Hawaiian boy standing beside it looks at us expectantly and holds up two fingers. The Skipper nods and the boy bends down and pulls two bottles out of the ice. Popping the tops, he hands them to us as the Skipper hands him a few dollars. The boy bows gratefully, then turns away.

"Hey Tyreen!" the shout comes from behind. We turn around to see two khaki figures advancing toward us. "Tyreen! You made it!" The figures come loping up in an alcohol-affected swagger. The figures stop in front of us, panting for breath. They're officers, but their uniform coats hang open, ties droop loosely round open collars, and their shirts cling to them with sweat. "How's this for a blowout huh?" the one on my left declares, rubbing his free hand into a well-tailored beard. "Was afraid you weren't going to make it."

'Thought you'd spend your last night running around in that Hollywood set of wheels with one of your rich girlfriends." The other taunts through a crooked smile.

"Now who said my girlfriends were rich?" The Skipper demands good-naturedly.

The two bearded officers exchange sly looks and burst out laughing. "Oh come on John! Everybody knows the score with you, out romancing the Admiral's daughter, borrowing her car and all that! I'm surprised she hasn't got Dad to transfer you to a desk job in fleet ops, that way she knows you're safe and can keep an eye on you!"

The Skipper starts shifting uneasily from side to side.

"But then,' the other one says, 'he'd have to give up his other two dames! Hell - little Admiralette might even get you under the crossed swords!"

"Gentlemen,' the Skipper says firmly, 'a man's private liaisons are just that, so shall we leave them as such?"

The two grunt and giggle like drunk teenagers, then one of them thumps me on the chest. "Who's this in his class A's?"

"Our new ensign." the Skipper replies. "Ensign Watts, these are Lieutenants Pierce and -'

"These are Lieutenants Walker,' one of them leans close to me, extending a hand, 'from the *Wahoo,* best boat in the entire fleet!"

"Second best." The Skipper corrects with a smile.

"You had one hell of a first patrol John." Walker says, sipping his beer. "I heard about Jamison. He was a good man. I'm sorry."

"Yeah."

"Tin-can?" Pierce asks.

The Skipper nods.

"He had a wife, didn't he?"

The Skipper nods. "Two months."

"Oh Christ!'

"Now she's a widow." The one named Walker says, shaking his head and looking down into the sand. "There's going to be a lot more of those before this thing's over."

"Listen,' the fellow named Pierce says, taking a more upbeat tone, 'in exactly two zero minutes our boat is challenging the *Skipjack* to a drinking contest, interested?"

The Skipper guffaws. "Thanks, but I've got some business to tend to. "

Pierce flashes an evil grin. "Okay, it's your loss." Turning away, Walker thumps me in the chest again. "Take it easy kid. You'll do all right, you're with one of the best!" They disappear into the crowd.

"Over half of the crew is missing,' the Skipper observes, 'must all be down at the Forbidden City."

The Forbidden City: Honolulu's most notorious whorehouse, frequented by servicemen of all branches stationed here in the islands. In my brief two days on Oahu that was one of the first things I learned. How times haven't changed.

"I haven't been there sir."

The Skipper looks at me and flashes an evil grin. "Yet!" He takes another swig on his beer, "I've got to get going."

Falling in step behind him we move through the crowd, which is becoming larger and out of control. Prone bodies lay on the sand in every conceivable position with a bottle or glass full of something clutched in hand. Crewmen saunter about in grass skirts, stumbling and staggering with every step. A group of petty officers have their own "whiskey waterfall"; one man stands upright with a bottle of whiskey, the rest crawl on their backs on the sand underneath him, and try to keep the steadily pouring stream of whiskey in their mouths. To let the stream hit the sand is the unpardonable sin, as the guilty party is subjected to a chorus of insults and diatribes. Over here a group of bluejackets is learning to *hula* with a group of Hawaiian girls, who giggle and laugh at the men's drunken movements. I notice the Skipper shaking his head as we pass by.

"Their families' back home wouldn't believe it!" He says, straining to rise over the noise level and shaking his head in disbelief. "You know what happens when you join the navy? You get corrupted! If you go in as clean as starched linen, you come out soiled for life. We live fast because we tend to die young. Hey - you hungry?'

After loading up some plates of local food, sudden wild gunfire splits the night. Frenzied yelling. Terrified screams as women run in all directions. Bodies dive into the sand. Somebody's moaning.

"Ah - Pike must be here." The Skipper calmly observes.

"Sir?"

"Pike, our torpedo and gunnery officer." The Skipper starts moving toward the offending sound. "Relax,' the Skipper says, glancing back at me with a smile, 'he does this all the time." I follow him, counting the rounds that are ticking off. Within one minute I count several dozen. Then several figures loom out in the darkness. A myriad of ear-splitting roars, accompanied by wild hooting and hollering.

"That's a hit!"

"The hell it was! The bottle's still there!"

"You're full of shit! You can't even see!"

"You shoot like I spit!"

Somebody's singing. There's a beach chair with somebody in it. Two men stand beside it. Beer bottles litter the sand around them.

"Lt. Pike!" the Skipper calls out.

"Here sir!"

The two officers turn around. Two I've seen before during my posting to the *Bullhead;* it's the cigar-chomping Lieutenants Mike Michaelis, and the pipe-smoking John Waldron. The

Skipper is motioning at the beach chair. "Pike, we have a new virgin aboard!"

The Skipper steers me over to the beach chair, in which a rumpled figure is sprawled out. He does not have the presence of an officer; hair plastered messily to forehead, uniform all tussled, and a .45 pistol in his right hand. Unfocused eyes creep over me. "Oh, so you're the new guy? - Oh hey thanks! " He exclaims, dropping the .45 into his lap, and reaching for the plate of food I've unconsciously carried over from the *imu* pit. *Hey - that was...*

"How long you been in the boats?"

"I'm new sir." I say, watching him attack my plate with a vengeance.

"Been on a patrol before?"

"No sir."

"Ever been out to sea in one?"

"Yes sir, in an "S" boat, but not in one of the newer "fleet" types."

Pike snorts and sets the fork down and produces a fresh clip from his pocket. He slams it into the handgrip and snaps the slide forward. "You familiar with a .45?"

"Yes sir.'

"Good. Let's see what you can do with this." He says, shoving the weapon into my hand.

Michaelis drains his beer bottle, takes a few steps toward the surf, and flings the bottle out into the surf. *Are they serious?* "Sir, how am I supposed to see that?"

"Got to train your eyes cutie-pie!" Pike declares, still munching. "You're maybe twenty yards from that bottle. If you can't see that how are you going to spot a masthead barely poking above the horizon?"

Michaelis and Waldron stare back at me with fixed faces. "Go on, give a try."

Taking a deep breath, I raise the weapon. But I can't find the bottle; it's too dark and there's too much surf. I stare for what must be a full minute. A few times it does bob up - or at least I think it does - before disappearing again.

"This is impossible! It only shows itself for a second at a time."

"Precisely." Waldron agrees judiciously.

"That's the whole idea." Michaelis states, moving up even with me. "About two points off you're line of sight. There....you see?"

I don't, and not particularly caring anymore I squeeze off a few rounds just for show anyway. Michaelis grunts.

"Missed." Pike declares, pulling on his beer. "Want to see how it's really done?"

I hand him the weapon and step aside. Raising the .45, he stares down the barrel for a brief moment - then pulls the trigger. The resulting crash causes an explosion in the water and dozens of little geysers fan out for ten or twenty yards.

"See?' he says laconically, through a shit-eating grin, 'it is possible. You have to believe Ensign."

It is then that I notice the Skipper has slipped away, vanished like a shadow into the night.

Lt. j.g. Billy Lemert turns up with each arm wrapped around the waist of a Hawaiian girl. Besides me, he's the lowest ranking officer aboard and serves as commissary officer. He is a veteran though of the first patrol. A flaxen-haired California-type with an affected swagger. He struts up to me, smacking me sharply on the chest, "This is your last night here for a while,' he says, flipping his arm back tightly round one of the Hawaiian girls, 'Make sure you make the most of it!"

"What do you have in mind?"

"You really need to ask - or do you need some help?"

I shrug. "I'm new here Lieutenant."

Nodding his head, he looks at me sideways, stepping off down the beach. "I'll see what I can do."

Michaelis reappears, sloppy and intoxicated - barely able to stand. Weaving from side to side like a tree in a heavy wind. "Lemme at 'em! Jap bastards! *Bullhead*'s gonna kick some ass!" He yells at the top of his lungs, waving his fist in the air.

"Disgusting spectacle.' A gruff voice snaps behind me.

I turn around A short but powerful looking man waltzes through the sand across from us. "This is Chief Petty Officer Schrier, he's Chief of the boat' Waldron says.

"You meet the Chief yet?" Michaelis queries, chomping on his cigar.

I shake my head. "No sir."

Waldron nods his head toward him, "Schrier is a Chief Torpedoman's mate. He's been with the Bullhead since she was commissioned." Waldron proceeds to give me a brief overview of the crew; there's a new kid Yeoman - a redhead by the name of O'Toole. The Boatswain's mate, a Kansan, Duffy's, who is reputedly the best sonarman around. But the really loud and wild ones are the Torpedoman's mates, Waldron says. A real rough bunch. There's Daschler - a fellow built like a brick house, a guy whose biceps are so big he has to cut holes in the upper arms of his dungaree shirts just so his arms will fit in. Head's as bald as the moon and he's probably got the biggest tattoo collection in the entire Pacific Fleet . "All 'piss and vinegar' with fists," is how Waldron describes him. Then there's 'Tashtego', who'd a full-blooded Sioux Indian who's real name is Johnston Malakachee. Waldron isn't sure when the 'Tashtego' moniker started, but the name is pulled straight from Melville. Could have made petty officer by now if he'd quit knocking the shit out of shore patrols. Waldron says he's usually in the brig when not at sea as he's a real fighter. Two other petty officers are Copenhaver - a constant tobacco chewer - and Harmison, who's a quartermaster. Close behind there are the Electrician's mates, commonly referred to as "E-mates". The Motor Machinist mates, "Motormac's", and the Firemen, Radiomen, and Seamen. All together the boat's complement numbers some sixty-five men. Every man is a specialist in one area or another, but ready at a moment's notice to step into another man's post.

"You're lucky Watts,' Waldron says, "I'll stack these men up with any other boat in the fleet."

*   *   *

"I'm sorry Lieutenant, but my hands are tied." The Warrant Officer's tone is curt and condescending, without the slightest trace of sympathy. In contrast, he seems to relish our predicament. "This is, 'he continues, glaring at us like some high and mighty government bureaucrat, 'the third time this week that you submariners have committed mayhem someplace with your wild parties and all! If *Bullhead* isn't raising hell someplace, it's *Wahoo*, *Grampus*, or *Grayback*! You people spend more time bailing each other out of the brig than you do at sea!"

"Chief,' Michaelis intones forcefully, 'I need those men! We sail at oh eight hundred."

The Warrant Officer's head twitches. "I say again sir, I'm sorry. These are serious charges." His eyes flicker from Michaelis to me and then back again.

"Charges?" Michaelis' eyebrows jump. "We are speaking in a *plural* sense?"

"Yes sir." The Warrant Officer dons a pair of reading glasses as he opens the folder in front of him. "Let's see here....disturbing the peace, drunkenness, assault, willful and malicious destruction of property-'

"Wait a minute - assault? Willful and malicious destruction of property?' Michaelis stammers, incredulous. "Who filed these charges?"

"The Hawaiians sir."

"And they're seeking damages."

"I might have known. How much?"

"Three hundred dollars and eighty-five cents."

"*What*? Chief there isn't that much money on the entire boat, even including the officers."

"Well, that's not my problem sir." The Warrant Officer takes off his glasses, lays them down and leans back in his chair, folding his arms across his chest.

"Where are the Hawaiians?"

"Down at the infirmary. They're pretty banged up."

"Oh lovely. Look Chief, we can handle this real easy, otherwise the Captain's gonna be down here breathing fire. Just -'

"Sir,' the Warrant Officer interrupts, 'there's nothing I can do. Unless the Hawaiians drop the charges, which I can't see them doing, it's up to a board of inquiry."

Michaelis takes a deep breath, desperate to maintain his composure. "Very well. I expect you have a list prepared of the accused?"

The Chief produces a sheet of paper. "Yes sir." He holds it out to Michaelis who snaps it out of his hand. "Torpedoman's mate Johnston Malakachee, Torpedoman's mate Harlon Daschler, Motor Machinist mate Jack Skjonsby....Christ Chief! There's close to thirty names here!"

"At least sir."

Michaelis looks up from the paper flushed with anger. "We'll be back."

Outside, Michaelis is beside himself. 'What the hell are we gonna do now? The Skipper's gonna nail our asses for letting things get out of control!"

"Well? How did it go?" Lt. Waldron, outside this whole time in the jeep, wants to know.

"Don't ask!"

The send-off *luau* unfortunately degenerated into a wild brawl. At first the melee included only naval personnel, but then rapidly spread, encompassing the Hawaiians. Guys were staggering around with guitars and ukuleles bashed over their heads. One fellow got his head stuck in a drum and almost suffocated. Then the shore patrolmen showed up, careening through the throng swinging nightsticks. Shortly everybody was just beating the hell out of everybody else for the hell of it. With so many packing .45's, it's a miracle nobody got shot.

Now Michaelis stands outside the brig wondering what to do. "And that stupid bastard in there won't be any help!' he snarls at Waldron, 'And besides, they have an attitude about submariners."

"Why is that?" I ask guardedly.

"When you figure it out, you tell me! They think we're too cliquish or something. But it really starts to border on harassment. Damn shore patrols are always busting up our parties and never go near anyone else's. Sometimes you really have to wonder just whose side they're really on!"

"I suggest you come up with an alternate plan." Waldron observes candidly, lighting his pipe.

"Oh that's brilliant' Michaelis kicks back sarcastically. 'Ya know Waldron, once in a great while you actually make sense!"

Waldron smiles. "Bless your heart."

"Stand at attention!" The Skipper's voice bellows at the ragged line of bluejackets drawn up inside the brig. He walks down each line slowly, as if conducting an inspection, gazing hard at each man. As a group they're a pitiful specter, most are still drunk and barely able to stand up. Their uniforms hang on them in various stages of disarray; torn and rumpled splotched with blood stains. The amusing thing is quite a few of them are wearing grass skirts round their waists. Probably still too drunk to even realize it. They're a pretty pathetic sight.

The Warrant Officer stands stiffly beside his desk with a self-satisfied look, all threats and impertinence.

"Well, we're all quite the spirited bunch this evening." The Skipper notes without humor, still strolling among the lines with a firm scowl on his face. "I hope you all enjoyed yourselves, because there isn't a sling big enough in the entire fleet to hold your asses!"

The Skipper strolls over to a thickset man in the first line with darkly tanned skin. He resembles a bear: dark eyes under thick eyebrows and a crooked broad nose. "How 'bout it Tash? What happened?"

"We were just drinking and having a good time sir...and then -' he breaks off and his eyes narrow in concentration.

"And then what? Speak up man!"

"I don't really remember sir. It's kind of in a fog."

The Skipper sighs and takes a step back. He pulls out a copy of the charges and begins reading it aloud. The vacant countenances disappear and are replaced with furrowed and creased brows and narrowed eyes. A few puzzled looks.

"I don't need to explain to you the seriousness of these charges,' the Skipper remonstrates, 'but my immediate concern is that this crew departs *as one* on time. I don't want to have to make do with second-hand replacements of questionable reliability."

The door behind us opens, and a captain in summer whites strolls in with a briefcase under his right arm.

"Hangman's here." Michaelis snorts quietly.

"Huh?"

"Brig officer." Waldron whispers to me.

The Captain struts over and reviews the charges. A few moments later he lowers the paper.

"Sir,' the Captain announces, 'I'm sorry but unless the Hawaiians agree to drop all charges I cannot release these men."

"By-the-book bastard!" Michaelis hisses quietly.

The Skipper crosses his arms and straightens himself up to his full height. "Captain, then I request these men be released to me under open arrest until a formal inquiry is convened."

Beside me both Waldron and Michaelis break into a broad grins.

The Captain looks pensive a moment as he produces a pack of cigarettes and places one between his lips. "That is possible,' he says, striking a match, 'but that decision would have to be made by a informal board of inquiry. "

"Captain, ' the Skipper interrupts, leaning forward, 'we sail at oh-eight hundred!"

A sympathetic look comes over the legal eagle but he shrugs helplessly. "That's the best I can do Commander Tyreen. We have protocol."

The Skipper sighs again and stares into the overhead, his face completely blank. "He's really holding it in." Michaelis says under his breath.

"What d'you mean?"

"He's got a temper, but he won't blow. He never loses control."

The Skipper suddenly looks back at the Captain. "Can we get the Hawaiians in here Captain?"

The Captain nods. "I believe so sir. Warrant Officer?" The Warrant Officer calls over a shore patrolman and instructs him to bring the Hawaiians back from the infirmary.

"What gives?" Michaelis hisses.

Nobody has the slightest idea. We stand around like wooden mannequins until the shore patrolman reappears with the Hawaiians in tow. Some short and stout, some tall and thin, they shuffle in with more than varying degrees of agony on their faces. They've been in a fight all right; black eyes, cracked and bloody lips, and bloody noses. They are drawn up in a line just across from the bluejackets. One Hawaiian is a little older than the rest and stands at the front of the group. He looks familiar, and then I recognize him - it's the fellow to implored me to "kill Japs."

The Skipper studies them out of the corner of his eye and shifts the cap back on his head. "Who threw the first punch?" he asks finally.

"He did,' the Hawaiian in front replies, pointing at Tashtego, 'the big red one there."

The Skipper glares at the Torpedoman's mate. "Is that true Malakachee?"

The Torpedoman's mate frowns, then blinks. "I really don't remember sir."

"And him too!" another one of the Hawaiians exclaims, pointing at Daschler.

"How 'bout it Daschler?" the Skipper demands. The Torpedoman's mate merely lifts his eyebrows and shakes his baldhead. "Couldn't really say sir, it's like Tash said, it's all kind of foggy."

With a sudden intake of breath the Skipper starts pacing again, then pauses when he sees the

Chief. "Chief - ' he says with regret, shaking his head, 'how could you?"

Chief Schrier glumly shrugs his shoulders. "Sorry sir."

"Do you remember anything?"

"The last thing I remember sir is drinking punch,' the petty officer says, shifting uneasily from foot to foot, 'everything else is a blank."

Michaelis groans under his breath. "We're screwed!"

"Why doesn't anybody remember anything?' the Skipper exclaims. 'Why the sudden case of amnesia?" He walks down the second rank and pauses at the Boatswain's mate. "Duffy? You suffering amnesia too?" Duffy sighs heavily as his head rolls. "I....I....uh,' the Skipper stiffens and leans close to him. He sniffs a moment, then glances back sharply at the Hawaiians. "So nobody remembers anything huh? Is that right?" the Skipper demands sarcastically.

Nobody says a word. The Hawaiians suddenly begin to fidget.

The Skipper strides over to the Captain and the Warrant Officer. "Gentlemen, I'd like to file countercharges against the Hawaiians for unauthorized and illegal distribution of grain alcohol to my men."

The silence is deafening. It's common knowledge that the use of grain alcohol is illegal by all naval personnel. Anybody getting caught with the stuff is really in the shit.

The Hawaiians immediately begin chattering fearfully amongst themselves. The Captain studies the Skipper warily. "How are you so sure?"

"*It's coming through my Boatswain's mate's pores*, that's how I'm sure! Captain, if you will accompany me to the sight of the *luau*, I'm sure you will find the punch there spiked with it. Empty bottles should not be hard to find."

The older Hawaiian is suddenly waving his arms. "Sir....sir...we respectfully wish to withdraw all charges against these men!"

The Skipper cackles sarcastically.

"You sure about that?" the Captain wants to know with a guarded look, but the Hawaiians couldn't be any more enthusiastic. "Well then,' the Captain says, adorning himself with his cap and picking up his briefcase, 'that settles it."

    *   *   *

The white sign reads *U.S. Submarine Base, Pearl Harbor* in black lettering. Lemert slows the jeep as we come up to the gate. A marine sentry steps out, glances at our passes, and salutes smartly. Another marine sits behind him, next to a .30cal machine gun. Its barrel gapes menacingly at us.

Inside, the area is bustling with activity, trucks to and fro laden with everything from fuel tanks to large pieces of metal that twist and corkscrew in every direction.

"Scrap from the attack,' Lemert explains, as if reading my mind. "Everything that can't be salvaged or raised gets put to the cutter's torch. It'll take years to clean up this mess. I can't understand why the Jap's didn't take out the Sub base? They blast the hell out of everything else, why leave the subs untouched? Or the oil drums - they missed those too."

Lemert neatly maneuvers the jeep between two large flatbed trucks parked on either side of the road. Suddenly a familiar white Speedster roars in front of us. "It's Tyreen!"

Seeing us, the Skipper waves as several greasy and oil-spattered workers on the back bed stare down at the car open-mouthed, as if it were a mirage - an oasis on wheels. How out of place it does look on a military base. The people who stop and stare probably expect to see Robert Taylor or John Wayne behind the wheel, instead of an ordinary naval officer.

The Skipper pulls the car into a parking space outside a long row of buildings. Lemert pulls the jeep into the adjoining space and kills the engine. "That's the last time we'll drive anything on land for awhile.' He notes with humor, grabbing his sea bag out of the back.

Hopping down to the pavement, I look around. The buildings in front of us are the machine shops, full of welders, cutters, riveters, pipe fitters, and other dockyard workers whose sole duty is to keep the submarines ready for action at all times. The place has almost a blast furnace look to it. The weathered paint is cracked and peeling where welding or cutting torches haven't blackened it. The smell of oil, grease, and acetylene mixes with the tar and creosote of spare pilings to produce a stinging and acerbic aroma.

The Skipper's moving toward us. "Morning boys!'

"Good morning sir."

The Skipper hefts his sea bag out of the rumble seat and we move - three abreast - toward the shops. Metal bushings, old shavings, and tar-stained gravel crunch underfoot. From the shops comes an ear-splitting machine gun report of a riveting hammer. We almost stumble over a pile of new pilings, their sides shiny with fresh coats of tar and creosote. The Skipper navigates through this obstacle easily. Lemert and I fall a few steps behind, carefully minding not to trip over the greasy poles. Passing over them, we step up and onto the cracked and crumbing concrete floor of the machine shops.

The insides are filthy and devoid of any aesthetic value. Naked electric light bulbs hang from a ceiling composed of steel "I" beams. A snake-like configuration of cables crisscross over the floor in every direction. A deafening whine of welding machines and machine lathes. Just a few feet to my left, a welder hunches over a large piece of steel. A large shower of sparks shoots out away from him. A loud hiss, like steaks barbecuing on a grill. A smell of burnt steel.

Then, out of the dark cavern-like tomb and once again into the bright morning sunshine; before us lay the submarine piers. The long sleek boats rock gently at their berths. Crewmen and dockyard workers pour over them like worker ants swarming over a honey-topped mound. Jeeps and trucks race past, a few towing torpedo trailers behind them. Others are laden high with every other type of supply imaginable. The entire wharf is a beehive of activity.

There are several generations of boats moored at their piers. A few of the old "S" types built just after the last war and into the nineteen twenties. Though extremely small and equally as cramped, ComSubPac is so short of boats that everything that can fire a torpedo is being pressed into service. Then there are the "fleet" boats, like ours; larger and with a much greater range than the old "S" types and packing a much greater punch in firepower.

Just in front of us is a pier unlike all the others. Constructed out of concrete, it rises higher in the water than do the rest - it's a dry-dock. We skirt around it, but close enough to see a small army of dockyard workers pouring over it with long-poled paintbrushes. Others - equipped with acetylene torches - are in the process of cutting holes in the sides of the hull above the waterline right around where the main vent holes - which allow a submarine to dive - are for the ballast tanks.

From somewhere comes the sound of bagpipe music. Bagpipes - out here?

"You see that?' Lemert asks, pointing with his arm and raising his voice to be heard over the crackling of acetylene and welding torches. "They're cutting extra limber holes. That'll reduce diving time.' He points at the new holes being cut in the tops of the superstructure. "Limber holes are where the air escapes from the outer superstructure, trapped air can hold a boat to the surface. That's what we don't need."

The submarine, an extremely complex piece of machinery, able to do what no other ship in the world can do; freely give up and regain its own buoyancy. This is accomplished through a system of ballast tanks which entirely surround the submarine's pressure hull, the inner steel casing in which the crew live and carry out their duties. The pressure hull is not only watertight but also pressure resistant to resist the weight of the water surrounding it. Water is the heaviest thing known to man. Measured in pounds per square inch, the weight of water is such that at deep depths can crush a steel hull as easily as a man does a beer can. Therefore, every boat has its limit as to how deep it can go. The fleet boats are rated to a depth of 300 feet, though skippers do take their boats deeper. Every boat though has its limit. Those that have been to great depths can never be quite sure they've reached the limit. A crew only finds out the true crush depth when a screeching hull implodes, and they of course never live to tell about it.

Regulated through a system of pumps and levers, located inside the pressure hull, the inflow and outflow of water in these tanks will produce buoyancy, or take it away. These tanks have two sets of vents, one at the bottom of the tank that allows the inflow of water, and one at the top that allows the air to escape. On the surface, the main ballast tanks contain air. The vents are closed, both top and bottom. In wartime, when a split second can mean the difference between survival and a cold, watery grave, skippers often patrol on the surface with the bottom vents open and the top ones closed. This enables them to dive that much faster. A condition known as "riding the vents"; the air doesn't leak out due to the seal created by the water at the bottom of the tank and the closed vents on the top.

To submerge, the vents are opened which allows the air to escape at the top and permits water to enter from the bottom. The tanks fill, the buoyancy is lost, and the boat dives. To submerge the boat is not enough. Stability is imperative. Accomplishing this task are tanks at either end of the boat called trim tanks. By pumping water through the trim system into the tanks, something known as compensation, an even keel is attained. Submarines also have variable tanks. These are ballast tanks not carried completely flooded when submerged, and whose contents are used in compensation of the boat.

The idea that a ship can willingly give up its own buoyancy and regain it on its own whim is astounding. It always seemed to defy the laws of physics, when simple physics proves it remarkably easily. Studying the main ballast tanks that stick out of the side of the boat like saddlebags, a movement below catches my attention; the underwater sound heads are lowered. These lie below the forward torpedo room. The bow diving planes, which affect the depth of the boat, are rigged out and are moving slowly up, then down. Now a metal scraping sound; one of the torpedo tube shutters slides open, only to close a moment later.

"There she is - that's our girl!"

Here we are - pier No. 9. Lemert has stopped and stares admiringly at the sweeping, elegant lines that grace the three hundred an eight-foot long steel hull moored alongside the quay before us. The U.S.S *Bullhead,* a Tambor-class boat. Her prow, rising majestically up out of the water begins a slow, easy descent down her length that tapers at her rounded stern. Her rounded conning tower sits squarely on the wooden deck a bit forward of amidships, bordered at either end by s steel railing, or "greenhouse." The jagged lines above are courtesy of the business ends of her two periscopes and accented by one of her two radio antennae, the fixed model just aft of the search scope. The other antenna - a flexible cable - runs from the top of her periscope shears to the bow. The scalloped-shaped cuts of the limber holes show gray in her black hull. Similarly scalloped openings in the bow, right at the waterline for the bow buoyancy vent look very much like a row of razor-sharp sharks' teeth. On the surface she's powered by four Fairbanks-Morse 38D81 diesels of 5400 Hp respectively, and four electric motors - GE 2740's - give her way when submerged. At top speed she can make 20 knots on the surface and 9 knots submerged. Six torpedo tubes forward and four aft, and a full complement of 24 torpedoes, or "fish." These are the best boats in the fleet, long-legged enough to reach Japanese home waters and able to patrol up to ninety days. Mounted forward of the distinctly cut conning tower, is the 3-inch deck gun.

The source of the bagpipe music reveals itself, a sailor - with a set of pipes draped over his left shoulder - is waltzing back and forth along the quay, playing.

"Who's that?" I ask, pointing at the plodding figure with the set of pipes over his arm.

"That's McGowan - one of the helmsmen. He's s Scot. We're the only boat in the Pacific Fleet with our own piper. C'mon, let's get aboard."

Grabbing my bundle I stumble unsteadily behind him toward the narrow gangplank that spans the submarine's deck and the pier. Stepping onto the teak planking that makes up the *Bullhead*'s deck, I notice a colorful, Disney-esque emblem painted on the side of the conning tower. Under closer scrutiny, it's the head of a snorting bull, complete with long horns and a fish's swishing tail, clenching a red-tipped torpedo in a fiery grin. On his head, right between the horns, he wears a white sailor's cap. Whoever did this is a pretty good artist.

"Like that?" A proud voice asks from above.

I look up to see the XO leaning on his crossed arms over the bulwark of the bridge. 'Chief Schrier's idea. He paints a little." The XO leans a bit further out and examines it upside down. He thrusts out his jaw and nods approvingly. "Damn fine job."

Probably the quickest and shortest route into officer's country is through the gun access hatch at base of the conning tower. Skirting around a group of crewmen in the process of loading 3-inch shells for the deck gun, I step down the narrow ladder that leads into the control room. Hefting my sea bag like a harpoon, I follow Lemert's lead and cry "Look out below!" Then scramble down after it.

The difference between the outside air and the air inside the boat smacks into me like a bucket of ice water in the face. Inside the boat the air is hot and humid. The diesel fumes are almost overpowering. Behind the diesel smell is something akin to a football team's locker room. At the bottom of the ladder, I notice it's not quite the same control room of a few days ago. The endless tangle of cables, pipes, switches, and levers snake all around just as they did before, but now the room has become jam-packed with boxes of food and other accouterments; charts, ammo, small arms, some clothing, and boxes of another type that I can't make heads or tails out of. The Skipper's over by the chart table in deep conversation with the XO.

"All set Ensign?" the voice startles me. Turning around, I find myself staring into the Chief's face. His powerful body looks coiled as tight as a spring.

"Yes Chief."

His bright blue eyes dance with excitement, "Stow your gear then, we cast off in forty-five minutes." He quickly pushes past me and into the control room, haranguing a few seamen for ill placement of boxes of provisions.

The forward battery compartment also doubles as the officer's quarters. All five of the ship's officers will share this small enclave of bunks and small lockers for the duration of the patrol. Below the platform deck are the 126 cells of Exide batteries, which will give us half our power when we are underwater. The other half comes from the 126 cells in the after battery compartment that doubles as the crew's quarters. I begin to search for my bunk, but am immediately interrupted by a metallic crackling. The XO's voice suddenly booms over the ship's loudspeaker, "Attention - all hands to form on deck on the double!"

Five minutes later, the crew stands in formation - straight, even rows on the fantail - all squinting in the bright morning sun.

The Skipper stands before us. A flock of seagulls flutters overhead, their lonely calls breaking into the silence on deck and the sounds of the workmen in the machine shops on the quay, even McGowan's piping has stopped. "You all see the pile of shit on the bottom of the harbor?' he asks, pointing toward "Battleship Row", 'You know what it used to be. Let it be a lesson to all of you how the Nips conduct business. The Nip doesn't seem to think Americans can fight. They think we're too soft, too fond of luxury. I know they're wrong. What do you think? We lost a fine officer on the last patrol. Captain Jameson believed in carrying the war to the enemy, and for that he paid with his life. Leaving a widow after two months of marriage. This is just the first round in this fight, but it's high time we get a little payback. Not only for what they did to the fleet, but for what they inflicted on Mrs. Jamison. So I ask you, are you with me?"

A spirited roar as sixty-five men speak as one. "Aye-aye sir!"

The Skipper whirls around. "XO, put us in departure position, all hands to their stations! Stand by all lines!"

This patrol will be a school of sorts for me. Since I am to become "qualified in submarines," I must learn how to operate every piece of machinery in the boat. This will qualify me for my "golden dolphins'" insignia, meaning acceptance into the brotherhood of the silent service. The XO heads toward the bridge, and I am not far behind. I scramble up the ladder leading to the cigarette deck, past the .50cal mount and onto the bridge.

The XO leans against the bridge bulwark, scanning the boat with his eyes. He notices my approach and offers his hand. "Watts...right?"

"Yes sir" I say, taking his hand. Could this be the man of the night before, loaded to the gills and barely able to stand up?

"Good to have you aboard."

"Thank you sir."

"Skipper informs me I'm to get you qualified in submarines?"

"Yes sir."

"This your first crack at the Japs?"

"Yes sir."

He lifts up his cap, smoothes down his black hair and replaces it. "Had a tour of the boat?"

I nod and reply when I first came aboard.

He smiles. "I think you'll find she looks a shade different when she's loaded to the gills. Go ahead, have another look. It'll be just a few minutes till we're in departure position."

Eagerly I disappear below, casting my eyes on a mind boggling variety of instruments, dials, gauges, and switches. In the middle of the tower are the two periscopes; a large search scope and a smaller attack scope. To starboard are the periscope hoists, the sonar and hydrophone gear, and one of the newest inventions, the Torpedo Data Computer; a device that calculates speed, angles, and bow set-up for firing torpedoes. To port is the firing plunger for the TDC, and directly behind me is the conning tower steering stand for the helmsman, gyro compass repeater, depth gauges, and the engine annunciators. The mirror-bright metal scopes reflect the sunlight that shines through the hatch, creating a bright sunburst on the tower wall. Moving to the ladder I lower myself into the control room bustling with activity. All the information I crammed into my head at sub school begins to flood back; fleet boats; eight major compartments that comprise the pressure hull. All watertight fore to aft; forward torpedo room, forward battery compartment, control room, after battery compartment, forward engine room, after engine room, maneuvering room, and after torpedo room.

The control room is the nerve center of the boat and a veritable maze of all types of machinery, for it is from here that just about everything in the boat is controlled. Both sides of the compartment are crammed full of steel and copper piping, manifolds, switches, levers, and circuits. In the overhead - the ceiling of the compartment - it gets even more crowded. All ventilation pipes, exhaust and compartment air salvage lines weave a twisted path above our heads like so many snakes in a pit. Throughout the boat, ducking is at a premium. You could easily give yourself a concussion on these bare steel pipes.

Waldron, Pike, and Michaelis turn up. Of all, only Pike is feeling the effects of last night's binge. Waldron informs me through a suppressed grin that he was loaded for bear before setting one foot into the Forbidden City, and was rescued by the Pharmacist's mate a mere two hours ago.

"You wouldn't think it was so funny if it was you." Pike mumbles, wincing at the sound of his own voice. "You wait, one of these days we'll be fishing you out of some godforsaken hole."

Waldron produces a pipe from his pocket and inserts the stem neatly between his teeth. "Not likely."

"Hey new guy,' Michaelis points out, 'Waldron here's our thinker, so we direct all our more intellectual problems to him. ComSubPac only put him on board to keep the rest of us out of trouble."

"Or to irritate us,' Pike adds painfully, wincing as he glances up at the naked light bulb hanging above, 'One of these days we'll figure out which."

"How is it I can succeed in one and not the other?" Waldron shoots back playfully.

Another figure in khaki looms up from behind Michaelis with a clipboard in hand.

"Watts,' Michaelis says, grinning at Pike's hangover, 'this is our engineering officer Lt. Schumacher. He spends most of his time back in the maneuvering room with all his electricity. He's definitely a guy you get a charge out of!" Michalis cracks up at his own joke.

Schumacher simply shakes his head. "Arthur Godfrey you are not.. Hi Watts - nice to meet you." I study his face; long, with deep set eyes under heavy eyebrows, high cheekbones and a hooknose, he looks like a hawk.

The ship's loudspeaker suddenly crackles, "Harbor stations: maneuvering watch on deck! prepare for departure!" My sojourn through the boat is now at an end. Our little party breaks up.

Turning around, I clamber up the ladder into the conning tower.

"Permission to come onto the bridge?" I ask, peeking my head over the hatch rim.

"Granted."

On the pier, seamen in dungaree shirts and trousers - their white caps brilliant in the sun - scramble around readying the lines to be taken in. The XO watches them intently, then turns and glances aft. I notice that most of the bluejackets sport beards, another telltale sign of a submariner. We're the only branch of the navy still allowed to have them. The XO leans over and yells down into the open hatch, "Standby No.1 and No.2 main motors!'

The shrill notes of McGowan's bagpipes begin again. He's here on deck, standing just forward of the three-inch gun.

Suddenly, the Skipper appears seemingly from out of nowhere. He glances around with a frown and takes the report from the XO. "Sir, all lines standing by. No.1 and No. 2 main motors standing by. All clear for departure."

The Skipper nods as he lights a cigarette and drapes his arms over the bridge bulwark, "Thank you Mr. Bainbridge.' He pauses a moment, looking around - from stem to stern. "Cast off No.1!"

The XO leans over the bridge and repeats the order to the men at the bow, who immediately begin hauling in the thick hawser from the pier. A light breeze blows up and caresses my face, bringing with it the aroma of salt, oil, and rotten fish. A few dockyard workers standing on the pier watch us. Their gazes seem solemn, almost reverent. Off to the right, the bright sun glints off something - I look closer; brass instruments, white uniforms, a man off to the side holds a pair of large cymbals - it's a band. Suddenly the conductor waves his baton and immediately the band crashes into a spirited rendition of "Anchors Aweigh", drowning out McGowan's bagpipes.

"Cast off No.2!" The Skipper bawls out commands for the engine room. "Left full rudder, port ahead two-thirds, starboard back full!" Now the boat begins to swing away from the pier. I lean against the steel side of the bridge and watch as our bow neatly parts the quiet harbor water.

Behind us the band launches into "Sink 'Em All." But still McGowan keeps it up on deck with his pipes, refusing to be squelched.

Even from the submarine base, the tall, gangly necks of the salvage derricks are visible along what used to be 'Battleship Row.' Multitudes of them, so that the skyline looks like a cross between a construction site and an oil field. All there for the same reason, salvaging the scrap and cleaning up the mess from December 7th. Not yet a month ago. A shiny sheen on the water catches my attention, it's an oil slick. The whole harbor is lousy with oil, leaking from the torn and broken ships that used to be the Pacific Fleet. The shiny and greasy liquid clings to our starboard saddle tank like frosting on a cake.

"I want all hands not at their stations below up on deck,' the Skipper growls, 'I want 'em to remember what we're fighting for." The XO repeats the order through the open hatch, and a few minutes later the deck bursts with crewmen staring at the blown up, burnt-out, and twisted relics of once proud ships.

McGowan's wailing pipes abruptly cease. I don't know the reason why until I look down. His cap is off, and held across his chest in reverence.

Off to port is what once used to be a destroyer, a "four-stacker" so-called because of their four smokestacks. One stack has completely vanished; the only remnants of it are the sheared pieces of steel at the base of the pipe. The second is blown in half, blossomed out like a sick flower. The third is full of holes like Swiss cheese, and the fourth is bent grotesquely forward. I notice that the bridge is gone and that there is no bow to speak of ; this ship's magazine must have exploded. Here's one destroyer that won't be sailing anymore.

"That used to be the *Shaw*,' the Skipper seethes, 'at least before the Imperial Navy got through with her."

"Lousy fucking bastards!" the XO spits.

The Skipper stares at the destruction. "Well, they want a war, and by God we're going to give 'em one!"

We round ten-ten dock, so named because of its one thousand and ten foot length. Wisps of smoke still can be seen rising from some of the huge battlewagons that burned for days. The steel becoming so hot I heard, that it glowed, visible from miles.

The XO clears his throat. "I've heard some of the salvage guys talking about the tapping they hear coming from inside the ships. Christ almighty! How'd you like to be entombed in burning steel?"

The Skipper sniffs violently. "How long will it go on? Will they tap for months? It's already been weeks. If they don't get them out of there soon, the lack of food, water and air will surely silence them."

Over there is the twisted superstructure of the *Arizona* where so much of the tapping is heard. What is it like to be trapped in a dark tomb, shrouded in steel? What thoughts must cross the minds of those who find themselves in such a horrific situation? Will they survive? What will become of them? Will their families ever know what has happened to them? Will they be found or will their bodies lie and rot inside this metal sarcophagus until it's just a pile of disjointed bones? Ideas that make your skin crawl. Horrible, the eternal darkness, the cold metal; I involuntarily shudder.

From the blackened and torn ships come the hissing of acetylene cutting torches. Fiery sparks shoot out over the water in a colorful cascade of red and blue, instantly vanishing when they hit the water. Workmen in blackened overalls are visible, looking like hideous creatures of the deep with their mouths and faces covered by goggles and masks to protect them from the toxic fumes, greasy smoke, and metal dust.

There, coming up now is the bare steel hull of the *Oklahoma*. She lies keel up. The torpedoes that tore into her side rolled her completely over in minutes, taking most of her crew with her. Harbor boats ring her side. Cables crisscross her black hull and run along the keel. Suddenly all cursing and talking ceases. The deck has become as quiet as a funeral parlor. The sheer enormity of it sinks in; *Oklahoma*, behind her *West Virginia, California;* all twisted smoking wrecks. This wasn't war - it was murder. Tales of Japanese planes strafing in the water helpless men desperate to escape their doomed ships.

"Motherfuckers!"

"Take a look, take a good look,' the Skipper snaps, 'and keep it right *here*." He slaps his chest hard.

I notice McGowan licking the mouthpiece on the stem of his bagpipe. A note shrills and he begins playing "Amazing Grace."

A destroyer approaches off to port, steaming up harbor and passing close alongside. Several of their crew stand against the side rails looking down on us with a mixture of wonderment and disgust. To the regular surface navy submariners are a mystery. They do not comprehend why anyone would willingly serve in these "iron coffins." Surface sailors, accustomed to the large cavernous spaces found on surface ships, are horrified by the idea of being shut inside a steel pipe for weeks on end. The thought of never seeing a ray of sunlight abhors them. A simple fact is we have more in common with our counterparts in the Japanese submarine force or the German U-boat arm than our own surface fleet.

The destroyer's diesels churn the water into a milky froth. The water doesn't stay foamy for long, all the oil in the water has seen to that. Strange, the oil is like blood; the blood of torn and broken ships, the blood of drowned crews.

Approaching the harbor mouth, the water becomes more turbulent. The ceaselessly energetic ocean meets the quieter harbor and Back Bay water. Lighting one of his Chesterfields, the Skipper runs his hand through his tangled mop of blond hair and replaces his cap. He leans over to the hatch, "Bridge to engine room, standby to engage No.1 and No.2 main engines." When he gives the order a moment later, a thunderous roar shakes the boat. Looking aft, the water now churns as white as snow on a mountain. Blue-gray smoke pours from the engine exhaust ventilators on both sides of the hull as boat lurches forward.

The Skipper orders the ship rigged for dive, effectively ending the crew's time on deck.

McGowan promptly folds up his pipes and disappears into the lower conning tower hatch. Now the boat is readied to dive at a moment's notice. The Skipper then orders the Chief to flood the negative tank. This tank gives the boat both negative buoyancy and its initial down-angle. I remember: flooding the main ballast tanks submerges the boat enough to make it roughly neutral in the water. The negative tank gives the boat the necessary weight to attain depth fast, so the boat would not linger at the surface. Once the boat has attained the desired depth, the tank is blown dry with high-pressure air and the bow planes regulate the depth.

Roused from my thoughts by the XO, who points to the patrol boat off the port bow. Not a large warship, about the size of a rich man's yacht. She idles, tossing and bobbing in the swell before turning and beating her way out to sea. We fall into line astern of her, our speed increasing.

A movement through the hatch, Lt. Michaelis comes up to assume his position as officer of the deck. The XO disappears below mumbling something about looking over his charts.

"Commence routine below Michaelis." The Skipper orders. A pair of binoculars is handed up from the conning tower and Michaelis hands them to me, saying "Lesson one, when on the bridge, always be on watch." So class has begun.

Lemert appears. He's to be quartermaster of the watch. He nods at me, saying not a word. A greenish tint has appeared in his face. The Skipper notices him.

"Too much swimming last night Lemert?" He grins as he accustoms himself to the increasing motion of the boat. The Skipper stands about a foot away from the bridge bulwark, his feet apart - assuring a low center of gravity - and sways easily as the groundswell lifts and rolls under the boat. The groundswell is long and rolling. I watch as our bow rises and falls as it climbs up the hill, crosses the top, and then plunges into the valley on the other side. Each time the bow plunges, it throws up a wall of white foam, which the wind soon carries onto the teak planking of the deck, darkening its already rich deep-brown color. It reaches us on the bridge - licking my lips I taste the salt.

"Funny thing seasickness,' the Skipper observes, 'Some people are extremely susceptible while others can go through a full-blown gale with a ten sea running and never feel a twitch. Apparently it has something to do with the fluid in your inner ear." With every sweep of the binoculars, I steal a glance in his direction. From somewhere he has produced a cigar, and begins meticulously unwrapping the cellophane from around it.

I find that the binoculars, held for a period of time, soon become damned heavy. I begin to feel the strain in my triceps. I shift the weight of the glasses to my left hand and flex out my right.

"Make a sweep, lower your arms and stretch them out. Then repeat." The Skipper instructs. "It's the only way you'll make it through a watch." He's rolling the cigar around in his mouth, wetting the end before biting it and spitting it over the side. "I'll bet within the hour, half of the crew will be green and vomiting. Too much firewater last night."

"I made sure the Chief has plenty of empty pails in every compartment just in case." Michaelis adds matter-of-factly. And what about him - Michaelis? He could barely stand up himself last night. Must be feeling a bit queasy himself about now.

The Skipper looks thoughtful and puffs on his cigar, rocking back and forth on the balls of his feet to the motion of the boat. The roar of the diesels suddenly muffles - the exhaust ventilators must have been submerged in the swell. A moment later they break free and once more the loud throbbing continues.

"You know there's lots of ways to get killed out here.' The Skipper states flatly. "Submarining is, by nature, inherently dangerous - even in peacetime. Remember what happened to the *Squalus*?"

The *Squalus* was a *Salmon*-class boat that went down off Portsmouth, New Hampshire just two years ago. During a dive the main induction valve - where the diesels draw air from outside the boat - failed to close. The after compartments flooded and the *Squalus* went straight to the bottom almost three hundred feet below, killing twenty-six men trapped in the after compartments. The thirty-three men that were able to survive only did so by sealing the watertight door to the flooded compartments, in effect cutting off escape for those aft. But what else could they could have done? Had they not sealed the door - all hands would have been lost. What would it be like? To be trapped in a sealed compartment with bone-chilling seawater pouring in? Nothing left to do but make your peace with God.

Seagulls cry and screech as they hover around the boat.

A sudden retching sound from aft. I turn around. The movements of the boat combined with the hangover have finally become too much for poor Lemert.

"Impressive Lemert!' Michaelis declares as the Skipper cracks up. Michaelis is waving his arm around wildly pointing to his watch. 'Almost an hour! Better than last time." The Skipper leans over to the gaping hole that leads to the conning tower. "Quartermaster, have the Chief make a notation in the ship's log. Lemert held it down for almost an hour!" He laughs uproariously as he turns to Michaelis and glares at him expectantly. "Well, how about it?"

"I'm perfectly fine sir." He replies confidently, throwing down the gauntlet in front of our commander.

"Nonsense.' The Skipper contradicts. 'As tight as you were last night? It's only a matter of time."

Apparently there's some sort of bet going on, to see who gets sick and throws up and who doesn't. The Skipper confirms my hypothesis when he instructs the Chief to tabulate a head count of how many of the crew are using the Chief's vomit pails. The answer is not long in coming, so far two out of five men.

"Excellent! 'The Skipper chuckles, content with himself, 'More than halfway there!"

I've heard that submariners have a strange sense of humor, but this takes the cake.

An hour later the Skipper breaks the silence by calling the radioman to the bridge and dictates a signal to our escort. "Will commence a trim dive in five minutes, tell them to execute exercise in exactly two zero minutes. Will maintain present course of three zero five degrees, speed four knots, depth one two zero feet - got it?" A Radioman named Swensen nods as he jots it down on a small note pad.

"Now repeat it back to me."

After Swensen disappears, the Skipper begins by ordering the lookouts below. The two lookouts on either side of the periscope shears duck underneath the railings and disappear down the hatch.

"Clear the bridge!"

This means me. I let the binoculars dangle from the strap around my neck and take the conning tower ladder two steps at a time but it's not fast enough. Michaelis painfully treads on my fingers as he follows behind me. Two sharp blasts on the klaxon.

"Take her down!"

"Christ Watts! Move your ass!" Michaelis roars at me as he stumbles over me on the conning tower deck. I roll off to the side. The Skipper is already there, and then Lemert who is the last man through the hatch. The quartermaster leans hard on the lanyard, pulls the hatch to, and then scrambles up the ladder to make it fast.

I hop down into the control room. A crewman stands in front of the "Christmas Tree"; the condition board that shows the status of all hull valves, vents, and hatches. He flashes the words "Green board!" to the Chief.

"Flood!"

I hear the hissing and rush of air as the main ballast tanks vent and the gurgling sea rushes in from the bottom.

"Pressure in the boat!" The hull is now sealed.

The Chief stands just behind the two planesmen, who regulate the bow and stern plane controls. "Twenty-two degree down angle on bow planes, six degrees down bubble on stern."

The Skipper shifts his cap on his head and leans back against the periscope housings behind him. "Make your depth one zero zero feet Chief."

"Proceeding to one zero zero feet aye." The Chief responds, not taking his eyes off the inclinometers, which indicate the angle of the boat's dive.

"Passing three zero feet sir,' this from the bow planesman. Michaelis appears and takes over the diving controls from the Chief. He elbows me in the ribs, "Soak in everything I do, okay? Shut bow buoyancy tank, open safety tank and vent to the sea.' Michaelis handles the phrases effortlessly and efficiently, as if he'd been born for only one purpose.

"Safety open. Venting aye!"

Michaelis waits five seconds and then orders it closed. The tank is now dry.

"Close all vents!' A split-second later, "All vents closed aye!'

It's eerie. It's as quiet as a grave in here. Except for a few coughs, clearing of throats and the like, you wouldn't know there were human beings alive inside the boat.

"Passing eight zero feet sir.'

The only indication that we're getting deeper is the needle on the depth gauge, which moves around the dial as if powered by some unseen force.

"Blow negative to the mark. Cycle the vents Mike.' The Skipper orders. Blowing the negative tank will halt the boat's negative buoyancy and make us roughly neutral in the water. Now, the bow and stern planes govern our depth and angle.

No more throbbing diesels, only the barely audible humming of our electric motors.

The Skipper produces a Chesterfield from his shirt pocket and lights it. "All ahead two-thirds.'

"All ahead two-thirds. Aye!' The ringing of bells as the indicator on the engine annunciator clicks over. The Skipper blows smoke at the twisted tangle of cables and pipes that hang over our heads. "All compartments report for watertight integrity."

The order passes via the boat's intercom system - the IMC. Moments later the compartments begin to report in. "Forward torpedo room all secure...after torpedo room all secure....maneuvering room...all secure....' and so on down the line until the Skipper checks his watch. "Proceed to one two zero feet."

Michaelis repeats the order and orders the bow planes down ten degrees and five degrees down bubble on the stern planes.

"Helmsman, course?" the Skipper asks as he cocks his ear toward the yawning hole above the ladder that leads to the tower.

"Course is three zero five degrees Captain." The disembodied voice replies. Normally, the helmsman pilots the boat from the steering position in the tower. There's another one down here in the control room of course - in case of emergency.

"Very well, keep her so."

The boat has arrived at depth, one hundred and twenty feet of water above the keel. Michaelis orders the bow and stern plane controls eased back so that the boat glides evenly through the water. "Now let's get this girl trimmed out."

Through the trim controls and the trim pumps, water is pumped forward and then aft to achieve a balance. Much like a carpenter and his level, the boat must be balanced so that the bubble hovers within the hash marks specified. I find myself staring at the depth gauges on the metal plating in front of the plane controls. There are three depth gauges, two go only to one hundred and sixty feet, and another smaller one has readings and hash marks on it all the way up to six hundred. Six hundred? That seems like a bit of a stretch. Electric Boat Company in Groton has given us a guarantee of three hundred. Granted, many times a boat will need to go below the guaranteed depth, but twice as much?

A few reports of leaks come in; valves, a few pipefitting, seals that need tightening down - nothing that can't be put right with a few turns of a wrench. The water pressure is making its presence known. Even here, almost at the middle of the twentieth century, there are limits on the things man can do

"Boat in balance." Michaelis's words suddenly thrust me back from my thoughts. The trimming process is over. The Skipper nods silently, apparently satisfied. I glance around - those affected by the motion of the boat and last night's alcohol are now getting a reprieve. The boat neither pitches nor rolls. We glide through a soft cushion of water. An awful stink hangs in the air; the putrid odor from the Chief's vomit pails. The pressure inside the boat exasperates it, causing it to smell worse than it would if we were on the surface drawing air into the boat.

I notice the Skipper is suddenly very interested in his watch. He and Michaelis exchange a knowing look. "How far off?" Michaelis wants to know.

"No more than a minute."

From the crew's mess aft comes the sound of boisterous laughter. I catch fragments of the sexual antics of several crewmen at the "Forbidden City" last night.

CRACK WHAMM! The boat shakes from stem to stern. The floor plates beneath my feet jump and clang together. The boat rocks to starboard, then slowly comes back onto an even keel. Bombs? Collision? Can't be - not at this depth! Visions of foaming water pouring through the bulkhead into the control room send sharp pangs of fear up my spine. Is this the way it will end? Drowned not a hundred miles from Pearl Harbor?

The Skipper's voice pulls me back, "This is the Captain,' he addresses the crew over the loudspeaker, "Men, that sound is something you will become very familiar with - depth charges. They are the primary weapon of your enemy. Our escort dropped those about two thousand yards off the port bow. In action they will come much closer than that. Believe it or not, you will become used to them. You must. Or else you are no good to us here. That is all."

Silence in the control room. The Skipper glances around at all of us, exchanging knowing looks with the Chief and the XO, who have surely been through it before. I can only imagine what my own face must look like. The shock, the sound, the feeling is indescribable. Michaelis leans over to me. "Won't be long 'til you experience the real thing."

"Prepare to surface!"

Three blasts on the klaxon; compressed air hisses into the tanks and the bow tilts upward. "Bridge watch stand by!"

This means me. I grab my binoculars and cap from underneath the chart table and head up the narrow control room ladder into the conning tower.

The boat begins roll and tilt from bow to stern.

"Tower free,' Michaelis reports. 'Equalize pressure!"

A low humming begins as the low-pressure blowers engage, drawing down the excess pressure from inside the boat. "We do this as a safeguard,' Michaelis explains, "As normal operation of the boat may result in a consequential rise in pressure as certain tanks vented inboard or air is bled into the boat. For example, without equalizing the pressure beforehand could cause somebody opening the bridge hatch to be literally blown out of the boat."

The cry comes up from the control room, "Pressure equalized!" Since I'm the junior officer on board, the Skipper decides to have me open the hatch to the bridge, instead of the quartermaster, who usually does it. "On your way to being 'qualified in submarines." He grins.

"Tower free." Michaelis again. I hop up the ladder and swing the hatch wheel. I make the mistake of looking up as I fling open the hatch - a jet of water roars in from the bridge, hitting me full in the face and soaking me to the waist. It crashes on the floor plates below. I hear somebody behind me laughing. The Skipper roars at the top of his lungs, "Up! Up! Move!" as I scramble onto the bridge. Rivulets of water cascade aft toward the cigarette deck. The boat is at a sharp angle. The steel decking of the bridge is wet and slick. I catch a glimpse of our bow rising up out of the water, like a whale, she breaches. A steel prow at a thirty-degree angle. Foaming water parts to reveal the glistening teak decking. The shiny gloss of seawater soon scurries off back into its domain. The water around our saddletanks glistens as white as newly fallen snow. The boat's angle begins to ease as the stern breaks surface. A glance aft; our gray steel hull emerges from boiling water that swishes and swirls out of every limber hole in the superstructure.

A blue sky with clouds that look like puffs of whipped cream. Deep blue water. A shiny black steel hull surrounded on all sides by shimmering water; a portrait of serenity worthy of a

Monet.

The Skipper orders the main induction valve and hull outboard ventilators to be opened. A throttling roar and shaking once again overtakes the boat as the machinists' aft crank over the diesels. Blue-gray smoke coughs through the engine ventilators. Chief Schrier appears for a quick smoke as two lookouts climb into the periscope shears. Lighting a cigarette from my lighter, he explains to me, "Above you you've got Torpedoman Daschler and the Boatswain's mate Duffy. Duffy is also our soundman - and he's one of the best around. His ears are so good he can identify a type of ship simply by the sound of her screws. We almost lost him after the last patrol. It's normal to transfer some men between boats, that way the less experienced crew is able to have a few seasoned men in their ranks. But when Tyreen heard they were going to transfer Duffy, he really went ape. He carried it as far as ComSubPac. The Skipper swears by him."

"True -' the Skipper interjects, glancing up at the Boatswain's mate with a look of affection. "It's like a woman that you meet and want to marry. When you find a good one - you don't let 'em go."

The Gunner's Mate now appears out of the hatch with drums of .30cal ammunition for the machine guns. First he attends to the one on the port side; a scraping of metal on metal, followed by a clang as he locks and chambers the belt. He moves to the starboard gun and repeats the process. His task completed; he disappears below without a word.

In the interim, the Chief has finished his cigarette. "Much to do - must go." He says, flicking the butt over the side.

The Skipper glances at his watch and leans over the open bridge hatch, "Secure low-pressure blowers!" The Skipper requests a confirmation of course from the helmsman.

"Course three zero five degrees sir." The conning tower talker watch in the conning tower relay the answer. The petty officer in charge there in the tower is a voice link between the bridge, conning tower, and control room when on the surface, and conning tower and control room when submerged.

The XO appears and requests his sextant be handed up. Apparently he wants to get a sun line. Moments later the instrument in gingerly lifted to the bridge. Lifting it to his eye, he aligns it with the horizon.

"It's rather ironic if you think about it,' I say, watching him, 'here we are in the middle of the twentieth century and still navigating like Magellan did when he rounded the Horn."

The XO grins. "Some things never change, do they? Centuries ago, explorers figured out that by measuring the height of the sun above the horizon, a *line of position* can be taken; the angle being measured in degrees. This line of position will gives us a track, which is plotted on the chart. But that's only part of it. Tonight, we need to take another bearing on a star, called *a star fix*, and plot it's bearing from information contained in the Nautical Almanac. This book contains figures for exact positions of the heavenly bodies at exact times and exact dates. This information once plotted, will bisect the track given us by the sun and we will be able to plot the boat's position on the chart. All nice and neat huh?"

Finished, the XO hands it below and climbs in after it to attend to his charts. Silence on the bridge. The Skipper sways to and fro with the motion of the boat. The lookouts bury themselves in their binoculars. Lemert coughs loudly now and then and clears his throat. Probably attempting to keep whatever remains in his stomach down.

We soon begin to overtake our escort. He's cutting speed and readying to alter course and head back to Pearl. Passing him astern of him, we exchange a few waves and shouts as they fall behind in our bubbling wake. A seaman stands behind a .50cal mounted forward on the escort, waving wildly so we see him. His mouth is open and yelling. It takes a moment for his words to reach us. "Good hunting!"

I watch as the escort turns, and with a final wave begins chugging back towards Pearl. The Skipper orders engine speed increased. Our bow neatly parts the deep greenish-blue water and transforms it into a veil of white that looks as pure as a bride's wedding dress.

Waldron appears to take over the deck and lights his pipe. Letting it droop by the stem from the corner of his mouth, he scans the horizon with his glasses. Waldron reminds me of a character in Herman Melville's *Moby Dick*. The ship's first officer was a fellow named Stubb - also a pipe smoker - a happy-go-lucky type. The pipe that dangles from his mouth is unusual for someone of his youth, but it suits him.

Word comes up from below, lunch is served. Since I'm an extra man on the bridge, I can go below with the Skipper.

The tiny wardroom doubles as the officer's mess; located in the forward battery compartment just aft of the forward torpedo room. A table - fixed fast to the floor - is in the middle of the room with bench seats surrounding it. The Skipper, Pike, Schumacher, the XO, and myself all crowd around the table. It's funny, even though it's called the wardroom, a "room" is something this little enclave aspires to be. On the after partition that separates our bunks and Chief Petty Officer's bunks from the wardroom, a row of small cabinets hang.

We jostle and elbow one another in a quest to find the most comfortable position. The steaming plates already lay before us, chicken fried steaks with mashed potatoes, gravy and green beans. The best food in the navy is to be had by submariners, it being the most hazardous of duties.

The wardroom tilts up and down. This far forward it catches the motion of the bow as it rides up on the swell and drops into the valley on the other side. Must be impossible to eat in here if the boat is plowing through a heavy sea. I notice dime-size holes all around the edge of the table for table support rails whenever the weather gets bad. If things get that rough, I can't imagine wanting to eat anyway.

The steward comes in with a coffeepot and dispenses the piping hot liquid all around. I sip it and immediately stiffen. I'm accustomed to strong but this stuff is lethal. Across from me the Skipper chuckles. "One thing about Jonesy's coffee, I think if we'd replace the water in the batteries with it, it'd double our time underwater."

"When I get out of the navy,' Schumacher comments, chewing with bulging cheeks, 'I'm putting Jonesy under contract to make the stuff by the drum full. Then I'll turn it around and sell it back to the navy as an engine oil lubricant!"

Jonesy's baldhead suddenly appears through the partition from the pantry. A narrow cubicle a few feet wide by about as many long, it lies sandwiched between the forward bulkhead and the wardroom. "Slapping the hand that feeds you again eh? Sirs, if you don't mind me saying, you really got nerve!" Jonesy screws up his lined face in a twisted grimace of mock anger.

The XO chuckles in amusement. "Hey Jonesy - cruisers bounce you to destroyers, who bounced you to minesweeper, who bounced you to us! You tell us who has the raw end of this deal."

"We did!" Pike grunts, 'and suffer because of it." Grunts and giggles of agreement all around. Jonesy abruptly disappears into the panty. When he appears again, he holds a coffeepot in his right hand and waves it around, "You see this? You know what this is?"

"An instrument of torture?' the XO cracks with heavy sarcasm, 'Or weren't those outlawed by the Geneva Convention?" Schumacher suddenly gags as if he's going to spit the contents of his cheeks all over the table.

"No!' Jonesy waves it around again, 'This is a U.S. Navy coffeepot, to be filled with U.S. Navy coffee! If you can't handle it I'm sorry, but regulations don't allow me to carry Kool-Aid on board!"

The Skipper grins. Sitting with arms crossed, cap perched on the back of his head and a smile as broad as our beam, it's clear he's enjoying the verbal sparring. "Game, set, and match to the ship's cook!" He declares.

"Thank you sir!' Jonesy crows, bowing his head to the Skipper. 'Well then, since the rest of you don't appreciate me, maybe I ought to just go and cook for the Japanese!"

The XO swallows his coffee, "You do that and the war would be over in a week!."

"No-no-no!' Pike exclaims, 'That'd make us all war criminals!"

Jonesy disappears now altogether.

As the men finish up their meals and pour cup after cup of coffee down their throats, the Skipper orders the Chief to put a record on the boat's turntable. Johnson, the steward, reappears to carry away the dirty plates and top off our coffee mugs.

"Which one?" the Chief inquires, halfway in the gangway, to which the Skipper merely shrugs his shoulders, responding "surprise me."

After about a minute the unique vocal harmony of the Andrews Sisters wafts through the speaker. Pike motions toward the Skipper. "Look out, when he's in one of his quiet moods, we get Brahms and Handel."

Pike retreats back into his cup of coffee as the Skipper eyes him with interest. "Surely you have nothing against a little culture Lieutenant?"

The XO rolls his eyes and nods toward Pike. "You can he when he's into Spike Jones?" Producing an indignant look from the torpedo and gunnery officer, who demands to know what is wrong with Spike Jones.

He never gets his answer. The Chief reappears with the word that the lookouts have spotted something off the starboard bow.

In less than a second the Skipper is on his feet.

Half a minute later we're on the bridge. But it's a false alarm. Through an embarrassed grin Michaelis reports it's a solitary sea turtle.

So much for the excitement. Later though, I can't help but think how lucky that turtle is. He's at home, and has the entire Pacific Ocean to swim in; no watches to stand, no ships to sink, and no war to fight.

Only humans create war.

    *   *   *

I learn from the XO that the boat will make a stop at Midway Island to top-off our fuel tanks. Midway Island is 1200 miles from Pearl Harbor. At top speed on three engines, that's a four-day run. Of course, it means our diesels will be sucking fuel like mad, but since we're to refuel, it doesn't matter.

I get the Watch bill straight in my head. There are three watches; First, Second, and Third; each led by one of the ship's officers. Pike has the First, Michaelis the Second, and Waldron the Third. So each man is on watch four hours and off for eight. The Skipper doesn't stand a watch per se, as his duty goes round the clock and he may stay on duty for days at a time.

Later, I take a turn forward so Pike can show me the forward torpedo room. Passing through the oval hatch in the forward bulkhead, the compartment is a mass maze of pipes, cables and reload torpedoes with thirteen bunks for the torpedomen crammed into every inch of available space. There's practically no space left for them to sleep, let alone move around. A small steel pipe made even more stifling by the technical wizardry protruding from the ceiling and walls.

Pike shows me the torpedo blow and vent manifold in the center of the overhead barely a foot from tubes' one and two. He explains that this manifold controls the 225lb. air banks forward which are used to fire the Mark XIV torpedo in each of the six forward tubes. He leans back and taps one of the steel lances with his hand. "The Mark XIV is a 21inch whitehead-type torpedo, basically a copy of the Mark X, that we had during the last war. It carries a warhead of five hundred pounds of TNT, has a range of 4500 yards at 46 knots, or 9000 yards at 31 and a half knots,' he pauses to clear his throat. I glance around at the "torpedo gang," who stare back at us with bored looks.

Daschler - he of the enormous tattoo collection and bulging biceps - sits on his bunk with a cigarette between his lips. Next to him lays a torpedo on its storage racks. Strange bedfellows indeed. Imagine, sleeping next to 500 lbs. of high explosive.

"These are steam torpedoes." Pike continues in his high-pitched southern accent. He stares at me, as if to make sure I'm getting every word. "Which means they are driven by steam generated by the combustion of alcohol and water in compressed air, savvy?"

I nod absentmindedly.

"As the alcohol burns, it leaves a highly visible trail of bubbles in the water, which means you can see 'em, which is good for the Japs and bad for us. Any Jap skipper with a good eye can spot 'em coming and turn in time to avoid getting hit and - ' the corners of his mouth now turn down as if he'd bitten into a sour apple, ' - they also provide a great bearing on our location for any Nip tin-can that might be in the area."

'Tin-can' - he means the destroyer, our ultimate nemesis.

"So,' he continues, 'if there's a destroyer in the area, when we shoot we immediately hightail it in another direction." We both have to grab onto a handhold as the bow suddenly rises up on a large swell. The entire compartment tilts aft, then just as quickly drops forward. Pike and I hang onto the manifold above us to keep from stumbling into the heavy brass torpedo tube doors.

Pike shifts his weight from one foot to the other, then shoves his cap back on his head.

"The torpedoes are checked daily, during the trim dives. First we go over the ones here in the racks. Then, we pull the ones in the tubes out and make sure all systems are go with those; motors, alcohol, air banks, and the gyroscope. We always have to dive to do it because otherwise there would be too much tossing around in here - '

As if to punctuate his comment, the bow again dips severely. Once more we grab a hold of the manifold to steady ourselves. Pike nods his head. "See what I mean?"

"Now -' he says, turning once again back to the tubes, 'We have six forward. On the port side the tubes are evenly numbered two, four, and six. On the starboard side are the odd numbered one, three, and five. Course you only see tubes' one to four now. Tubes' five and six are beneath the deck plates, look here -' he bends down and pulls up one of the heavy iron plates that make up the grating of the deck. With a creak and a sound like sliding slate, the plate comes up. I can see the shiny solid brass inner door that covers the breech of torpedo tube number five. A few feet back lies the dull, gunmetal muzzle of the reload torpedo. The naked electric light reflects harshly off its oily exterior.

He looks at me expectantly, as if awaiting some type of revelation. I simply nod. Satisfied, he slips the deck plate back into place and continues.

"These tubes are closed on the outside by, as you know, a outer door similar to the inner door which can be opened by the cranks you see here - ' he points to the objects in question, '- as are the outer door shutters - opened by these cranks here -' his hand moves correspondingly to two large metal pins sticking out of the overhead, '- and when the tube is flooded, these glass ports on the outside of the inner door will turn green. The senior torpedoman will then flash a message to the tower - or bridge as the case may be - affirming tube is ready to fire. You still with me?"

"Yes sir." I can't help but notice the torpedomen in here, stare at Pike with a mixture bored and amused looks.

"Now, the tubes can be fired from either in here at these switches -' he points to the firing levers on the front of the manifold, '- or from a master switch located in the conning tower next to the TDC. That doesn't concern us though, that part is up to Tyreen.'

He takes a step back and puts his hand on a ladder leading to the top of the pressure hull.

"This is the forward escape trunk. It has two hatches, one on the top of the deck, and another at the top of the pressure hull. In the event of an emergency we can flood it, and get men out of the boat two to three at a time, using their Momsen Escape Lungs." A smile creases his lips, "Remember the big training tank at New London? The instructors put you in a chamber similar to this, flood it, and up you go using the Momsen Lung."

A moan comes from one of the bunks.

"Somebody still tight from last night?" Daschler queries belligerently from his bunk, "I can't believe I put to sea with this bunch of mama's boys! A smooth sea and they're puking! I hate to see what happens if it gets sloppy out here."

A tanned figure stirs to my left. Lifting up from the prone position on his bunk, he sits upright and glares around menacingly - it's Tashtego - the full-blooded Sioux Indian.

"You throw up in my torpedo room, I'll bash you're head in!" The words come slowly with an emphasis on the word "my."

Daschler leans out over his bunk, "Ya hear that! Now if you throw up, fart real big so "Tash" here doesn't smell it! Everybody got that?"

A new fellow leans down from his bunk in the overhead, "Hey Lieutenant, what's this "Gooneyville Lodge I keep hearing about at Midway? We going to stop there?"

Pike shakes his head. "Sorry Cutter - just long enough to top off our fuel tanks."

A groan suddenly emanates from one of the other senior torpedomen. "That means we've got to traverse the Pacific without a final send - off bash! No booze till Pearl huh?"

"I would've thought you'd had enough booze for a while after the way you were last night Howe!" A disembodied voice cries out from one of the bunks.

"I only sober up to find out where I'm going to get drunk again! And besides, with the Navy putting you on the wagon for weeks at a time,' Howe retorts angrily, " I'm just like one of my torpedoes, got to have enough alcohol to keep moving!"

Daschler suddenly lets out a high-pitched cackle, "You were moving pretty good enough last night at the Forbidden City without a drop, so what gives?"

"That's different!"

"How so? Come on...fess up!"

The conversation suddenly turns bawdy. Our business completed in the bow compartment. Pike and I retire through the bulkhead, leaving the "torpedo gang" to their business.

"Now let's get you a close-up at the batteries.' He says, lifting up the removable panel located in the middle of the passageway's aisle. Shifting the cap on his head, he lowers himself down into the hole. Follow me."

Dropping down into the lower portion of the compartment is like entering a subterranean catacomb. All I can see are the vague outlines of giant hulks protruding from the floor, only faintly illuminated by the light coming down through the open entrance panel.

"Wait,' Pike's commands, and I hear him moving along whatever it is that we're standing on. A scraping sound follows, and then a set of lights comes on, not bright by any measure - only enough to navigate your way around. "There....that's a little better,' I look down. We stand on a narrow catwalk sandwiched between the gargantuan lumps that are the batteries. I notice thick bundles of cables criss-crossing in every direction, looking like the wriggling bodies of a thousand or so snakes. The exterior of the cells is probably a creamy-white color, but looks dirty-gray in the faint light. The bulky rows in the center nearest us are on one level, then the rows directly outboard of the center rise almost a foot higher. The battery tops wedged right against the inside of the pressure hull are yet even higher; as if the shipwrights had not figured each battery cell's width into their designs and had to literally squeeze in the last two rows of cells.

"Now,' Pike begins, taking a deep breath, 'in here you have one hundred and twenty-six cells right? Each battery tank....these here,' he explains, tapping one of the gray hulks with his boot, 'Consists of six fore and aft rows of twenty-one cells each. You can see by the layout it's a tiered system. The cells are joined in a series by inter-cell connectors while the cells at the end of the rows are linked by....of course....end cell connectors. Now,' he says, moving to a control panel about thigh height above the catwalk, 'the ones for the after batteries are located in the after end of the crew's quarters. But remember these are only for use in an emergency, such as in a fire - where we run the danger of a rapidly expanding electrical fire."

Pike stares at me a moment - blinks - then continues.

"Also, each battery is fitted with an exhaust ventilating system in order to remove battery gases. The air required for this system is drawn from intakes located at opposite ends of each compartment. The free air in the compartment is drawn through the filling vent connection of each cell. The cells are connected by soft rubber nipples-' he can't resist a smirk here, '-to exhaust headers of hard rubber which extend fore and aft for each row of cells. The headers - in two sections - are connected to cross-headers which unite in a common exhaust duct. The exhaust duct from each battery is led up to and through the deck to the inlets of two fans which are mounted on the hull overhead in the battery rooms, just above us."

Pike - the walking encyclopedia of submarining.

"The fans -' he continues without missing a beat, '- are rated at five hundred cubic feet per minute at two thousand seven hundred rpm's. Each has its own independent drive, with the motor for each being controlled from the maneuvering room. Armature resistance governs starting and speed regulation. Each armature circuit includes armature resistance, and there is a damper that allows the fans to operate singly or together, which exhaust into the ship's exhaust line. The quantity of air moving through the ventilators is measured in the maneuvering room by means of two airflow indicators marked in cubic feet per minute."

He pauses and takes a deep breath. "Make sense?"

"Oh certainly." I lie.

"Okay,' he says - and I'm not sure if there isn't a hint of a smile on his face - 'There's airflow through each individual cell. The flow of air through cells of each battery compartment achieves equalization by means of adjusting regulators installed as an internal part of each filling vent cylinder. We - and by that I mean nobody on board - ever messes around with the settings. The yard determines their proper adjustments and sets them accordingly. We're not to touch them."

He stops again and looks at me. I stare back blankly.

"Those rubber nipples incidentally, are never to be twisted. A twisted nipple interferes with the airflow and -' he starts snickering, '- it's not kind to do that to our girl, now is it?"

This dark, labyrinthine-like cavern, who could know the technological secrets it holds?

"Let's keep moving,' Pike declares, motioning me up with his hand.

Into the control room. Pike steers me over to the port side of the room and stops right in front of the "Christmas Tree" - the hull indicator light board. The "Christmas Tree" name originates from the red and green lights that indicate whether the hull vents and openings are open or closed. A green board means all hull openings closed and the boat ready to dive. When the lights are red; we are either on the surface or not prepared for diving. When the lights flash green, all openings are closed and the boat is ready to dive. Directly below it are levers that control all main flood vents. To the left is the diving control station.

"Now -' Pike begins, 'here is where the bow and stern planes are controlled. They are operated hydraulically except when we rig for silent running. Then, we shift to hand power, by means of these levers here,' his right hand goes out and touches the two levers which disengage a clutch which separates them from the hydraulic line. Two large stainless-steel wheels control the angle of the planes."

"This is the trim manifold here,' Pike says, moving his hand to the left of the diving controls, to several rows of steel squares with large brass nuts on the top, 'where we pump water throughout the boat to achieve a neutral equilibrium. Beneath the deck plates here,' Pike taps a grating with the toe of his boot, 'is the pump room. All your low-pressure blowers, IMO pumps, trim pump, drain pumps, hydraulic accumulators, refrigerators, IC generators, and air-condition machines are squeezed into a little area down there barely big enough to stand up in." He pauses for a breath and looks at me. As he is about to go on Quartermaster Harmison pokes his head down through the conning tower hatch.

"Lt. Pike to the bridge!"

So Pike turns me over to the Chief, whom he instructs to take me aft. Apparently the Chief is a 'plank owner' in the boat. A plank owner means anyone who has been with a ship since it's commissioning. If anyone knows this boat stem to stern it is the Chief.

As Pike takes leave of us and heads for the bridge the Chief holds up a thick forefinger - wait. He is checking through what appear to be fuel logs. The Chief could easily be a boxer. His body is not large, but taut and powerful. It is a marvel he stays so much in shape. In a submarine, after weeks at sea with no activity besides going on watch, the muscles in the body tend to go slack. His deep, golden tan is either from spending a good amount of time on the bridge or sunning himself in port between patrols. His black hair closely shaved, when he takes off his white-topped cap with its verdigris-tinged gold anchor insignia, the look is as if he has five o'clock shadow all over his head. I notice the forefinger steadied for a moment in the air has that look of a long period in a greasy, oily environment. Both are ingrained into his skin.

He grunts suddenly and tosses the fuel log down on the small shelf that holds most of the boats' necessary books. He shifts his cap and regards me with an expectant eye. "So, we're to have a look aft eh Ensign?"

"I think that's the idea Chief."

The Chief's blue eyes glow brilliantly. "Come with me!"

"That's a neat little character on the conning tower Chief.' I say, following him through the after bulkhead.

He stops and his eyes light up. "You like that?"

"Very much."

"It's my catharsis in a way. I love losing myself in drawing, sketching and painting. The one I'm most proud of is the one I did of my wife. It's on the panel at the foot of my bunk, so it's the last thing I see before I go to sleep and the first thing I see when I wake up. Remind me and I'll show it to you."

As we navigate through the after bulkhead, he points out the radio room. "All incoming and outgoing radio traffic goes through here." As we move through the hatch coaming, my nose suddenly detects cooking odors - here's the galley - and Jonesy, who gives me an irritated look as I pass by. Then the crews mess with its four small tables and just as large benches. I duck my head just in time to avoid slamming it into the skirt of a hatch that protrudes from the overhead. The Chief taps the rim with the palm of his hand.

"Main deck access hatch, right now it's full of potatoes. On these long Pacific cruises we have to cram provisions into every spare nook and cranny - and in submarines there's not too many of those!' He pauses as he adjusts his white cap. 'Just aft of the after battery compartment - which doubles as the crew's quarters - we have a head and two showers.' He grins sarcastically, 'Showers the Navy obviously meant to be used in port only, because they're also stuffed to the rafters with provisions."

He's watching me intently, like a schoolmaster does a pupil. His blue eyes seem to stare into the back of my head. "So you see Ensign,' he continues, 'there's not much similarity with the surface fleet."

I can only nod in response as the Chief taps the floor plates with his foot.

"The magazine's right below us; all ammunition for the deck gun, .30 cals, and small arms are stowed there. Right back in here,' he pauses as he opens a narrow door, 'is the crew's quarters. Thirty-six bunks and a few inches for their necessities that the Navy likes to refer to as lockers. Beneath us - one hundred twenty six cells of Exide batteries, the after battery compartment."

As I step into the compartment, the aroma of sweat, body odor, vomit, and cigarette smoke is almost overwhelming. There is also a strong smell of diesel exhaust. It is such that I can almost feel the hair in my nose curling. Once again, take the nose out of operation and breath through the mouth.

The Chief stops. "Only thirty-six bunks in here.' He notes with regret, 'Since we have a complement of sixty-five men, we have a system known as 'hot bunking', that means one bunk for every two men. One sleeps while the other is on watch. In the torpedo rooms it's worse, the men have to triple up.' The Chief shakes his head sheepishly, 'One of these days they'll design a boat with enough bunks for each man in the crew, so that the man coming off watch won't have to crawl into the other man's sweat."

Off-duty sailors lounge in their bunks. Some read, a few play poker, but most are still fussing about with personal articles. The Chief steps easily over the clothing, sea bags, and accumulated junk that has not yet been stowed properly. "All right, let's get this compartment squared away! I will not tolerate my boat being turned into a hog pen. C'mon! Snap to it! Let's go!" Groans and mutterings answer him all around.

He suddenly lets out a yell as he stares down at the floor plates.

"What the hell is this?"

I step around him to see a puddle of reddish-yellow liquid on the floor plates. It rushes to one side, and then the other, moving with the motion of the boat. My momentary confusion evaporates when the vile aroma of stomach acid reaches my nose. Gorge suddenly rises in my throat. I look away.

One of the men looks up from a "Lil' Abner" comic book, "Oh, Myers isn't feeling too well -it's his first time at sea." The sailor motions to a figure next to him curled up into a ball.

The Chief sputters with rage. "Get off your filthy ass and get this shit cleaned up NOW! You puke on my floor - you clean it up! I'll be back in here in five minutes! If this shit isn't up so help me God I'll rub your ugly face in it! MOVE!" The men vault out of their bunks as if at gunpoint. The Chief shakes his head as he continues aft. "Jesus, Mary, and Joseph!"

Moving aft, the rumbling of the diesels gets increasingly louder. It can be heard and felt all over the boat, but now - in here - it's almost deafening. Everything vibrates. The floor plates beneath me feel like they're moving on their own accord. The hatch before us is closed. The Chief stops. "Ya hear that?' he says, half-yelling to be heard over the din, 'that's music to the ears! You want to see our girls in action?' the Chief beams proudly, as if getting ready to show me his first-born. He reaches down and turns the crank on the watertight door and opens it.

All at once the roar envelops me; thirty-two cylinders in the two engines all slamming away at once. The noise is such I can't even hear my own thoughts. As I step into the forward engine room the Chief leans back and closes the hatch behind us, locking the engine noise in this narrow cubicle. There are two men on watch in here. They stare at us expectantly. The Chief leans close to my ear and yells at the top of his voice to make himself heard over the furious racket - I catch every other word, "That....Motor.... Mates....--grew....--sby,'

I shake my head at him - not getting it. He tries again.

'MoTOR...MachinIST...MATES....PETTI-GREW....AND SKJONS-BEE." He leans back and looks at me.

I nod - got it!

One of the men moves up to the Chief. He and the Chief exchange yells for a moment. How the hell can anyone hear anything in here? Lip-reading must be at a premium. The man turns and half salutes. I merely nod my head in acknowledgment. Submariners dispense with the stiff, military etiquette that is the norm on surface ships. Here informality is the rule.

The man is wiping his hands with an oil soaked rag. Behind him, the other engine room mate has the cover of the port diesel open. The engine rocker arms driving the pistons inside the cylinders move so fast that they are nothing more than a blur. It all begins to come back to me; the diesel engine differs from an internal combustion engine - like a gasoline engine - in that it has no ignition system or spark plugs. It relies solely on the heat of compression to ignite the fuel forced into the cylinders under pressure and atomized. Each engine is of the two-cycle diesel type. The engines on the port side are for left-hand screw rotation, and those on the starboard side drive the starboard screw on a right-hand rotation. The diesel engine burns a mixture of fuel oil and air, and injected air is from the boat's high-pressure 3,000 lb. air system. But before the air is admitted to the engine, it first goes through a reducing flask, which brings the pressure down to 500 lbs. Air is then injected into the cylinders, causing the first internal explosion. The high-pressure air is shut off, as the engines own momentum carries each controlled explosion into the next. The air for the cylinders is provided by blowers, which sit right above the diesels. Their shiny metal exteriors reflect the opposite sides of the compartment in a warped specter. These have a dual purpose in also carrying away the burnt gases from the same cylinders; a function known as scavenging, a constant, uniform supply of air furnished at the rate of - what was it? Oh yes! 5,630 cubic feet per minute!

Now, the engines do not drive the propeller shafts directly. Each engine drives a generator that supplies electrical power to drive the four main propulsion motors, located under the floor plates. A reduction gear drives each of the two propellers, two pinions driven by the propulsion motors and a slow speed gear connection to the propeller shaft.

The fellow standing over the uncovered port engine nods his head, apparently satisfied, and settles the cover back into place. He fumbles in his greasy and oil stained dungaree shirt and produces a pack of cigarettes. Selecting one, he places it between his lips with grease and oil-blackened hands. Lighting it, he sits down on a toolbox and regards us with feigned interest.

The Chief shouts something in my ear. I look at him and shrug - missed it. He tries again and this time it reaches me, "THEY'RE....PURRING....LIKE....KITTENS!" The Chief motions with his arm and heads toward the after bulkhead. Onto the after engine room. I nod at the machinist mate next to me. He grins back, his teeth showing a brilliant white behind a greasy and exhaust blackened face.

The infernal roaring continues unabated in the after engine room. In here are diesels number three and four. The Chief leans close and yells to me that we have three engines on propulsion and one on charge, or "putting juice in the can," as calls it. The two skinny machinist mates in here, Hartmann and McClusky - along with a petty officer - are as black with exhaust, oil, and grease as are their cousins in the next compartment. The petty officer - whose name I think is Copenhaver - tests the petcocks on each side of the engine. Copenhaver is a daguerreotype of an 1890's gentleman personified; complete with a fastidiously waxed handlebar mustache. Each time he opens a petcock, a blue flame shoots out. He looks at the Chief, who nods his head approvingly. The man takes a step forward and engages in a shouting match with the Chief - I can make no sense out of it due to the noise level. He leans close as the Chief directs orders into his ear. As he stands there, he produces a pouch from his back pocket. Unzipping it, his hand disappears into it for a few seconds. It reappears with a neatly kneaded plug of tobacco held between his thumb and first three fingers. His left hand comes up, holds his cheek open, and into the void disappears the plug of tobacco. Copenhaver's right cheek now protrudes out over his jaw as if he held a baseball inside of it.

Finished for the moment with their antics that could easily pass for a game of charades, the Chief nods his head once again. And on we go through the after bulkhead.

The next compartment is the maneuvering room; "Schumacher's hole" the Chief calls it. Schumacher stands in front of the maneuvering stand, upon which are the main propulsion controls. He studies them like a doctor does X-rays. Directly in front of him are ten levers, and above them a board of gauges of various types, engine telegraph indicators, voltmeters, and a host of switches and dials. Getting 'qualified in submarines' is not something that's going to happen overnight. It will take me the better part of the patrol just to become familiar with all this technological wizardry.

Everything in here vibrates and pulsates with energy from the diesels next door. Even as the Chief closes the watertight door, my head still resounds with the roaring and rumbling courtesy of Fairbanks-Morse.

Schumacher gives me a friendly grin and a wink as he busies himself with tests of all the different gauges and dials. The Chief once again becomes the narrator, "In here is where we control the e-motors when we are submerged.' He taps the deck plates with his foot, 'These are located under the deck plates in what is called the motor room. These gauges you see tell us our ampere output and wattage, and let us know how much juice is in the can,' once again pausing for effect. I am beginning to feel like a sponge, trying to soak up all this information in as short a span of time as possible. He goes on to tell me of all the functions that take place in here. Some stick in my head, others go out my other ear. I'm reaching a saturation point. All of it is so complicated.

Then it's on into the after torpedo room where I get the chance to become more confused: four torpedo tubes in here. Also an escape and rescue hatch, identical to the one in the forward room. A stern plane tilting mechanism in here for emergencies, similar to the one forward for the bow planes. And more bunks, gauges, valves, pumps, pipes, flappers - the list are endless. The torpedomen back here - oblivious to my confusion - go about their business getting everything in the compartment squared away.

Curiously, I've noticed that in every major compartment is a good-sized wood box stuffed with a multitude of pineapples, oranges, papayas, coconuts, and grapefruits. My guess is that these are preventive measures against scurvy. Scurvy, a condition resulting from a lack of Vitamin C. My mind forms an immediate picture of gaunt figures painfully treading the decks of sailing ships in the days of old. Their hair falling out, open sores festering, each man counts with excruciating regularity as his teeth fall out one by one until dissolved to futile process of mashing his food with bleeding gums.

I notice that the further you get aft, the more you experience a creeping feeling of isolation from the rest of the boat. The control room seems a mile away, the conning tower ten miles, and the bridge a thousand. Of course there is the speaker connection with the bridge and conning tower, but it doesn't seem to matter. If anything goes wrong with the boat and she sinks - like the *Squalus* did three years ago - there is little chance of getting out alive. The reason being if the main induction valve water floods the engine rooms, it will seal off the rest of the boat. And when that happens, the stern is the first thing to go under - which rules out getting out of the hatch. Those fellows forward can scramble out of the bow before it goes under. But aft, you're trapped. The only way out is the Momsen lung, that strange breathing apparatus that the crew would don and then make a break for the surface.

The grand tour is now at an end. As the Chief and I work our way back forward, it strikes me that each of these compartments are as alike as they are different. Each has its own specialized purpose, and manned by the same sweating, putrid men that breathe the same foul air. I even comment to the Chief about the boat's inherent odors. He laughs mischievously as he regards me with his piercing blue eyes. "You've smelled nothing yet sir, wait until our next trim dive, when the sanitary tanks - which collect all the shit from the heads are blown to the sea. While the contents are vented outboard, the air that we blow them with is vented *in*board."

I can hardly wait.

All the bunks in here are on the port side. I'm on the top, and Lemert is on the bottom. I find out that Waldron's bunking in here too. Across the passageway are the Skipper's quarters. Our only privacy is a thin curtain pulled across the opening when one of us sleeps. Aft of us is the control room, and forward is the bow compartment. If the hatches are open, you can hear everything that is going on and being said. From forward comes the sound of boisterous laughter. Apparently two nights before our departure they drank three marines under the table.

"I'm telling you, you shoulda' seen 'em, these freckle faced teenagers come up and tell me and Howe here that marines are the best and all this shit. Well, I say to this one who's all puffed and important, if he's so big and tough - why not challenge me and 'Howesy' to a few rounds."

A chuckle of disbelief, then "And they did it?"

"Not only did they, but paid for all the rounds! I'm telling you if the war's left up to little one's like them, the Japs are gonna kick our ass! Anyway,' he says, sounding delighted to have an audience 'By the time we're finished...me and 'Howesy' are still standing and feeling fine. But two of the leathernecks are passed out and one is on the floor puking all over himself."

"Unfair. They were straight out of boot-camp."

"So what?" Says Daschler, incredulous that Tashtego is raining on his parade, "They challenged us! We were minding our own business!"

"Not fair. They were too green. Now I'd like to see you take on a few China marines and see how well you do. Try playing with the big boys for once."

A ripple of laughter comes from the compartment. Daschler's rising balloon has just been stuck with a pin.

"Big boys? Hell - I'd like to see how straight you stand after fifteen shots of bourbon!"

"Fifteen!" Somebody exclaims.

"Straighter than you my friend."

"And how do you know that?"

"I am a stronger person inside,' Tashtego replies confidently, 'You are not as strong as I am."

"Hah! We'll settle this right now - when we get back, you and I are gonna go head to head - not with whiskey - but with white lightning! Then we'll see who's the strongest!"

I can almost picture Tashtego screwing up his face as he repeats in confusion "White lightning?"

"Yeah - from Tennessee! Home-brewed double rectified bust-head!"

"Do I hear a challenge?' Place your bets on this one while there's still time!"

"Time? Shit - we got the whole goddamned rest of the patrol! Cool off Garn, you can soak everybody for money later."

"Opportunity waits for no one little one!" Garn cackles.

And on it goes. They certainly find a lot of things to talk about up there.

A little while later Waldron issues me something that may save my life someday, the Momsen Escape Lung. It consists of a bag charged with oxygen from the ship's salvage air system, that flows to the user through a rubber hose attached to a rubber mouthpiece. The wearer then breathes normally through the mouth. A clip that goes over the nose prevents water from entering. The apparatus straps around the front of the chest. Wearing this contraption makes you look like some type of hideous beast from the deep.

"Permission to come on the bridge?"

"Granted!"

The wind that blows over the bridge brings a welcome relief from the fetid air below. It is amazing how one can take things for granted; fresh air, spacious quarters, and a comfortable bed....

I take up station on the port side, on the Skipper's left. Waldron is on his right; his pipe still clenched between his teeth. Looking out over the bridge bulwark lies the vast expanse of the Pacific, the long and low rolling groundswell meets our bow head on. The sun has shifted in the sky during the time I was below. Earlier it had been just off our port bow; now it is on the port beam. I glance at my watch - 1500 hrs - midday. My stomach rumbles, reminding me mess isn't until 1800 hrs. Three hours till then, so I reach for my cigarettes. A cigarette is always good to stifle hunger off for a while.

The sky is a brilliant deep blue and almost cloudless. A few fleecy masses float to the northwest, steaming across the blue void as if pursued by some unseen force. The unseen force is the wind, which blows cool and salty.

"So what brings you into the boats Ensign?" The Skipper's voice brings me back into this world.

"Reading about the U-Boat campaigns of the last war."

The Skipper nods his head as he listens. "Ever heard of Otto Weddigen and the U-9?"

"Wasn't he the fellow that sank three British cruisers in one afternoon?" Waldron asks from behind his binoculars.

The Skipper nods his head slowly. "HMS *Hogue*, *Aboukir*, and *Cressy*, all torpedoed and sunk within a space of three hours. In three short hours he single-handedly changed the face of naval warfare."

"So much for Britannia ruling the waves!" Waldron cracks with a chuckle.

The Skipper shakes his head; "this fellow Doenitz is no idiot." He lets his glasses hang from the strap around his neck and leans back against the periscope housing. "The truth of the matter is, ' he begins slowly, carefully selecting each word, 'Surface warships are obsolete. Battleships, cruisers, frigates...they're all passé`. The only surface warship really needed anymore is the destroyer, for anti-submarine action, and maybe aircraft carriers. But those are so vulnerable they practically need an entire fleet to defend them. The big battlewagons we have now are steel versions of ships of the line back in the eighteenth century. There's no place for them now. But submarines - look what the Germans are doing with them now!

"But -' Waldron interrupts, 'it didn't work for the Germans in the first war."

The Skipper nods again. "But the reason was because they did not possess enough of them. If their U-Boat offensive fails again, it will be because they did not have enough of them at the critical time! With a large fleet of submarines a country can stop everything.' The Skipper pauses to collect his thoughts.

"For example,' he says, a bit of sarcasm lacing his deep, baritone voice, 'they called the new classes of submarines 'fleet boats,' Why? Because the idea was for them to operate in conjunction with the fleet - they're primary targets being warships! Nobody ever said anything about shooting up merchant shipping, which is a country's lifeline! And the big shots at headquarters all went through the last war,' he shakes his head dejectedly, 'Didn't we learn anything from the Germans? It's absolutely amazing!"

Following his lead, I politely point out that the very idea of submarine warfare was abhorred and considered barbarous by the devotees of the surface fleets, and that in some quarters resistance still runs high.

"That's true." The Skipper agrees. "And those are the very people who's ships submarines have made obsolete,' he looks at me with a knowing glint in his eye, 'what would you do if your job was on the line Ensign?" The Skipper shakes his head again and waves his arm. The subject is closed.

The Skipper leans over the open hatch leading down into the tower and requests a sounding. After a moment it comes back, Schumacher voice sounding hoarse as he yells up the hatch, " Just over a hundred and fifty fathoms sir!"

"We passed the hundred fathom curve about an hour ago sir" Waldron says from one corner of his mouth, his lips straining as he clenches the stem of his pipe in the other. The Skipper nods his head slowly.

"All right, let's take her down and see how the seals, valves and outboard plugs hold out,' he glances over his shoulder, 'lookouts below!"

The Skipper climbs down from the tower. He pauses, lifts his cap and runs his hand through his tangled mop of hair, then cocks it back on his head at an angle. If the navy got smart, they'd put him on recruiting posters. His face could no more be perfect than if it had been painted by an artist, lean with fine bone structure and kissed by the sun, salt, and wind. Even at his young age, he's already developed those peculiar lines around his cheeks and forehead, and the crow's feet near his eyes that come from staring into the sun too long. That legendary weathered look of a seafarer from years of exposure to the elements.

"Take her down Mr. Waldron. Level her off at two zero zero feet."

Waldron gives a slight nod of his head. "Level off at two zero zero - aye sir."

The Skipper props his foot on the ladder leading to the tower and glances at his watch. "Open bulkhead flappers and re-circulate."

The sonar sounding said it was a little over a hundred fathoms. So, if a fathom is approximately six feet, that's six hundred feet. The Pacific is both incredibly vast and deep. If all the world's continents were placed in the Pacific, there would yet be room for another continent the size of Asia. The ocean that embraces our boat and buoys it up covers more than a third of the world's surface.

"Passing one zero zero feet." Waldron begins sucking air through his pipe, making a sound akin to fat in a fryer. The two planesmen, engrossed in their controls, rivet their eyes to the plane angle indicators.

From somewhere comes the sound of water dripping into the bilge. The Skipper's eyes narrow and he tilts his head, "Chief" There's a movement behind me. The Chief starts off in the direction of the offending sound.

"Passing one five zero feet."

I study the backs of the planesmen. Theirs is not an easy job. They must control the depth and angle of the boat so precisely at all times, so that the boat is on an even keel. Their movements of the planes must neither be too much nor too little, just enough. Too much movement will throw the boat off and by then it's too late - at periscope depth the Skipper would be blinded as the scope end went under the surface. It could completely foil and attack and endanger the boat. So the planesmen must be very precise in their movements.

The Chief reappears. "Packing gland" is all he has to say.

"Passing one seven five feet." In my right hand I grasp the rungs of the ladder leading into the tower. The metal is cool, and a little clammy.

Waldron sighs, as if contemplating a momentous decision. "Blow negative to the mark!"

Behind me, Seaman Andersen is on the boat's high-pressure air manifold. He immediately begins twisting the valves that control the negative tank. A low hiss becomes a roar as the high-pressure air is vented into the tank, forcing the seawater out the bottom. His exertions completed, he turns around, "Negative blown sir."

Waldron's pipe crackles in the still air. "Leveling off at two zero zero feet sir." Two hundred feet of seawater above the keel. After some slight trimming, the boat is on an even keel. "Boat in balance sir." Waldron reports.

The Skipper is silent. A few moments pass by with only the humming of our electrical motors to keep us company. Then he splits the quiet by clearing his throat and ordering Waldron to take the boat deeper, to make sure "all plugs, valves, and packings can take the stress."

I watch the needle on the depth gauge in the center of the diving controls. The markings denote from two hundred to a hash mark three quarters of the way away from the three hundred mark - two hundred and twenty five feet. It continues to move two hundred fifty, then two seventy-five. Then, three hundred feet.

Something pops. I look around. The Skipper gives me a reassuring look, "Just the woodwork. There's a lot of air in the paneling and the deck."

Not wanting to appear in the slightest way frightened, I shrug nonchalantly.

The gauge needle continues to move. Three hundred twenty five...three hundred fifty. A sudden shudder runs through the hull. More popping noises. The ocean is pressing in on every square inch of our steel pressure hull with all its might.

Almost four hundred now. Another shudder - worse than the first. The sound of creaking metal. I catch a few alarmed looks from some of the men around me. Even Waldron glances expectantly at the Skipper. It flashes through my mind: *Electric Boat Company guarantees three hundred feet.*

Suddenly, a loud crack and a taut metal cable bounces in the wind. I steal a glance at the Skipper - his face betraying no emotion. He stares, poker faced, at the diving controls.

The needle on the depth gauge is rapidly approaching four hundred and twenty five feet. More popping noises. Creaking metal; like un-oiled hinges. Waldron's glances are more frequent now.

"Deeper." The Skipper tosses out the word as if it had no meaning to him at all. He's the epitome of calm.

A few nervous coughs, clearings of throats, and shuffling of feet. Are we all thinking the same thing? What would happen should the hull give way? What would it be like to die that way, trapped inside an imploding submarine? Screeching metal, jets of ice cold water streaming in as the hull crumples, the pressure such that it could cut a man in two in seconds. Pipes bursting; more water, oil, hydraulic fluid. The screams of men drawing their last breaths.

The popping is now excruciating. The steel groans in pain.

"Level off at four seven five." Finally the boat levels onto an even keel. The seaman on the high-pressure air manifold vents a predetermined amount from the main ballast tanks. This is a must. As the boat goes deeper it becomes heavier. Simple laws of physics. The hull compression caused by the outside pressure actually makes us smaller and therefore less buoyant, so to maintain a roughly neutral state, we must blow some of our ballast to compensate.

"All compartments report." The Skipper directs. It takes a few moments for the reports to start coming in. A few leaks from valves and fittings, packing glands that need tightening down, etc. We're still in one piece.

The Skipper glances around the control room, "She must take this depth." He grins slyly over at Waldron, "They build them solid in Groton."

"Indeed they do sir." Waldron grins.

The Skipper orders the sound heads rigged out. Located beneath the forward torpedo room where they are least affected by our own noise. Topside there is also the JP hydrophone, which the soundman can turn by means of a lever located above the sound controls.

The Skipper moves up the ladder into the tower. He pauses just before taking the last rung, "Ensign. 'Apparently he means for me to follow him. I double-time it up the ladder.

In the tower the Skipper leans against the periscope housing. Schumacher stands near the small chart table, and Boatswain's Mate Duffy is at the sound controls. Boatswain's Mate - a rank that on a surface ship carries much weight, since they were traditionally responsible for the ship's rigging. Not much rigging here on a boat like this.

He sits with a pair of earphones over his head, snapping the lever around just in front of him. On a dial below him are a series of numbers, like a compass. This is so the soundman can give bearings to the sounds that come over the line. Duffy's right hand grasps the lever, turning it ever so slightly. His face is screwed up in concentration; a thoughtful frown creases his forehead. A few moments pass as Duffy twists his lever this way - then that. His frown disappears. He looks up at the Skipper. "All in order sir."

"All right. That'll do for now." The Skipper glances around at each of us in turn, as if to size us up. He looks satisfied for the moment.

"Surface."

I feel a bit like a fish out of water, totally out of my element. I must learn everything as fast as I can, for everything on the boat has a specific function. Nothing is superfluous. Just as the machinery and technical wizardry in here are products of much trial and error. The end result is everything in the boat has its purpose; it is the same with her crew. Every man right down to Jonesy has a specific job to do. And he executes that job better than anyone else does.

"It'll takes a little time to sink in Ensign, just go with it." The Skipper remarks, as if reading my mind. I can't tell whether the pun was intended or not.

"Passing two five feet. Tower clear,'

"Equalize pressure." The Skipper says over his shoulder. Harmison breaks the seal and allows the excess pressure in the boat to escape. The resulting blast of escaping air causes a brief wind through the boat. Dust, papers, and some loose cork insulation are suddenly lifted into the air. The wind dies as suddenly as it came. Harmison undoes the dogs and flings open the hatch, a jet of water shoots through the open hole. He jumps away dripping to make way for the bridge watch. The OOD is first, followed by the Skipper. I am two steps behind him.

We hear the Philippine situation is fast turning from bad to worse. The Imperial Japanese continue to sweep all before them. The islands are completely surrounded by the Japanese Navy. Hope for the garrison is slim. But hope is all we have right now. We laugh, joke, and carry on because we do not want to think of what is reality - our fellow countrymen are dying there and we can do nothing to stop it. We are powerless. Even money is on the Japanese invading the West Coast within the next six months. How will it all end?

The Skipper looks completely disgusted. Tossing back the last of his coffee he drops the cup heavily on the table. Without a word he gets up and leaves the room. An embarrassed silence follows. We stare into our cups and trays so as not to have to look at one another.

The XO is first to break the silence by clearing his throat. He doesn't look up, but stares at his tray in front of him. With his fork he pushes the remnants of a potato around, making tracks in the brown gravy. "Tyreen's got several friends stuck in the Philippines. Three have already been killed and two others are crippled for life. He just received word about it this morning."

Putting down his fork, he stares vacantly in front of him. "All the signs were there. You would have thought someone would've put their finger on it." Angrily, the XO tosses back the rest of his coffee and without another word disappears into the passageway.

Michaelis whistles between his teeth. "Bet there are a few necks in Washington he'd like to wring."

"Isn't it funny,' Pike says thoughtfully, studying a fork on his plate, 'How the politicians are always the ones who make wars but never have to fight in them."

The steward appears and begins clearing away the plates and trays. Pike gets up, muttering something about the air flasks and torpedo alcohol. I might as well head to my bunk for a while. As I get up, the XO sticks his head back in with a book for me. The cover reads, in big block letters "ONI-208J IDENTIFICATION OF MERCHANT VESSELS OF THE JAPANESE EMPIRE."

"Learn that backwards, forwards, sideways and every other way. Got it?"

"Aye-aye sir."

I lie on the bunk facing the bow, my back against the pillow propped up against the partition behind me. Gingerly placing the coffee between my thighs, I crack open the manual. There are not pictures of ships in it, but rather silhouettes of them all colored black. Freighters, tankers, and tramp steamers - all laid out in black and white. The ship silhouette lies at the top of the page. Below this lie the ship's specifications: tonnage; both gross and deadweight, length, beam, draft, speeds, when constructed, type of propulsion, radius of vessel, potential naval value, and any remarks that might shed more light on the vessel. All Japanese merchant ships have the suffix *Maru* with their names, to denote them as merchant ships and not warships; *Kasugasan Maru, Katyosan Maru, Seiwa Maru.*

Engrossed in the manual, my concentration is interrupted periodically from the theatrics and boisterous laughter coming from the bow compartment. Daschler and Howe are once again indulging the rest of the torpedo gang in their sexual exploits while on shore.

"I'm telling you, her ass was - this big! Hair down to here. A brunette. Blue eyes. Would make Betty Grable cry."

"You're full of shit! She wouldn't have wasted her time with the likes of you!"

"To hell with all of you! The dame I've been with could be Katherine Hepburn's stand-in."

"Now who's full of shit?"

"Anybody up for some five-card draw?" The smooth even voice must belong to Tashtego. It has a note of resignation in it; he must be hearing all these stories for the hundredth time.

"Even money?" The aggressive, almost angry tone of Daschler.

"What else?" Tashtego replies. There is a commotion of moving about, bunks creaking, and men shifting around the compartment. A game is about to get underway.

I poke my head over the edge of the bunk. "Lemert?"

"Hmm?"

"Gambling allowed on board?"

"As long as it doesn't get out of hand. On these long cruises, sometimes you have to relax the rules a bit."

"Oh."

I sit back and silently sip my coffee as Lemert goes back to his book. Maybe by staring at the outlines in the ship recognition manual long enough, they will imprint themselves into my brain.

Sudden wild cursing from the bow compartment. Daschler's probably lost a hand. Daschler is one of those arrogant, aggressive types that are cocky and confident when everything goes their way, and when things don't, it's a conspiracy of major proportions. If it weren't for the countering effect Tashtego has, he'd probably try to dominate the rest of the men.

*   *   *

I awake with a start. Everything is strange to me - the room, the sounds, voices from somewhere, the bunk in which I lay is moving - where am I? It lasts only a second. A blurry figure leans over me. It takes me a moment to get my bearings. The figure wears an officer's cap, chiseled features, pipe protruding from the side of his mouth - Waldron.

"Ensign?"

"Sir?"

"XO would like you on the bridge."

"Yes sir."

Still disoriented, I slip down from my bunk, at the same time noticing Lemert lying in his bunk, novel fallen open on his chest, head back, mouth open and snoring. I grab my cap off the hook on the wall and follow Waldron out into the passageway. A roar of laughter comes from up forward, the poker game continues unabated in the bow compartment. It's like a bar, only the clinking of glasses is missing.

Into the control room. Moving around the small chart table, past the trim manifold and diving controls, and - grabbing a pair of 7x50's off the hook - head up the ladder into the conning tower. I can already smell the sweeter, fresher air up here even before I stick my head over the rim of the hatch. No more pungent aroma of bilge oil or body odor. The outline of the XO is just visible in the fading light.

"Permission to come on the bridge?"

"Granted."

I scramble up. Wonderful clean air fills my lungs and my nostrils; I breathe it in deeply and savor each breath. Surely mankind has for centuries taken our atmosphere for granted. One afternoon inside a submarine would cleanse all of any such ill-conceived notions quickly.

"Ensign Watts reporting as ordered sir."

The XO glances at me and nods his head, "Let's get you familiar with the bridge routine. Stick with Pike here through the watch."

"Yes sir."

"Pike, you have the conn."

"Aye-aye sir." The XO disappears below.

I quickly glance around. In addition to Pike, there are lookouts in the periscope shears just above us. Schumacher watches the great ocean rolling on past us from aft on the cigarette deck. Pike produces a pack of cigarettes and offers me one.

Lighting it, I lean against the steel bulwark of the bridge and stare out over a vast valley of gently rolling hills that approach out of the darkening sea ahead. With a shower of salty spray and a hiss of foam, the boat moves as gracefully as a ballerina does in a pirouette. Our string quartet the rumbling Fairbanks-Morse diesels, fading in and out each time the ventilators submerge in the swell. Behind us, the sun is slowly sinking below the horizon, a pool of scarlet created by its glow, which sparkles across the surface of the water like a thousand diamonds under a brilliant shining light. The red streaks of the fiery ball reach reverently skyward to the heavens, as if to remind mortal man once again whom it is to take credit for such natural splendor.

"This is the most dangerous time for us to be on the surface." Pike states candidly. "That damn sun in front of us, we're silhouetted on the horizon from behind. Keep your eyes open. Hear?"

Ignoring his challenge, I lift the binoculars to my eyes and scan the horizon; a dark green line above which is the deep gray of the darkening sky. The stars appear, small specks of light glittering in the heavens. The breeze that comes across the beam blows cool.

"Chilly." Pike concurs. The temperature must have dropped significantly from this afternoon. The sea is somewhat like the desert in that respect, during the day it can be a broiling furnace, so hot is snuffs out all forms of life. And in the dark of night, can become incredibly cold. I should send for one of my sweaters. I shiver again and decide to wait. If it doesn't bother Pike, I won't let it bother me.

A disembodied voice cries up from the conning tower. "Recommend coming right to two seven zero degrees sir!"

"Course two seven zero degrees authorized" Pike replies over his shoulder. We're still zigzagging. Every ten minutes or so, the routine varies so we cannot be tracked with any regularity. Our base course is now two hundred fifty degrees.

Pike gives the horizon another sweep with his binoculars, then lowers them and glances over his shoulder at the lookouts. Satisfied all is well, he turns back to the bulwark and leans against it, folding his arms in front of him. Though holding a relaxed and easy posture, I can still detect the fight in him. Pike always appears ready for a brawl, and even more eager for it to start. His lean, hard-bitten face belies his tender years, giving much the same impression as the Skipper's chiseled countenance that he's older than he actually is. I've also noticed Pike's face perpetually wears the curious expression of someone that's determined to ram his fist through the nearest bulkhead and was about to do it.

"Flashing in the water off the port beam!" The port lookout suddenly cries. Three pairs of binoculars swing in that direction.

"Left full rudder! All ahead flank!" Pike yells down into the conning tower from behind his glasses.

The boat heels sharply to port, I have to grab hold of the steel bulwark of the bridge to keep from being thrown off balance. Engine annunciators ring. The throbbing of our diesels increases with a sudden lurch. The hissing along our hull increases, the water boils. Pike mutters something unintelligible under his breath. A flashing object? The cold shiny steel of a torpedo broaching in the moonlight?

"There it is again!' Pike exclaims, 'Dead ahead!"

I see it, despite motion of the boat that constantly throws the binoculars around. A flashing - then nothing. There it is again! And again! A whole series of flashes.

Pike suddenly chuckles like a school kid. "It's a school of porpoises! Resume course two seven zero. All ahead full! Lucky that time." Pike says through cupped hands, lighting yet another cigarette. "I'd be curious to know in wartime just how many alarms have been sounded and crash dives caused by dolphins and porpoises looking like torpedoes and gulls looking like aircraft. Course you feel like an idiot when you make the mistake, but it's better to make an incorrect call than no call at all." He looks at me expectantly, shifts his cap on his head, and flicks a cigarette ash over the side. "Did you know there's really no such thing as a 'crash dive'? Dime-store novelists and Hollywood invented that term after the last war. What we do here is technically called a 'running dive.' This 'crash dive' stuff is all bullshit. But the term's caught on and not just with civilians. We do it too; everything is now a 'crash dive'. If you spot a plane, you 'crash dive' come across an enemy warship unexpectedly, you 'crash dive.' He chuckles and shakes his head sadly, 'You know funny thing is, I even catch myself saying it"

The Skipper calls up to the bridge, to find out what the maneuvering around was all about. In his quarters the Skipper has a compass repeater at the foot of his bunk, so that at any time he can at a glance, note our course. Pike recounts the school of porpoises for him. Apparently satisfied with the explanation, there is no further word from the conning tower. Pike shakes his head. "Tyreen's really on edge. It's almost as if he feels personally responsible for the life of every man, woman, and child in the Philippines. What we need is a miracle! If they can just hold out a little longer until help arrives. We need time, but it just isn't there!" Taking a long drag on his cigarette, he hunches his shoulders to ward off the chill of the breeze blowing over the bridge. "I know Tyreen pretty good,' he begins, staring vacantly in front of him. 'He's gonna hit hard. No quarter. He's gonna be relentless, like Grant at Petersburg. It's personal with him."

I feel him staring at me.

"You know, you could've shipped out with a lot of easier skippers than Tyreen."

"Meaning?"

"You'll see."

He pauses, momentarily lost in the rolling sea. The cigarette in his right hand glows brightly in the strong breeze coming over the bulwark. The boat rolls and swaggers from side to side as it beats its way through the swell. Sounds of diesels fading in and out, the hiss of foamy water.

"How do you feel about it? The Japs I mean?" I ask, the silence unnerving me.

Pike takes a final drag on his cigarette and flicks the butt over the side. "Kill 'em,' he says evenly. 'Kill 'em all."

*   *   *

In the wardroom. 0700 hrs. Breakfast. I sit across from Waldron, who takes his pipe out of his mouth for the first time today. It's funny; the only time Waldron doesn't have his pipe in his mouth is at meal times or when he's asleep. Earlier, when he rolled out of his bunk, before he put one leg into his trousers - he put his pipe into his mouth. It's as much an appendage as an arm or a leg.

The steward appears with plates full of scrambled eggs, bacon, and toast. We sip cups full of Jonesy's "lubricating oil." Michaelis shudders, "This stuff's beginning to dissolve my fillings."

No sign yet of the Skipper. Along with Waldron, Michaelis, and the XO - who's just down from the bridge for his morning sun line muttering figures under his breath - Schumacher joins us. One of Schumacher's most distinguishing trademarks is his habit of smoking these little Havana cigars. Wherever he is, like Waldron with his pipe, he usually has one of these little cheroot-looking things clenched in his teeth. He's from Louisiana I believe. Lemert says he first wanted to be a flier but flunked out of flight school after some inebriated barnstorming hi-jinks. He says the local squadron commander's daughter figured into the picture. Apparently the whole episode came pretty close to a court-martial. How he got out of it is a mystery. That's all we know. He plants himself at the other end of the table, and proceeds to send up clouds of smoke, causing the XO to give him an irritated look.

"You escorting a convoy or making smoke just for the hell of it?"

Engrossed in his own thoughts, Schumacher looks up with a start. "Huh?"

"Never mind."

Michaelis reaches over and grabs the salt and peppershakers in the middle of the table.

Thrusting his arm right in front of Waldron, who gives him a scathing glance for his apparent lack of table manners. Michaelis up-ends the salt shaker over his eggs and bacon. He has to beat on the shaker several times to get anything out; the high moisture content of the sea air causes the salt in the shaker to crystallize. The XO stares at him in amazement. By the time he puts it down it looks as if there is a dusting of snow on top of them.

"Why don't you make it easier on yourself and just unscrew the cap?"

Michaelis ignores the comment and gives his eggs a hefting dousing. His eggs are now pale yellow, white, with black spots. It resembles the pelt of a sick cheetah.

It gets better. Through the sliding partition to the pantry, Michaelis calls for a bottle of ketchup. He then tops off the foul-looking specter with a generous dollop of ketchup, and mixes it in until the entire plate is a thick, gooey mass.

Schumacher groans. "I'm gonna be sick!" While Waldron regards it more studiously, "Now that looks like something that escaped out of the bilge!"

The XO shakes his head and rolls his eyes skyward. "Bunch of freaks!"

"Can we get one of the Chief's vomit pails in here?" Schumacher asks, tearing a strip of bacon in two with his teeth.

"And this guy,' the XO remonstrates, pointing at Michaelis, ' - has the nerve to complain about Jonesy's coffee!"

"It's a soldiers' right to complain." Michaelis counters, in the process of downing his evil-looking plate.

If a play were produced using the officers as the cast, Michaelis would be the heavy. His slicked back hair and Italian looks effectively guise his east European birthright. He's even got the imbued arrogance of a criminal's superior mind, like some character out of Jimmy Cagney's gangster films. Pinstriped suit and violin case complete with a machine gun. When he looks at you sideways with one of his trademark "cold steel" stares, you wonder whether or not he practices these in front of a mirror.

There's no sign of Lemert. The XO informs me he took his breakfast on the bridge to get some fresh air. So, the atmosphere down here is getting to him too.

A few minutes later the Skipper appears. He waves away the steward who approaches with a plate for him. He looks very relaxed, the khaki shirt he wears open at the neck has obviously seen some time at sea. Faded, with a few stains here and there that bespeaks of oil or grease, and a bit rumpled from being washed too many times and starched too heavily. His trousers are of the same color, also showing their wear, and are tucked into British Navy half-Wellington sea boots that he came by somewhere. Cocked on his head is his cap, with its verdigris-tinged insignia, and he scratches at the one day growth of stubble on his face. He plants himself at the end of the table and calls for coffee.

The XO remarks the Skipper is developing his 'salty' look. We have not shaved, nor have we changed clothes. We all look similarly rumpled.

The Skipper glances at Michaelis's plate without reaction. He brings the cup to his lips, steam wafting up out of the cup. Blowing on it a bit, he takes a sip and glances up at the XO. "Base course?"

"Three hundred degrees sir."

"Speed?"

"Fifteen knots."

"Sea?"

"Three. Wind out of the northwest at seven. Clear sky. Barometer steady."

The phone buzzes. Waldron lifts it out of its cradle. "Wardroom?" He listens a moment, then replaces it in its cradle.

"Michaelis - Swensen has a wire for you."

"It's probably your doctor concerned about your sodium count."

"You're a funny guy." Michaelis hastily downs the last bite from his plate and disappears in the direction of the radio room.

The XO and the Skipper are soon involved in a discussion over our patrol area; AREA THREE by ComSubPac's definition; an area to the northeast of the Philippine Islands that interdicts the shipping routes leading to Japan. "With the current fight going on there, there shouldn't be a dearth of targets. Plenty of transports, but heavily escorted.' The Skipper observes philosophically. 'The Nips won't be asleep at the switch, you can count on that." His left arm is crooked back on the arm of the seat. His right braced on the table with the ring of the coffee mug grasped between his thumb and first two fingers. He stares above our heads as if seeing something oblivious to the rest of us. "Drills gentlemen, drills and more drills. When it's time to butcher the hog, the skewer must be sharp."

He isn't kidding. Five minutes later I'm on the bridge as the Skipper begins the drills. We go with a full bridge complement plus an extra man - me. The Skipper stays below in the conning tower with a stopwatch, and yells up through the open hatch, "Any time Pike!"

Pike glances around. "Lookouts below! Clear the bridge!"

Two blasts on the klaxon. Ear-splitting blasts of air as our vents are opened. Before ducking down into the hatch, I see the white boil around our hull and feel our angle begin to incline sharply.

"Take her deep - fast! All ahead emergency! Rig for depth charge!" Pike yells down the open conning tower hatch. There is a sudden loud banging through the boat as watertight doors are slammed shut and sealed. The conning tower hatch slams with a metallic ring. The wheel on top spins madly as it is made fast from the control room. Now the only contact with the rest of the boat is through the telephone talker, manned by Yeoman O' Toole. The earphones and attached mouthpiece that hang round his neck are almost too big for his small head.

"All compartments report." Pike says, glancing over his shoulder as he leans against the shiny steel housing of the attack scope. O'Toole repeats his order into the microphone. A moment passes. O'Toole raises his hand to his left earphone; I catch pieces of garbled metallic voices. The compartments are reporting.

"All compartments report rigged for depth charge sir."

The Skipper snaps the top of the stopwatch and looks around at us with an unsatisfied gaze.

"Almost a minute and a half, way too slow. We need to shear off thirty seconds for starters." He's shaking his head. "This is what happens when a boat's in port too long. The crew gets soft. We'll do it again! Surface!"

And on it continues. For four hours the Skipper runs us ragged. Each time is no better than the one before. How many times do we hear, "No good, try it again!" Up and down, like a yo-yo on a string - only to have the entire process begin anew. Finally, near midday, after our umpteenth time, he snaps the button on the stopwatch and says, "Better that time."

Is it over? Are we to be reprieved?

Hardly. A new drill commences, "Battle Surface, Gun Action" that proves to be even more demanding. When the boat breaks surface, it's up and out to man the three-inch gun forward, set up the .30cal Lewis guns in their mounts forward and aft of the bridge. Again, the remarks are the same, "Too slow - no good! Do it again!' It continues on well into the afternoon. The Skipper details me to learn all I can about commanding the deck gun, so I accompany the gun crew out of the gun access hatch each time we break surface. It goes on until the crew has the first round loaded and ready to fire in just under a minute, which the Skipper says is still unsatisfactory. "In forty-five seconds the crew should have the first round loaded and ready to fire." He remonstrates. "It can make the difference between hitting the enemy and being hit ourselves."

1600 hrs. The Skipper calls off the battle surface drills for the day. Not because we've become experts, but because the exercises have depleted our air flasks of high-pressure air. With two engines on propulsion and the other two putting juice in the can and charging up our compressed air supply, we stand down from battle stations.

An odd feeling begins to overtake me, that of being out of place among my fellow officers.

Unlike me, they are all qualified submariners. Just learning the ropes, I can add little of any importance to anything I do. I feel reduced to a spectator in an important game in which I should be playing. They all seem so cocky, confident, and sure in their tasks. The harsh reality is, I am really a supernumerary on board. A spectator, whose job it is just to watch and learn all I can. Really the only time I feel of any worth at all is when I am on the bridge and can act as an additional lookout. This feeling of worthlessness is at its worst when we are running submerged, since I have nothing to do besides stand around and watching everyone else.

Later, in the wardroom, the Skipper inquires if I play chess. As I respond in the negative, he shakes his head. "We need to put that right. Every good submariner should know chess backwards and forwards." He directs me to retrieve a chess set in one of the cabinets behind us. Withdrawing a wooden chest from the cabinet it almost slips from my hands. It must weigh close to forty pounds. I set it on the table. The Skipper slides it over and opens it. Then I see the reason for all the weight; the board is made of reinforced plywood and has a double section steel base at least three-sixteenths of an inch thick. The chess pieces - all wood - have a thick square steel base attached to them. The Skipper unfolds the board and lays it on the table. It touches one of the pieces lying nearby on its side. The piece suddenly rights itself on the board with a metallic *click* - it's magnetized. The Skipper looks at me expectantly. "Neat little arrangement complements of Chief Schrier. He got a little tired of having to get on his hands and knees to pick up the pieces that scattered all over the deck every time the boat rolled."

"Chess,' he says, lining up his white pawns on the board, 'Is the ultimate game of war. Strategy is paramount."

The pieces are now set. The Skipper takes off his cap and lays it on the bench beside him. At the same time running his hand through his tangle mop of blond hair. He produces his cigarette case and the matching gold lighter, lights one and settles back to enjoy the game. He regards the board for a moment, then slowly reaches up and moves his first piece - the pawn right in front of his knight. He glances over at me with a knowing look.

"You don't follow me, do you Watts?"

I don't and admit it. In the interim, the XO has moved the black pawn right in front of his rook. The Skipper studies the board a few moments, then moves the pawn in front of his other knight.

"Tell me,' he says without looking up, 'What makes a good hunter?"

I shrug. "Stealth, a good eye, love of the hunt.'

The Skipper nods slowly as he moves his rook up to the middle of the board; "you missed one that is indispensable. Can you think of it?"

I rack my brain. Clearly he is after something specific. I shake my head.

The XO shows not the slightest interest in our conversation. His attention is fixed solely on the board. He only looks up to sip his coffee and Lemert's totally engrossed in the December issue of *Collier's* magazine.

Only Waldron casts a kindred eye over to me and gives me a knowing wink. Apparently he too has gone through this at some time or another. He sips his coffee and glances at the game in between puffing on his pipe and flipping the pages of a *Life* magazine.

The Skipper eyes me over the rim of his coffee mug, a slight grin forms at the corners of his mouth. His eyes shine expectantly.

"Patience Ensign." He moves one of his bishops across the board until it intersects with one of the XO's rooks. Out of the corner of my eye I see the XO stiffen and wince; he never saw it coming. The Skipper picks up the rook and replaces it with his bishop. The rook is laid off to the side, looking lonely and forlorn all by itself.

"Patience,' he begins again, 'is what allows you to set up a proper attack. Fighting a war from behind a periscope is one of the hardest things to do. There are so many factors involved; sea conditions, target speed and base course if evasive maneuvering, escorts to worry about, approach courses to be plotted out, bow angles and so on. In effect it is much like a chess game.

If you move a space here, you must give up something over there. And you must choose your spaces carefully. A wrong choice, a wrong move, can cost you the opportunity to attack at all."

The motion of the boat has increased slightly. Nausea rumbles in the pit of my stomach. The wardroom rocks from port to starboard. The bow pitches, then wallows and yaws. I turn round and call into the pantry for more coffee and bread. I find myself wishing I were playing chess or something - anything - to occupy my mind and take it off my stomach.

It is clear who has the advantage in this game; the Skipper has a host of the XO's pieces lined up next to him inside of forty-five minutes. The XO has lost one of his rooks, both bishops, one of his knights, and nearly all his pawns. He is trying in vain to stave off defeat and protect his king with one knight, his queen, and a rook. The Skipper shoots him an irritated glance.

"You're not concentrating Mr. Bainbridge; you're better than this."

The XO nods dejectedly, like a schoolboy caught pulling pranks. "I know sir."

Ten minutes later it's over. Trapped in one corner of the board, the XO has no alternative but to capitulate. The Skipper, after another agitated look in the XO's direction, calls for more coffee and lights another cigarette.

"Get yourself together man! We'll have another go in a little while."

A hot searing flash suddenly runs through my gut. It is so sharp and so sudden I almost double over in pain, letting out a cry of surprise.

"What's the matter?" The XO inquires.

Holding my gut with my right hand, I struggle to get up, "nothing a trip to the head won't fix."

"Jonesy's coffee claims yet another victim!" Lemert exclaims, smacking the tabletop.

Excusing myself, I move out into the passageway and head toward the forward bulkhead. The officer's head is located in the rear of the bow compartment. Bending and stepping through the watertight door while the boat dips, falls, and rolls are almost too much to bear. I come close to losing control and messing myself; something I haven't done since the age of four. Now, duck the head and step through the bulkhead. There, now to the right -

"Evening Ensign.'

"Evening sir."

A few of the torpedomen notice my irregular gait and watch me with interest. A few giggles emanate from the group. Right now I couldn't care less. I fling open the door and clamber inside. The toilet is arranged up off the main deck plates a few inches, so I have to step up. My insides rumble fiercely. The pressure is almost too much to bear. I struggle with my belt - a fine time for the buckle to jam! I curse violently. The bow suddenly raises up - banging my head into one of the many pipes just inches above my head - then drops. The timing is perfect. As the buckle comes free, the trousers drop, and the sudden dropping of the bow slams me down squarely on the head as if I'd lowered myself. So, freedom at last!

Upon my return to the wardroom, the Skipper and the XO are engaged in a second duel of chess and the topic is unrestricted submarine warfare. Waldron notes with some humor that was the precise reason we went to war in 1914-1918 with Germany, and we are now waging the very same type of fight. Unrestricted submarine warfare is simply "sink on sight", instead of fighting under the rules and regulations of Prize Law.

The Skipper guffaws. "Prize Law! If there was anything more stupid thought up by a bunch of know nothing politicians, it was Prize Law! Meditate on this; Prize Law held that a submarine when sighting an enemy vessel would surface and fire a shot across its bow. This would cause the captain of the ship to heave to while the submarine sent a boarding party over to inspect the ship's papers and cargo. If it were "contraband" and would help the enemy war effort, the boarding party would direct the ship's crew into lifeboats, plant explosive charges and open the sea cocks and scuttle the ship. All fine and dandy,' The Skipper points out, 'Until the British merchant marine started arming their merchant ships with five-inch guns -'

"Also outlawed by Prize Law.' The XO adds with a grin, in the process of removing one of the Skipper's knights from the board. Our commander notes the passing of one of his gallant knights with irritation. "The result,' he continues, 'Was that the German U-boat skipper would surface and obey international law to his - and his boat's - own peril."

"The U-boat surfaces and the Limeys start shooting from a supposed 'unarmed' ship.' Waldron adds, joining the conversation. "No, finally and sensibly the German Admiralty directed all submarine skippers to think of the safety of their boats and their crews first, which led them to "sink on sight." And thus was born the phrase "unrestricted submarine warfare."

The Skipper moves one of his knights down the board, slyly taking possession of one of the XO's pawns. "To think that a submarine - the most vulnerable of all vessels - would blindly surface in front of an enemy ship and expose itself...' he merely shakes his head and leaves the thought unfinished.

"And the Q-ships?" Lemert chimes in eagerly.

"Illegal under rules and restrictions of Prize Law,' the Skipper snorts, 'but did they have them? You bet your ass! Did you know Q-Ships were directly authorized by none other than Winston Churchill himself! See? There's the head politician breaking international law! And he's got the audacity to call the Germans a bunch of criminals?"

Q-ships are disguised merchantmen designed to look as innocent and as helpless as possible, with false sides and structures that contain large caliber guns. In order to lure an unwary submarine skipper to the surface, these were concealed until a submarine surfaced. Then the false sides and structures came down, and more often than not the submarine went to the bottom.

Our bow rises and plunges as it cuts through each swell. In between the sheets of white foam that shoot out away from it lies the deep black undisturbed water just in front. Rippled, with a bit of curling at the wave tops as it seems to rise up out of nowhere and press against us, as if to impede our way forward. But then it makes contact with our steel prow and it too, becomes severed in a spray of white as our bow bites deeply into it. Angrily separated from its brethren, it swirls and swishes down our side. Parted further by our widening midsection, where it pancakes out into uneven widths only to come back at our hull once again to slap at it with increased intensity. The turn of our screws only causes even more vexation; it boils and froths until glistening white as fresh mountain snow, bubbling and hissing in its madness. Only when our rounded stern departs is it reunited with its family and begins to lose the fury it held only a moment before. It quiets down, the bubbling stops, the hissing quiets, and the rolling, wrinkled swell once again asserts itself as master of the domain. There is left not a trace of the *Bullhead*, nor any one of us. The sea resumes its ancient restless nature.

The sun begins to set. Peeking through holes in a billowing low-lying layer of cumulus clouds like shafts of heavenly light; searching out for some remnant of peace in a world at war. Behind us a thousand or so miles - a world away - our loved ones back home go about their business. Daily chores, work, children are going to school, people are falling in love, getting married, being separated by the war. Do they think of us? If we are sunk and all hands lost how will they know? The Japanese don't send messages to ComSubPac informing them of submarine kills. If we are lost it will only be known or assumed after we fail to put into port. ComSubPac will give us several days grace period to see whether or not we're just behind schedule, and then they'll list us as "overdue and presumed lost." How long until it's no longer presumed and it becomes "lost with all hands?" This claustrophobic steel pipe full of smelly men, provisions, technology and weapons sails into the dark and deadly waters controlled by our enemy.

What will tomorrow bring?

Stars now peek out of the heavens. I can make out the North Star, the Little Dipper, and right over there is the Big Dipper. It is no surprise that with such atmospheric clarity the XO appears a bit early for his evening star fixes. The sextant is handed up, and one of the quartermasters acting as his assistant, stays below in the conning tower with a stopwatch at the plotting table. The XO raises the instrument to his eye and proceeds to read off degrees for both Saturn and Jupiter. His task completed, his disappears below to do the plotting.

Night soon falls. The line of demarcation between the sky and horizon dissolves until nothing but blackness remains. Punctuated at frequent intervals by starlight that resembles so many precious stones gleaming in faint light. The moon's dull sheen comes off the black water, looking like silver paint dashed onto a sea of black ink that follows us no matter how many times we change course and speed. We are under its eye at all times. It never leaves us, this perpetual spectator of the sky. It colors the few clouds around it in gothic fashion, like the Scottish moors; a scene pulled from Sir Arthur Conan Doyle's *Hound of the Baskervilles*.

This rolling, restless water, how many times have its depths seen the falling and twisting hulks of broken ships, spiraling toward the sea floor miles and miles beneath the surface? How many times have the bodies of drowned seamen floated to the surface from their graves below because of the putrefying gases in their bellies that buoy them to the surface? Only to become food for the scavengers of the sea as the sharks, barracuda, eel, and even seagulls all have their day. Certainly this war is a windfall for the marine creatures that inhabit both the Pacific and Atlantic oceans, for they will feed well off the dead.

Out here time seems to stop. The creased wrinkles on the top of the waves have looked the same since time immemorial, all the great seafarers surely had become familiar with them: Vespucci, Magellan, Columbus, Cook. All have seen the sea in its various moods. Always the same, yet always changing, from the Orkneys to the Cape of Good Hope, round the Horn to the Barents Sea, incessantly, restlessly moving. Swirling, rushing, crashing, tearing around the Four Corners of the globe. Spawning life for the thousands of creatures under her protective arms, and bringing death swiftly to those who do not heed her angry and restless character. The sheer raw power she possesses.

Clattering of sea boots on the ladder. The Third Watch is coming up to take over. After a short briefing on the sea, wind direction, course and speed, Michaelis disappears below.

A little while later a movement beside me draws me back from thought - it's Waldron, dropping down below the bridge bulwark to relight his pipe. In the darkness I study him; his movements are slow, self-assured, and precise. Relaxed at all times, he acts as if conning the boat was the most normal thing in the world for him. Will he always be this calm? What about when we are under attack? What will I be like under attack?

Forty-five minutes later comes a cry from our starboard lookout.

"Contact off starboard bow!"

In the blink of an eye I am at the bridge bulwark.

"Where?" Waldron demands.

"Two points off the bow sir!" I recognize the voice - it's the Gunner's mate.

Training my glasses on the area, I see nothing but rolling, wavering swell. But wait - what is that there? There is something there! Something several feet above the water!

Waldron is already fumbling with the compass repeater. He stares at it, then whirls around.

"Helmsman - come left to two eight zero! All ahead full! Captain to the bridge!" He snaps around, bringing up his binoculars to his eyes. Below us I hear the orders repeated. The boat comes round to port, the throbbing bass tones of our diesels increase, our prow cutting deeper into the swell. The breeze against our faces intensifies, bringing with it the salty spray from rising and plunging bow, which quickly fog over the lenses in my binoculars.

"Lens paper to the bridge!" I yell, trying hard to sound like a veteran. If my glasses are affected, surely all will be shortly.

Waldron stands riveted to his spot, craning his upper body over the edge of the bulwark, the binoculars glued to his eyes.

"That's no freighter!' he declares, sliding his binoculars into the TBT housing. With a metallic *click* they snap onto the base.

"Lens paper sir." The outline of the quartermaster's head and shoulders protrude from the hatch, in his right hand the lens paper. I snatch it from him and quickly rub the two glass lenses.

The clatter of sea boots on metal; the Skipper is here.

"What is it?"

Waldron rises up over the TBT. "Contact dead ahead. Range about eight thousand yards."

Frantically I raise the glasses to my eyes and immediately curse - the damn lenses are smeared now! I go at the lenses again with a vengeance. Wiping and buffing like a madman. The spray still coming over the bridge bulwark doesn't help, and now Waldron calls for more lens paper. If I don't get these stinking things clean, I can't see the target!

"Jesus!" Waldron spits, wiping his binocular ends furiously.

What dammit? I can't see a thing!

The Skipper suddenly stiffens as if a jolt of electricity had shot down his spine.

"The bastard!"

I get the glasses up. Finally! They're usable again. I stare out over our bow, straining to see what it is that -

"Sound general quarters - battle stations torpedo! Waldron - I have the conn." The Skipper's voice has an edge in it that cuts like a knife. The alarm sounds. I strain my eyes, not even blinking in case I might miss something. There it is again, the same protuberance as before, only parts of it visible at any one time.

"Sir,' Waldron says evenly, 'I wager my commission that's the conning tower of an "*I*" class Jap submarine."

An *I* class sub? One of those monsters? There's no mistaking our boats for theirs: *I* class subs are over four hundred feet long. Could it really be the enemy? The enemy responsible for the attack on Pearl Harbor and for the rape of Nanking?

"Is he tacking?"

"Doesn't appear to be." Waldron replies to the Skipper from behind the TBT.

The Skipper turns and shouts down into the hatch, "Make ready tubes one to four! All ahead flank!', the binoculars come up as the boat surges even harder through the swell. The roaring of diesels, hissing spray strikes me full in the face, my eyes start to sting and water as the Pacific salt finds its way into them.

The Skipper stands ramrod straight, staring ahead. The spray that comes over the bridge seems not to faze him in the slightest. Unblinking, he stands there holding the binoculars against his body to protect them from the spray. Waldron calls once again for lens paper to clear his spray-soaked binoculars.

"If we can inch up behind him,' the Skipper bellows, competing against the roaring diesels, hissing spray, and whistling breeze, 'Close enough before he spots us and pulls the plug, we've got a good chance to kill him!"

A few minutes later the Skipper sputters a stream of obscenities and orders our speed cut back, 'Making too much goddamned bow wave! He's bound to see it!"

I find myself grasping the rim of our rounded steel bulwark so tightly my hands begin to go numb. My knees shake with excitement. The enemy is here, pitching and yawing in the rolling sea before our torpedo tubes. The torpedomen forward have flooded them, now all that is needed is to open the outer doors - a final bearing - and one of our tormentors will be headed to the bottom.

My shivering increases. Not only my knees, but also now the binoculars shake in my trembling hands. I silently thank the Creator for the darkness, which hides my quaking limbs from the Skipper and Waldron.

"Range?"

"Seven two - double oh!"

"If we can get in below two thousand -'

" - It would be better." Waldron declares, finishing the thought. "We can shoot at a further distance. But at this angle - our bow on his stern - the target is real slim. It doesn't offer a wide target area like he would if came at a sharper angle horizontal to us."

I keep the elongated steel structure that is our enemy in my binoculars, periodically losing it among the wallowing white peaking crescents that caress the top of the rumbling swell. A shower of spray comes over the bulwark. I snap my eyes shut as it strikes my face like pattern of pellets. My shirt is already soaked through and stuck to my skin, the salt water running down my face like tears and dribbles off the end of my nose. I feel a band of moisture around the top of my head. Shifting my cap, I find that its stiff canvas-like material is completely soaked and heavy with water. I grab a hold of the steel structural support behind the bridge several times to retain my footing as the bow dips steeply into the valley following a swell. The steel lives; it pulsates with life from our diesels. The lubricating oil that cools the engines it's blood, the oil in our fuel tanks its nourishment, the crew it's vital limbs, and our commander its beating heart.

Waldron coughs and snorts as another shower of spray shoots over the bulwark and finds its way into his face through the spaces around the TBT. He curses and continues to fumble with it.

I can imagine what the feeling is down below. For the men - the Chief, McGowan, Swensen, Howe, even hard-as-nails Daschler, the entire ship's complement - a euphoria; a strike back at the those that would defile a nation and murder men. Revenge for December 7th. We are now able to come to grips with our tormentor.

The Skipper leans a bit toward Waldron, his eyes not leaving the bobbing spec several thousand yards ahead of us. "Any change in course?"

"No sir, he's still steady on two seven zero. Making about fourteen knots."

The Skipper gives a grunt of disbelief. "Are they really that complacent? What the hell is wrong with them? No evasive maneuvering? It doesn't make sense!"

A dull thump as a wave smacks against our starboard freeboard and with a hiss like cold water on a hot plate another shower of Pacific spray splatters across the bulwark. Again and again I wipe a sodden lens cloth across my binocular lenses. It seems to come over with increasing frequency; the breeze has intensified. All of us - the Skipper, Waldron, and the lookouts - are completely soaked. Our wet clothes cling to us like leaves in tree sap.

"Range?" The Skipper asks out of the corner of his mouth.

"Six two double-oh!"

The Skipper glances at his watch for a good half-minute. In the darkness it is next to impossible to make out the face. He jerks his head back, "Damn! It's taking too long!"

"Should we increase speed sir?" Waldron says, stepping out from behind the TBT for the first time in ten minutes.

The Skipper remains quiet. In the moonlit glow on the bridge I can almost see his jaw set and begin to shift from side to side, as he does when thinking. "No. We do that and he's bound to see us for sure. At this speed it'll take us longer to get into a good position, but if he's stupid enough to maintain a straight course in enemy waters, he just might not see us."

Minutes drag like hours. The bobbing steel structure up ahead never seems to get any closer. And what happens if they see us? Are we in as much danger as he is? Will they dive or stay on the surface to fight it out? "*I*" class boats have stern tubes. Are the chances of him hitting us the same as us hitting him? Would they pick us up or leave us out here to drown? Would the Skipper pick them up if we hit them first? I can't imagine it.

My eyes burn like fire, the skin of my face feels tight and taut; salt is finding its way into every crack and crevice above my waist. My trembling continues, but now for the additional reason of being cold. The ends of my fingers are numb. I squeeze them with all my might around the handles of my binoculars just to get some feeling back. My shirt is now so thoroughly soaked that water continuously drips down onto my thighs, and down the inside of my trousers into my sea boots. Rivulets of water runoff the brim of my cap. With every movement I feel stiff and cold. Maybe I should call the quartermaster for oilskins, but I'd still have the same drenched shirt on and still be cold. Neither the Skipper nor Waldron has made any noises about foul-weather gear yet, so I steel myself and take the whipping spray head-on.

Still the structure bobs in my binoculars. I can now make out the line of the deck and can just make out his bow when it takes a large swell. A plume of white foam shoots out from either side as his prow cuts through the sea. I perceive more than I can see figures in the after part of the conning tower.

"Shit!' the Skipper roars, 'He's saw us! He's pulling the plug!"

"Damn!" Waldron hisses through clenched teeth.

Sure enough, the deck line disappears into the sea and the rolling swell rumbles over the now submerged deck and crashes against the tilting conning tower. The enemy's stern raises up and tilts forward.

The Skipper curses again. "Lookouts below! Clear the bridge!"

Now it is we who must get under so as the hunter, we do not become the hunted.

In the conning tower, the Skipper braces himself against the shiny steel housing of the attack periscope and orders the boat to sixty-three feet. He looks even thinner now that his clothes are soaked through and cling to his wet skin. Water drips steadily off the brim of his once khaki cap, now a dirty gray. Binoculars still hang from their strap around his neck. He glances back at Duffy, who's at the sound gear and has already ordered the sound heads rigged out.

"If we can get a good sound bearing, we just might be able to get a shot at him."

"That's gonna be tough." The XO, now at the small plotting table, mumbles under his breath.

Pike stands itching for a fight at the TDC. I've heard some of the men recently refer to him as "old' blue light," for the way his eyes light up in combat. A nervous cough beside me - it's O'Toole.

We all stare at Duffy at the sound gear. He sits, earphones placed over his head, carefully moving the wheel above him that turns the JP hydrophone up on the deck.

"What was the last bearing?" He asks, with a sideways glance.

"Two seven zero." The Skipper replies, taking off his cap and squeezing some of the water out of it. The liquid hits the deck loudly and immediately begins running toward the front of the compartment. It's our steep down angle that does it.

"I've got screw noises,' Duffy says, his right hand pressing the right earpiece closer to his head, 'at about two four zero....wait a minute! It sounds like he's blowing something,'

The Skipper's brow furrows. "Is he blowing his negative tank or trimming?"

Suddenly Duffy's lean face goes stark white and his eyes almost burst from their sockets. "Torpedo in the water! Bearing two six five!"

The Skipper whirls around, "All ahead emergency! Flood safety! Take her deep! Sound collision!"

The boat tilts sickeningly forward. I grab a hold of a lubricating oil pipe in the overhead to keep my balance and watch the needle on the depth gauge slowly creep over the dial as the alarm sounds over the speakers. A disembodied arm reaches up from the control room, grabs the handle of the hatch and slams it shut. I glance at the depth gauge; the goddamn needle creeps as slowly as if it were immersed in molasses! We seem stuck at this depth! The boat won't respond! My God - what happens if we're hit? Will we hear the exploding warhead of the torpedo? Or just the rush as the green Pacific comes roaring in to drown us all? A torpedo hit to a submarine is a fatal wound, were just too small to absorb that type of punishment.

Suddenly everything begins to fade away. Next to me the XO shouts something but it doesn't register. I feel myself shaking, sweat runs into my eyes, stinging more and more every second. I feel like I'm in another person's body, watching the scene unfolding in front of me. The dials and gauges on the compartment's side mean nothing to me. I feel myself sliding into that dark abyss of fear, where nothing exists except the animalistic instinct for survival.

All is quiet. No more alarm. No speaking - only breathing. A strange whirring sound comes from somewhere. It gets louder. With a shudder I realize it's the Japanese torpedo. I glance at the compass repeater; it still shows two seven zero! Isn't the Skipper going to change course and get out of its way? Or is he a madman, like when he said something about "making a life out of cheating death?"

Our Ahab leans against the periscope housing. He slowly scratches at his lengthening beard. His eyes stare straight ahead, but have that glazed look of being unfocused. The thrashing propellers of the torpedo are becoming louder and louder. I quickly glance at the depth gauge and silently will it deeper one hundred feet.

The XO looks up, listening. Duffy sits at the sound gear with a furrowed frown on his face, the yeoman keeps his gaze trained on the depth gauge, and Pike examines the floor plates with crossed arms. The helmsman's face I can see nothing of as his back is to me.

The sound becomes louder, coming ever closer. I can almost see the steel lance arcing through the dark water toward us, following our every move. Quickly I shake myself and push the apparition from my mind.

Not a word, not a whisper, only the whirring, thrashing of the torpedo's screws. Where is it? How close? At the university I learned water transmits sound at about three times the speed in air, an incredible rate.

The sound is right outside these steel walls. The droning grows, until a decibel level is reached where it could be right in the compartment with us and be no louder.

The Skipper shifts his head a mere fraction of an inch. His eyes still dazed, unseeing. "Bearing?"

Duffy glances up at the azimuth ring around the direction wheel. "Constant. Two seven zero."

I suddenly have to gulp for air. In my state of abject terror I have forgotten to breathe.

The horrid sound reminds me of a machinist's lathe, turning over at twice-normal speed. It is everywhere - all around us. Was there more than one torpedo fired? I notice the yeoman; eyes are closed tightly shut and he mumbles something silently. Is he praying? I close my eyes and wait for the inevitable.

But it does not come! The droning moves on aft past us. The Jap has missed after all! The yeoman explodes into a sigh, the XO nods with relief, and Pike no longer studies the deck. The Skipper's eyes now look more focused than a moment ago. The horrible droning continues, but it is fading further aft.

We have survived.

Duffy works the JP wheel like a craftsman toiling on an intricate carving, ever so slowly, bit by bit - to all points of the compass. "Screws receding at two three zero.'

"Range?"

Duffy shakes his head. "Four thousand plus."

The Skipper shifts the cap on his head and runs a hand through wet hair. "Secure from collision. We'll listen awhile.' He glances around at us with an amused look on his face; " anyone who needs to go change his trousers may do so." And a sudden burst of nervous laughter echoes around the conning tower as tightly coiled nerves release their vise-like grip on our souls.

The Skipper - a pillar of immovable steel in the face of danger melds into an assuaging valve of respite in its wake.

We listen and try to get a fix on him for three hours, but it's no use. The enemy has slipped away into the black depths of the Pacific. Like us, he has lived to fight another day.

The Skipper orders the helmsman to resume our course to three hundred degrees before heading for the wardroom and a cup of coffee. After he disappears, still mystified as to why the Skipper did not change course after that torpedo was fired, I inquire of the XO about it.

"That's precisely what that Nip skipper was banking on,' he slyly grins, fiddling with his dividers and ruler over the chart table. 'If we had turned either way, we'd all be dead now. That fish passed down our starboard side, no more than two hundred feet from the boat."

"But how did he know?" I persist.

The XO shrugs. "He just knew. The toughest shot in the world is a bow-on or stern-on, since the target becomes so thin. If we had exposed our broadside -' he winces and leaves the thought unfinished.

I look over his shoulder as he plots our position on the blue paper of the chart. Blue for water and here and there little white outcroppings that are islands. He mumbles something unintelligible and places his dividers down on the chart. One divider end is placed over one of these white irregular circles with a name printed in black beside it - Midway Island - the other stretches out to a position I think we're intended to be.

"Is that us?" I ask, pointing to the divider that stretches out over the blue portion of the paper.

"Mm Hmm....' he grunts, his mind still figuring and far away.

A separate sheet of paper by his right hand I notice is covered with trigonometry problems and logarithms. He slowly rises up. "This is going to make us a little late into Midway."

When engaging in his navigation duties, the XO is like a distracted scientist, oblivious to the world around him. Nothing exists for him but his chart, dividers, and protractor. As he leans over the chart, little furrows appear in his forehead and he purses his lips. His forehead shines with a slight glaze of perspiration. When he's really into it, his bottom lip will disappear under his front teeth. Then his two front teeth begin to saw away at his lip - back and forth - to one side and then the next. I don't think he's even aware he's doing it.

Pike hovers around Duffy at the sound gear. Duffy sits with one hand on the direction lever and the other pressing an earphone tightly against his head. His eyes closed, his face screwed up in a grimace of intense concentration. Pike seems to be studying him as closely as a jockey does his steed.

Waldron leans against the attack scope housing running a comb through his soaked and matted hair. He glances around, notices me and gives me a reassuring nod of his head. "Hey - you just got to tangle with the bad guys!"

I force a grin back; hoping my composure fools him. Inwardly, I still shake like a leaf. For the first time in my life, another human being has attempted to kill me. Nothing else imaginable brings the reality of the situation home, as does that one thought. This is real. It is not a drill; it is not an exercise. Had the torpedo struck, this very moment we would all be dead. I tremble, yet I am not in the slightest bit cold. The blood pulsating through my veins feels like ice water. Is this the way it is? Under fire for the first time? Does every man feel this way or only a few? None of the other officers displayed any emotion during the attack, granted this is not their first time under fire. Only in the yeoman could I detect fear.

I would give much for a stiff drink and a cigarette right now.

For the time being we're to remain submerged. To surface with an enemy lurking in the depths so near would be tantamount to suicide.

I clamber down into the control room. Lemert is there, looking bored and leaning on the ladder leading up into the conning tower. In front of him are the men at the diving controls - the Gunner's mate and Electrician's mate Garnett. The Chief is off to the side, keeping an eye on the various gauges and indicators on the blow manifold. With arms crossed and head tilted back, he looks like a schoolmaster keeping an unruly student under a watchful eye.

Copenhaver appears. Wiping his hands that are almost black with oil and grease, he exchanges a few words with the Chief, then disappears. Before he goes, I notice his hair - which earlier had been a light brown color - now looks almost black. As he passes by me and gives me a friendly grin, I notice a line of what looks like soot just below his hairline on his forehead that gleams with perspiration. This 'soot' is oil film and residue from the diesel fuel being combusted in our engines. Human hair must attract it like a magnet.

I lay in my bunk for what seems like hours, seized by my own mortality. The Skipper's coolness, Pike's fixed gaze, and Waldron's unemotional countenance, the XO's distraction, the praying yeoman; into which category will I fall? Am I like a horse of old, which had to gradually become accustomed to the roar of battle or will every encounter leave me quaking in my sea boots? Surely others in their first engagement must feel something similar to this.

Try as I might, each time I close my eyes I hear and see a dull gunmetal projectile tearing through the water. The nerve-wracking sound of its counter-rotating propellers follows our every move. Nowhere to hide. The inevitable explosion. Foaming water, icy cold. A forty-five degree list as the boat takes its final plunge toward the bottom: screams, darkness, death.

"Lemert?"

"Hmm?'

"How did you feel after the first patrol - with Jamison getting killed and all that?"

I hear Lemert put his book down. "Don't tell me - let me guess you were a raw nerve when that Jap submarine shot at us."

"How did you know?"

"Easy Watts, it's your first time under fire. It's not an easy thing to get used to - if a man ever can get used to it!"

"I imagine having someone trying to kill you is pretty hard to get used to."

"Probably have to be some sort of psychopath if you did."

"How were you - the first time?"

"You really want to know?"

"Would I be asking if I didn't?"

He chuckles. "You promise never to tell anyone this?"

"Yeah - what?"

"You sure?'

"Lemert c'mon!"

"Okay. I got so scared - after Jamison bought it and during the depth charging - I pissed myself. Thank God I was sitting down. I was able to stay that way until we gave the Nips the slip. Then I came in here and changed trousers. Did you -'

"No. I don't think I could've. I swear to God I was so scared my ass puckered."

"Relax Watts, it's a normal human reaction. You're human. Feel better?"

"A little - at least I know it isn't irrational to be so scared."

"It would be irrational if you weren't."

"Thanks Lemert."

"Anytime. Don't tell anyone what I told you, okay?"

"I won't."

Sleep will not come. Several times I nod off for brief intervals but a restful period of unconsciousness evade me. I lay there quietly. Staring up at the maze of pipes above my head slightly illuminated by naked electric light peeking around the corners of the drawn curtain. The sounds of the boat are all around. The shouts, curses and hell-raising coming from the bow compartment as the torpedo gang indulges in a series of card games to help pass the time. The slight bustle of activity coming from the control room; rustling of charts and logs. Clanging and squeaking of metal as valves are closed and opened. The thumping of our trim and bilge pumps. The barely audible humming of our electric motors. All humanity and machinery. The conversation in the bow compartment turns once again to our scrape with the enemy.

"Maybe he was scouting for another Pearl Harbor attack."

"Hell no! Why attack Pearl again? The bastards already got a clean sweep all the way to the west coast, all they've got to do is invade, and just walk right in. And what are we going to stop them with, the Orange County Temperance Union?"

"Be in better shape than some of the military units I've seen, bunch of mama's boys! Half of 'em can't even handle a rifle properly." Daschler remarks with a bitter edge in his voice. "And I ought to know, I pulled a stint in the Marines a couple years ago."

"Really?' somebody asks surprised, 'I didn't know that."

"What did you do?" Somebody else asks.

"Infantry.' Daschler responds, 'I was a squad BAR man."

"What's a BAR?"

"Browning Automatic Rifle! -' Daschler shoots back. 'Where the hell have you been?"

"How the hell did you wind up in the navy?"

"I got sick of having to carry two tons on my back and lug that BAR around - things a goddamned cannon! No jobs in the civilian world, you know with the Depression and all. I figured out that the navy had it easier. You don't have to march around anywhere, on a ship you get a free ride. No field packs, don't have to worry about having your boondockers just so, the food's always hot, and you're not up to your knees in mud or snow. A better end of the deal. And since the Marines are part of the navy, wasn't all that hard to get a transfer. So I put in for sub school at New London."

"Why?"

"I heard they needed people. Battlewagons, cruisers, and destroyers were all full up. And somebody said they were looking for people to be submariners, so here I am. Worked out better anyway. Here were members of a select group. No other arm of the navy can lay claim to that."

"You don't miss it?"

"What the Marines? Hell no! You try infantry training sometime!"

"What's wild again?"

"Your stinking breath for starters!'

"Kiss my-'

"Sevens asshole! Sevens are wild! You wanna play? You pay attention!" Daschler scolds.

"Yeah? Up yours!"

A brief pause.

"Why don't you come out with something original once in a while huh? You remind me of -'

"Shut up and deal!' For the first time Tashtego raises his voice, 'You want to talk shit? Do it in the head!"

"Where do you think we're headed?"

"Discards?"

A sigh, "Someplace that's not - dealer takes two - all that friendly."

"What does that mean?"

"Relax Buckley, you got another war to go to?"

"Well, the Pacific's a big ocean, there's lots of places to go."

"What's it matter? You won't see it anyway cooped up in here - I'll take three."

"Look,' Daschler says in a suddenly easygoing paternal tone, 'we're a submarine. Our job is to sink enemy ships right?"

"Depends on who you talk to."

"No - c'mon!' Daschler counters, ' I'm serious now! This boat's got a full load of fish, so think about it, it makes perfect sense for ComSubPac to send us someplace where we can sink the most ships right?"

Silence all around. Apparently Daschler is on to something.

"Coast of Japan?"

"I'll lay an even fifty bucks,' Daschler states evenly, 'We're on our way to the Philippines."

The sudden increase in sighing sounds like boilers being ventilated of excess pressure.

"I agree." Tashtego declares.

"Boys and girls, buckle your seat belts and get ready for the ride."

The rest of the game passes without the usual high jinks and bawdy overtones that I have become accustomed to hearing. Each man is preparing himself for what lies ahead. Daschler's logic is uncannily acute, and I cannot help but to notice that no one took him up on his bet.

"Bridge watch - stand by!" Pike's voice booms out in his southern drawl as I step over the hatch coaming into the control room. Up above the main hatch squeals in protest as the quartermaster loosens it. I glance at my watch - 0330 hrs.

"Equalize pressure!"

Another squeak is followed by a pop like a champagne cork, and my eardrums flutter as the excess pressure in the boat shoots out from under the hatch. The sound of water hitting the deck of the conning tower as the hatch is opened. Tramping feet as men move up the ladder and through the hatch.

"Lookouts to the bridge!'

Our steep up-angle begins to ease out as the fantail broaches. Now I no longer need to hold on. The two fellows at the diving controls, Swensen and Howe, hop off their little stools, grab a pair of binoculars each, and bound like deer up the ladder into the tower.

I skirt around the plotting table, heading toward the coffee maker that sits back in the crew's mess. Just forward of the after bulkhead is the radio room. Glancing in just as I pass by, I catch a glimpse of the radioman sitting in front of the radio gear with a paperback novel in hand. On his head rests a set of earphones. Only one is over his ear. The other is left off for orders. A half-stumble through the door as the boat tilts to starboard.

The steward is grumbling something under his breath and turns around to open the long, shiny steel lid of the oven behind him as I pour coffee from the coffee maker into a cup. There is an aroma of baking dough; smells like pastry.

"Second batch done yet?" an expectant voice asks behind me.

"In a minute!' the steward impatiently snaps, 'These things are hot - better let them cool awhile."

"I'll take my chances." the voice replies self-assuredly.

Turning around I see a large metal tray with dozens of little cow-pie looking configurations piled on it - it is Danish. On some the steward sprinkles with powdered sugar, some are left plain, and some even have cheese in the middle. Selecting a medium-sized one, I ease myself down onto the bench seat at one of the tables.

"Morning sir," one of the crewmen says as he slides a large can down towards me, "They're real good with preserves on them too."

Thanks,' I say, glancing at the can - blackberry preserves. Taking the accompanying spoon that sticks out of it at an angle, I smear a healthy dollop of it on top of the Danish.

"I'm E-mate Paxton sir,' the man says through a mouthful of pastry and preserves, 'This is

E-mate Garnett, and -' pointing to the table next to us, 'Seamen, Matthews, Quinn, and Myers."

We all nod politely and force greetings to one another through stuffed cheeks. I've certainly seen them before, yet I still don't know all their names.

E-mate Paxton finishes his pastry in three large bites and reaches for another still chewing. He glances over at the table next to us where Quinn, Matthews, and Harmison are seated. Another large can that I take to be preserves is in front of them. Paxton points to it with his blackberry-stained spoon.

"What kind is that?"

"Strawberry." The smaller of the two - Quinn, I think - answers.

"Gimme." Paxton is up and garnishes the pastry heavily with the sugary mass. I cannot help but to notice that all of them seem to be indulging themselves like condemned men at a last meal. They eat like a pack of ravenous hounds.

"This your first time out sir?" Garnett asks from behind his coffee cup.

"Yes.'

He rolls his eyes skyward, "Hope this patrol won't be like the last one!"

"I just about shit my drawers when that shell hit us." Matthews admits.

"Just about? I definitely changed my drawers that day!' Garnett muscles in, 'then when the Skipper got killed -' he puckers his lips and blows out slowly.

"Yeah,' E-mate Paxton agrees, 'thought we were all goners when the Skipper bought it, but then Tyreen stepped in and we came out all right. Even blew that Jap tin-can to hell.' His chewing slows as he stares in front of him a moment in silence. "Tyreen saved our asses!"

I start on my third pastry, Paxton and Garnett are already on their fifth or sixth. Where it goes is a mystery; both are as skinny as lamp posts.

"Hey -' the steward snaps, leaning forward over his burners with a long scowl, 'You pigs leave some for the off-coming watch! I only do this once a day!"

"Why do you think we're here now, you mutton-head!' Paxton spits back, 'If you'd do this on a regular basis we wouldn't have to get up before the crack of dawn!"

"Besides,' Garnett offers peacefully, 'You should be flattered we like the way you bake."

The steward waggles a dough-topped finger accusingly. "Just leave some for the off-coming watch!"

"Crap!"

A little while later there's some excitement. It appears we've sailed from Pearl Harbor with some unwanted passengers on board, an entire host of cockroaches. It seems that Johnson the steward was pulling some potatoes out of the hold and a whole nest of the vermin just exploded, running in all directions. The Skipper is beside himself and hauls Jonesy up before him, demanding an explanation. But Jonesy is dumbfounded, shaking his old head from side to side and assuring the Skipper nothing brought aboard during provisioning gave him the slightest cause for concern.

But it gets worse. The disgusting insects are found in both fore and aft torpedo rooms - the entire boat is infested. The Skipper is sputtering with rage, and orders bait laced with poison placed at different points in the boat. The entire crew gets into the act, everyone off-duty goes on a mass cockroach hunt with hammers, wrenches and anything else they can lay their hands on to smash the vile creatures into pulp. It really turns into a big sport, Daschler and the Pharmacist's Mate are already vying for the most kills. And Cutter, Buckley, and Harmison start a pool for the biggest number of roach corpses collected. The sickening scum are found everywhere; in foam mattresses, lockers, the heads, and especially the bilges. Into these, large amounts of diesel fuel are dumped, causing the atmosphere in here to become even heavier and more suffocating.

If for nothing else, it keeps us busy for a while.

That afternoon at 1300 hrs. Midway Island hoves into view. I am on the bridge with Michaelis. A brown, craggy protuberance rises above the endless rolling and dipping valley that is the sea. Broken here and there by curved lips of white foam as the wind creams the tops of the highest peaks. Like an oasis - a single point of land amid a vast ocean desert.

Michaelis peers at it through his binoculars, adjusting our course. "Helmsman, come left five degrees rudder, steer two niner five."

"Left five degrees. Steering two nine five aye sir!"

"Quartermaster, notify the Captain we have Midway Island in sight."

"Aye-aye sir."

Michaelis drops his binoculars and fishes in his shirt for a cigarette. "Ever been to Midway?" he asks, digging in his trouser pocket for his lighter.

"No sir." I reply flatly. What a dumb question. When would I ever have had the reason to go to Midway?

"Used to be a way station for the China Clipper planes back in the twenties and thirties,' he says, taking a long drag on his cigarette, 'that's how it got its name. The old Pam Am hotel is now the Gooneyville Lodge, the submariner's hangout. It's named for a strange species of bird, called a 'Gooney' bird, that's found only on Midway Island."

Groups of gulls suddenly appear and find something interesting about the boat. They hover, fluttering around first the bow, and then move aft, shrieking and crying in their lonely wind song voices. What can they be looking for here? This steel structure of war offers nothing for them. They could though find excellent nesting possibilities here in the bridge. With its tight corners and no overhang, what more could they ask for? And the periscope shears, that too would make a wonderful nest, though it offers little protection from the wind. The gulls would actually have a better time on the bridge than us humans, they're much smaller and could hide from the elements. As for us, we're completely exposed.

The quartermaster calls up, the radio room has a message in need of decoding. After passing the conn to the Skipper, Michaelis disappears below.

The Skipper plants himself behind the bulwark, reaches for a cigarette and offers one to me.

As I place the cigarette between my lips, my hand brushes the five-day growth of stubble on my face. This is probably the longest time I have gone without shaving in my life. I feel unkempt, and probably smell like yesterday's cigarettes and last week's body odor. It will feel good to get a shave and a shower once we get onto Midway.

"Permission to come up?" It's Michaelis.

"Granted."

Michaelis steps out of the hatch with a piece of paper in hand.

"Sir,' he says holding it out to him, 'It's from ComSubPac."

The Skipper glances at him and takes the offered piece of paper. Michaelis glances over at me and silently gives a twist of his lips, then shakes his head.

The Skipper's eyes narrow and furrows form on his forehead as he reads the paper. Then, he folds it and turns toward the hatch, "Michaelis, you have the conn."

"Aye sir."

After he disappears below, I turn to Michaelis. "What's up?"

"Our turn-around time has been halved, due to deteriorating situation in the Philippines,' he says, reciting from the message already memorized, 'U.S.S *Bullhead* will complete all refueling and necessary reprovisioning and put to sea within eight hours of arrival, by order Commander, Submarines, Pacific Fleet."

"Eight hours?"

Michaelis merely shrugs. So much for a tour of the island I guess. "What was our turn-around time before?"

"Twenty-four hours. Things must really be bad out there."

Down below I hear the crackle of the ship's loudspeaker as the Skipper announces the news to the crew over the 1MC. A chorus of groans accompanies the news.

Michaelis sighs, "It's gonna be tight, top off the tanks, load extra provisions, and get everything squared away in eight hours. No down time."

In the meantime, the seagulls lose their interest and desert us. We are alone on the sea.

I stand on the bridge, drinking in the smell of the sea and the wonderful coolness of the night. Under the full moon the water sparkles like quicksilver; an endless panorama of blinking light. The swell coming up the inlet begins to slap against our side, causing the boat to shudder and sway. Every now and then a hiss as spray mates with our deck. The Skipper stands beside me, his Army Air Corps leather jacket on, staring sightlessly out over our bow. His hands are jammed deep into the jacket pockets; his cap jauntily cocked on his head. Though so close, he is far away. Behind me, one of the lookouts coughs and clears his throat. The bridge is eerily silent. This is it, the finality. We are going to war. Our departure from Pearl was but a jump-off; now it is the real thing. From this point onward we are on our own. We are a lone wolf on an endless hostile prairie. Bloodthirsty hunters will lurk on all sides. We have only the boat and one another.

"Right ten degrees rudder. All ahead full!" the Skipper directs over his shoulder - ever mindful of the tops of the coral heads poking above the water. The boat inches out of the atoll inlet. Our bow climbs atop a steep swell and plunges down into the trough on the other side, neatly parting the black water into two inverted "J" shapes of glistening white. The bass baritone of our diesels increases. The steel of the bridge vibrates and throbs.

"Quartermaster, make course two seven five degrees!"

"Two seven five degrees....aye sir!" a voice repeats, sounding hollow in the conning tower. I cannot tell who it is.

"Lieutenant Michaelis, you have the deck. Commence zigzag pattern at infrequent intervals. No more than ten degrees off the mark, we've got to make it to the patrol area as quickly as possible."

"Aye-aye sir." Michaelis replies as he steps up to the bridge bulwark.

Even after passing the conn to the Lieutenant, the Skipper remains on the bridge. Staring silently out over our bow, only his knees steadying him against the perpetual swaying and tilting of the boat. The breeze that comes over the bulwark chills down to the bone. Cold - like a grave.

Book II:

Into the Jaws of the Tiger.......

I awake with a start. Voices and movement in the passageway stir me out of sleep. A few moans and exaggerated yawns; it must be the changing of the watch. So it's probably about 0400. A bustling of activity accompanied by cursing. A tramping herd of half-awake zombies heads aft.

"Idiot! - watch where you're going!"

"You know I always like to start a day by cracking somebody's skull!"

"Shut up! You'll wake the officers!"

"Hell, if we're up - they're up!"

"I'm gonna enjoy being a *lack* of character witness at your court martial!"

"Just get your smelly ass outta' the way!"

Their voices fade in among the endless chatter of the control room and Lemert's snoring. I lay quietly in my bunk, staring at the endless maze of machinery above my head. The Chief's voice, audible from the control room, instructs a man at the pressure manifold to make ready to blow sanitary tanks. Apparently there's a trim dive coming. The sanitary tanks - what was it the Chief had said about them?

With a sudden loud hiss the contents of the tanks vent to the sea. Then, with a mighty fart - the air used to blow the vile contents to the sea is vented back into the boat. Smell of urine and feces. No hope of getting back to sleep now.

The klaxon sounds, a roar as water rushes into the tanks. The boat tilts down by the bow, sliding me forward in my bunk. I hear the water outside gurgling into our superstructure above the pressure hull, sounding like a thousand glasses of water being filled simultaneously. Then, a hush - a muffled thumping gets further and further away as the boat slips underwater. Our steel home is quieter now; even Lemert's snoring seems more subdued. Alas, no more rolling or pitching. We descend quietly into the depths.

Quiet from the control room. Then a tapping sound and the Chief's voice again. "Pump fifteen hundred fifty pounds forward."

A heavy thumping begins; the trim pumps engage. The Chief compensates for the extra weight in our fuel tanks. I conjure up in my mind the intricate tank arrangement diagrams the XO has issued to me. There are normal fuel oil tanks, clean fuel oil tanks, lubricating oil tanks, fresh water tanks, battery water tanks, main ballast tanks, variable ballast tanks, sanitary tanks, water round torpedo or "WRT" tanks, trim tanks, safety and negative tanks; the list seems endless.

The variable ballast tanks accomplish trimming. Pumped dry or flooded through action of the trim manifold and the spidery network of pipes that originate from it. Interestingly enough, the diesel fuel in our normal fuel oil tanks sits on top of water. The chemical properties of both make it impossible for the two to mix. And since maintaining weight in a submarine is of the essence, seawater enters through the bottom of the tanks so that the diesel fuel floats on top of it. Diesel fuel is lighter than water. As the fuel burns in the engines, the water level gets correspondingly higher. In this way the boat stays heavy, assuring a quick dive. Failure to compensate for the change in weight - through fuel consumption, consumption of food, expenditure of shells and torpedoes - the boat gradually lightens and would be unable to dive. Try cocks extending into the pressure hull indicate the fuel content of the tanks. These act as a safeguard so as not to inadvertently draw seawater into the fuel pumps. Oddly enough this entire process leaves the boat heavier when she returns from a patrol than in departure.

The thumping trim pump abruptly stops. "Blow negative to the mark."

A hiss becomes a roar. Then a gurgling, and silence.

"Negative tank blown sir." Sounds like Copenhaver - he of the fancy mustache.

But the Chief is not yet finished. "Pump seven hundred aft." The hollow *whump-whump-whump* of the trim pump begins again.

We stay down just long enough for the Chief to get the trim right. Then we're back on the surface whipping our wake white as our screws beat it into a froth at a steady fifteen knots. Now, there's much more movement in contrast with the soft cushion of water both above and below us when submerged. Our hammering diesels send life pulsating into every weld and rivet.

The boat lives.

I can't sleep anymore, so I might as well just go up onto the bridge. As I hastily throw the nearest clothes on, it strikes me how much naval protocol suffers at sea - at least in submarines. The clothing I wear isn't regulation. In fact, on any other type of ship we'd be up on report. I still wear the regulation khaki trousers and shirt, but throw a ratty blue civilian sweater over it, sea boots only half laced up, and a light jacket I picked up somewhere. Before going out I pick up my cap and examine it. It looks so crisp and new compared with the other officers' caps. Theirs all have that weathered and worn look to them. A spatter of grease and oil here and there, the canvas bleached and faded where the sun has kissed it for hours at a time. Salt streaks where the seawater has worked its way into the fabric. A creased and crinkled brim, and the greening of the insignia as verdigris takes hold. Mine looks as though it just came off the haberdasher's rack. It really makes me stand out as the new kid on the block. Couldn't I weather it?

Holding the cap with the front facing me, I take it in both hands and squeeze it together several times. There, that'll loosen up the headband a bit. I wiggle and shake the brim, creasing it in the necessary places. I even go so far as to drop my cap on the deck and trod upon it several times, hoping to transfer some of the oil on my boots onto it. Picking it up, I feel around the brim. It's better, but it still has a long way to go. I put it on my head and check the outline of it in the mirror. No good - can't see well enough. I reach over and part the curtain by several inches. This lets in enough light so now I can see. I study myself in the mirror, hardly the archetype combat veteran. I still look so wet-behind-the-ears. I try cocking the cap to one side and then another. This is better, but I remember back in training during an inspection a reprimand of a man in our unit for wearing his cap cocked at an angle. Apparently only combat officers wear cocked caps, but does being onboard automatically qualify me as a "combat" officer? Or does that only happen once we've shoved a few enemy tons to the bottom? I don't know, so I'll give it a bit of an angle.

Before I go up to the bridge, I ease my way back into the crew's mess and grab a cup of coffee and Danish. Seamen are clustered around the tables. Quartermaster

Harmison sits at the closest one, wolfing down Danish in one hand and holding a thick Havana cigar in the other. "Morning sir."

"Morning. Making sure the Danishes are okay for the off-coming watch?"

Mischievous grins all around. Out of the corner of my eye I notice the steward look anxiously over at his disappearing mound of fresh Danishes. "Hey - !"

Having lit the fuse; I make my exit.

"Permission to come up?"

"Granted!"

Holding the mug of coffee in my right hand and clenching the Danish between my teeth, I move up the ladder steadying myself with my left hand.

"Well well - 'Pike observes with a grin, 'look what bubbled to the surface." He pauses, looking at me curiously. "Your cap's crooked."

Damn! Feigning ignorance, I shift it back straight. It was worth a try.

Like the Skipper, I notice Pike has one of those Army Air Corps leather jackets on. Where do they get these things? To my knowledge they are not standard issue. Do they all just come by them by accident or is it some clever underhanded plot to bilk the Air Corps for sea wear? No wonder submariners have such a bad reputation with everybody.

My Danish catches Pike's interest. "What's that you got there?"

I impart the story of the steward, the crewmen, and the Danishes.

Pike is beside himself. "And they're down there scarfing them all up by themselves?"

I nod.

"The ingrates!" At once Pike plants himself over the hatch. "Danishes and coffee to the bridge!" He says it with such vehemence it could be a battle command. "Lousy bastards in this crew wouldn't give a drowning man a glass of water."

The sun is not yet up. The wind is strong enough to curl the tops of the waves white - like vanilla icing. This contrasts starkly with the oily blackness of the sea, creating simmering, flashing rods of white on a plain of black velvet. They appear and disappear just as quickly as they form, seeming to well nigh wink at us. Now and again the wind will cream the top of a swell just as we come upon it, causing it to slap against our steel side, producing a hollow reverberation.

Footsteps on the ladder, it's the quartermaster again. An umbilical cord now connects Pike with an unceasing flow of coffee and Danishes from the galley. At the rate he wolfs them down, you'd think he was a sugar addict. "At yeast I won't be hungry anymore!" He cracks, then roars with laughter for five minutes at his own joke.

I shiver. I pull my jacket up tight and cup my hands tightly around the warm sides of my coffee cup.

A few minutes pass by in silence. A sufficiently stuffed Pike busies himself with the horizon; Buckley and Tashtego above us in the periscope shears stay busy with their assigned sectors. Schumacher has stepped up for a breath of fresh air; he's lounging on the cigarette deck. I step around the periscope shears and move up beside him, not knowing quite what to say.

"How long will it take us to reach our patrol area?" I pose.

The engineering officer shifts, looks at me glumly, and then shrugs. " 'Bout a week. A good seven days at cruising speed."

A few more minutes pass in uncomfortable silence. Schumacher is a lot like the Skipper, taciturn and mysterious. I'll try again. "Should be a pretty good area." Even in the darkness I can detect Schumacher's questioning gaze. "For targets I mean.' I add, pressing the point, 'With the Japs marching down Luzon there's bound to be plenty of shipping."

I see Schumacher's hawk-like profile nod slowly. "Oh yeah - but that comes with a price. I guarantee the whole area's gonna be lousy with destroyers!" At the word 'destroyers' - he almost spits. "I hope it's nothing like the first patrol, ' he continues, staring into the darkness, "those fucking destroyers! That's how Jameson bought it."

"What happened?"

He takes a deep breath, then lets it out in a long sigh, like a venting ballast tank. "We'd been tracking a small convoy on the surface, three, four average size steamers, 'bout eight thousand tons. They had one escort that we could see; he was on our side of the convoy - between the freighters and us. So we commenced an end-around - ' he looks at me to make sure I understand, '- that's a run at flank speed ahead of the convoy for a better firing position,'

"I know."

'Anyway, it was about 0300, blacker than a cat's ass with rain coming down in sheets. Couldn't see more than a thousand yards in any direction. Tyreen was below on the plot, Pike was officer of the deck, Jameson had the conn, and I was helping out on the TBT. Then, one of the lookouts, "Tash" in fact -' he nods his head toward the dark outline a few feet above us, ' - starts screaming at the top of his lungs there's a destroyer coming right at us just off the port bow -where the hell he came from nobody knows. I glance over and all I see is this huge steel prow with a bone in its teeth looking like he's going to ram. Then there's a bright orange flash and the sound of tearing metal. Pike was on top of things because he had the rudder hard over to port. I never even heard the diving alarm sound, but suddenly I notice the boat's down by the bow and water is pouring into the bridge,' a brief pause in the nightmare. He raises his cap, and runs his hand through his hair. Though physically unscathed by the experience, it is evident that scars have been seared deep into his soul. "The shell from the destroyer, probably a five-inch - either a dud or the metal framework around the bridge was too thin to set if off. It just tore right through him without exploding. The last thing I saw was a torso without a head or shoulders. Shell just tore him right in half. Poor bastard. Then I slammed the hatch and dogged it down. Four hours of depth charges after that. Didn't think we'd come out of it. Nobody did."

He shakes his head slowly from side to side, as if still trying to comprehend the experience. He stares vacantly out over the white trail emanating from our stern. I know he won't say anything more.

The mug of coffee in my hands has gone cold. I look down at it; the liquid is black and moves heavily, like blood. A spasm of revulsion courses through me. I dump the contents over the side and scramble below.

Tuesday. Our fifth day out of Midway. After lunch the Skipper commences drills once again, diving deep and rigging for silent running. The Skipper alternates between standing in the conning tower or the control room, always with his stopwatch. He drives us relentlessly, constantly haranguing, cajoling, and pushing us ever faster. His drive is that of a man possessed. I begin to envision him as our Captain Ahab as he hones our minds and bodies to a razor-sharp edge. His preoccupation is acute. He sees our goal before him as total as Ahab saw the slaying of the White Whale - our survival and the enemy's destruction.

Nearly crushed three different times coming down the tower ladder by Michaelis, who dives in behind me slamming the hatch onto its seat. I soon learn to not take the rungs on the ladder at all. Grasp onto the sides instead, place the insteps of your feet around the outside metal bars, and slide all the way down using your hands and feet to maintain balance.

Following these are crash dives to periscope depth - fifty-five feet to the keel. To get our bow down faster, Chief Schrier pulls the neat trick of flooding the bow buoyancy tank before venting main ballast tank number seven located outboard of the after torpedo room. This, together with the accumulating weight in the main ballast tanks forward, causes the boat to swing quickly downward as if on a pendulum. The deck just drops out from underneath you; everyone from the after battery compartment forward has to hold on tight lest they go tumbling into a bulkhead.

On the last dive the Skipper orders us down to ninety feet. Pike taps me on the shoulder, "Come on cutie-pie, time to check and service the torpedoes.' We head toward the oval hatch leading toward the forward torpedo room. Chief Schrier heads aft to oversee the same thing in the after torpedo room. The Skipper instructs me to go along with Pike, so that I can learn as much as possible about "our most important passengers' as he refers to them.

Moving toward the bow compartment, there is a noticeable increase in the amount of cursing and shouting. Stepping through the hatch coaming, I see the compartment has taken on an entirely new look. Gone are the lowered bunks and signs of human habitat. The bunks have disappeared, the floor plates are gone, and the torpedoes in their racks swung out from the wall. The harsh electric light now gleams dully off oily, gunmetal exteriors. Greasy, naked-to-the-waist torpedomen hover around them like mother hens. The whole compartment now resembles one of those machine shops back in Pearl. Pike crows like a rooster, attempting to be heard over the din. Cursing and shouting, torpedomen wrestle three thousand pound torpedoes into position for servicing.

Daschler stands a few feet away, uncoiling the hose of an air compressor line, his shiny baldhead glinting with sweat. The naked lady tattoo on his thick, hirsute forearm is like a "bearded lady" circus attraction. Tashtego stands over by tubes two and four, checking the block and tackle arrangement for the chain fall in the overhead. Next to him are Garn, and the bearded Hood, Buckley and Reece.

Pike motions me over, shifts the cap on his head and begins, "The Mk XIV torpedo is divided into five sections, this is the warhead,' he says - patting the tip of the missile. 'The air flask takes up most of the midsection. The midsection contains the combustion flask and the igniter for the motor, and then the complicated after body - '

"Oil tank - ' I interrupt, smiling proudly. "Motor turbines, depth engine, gyro steering engine, immersion mechanism, starting lever, and depth index."

Pike looks surprised. "And the tail section?"

"Exhaust manifold." I say with confidence.

Pike nods. "Very nice Watts, you're no dumbshit - I appreciate that. Now, they detonate in two ways; one by means of a magnetic exploder, set off by the ship's magnetic field as the torpedo passes underneath it. The idea behind this being that the force of the explosion is vented straight upward, in effect breaking the back of the ship, or by means of a contact exploder which explodes the warhead as it strikes the ship's side. The torpedo has to travel a minimum of four hundred sixty yards before striking a target, so that the warhead arms. This happens by means of an impeller on the underside of the torpedo head. Spun by the flow of water passing through it; the firing pins of the detonator rotate into the proper firing position. Savvy?"

Quite complex, these hollow steel tubes; in reality they're smaller versions of a submarine; their cargo high explosive instead of men. Just a hiss of compressed air that moves them up about one to two inches in the tube, allowing the tripping lever in the bottom of the tube to trigger the torpedo's motor. Then they drive on their way by means of double solid brass counter-rotating propellers. By way of their gyroscope, they can run straight or veer off to a maximum of ninety degrees in any direction. Depth is pre-set by means of the depth index. Modern marvels of twentieth-century technology. A cartoon taped to the inner door of number one tube catches my attention. It's of a man and a woman sitting in a bathtub facing each other. With big smiles on both of their faces, the man says to the woman, "and that's how the Mk XIV torpedo works!"

The speaker on the bulkhead crackles - the Skipper wants to know how much longer the torpedo gang will be. There's anxiety in his voice. He's chomping at the bit to get back to the surface. Underwater here we can make little headway, and it's a long run to our patrol area.

Pike abruptly abandons me and turns his full attention to getting the torpedo servicing complete. Instead of just overseeing the operation, he joins in to hasten its completion. He follows behind the crew chiefs and double checks their work. Tashtego tests and inspects the alcohol and air levels for the fish on the starboard side - Daschler on the port. Reece inspects the oil tank and immersion mechanisms. Hood the gyro steering mechanism and the igniter, and on it goes until all the compartment's torpedoes have been serviced. With more swearing and cursing, the fish are hauled back into the tubes, the racks moved back into place, and torpedoes swung back on the racks. Exhausted and dripping perspiration, the torpedo gang stands down.

Pike stands in the middle of the compartment wiping oil from his hands with a near-black rag. He lifts up his cap and wipes his forehead with his sleeve. "That's it for today."

"All that pumping and I didn't even bust!" Somebody cracks.

"Well use thirty-weight oil on your hand next time!"

"Fuck you!"

Pike sends word to the Skipper - torpedo servicing completed. Within seconds we're heading toward the surface.

After the evening meal, we sit around the wardroom table and try to keep from being bored. We smoke one cigarette after another, down cup after cup of coffee, and stare at each other in stupored passivity. The Skipper sits in his usual place, at the end of the table flanked by Pike and Schumacher on one side, Michaelis and I on the other. Waldron puffs thoughtfully on his pipe at the other end. Schumacher is flipping through the latest issue of Stars and Stripes newspaper that he picked up on in Midway before our departure. The front page reads, "Germans closing in on Moscow. Stalin vows fight to last man and last round."

"You know it's funny,' Pike begins, looking over at the newspaper from the other side of the table, 'remember back in 'thirty-nine when the Russians invaded Finland and everybody condemned them? How they were the big bad guys for doing that and carving up Poland with the Germans? Then how did Stalin get to be such a good guy all of a sudden? Hell, in some newspapers they call him "Uncle Joe."

"A mere alliance of convenience,' Waldron observes thoughtfully, 'When the war's over, we'll go back to despising them again."

"I'll tell you what bugs the hell out of me,' Schumacher snaps, lowering his paper, 'we're at war with the Japs, the British are at war with the Japs, then why in the hell aren't the goddamned Russians at war with the Japs? We're supposed to help them in *their* fight but not help us in *ours*? Bunch of shit!"

"Don't waste your time with politics boys -' the Skipper instructs, '- just remember our job is to clean up the mess that they create."

The spell breaks as the steward comes in to refill our cups. He dumps ashtrays full of cigarette butts so that we can refill them once again.

"Jonesy got any Danishes back there?" Michaelis wants to know, typically thinking with his stomach.

"Do you ever think of anything besides eating?" Waldron interjects, lowering his pipe from his mouth for the first time since the meal.

"Women." He responds with a leer.

"Now it's established." Waldron admits, reinserting the pipe stem into the corner of his mouth.

Clutching his coffeepot and a dirty plate or two, the steward exits.

"Says here that Hollywood stars are lining up to join in the USO.' Schumacher reads, still perusing his newspaper. "Bob Hope, Marlene Dietrich, Andrews Sisters, Robert Taylor, John Wayne, Jack Benny, Burns and Allen, Spike Jones, Rita Hayworth, and Betty Grable, to name a few. The USO is planning to form touring groups and have them visit military bases to put on shows."

"Hooey for them!" Michaelis cracks.

The steward reappears, clutching a small pile of Danishes and two tins of preserves. Immediately Michaelis squeals with delight. As the steward plops them down in the center of the table, Michaelis selects a large one and commences munching.

"Is that all it takes to soothe the savage beast?' Schumacher wants to know. "A cinnamon Danish?"

"Well, you could always do what my girl back home does."

"What's that?"

"Hold me close."

Schumacher gives him a scathing glance and goes back to his paper.

The Skipper - our great Sphinx - cracks an amused smile. Odd fellow our commander. Anything he says you have to drag out of him. A quiet, reserved type yet you can tell there's always something going on behind his eyes - always thinking, always calculating. For example, while most of the others are pretty free in talking about their sexual exploits, the Skipper is at the opposite end of the spectrum. Like one of those old-fashioned types who don't subscribe to "kiss and tell." Yet I've heard through the grapevine that he has several girlfriends back in Pearl. Apparently that's where the Speedster came from. Michaelis says he's seen two of them - one a beautiful blonde and the other a stunning brunette. However, often the man who talks all the time has only that, just talk. The man who is quiet and reserved has everything. If you think about it, it's true. Still waters run deep.

A quarter of an hour goes by. After umpteenth cup of coffee the Skipper calls for the chess set. The steward pours him another cup as he and Michaelis set up the pieces for a game. Schumacher and I exchange looks - another sacrificial lamb being hauled to the chopping block.

They are not ten minutes into the game when the wardroom phone buzzes. Swensen has a wire in. Michaelis disappears in the direction of the radio room. A few minutes later he returns, and hands a slip of paper to the Skipper, who stares at it a moment. A crease forms on his temple. The interest in the chess game vanishes like smoke in the wind.

"Attack on AK,' he reads aloud, 'five thousand GRT. Two prematures, one dud; 10-05 N., 123-55 E.; Three hours depth charge bombardment. Light damage. Contact broken. CO *Sculpin*."

He stops and stares at the paper a moment. GRT is short for *Gross Registered Tons*, the method of merchant ship measurement in the Registry. An AK, that's a -

" Jap freighter." Says Schumacher, as if reading my mind.

"*Sculpin* - isn't that Chappell's boat?" Waldron wants to know.

Schumacher shakes his head, "Taking that type of punishment for dud fish! What rotten luck!"

"How could it be that only now malfunctioning torpedoes are being discovered?' I query. 'Why wasn't this taken care of before the war broke out?

"Because - ' the Skipper snaps with heavy sarcasm, 'In peacetime the torpedo warheads weren't tested. During training exercises, we'd shoot practice torpedoes with dummy warheads; the real exploders sat on a shop shelf! Bureau of Ordinance and the Navy just *assumed* they would work. Since they cost ten thousand dollars apiece they didn't want to blow them up."

"Hopefully there was just a bad batch manufactured." Waldron points out optimistically.

The Skipper shrugs slightly. "A chance but if this kind of thing keeps happening, unlikely." He gets up and disappears into the passageway. A moment later the sounds of his curtain being pulled to.

Yet again, the change of the watch startles me awake in my bunk. For what seems like hours I lay staring into the semi-blackness before me. Below me, Waldron lies in blissful slumber, though only for him. For me, it's like sleeping with a rusty saw slowly grinding across a log that never cuts. His snoring is so bad it's amazing that he doesn't wake himself up. And it, of course, doesn't stop with him. On all sides the stentorian noises of the night assail me, from the bow compartment and from the petty officer's quarters behind us.

Only from the Skipper's quarters is there silence.

I can feel from the vibrating steel all around me that the diesels are running at high rpm's. We're probably doing a brisk seventeen knots. At this speed, if any type of sea is running the boat doesn't yawl all that much. The bow knifes through a wave and drops like a stone into the trough on the other side, causing a momentary weightless feeling on the drop and then the shudder as the bow buries itself. There must be fairly strong wind topside. We're rolling fairly sharply too.

The Skipper is becoming more and more anxious about getting to our patrol area. Before I turned in Swensen intercepted two other messages off of the radio, both from Corregidor with the same underlying theme; "situation worsening: food, ammunition, and medical supplies all in short supply. Immediate re-supply imperative if force is to hold out."

It doesn't take a military genius to figure out that if the Japanese sustain this blitzkrieg drive of theirs and keep knocking us on our ass, the war - barely a month old - is already lost.

Rumble of voices coming from the bow compartment, thumping footsteps in the passageway, scraping and squeaking of metal that sounds like bunks being folded up.

"Let's go! Let's get started!" I don't recognize the voice.

"What's the problem? You have another war to go to?" Unmistakably Tashtego.

"No, I've got the next watch!"

More shuffling, scraping, and squeaking.

"All right,' Tashtego begins, 'Seven card-stud, deuces and tens are wild."

Another poker game - at this hour? It's possible I've shipped out with a boatload of vampires. Sound of a deck of cards being shuffled.

"Anybody hear about *Sculpin*? Attacked a Jap transport with dud fish!'

'Yeah - and got a couple of hours of ash cans on account of it!"

"D'you think all the fish are garbage?"

"I load 'em, unload 'em, and service what makes 'em go,' he replies evenly, 'I don't mess with what makes 'em blow - those exploders are classified. That's Lt. Pike's job. Besides, I almost lost my head on the last patrol for checking one out."

A moment of surprised silence. "What happened?"

The sharp, unmistakable metallic click of a Zippo lighter opening, then snapping shut. "After our first two attacks on the last patrol, Jameson ordered Schrier and me to pull the fish from the tubes and check each one of the exploders in the warheads. SubPac found out about it and went ape. Jameson would've had his ass chewed if he hadn't gotten killed. I guess only Pike is supposed to mess with 'em. Gave Schrier and me a hell of a going over."

"Where was Pike during this?"

"With us, he had us help him. I think SubPac had a few words to say to him too."

"Did he get reprimanded?"

"Don't think so, Jameson ordered him to have us help."

"Hey - c'mon! You wanna talk or play poker? Make up your mind!"

"What's wild again?"

"For the last time,' Tashtego says with a sigh, 'deuces and tens. You in or out?"

"In!"

"Then keep your ears open and your mouth shut!"

An hour later they're still at it. Those coming off watch replace those going on. A never-ending circle of cards, cigarettes, cigars, and personal affrontery. They exchange insults as easily as a man changes his shirt.

The XO glances at his watch, "Bout time for the Second Watch." He slides out from the table and gets to his feet. Silently he picks up his cap and goes out.

A glance at the chronometer - 0743. The on-coming watch always relieves the off-coming watch fifteen minutes early, in accordance with naval tradition.

The Skipper and I sit alone in the wardroom. He sits quietly, arms folded, staring in front of him. He is not here, but somewhere else. I pretend to read a *Collier's* magazine lying on the table. I don't want him to think I'm staring at him. So deep in thought is he that I doubt he even notices Pike and Schumacher come in and plop themselves down for breakfast, tossing their caps on the shelf below the cabinets.

"Mornin' virgin-boy!' Pike cracks, sliding in beside me.

Schumacher shakes his head wearily while eyeing his food. "One of these days the Geneva Convention's going to come looking for him."

The jabbing at Jonesy has no letup.

Pike grins evilly. "Man's inhumanity to man."

Chuckles and giggles as the steward trots in with plates for them. Pike takes a fork in hand and tests the waters; he pokes around checking the consistency of his food.

"That's the problem with having the first watch, breakfast is always warmed over."

Both Pike and Schumacher shoot cautious glances over at the Skipper. A few moments later he looks up and asks Pike for a condition report.

"Wind out of the southeast at seven,' the torpedo and gunnery officer says, his voice muffled behind a mouthful of bacon and eggs. 'Clear sky with intermittent high strato-nimbus clouds, temperature steadies at sixty-five degrees, sea a three, barometer steady. Visibility superb. A good twenty miles. Speed fifteen knots."

The Skipper nods his head slowly, sinking back into his meditative state. Pike gives him another guarded look, then goes back to downing his warmed-over breakfast. The steward appears once again, and asks if the Captain is sure that he wouldn't like anything to eat. Barely glancing up, the Skipper merely shakes his head again, saying nothing. After the steward retreats, the Skipper remains a few more moments - then without a word - gets up and goes out.

Sure that he's safely out of earshot, Schumacher leans over the table, "What's with him?"

Pike glances toward the passageway. "Lichty intercepted a wire last night from *S-36*, running on the surface; northeast of Luzon they got pounced by a couple of Jap

Zeros. Got shot up pretty bad, especially the skipper of the boat. Not sure if he's going to make it. Fellow's a classmate of Tyreen's from Annapolis."

So that explains the Skipper's melancholia.

"He'll snap out of it,' Pike avers, 'once we get closer to our patrol area. And then look out!"

"What do you mean?" I prod.

Pike grins evilly. "You'll see."

A bustling in the passageway. A knock on the metal partition.

"Yo?" Pike says warily through a mouthful of toast.

Chief Schrier's head and large shoulders appear in the access way. "Morning sirs, just wanted to let you know we're checking the specific gravity of the batteries in this compartment, so just mind your step coming out of here."

"Wilco Chief - thanks.' Pike says, downing the last of his eggs. Across from me, Schumacher has already cleared away his plate and is lighting up his second cigarette.

The loudspeaker crackles. Pike and Schumacher look up expectantly. The first few bars of brassy horns open a Spike Jones favorite called "Der Fuhrer's Face."

Schumacher immediately snaps up a spoon and begins jabbing the air as a band conductor, singing along with the record.

Ven the Fuh-rer says....Ve is der master race,

Ve Heil! thbbbt! Heil! thbbbt!

right in der Fuhrer's face!

Not to love der Fuh-rer....

ist a great disgrace!

So ve Heil! thbbbt! Heil! thbbt!

right in der Fuhrer's face!

*   *   *

The sun rises and sets. The waves and swell, always in their interminable, ever ceaseless march, pass on beneath the boat; rock it this way and that, buoying us up above a sea floor miles below. We go on watch and come off, and seemingly turn right around and go back on again. We shovel Jonesy's meals down our gullets, smoke too much, drink pot after pot of coffee, and breath in the same dank atmosphere day after day. A mindless existence.

As of yet we have done nothing to dent the massive Imperial Japanese military machine. We sail around burning up precious diesel fuel with nothing to show for it. Somehow I imagined it would be different than this. All the accounts of submarine war I have read lead one to believe that you're dashing about in swashbuckling style from one place on the map to another firing torpedoes and sinking ships. In fact, nothing could be further from the truth. Boredom is our ever-present companion and - thus far - only enemy.

And as time goes by, I feel more constrained and claustrophobic. My world revolves around my bunk, the bridge and cigarette deck, and the wardroom. No pleasure here of an after dinner stroll around the deck as in surface ships - if a man tried that he'd be washed overboard within seconds since our deck is nearly always awash. The lack of movement is foreign to me. If I'm not assisting on a watch all I do is sit around studying ship's manuals. It isn't natural - I'm beginning to feel like a pile of Jell-O. A good hard swim or some other strong physical exercise would feel wonderful. Still, I guess my lot is better than footslogging around some godforsaken countryside with a rifle in my hand and a hundred pound field pack on my back.

A little excitement stirs up about 1000 hrs. Swensen is one duty in the radio room, scanning the airwaves for any transmissions when he picks up someone known as "Tokyo Rose" - it's a Jap propaganda broadcast. I'm with the Skipper when he gets the word, and follow him toward the back of the control room. Swensen hovers over the radio set like a mad scientist over a chemistry set, fine-tuning until the signal comes in loud and clear.

"Sir,' Swensen says with a chuckle, 'you got to hear this!"

I lean against the wall and listen. "...That the American war making machine is now on the sandy bottom of Pearl Harbor, the Empire of Japan wishes peace, for all nations of the Pacific."

A cackle of laughter behind me - it's Pike.

'- and as soon as the imperialist American government realizes they have no hope of winning the war, we will all live together under the wonderful arms of the Emperor Hirohito. This war is of the Americans making and the tyrannical English monarchy. If the democracies do not realize this, we - the Empire of Japan - together with Adolf Hitler's Germany, will bring them to their knees!"

A chorus of sarcastic laughter breaks out all around - except for the Skipper. Instead, a deep frown creases his brow; "I'm going to make that Jap bitch eat those words!" He turns away and heads back forward.

Around 0900 there are rumors about that we're in Japanese waters. That irrefutable point is rammed home about forty-five minutes later when one of the lookouts screams, "AIRCRAFT TO STARBOARD!"

"Floatplane HEADING THIS WAY! CLEAR THE BRIDGE!"

Tearing, stumbling, falling down the ladder into the tower. Brief glimpse of the Skipper below in the control room at the base of the ladder, staring quizzically upward. Quick - roll out of the way of the ladder! Move damnit! Move!

I strike something metal with my back. A puncturing, stabbing pain. Involuntarily I cry out.

The boat is already sharply down by the bow. Motors full speed ahead.

"Hard right rudder!" Waldron's voice is sharp, but still maintains that level of self-assured calm. Does he ever get excited about anything?

The pain in my back begins to ebb. Sound of boots on steel. Somebody's coming up the ladder. The slow murmurs of voices. I sigh and breathe deeply, trying to push the pain from my body. What the hell did I hit?

"What was it?" It's the Skipper who came up the ladder.

"Floatplane.' Waldron remarks without emotion. "Single engine Mitsubishi-type. Seven...maybe eight miles out."

"Did he see us?"

"Ease rudder amidships, make course zero zero zero."

"More than likely,' Waldron admits. 'He was heading right at us."

The Skipper sniffs violently through his nose. "That means there's either a tender close by or some naval activity. Report depth!" He snaps.

I open my eyes. The world is on a tilt; I'm on my right side and the boat is still at an angle.

"Passing nine zero feet sir." The reply wafts up from the control room.

"Level off. All ahead half." The Skipper notices me, but his eyes seem to bore right through me. He glances over at the depth gauge on the side of the tower. "Now let's see if this Jap has any eggs in his basket."

We wait. The minutes pass, but nothing happens. Still, that's no comfort to the Skipper. "Might have been just a recon flight,' he says, looking disconcerted, 'but he's still got a radio, and can still make things hot for us."

"There must be a seaplane tender around here someplace,' Waldron broods, 'he'd have to come from something like that in the middle of the ocean."

I turn around to see just exactly what protuberance I impaled myself upon: the corner of an electrical connection box, lying at a sharp ninety-degree angle. Couldn't somebody have thought to coat the damn edges with rubber or something? Fucking idiots!

We wait thirty minutes, coming back around to our base course; two seven zero degrees. The Skipper is impatient. Chafing at the bit to get back to the surface to get speed on he orders us to periscope depth. He moves to the search scope, which is larger than the attack scope and is better for sky observation and takes a look - nothing. He snaps the handles back up and orders it lowered. "All clear,' he declares, shifting the cap back on his head, "Either he didn't see us, or he already reported our position and went home."

"In which case the best thing to do would be to clear the area as soon as we can."

Waldron adds.

The Skipper slowly nods his head in silence, his movements abrupt - machinelike. "Surface! Waldron, I want three engines on line, base course is two seven zero, tacking at infrequent intervals at your discretion. Understood?"

"Yes sir." Waldron replies - glancing at his watch. Moving over to the ladder, he waits. A pair of glasses is already around his neck.

"Tower clear!"

"Crack the hatch!"

The torrent of water from above hits the deck plates like the sputtering from a leaky shower.

For a temporary interruption of the tedium, one can take a turn in the crew's mess. The usual high-jinks are constantly in the air; card games and coffee drinking, cursing and storytelling - with each lie nullifying the last. Also, McGowan often sits in here practicing scales on his bagpipes. Instead of the usual black baseball watch caps the rest of the men wear, McGowan prefers a worn but still smart double-stemmed overseas cap with a tartan tail. During one of my rounds through the boat, I learn he was just two years old when he emigrated with his parents. He relates all kinds of experiences of growing up barely above poverty level in Brooklyn and learned to play the bagpipes from his father, who was a piper with the Gordon Highlanders during the last war. Producing an elaborately bent meerschaum pipe from his pocket, he stops the Chief and wants to know when we'll see some action.

In the process of heading aft, the Chief stops and regards him with a kindred eye.

"Action - is that all you Scots ever talk about? Aren't you supposed to be fighting the Germans?"

"Historically it's the bloody French - but we need to fight."

"How so?"

"Every man must have a hobby!" McGowan grins like a Cheshire cat and puffs thoughtfully on his pipe.

Later, I take a turn aft. In my off time at night I have been studying the boat's manuals prodigiously. At this juncture I know fairly well the forward torpedo room and it's components, as well as the battery system, but the vast array of complexity in the control room still confounds me. So, to give myself a bit of a break, I head to the forward engine room. Passing the lump forms in the bunks in the after battery compartment that is the off-watch, I pause in front of the watertight door and grasp the handle. The great roaring and hammering of the diesels sound like it's in here instead of in the next compartment. How the hell can anybody sleep through this? I pull on the door - nothing happens. Sealed? Upon closer inspection I can see that it's not. I'll try again. Using both hands, I grasp the curved handles of the solid brass door and pull with all my strength. Like the popping of a champagne cork the door frees itself of the frame. Then it dawns on me; the suction caused by the engines is so great that it creates a vacuum that grasps the door so tightly it forms a seal completely on its own. Wincing from the shattering reverberations, I step over the hatch coaming and into the compartment.

Hartmann and McClusky - of the Third Watch - are on duty. Hartmann perches on a small wooden stool next to the starboard engine with his back to me. McClusky hovers over what looks like a lubricating oil pump, a cigarette jutting from the left corner of his mouth. He looks at me and grins through an oil-smeared face and starts to get up. I motion him back down. With a somewhat confused look, he sits.

The heat is oppressive. Add to it the heavy aroma of diesel exhaust and stench of diesel and lubricating oil. Already I'm breaking into a sweat. The controlled explosions inside the cylinders, combined with the various pumps running and the exhaust lines, easily bring the temperature in here to a sweltering ninety plus degrees. I can see heavy blotches of sweat on both Hartmann and McClusky's heavily stained denim shirts, both of which have the sleeves cut out of them, and are worn as vests only halfway buttoned up. Hartmann notices me through unfocused eyes. Unbuttoning my shirt and shift the cap back on my head, I lean against the port Kleinschmidt distiller. Despite the infernal racket, stifling heat, and fumes, a ship's engine room has a certain ambiance. A sort of introspective solitude all its own. The noise is such it actually precludes communication with anyone else.

A shout comes out of the incessant roaring and reaches out to me. A bit surprised; I look around. Hartmann stands to my left over by the port engine and is pointing at his watch. I move over to him. He cocks his head and yells into my ear.

"TIME TO OPEN...CLOSE.... VENTS!"

I look at him. "WHAT?"

He mimes a screwing motion, "EXHAUST VENTS,' another screwing motion. Then I understand; he wants to grind the exhaust vents open and closed so that the carbon deposits that build on them from the diesel exhaust don't hold the vents open in the event of a dive. Through my studying I know this must be done every two hours, and sooner if the boat is running at high speeds as the carbon builds up fast. And woe to the engineer who does not keep the exhaust vents clear of such matter, for a diving boat with open exhaust vents has a one-way ticket to the bottom.

Hartmann looks at me expectantly. It suddenly dawns on me; he's asking me if I want to help. I shake my head, "OKAY!"

Seeing a satisfied grin behind his brown neatly trimmed beard, he turns and points to a set of valves on the port side above the engine. He turns his arm in another screwing motion. I nod - understood - and step over to them. Behind me, McClusky steps up to the set of valves on the starboard side. We can't do both of them at the same time, since the exhaust would have nowhere to go except back into the engines where it would asphyxiate them. So, with Hartmann at my side, I am to go first.

Hartmann motions in a clockwise direction, then counter-clockwise, and back again. This is the grinding motion apparently necessary. With both hands on the steel valve wheel, I turn it to the right. Resistance is heavy, to get the valve to move I really have to put some elbow grease into it. Finally, the valve won't turn anymore - now it is closed. I begin to turn it in the opposite direction, the valve fighting me every step of the way. By the time I get it in the open position once again, sweat is streaming down my face.

I complete this process five times, allowing Hartmann each time to check it. He spins the wheel around, checking the resistance. Satisfied, he gives me a nod and turns around to give McClusky the go ahead.

Finished and drenched in sweat, my heart thumps heavily in my chest. And my hands are stained black from the carbon on the valve wheel. Here is one compartment that gets plenty of exercise. I allow myself to sink down on Hartmann's little stool to catch my breath.

A dirty rag lies next to me on the deck plates. I pick it up and try to wipe the worst of the blackness from my hands. A wasted effort - the rag is thick with grease and I only succeed in smearing it all over my palms. Cursing silently, I grope around for another as McClusky stumbles by and stops in front of the various gauges for the starboard engine. He taps the glass cover of one with a black finger. Apparently satisfied, he leans back against the starboard Kleinschmidt Distiller and produces a pack of cigarettes. I study him; a tall fellow with a slight build, he has to move around everywhere in a perpetual stoop - or else he'd bang his skull against the low overhead. I don't think he's very far into his twenties, but with his full beard he looks easily forty or better. I've heard the bluejackets have maliciously given him the nickname "Boris' - after Boris Karloff, the horror movie actor.

Two men about my age. Where are they from? What did they do before the war? A wife? A girlfriend? I know so little about them. Uprooted from every corner of the country and dropped into this smelly steel tube crammed with electronic wizardry. This entire experience is probably as bewildering to them as it is to me.

I have the answer to one question as I move toward the watertight door. McClusky still leans against the distiller smoking a cigarette, but now he has his wallet out. Stealing a glance over his shoulder, he stares at a picture of a radiant young girl - maybe nineteen or twenty - sitting on a park bench, legs crossed and holding a flower in her hand. McClusky glances at me and grins proudly. I nod approvingly and give him a pat on the shoulder. I wonder if she knows about his nickname?

Home. A girl. Love. Our embodiment of utopian happiness.

Next morning - our eighth day out of Midway. Dozing in my bunk, I am halfway between that state of unconsciousness and lucidity when a cry comes down from the bridge, "Pod of whales off starboard bow!"

Instantly awake, I bolt for the bridge.

Our bow knifes through an unbroken, rolling plain of deep beer-bottle green made luminescent by a dazzling fiery ball of the morning sun. Looking off to starboard even without binoculars, I spy a dozen or so sprays of fine mist in the air; they hover a moment and disappear. Faint black humps in the water are visible at a time.

"They're whales all right,' Pike declares, handing me a pair of glasses. Look at the size of those spouts."

"Way too big to be dolphins.' one of the lookouts declares flatly.

Pike whirls around, incredulity written all over his face. "Look out man! You're meant to be on watch! Pay attention!"

I peer through the glasses. When the swell allows for a decent glimpse, large log-shaped tops that seem to slant on a slightly steep angle down into the water. They're maybe two to three thousand yards out. It's a big group - I start counting and reach seventeen before commotion behind me causes me to lose count. People keep coming through the hatch. Everybody who can find an excuse is up here - Chiefs' Schrier and Pitcairn, the XO, and even the little red-haired Yeoman O'Toole. Waldron - who just had the last watch - appears a moment later, with a cup of coffee and puffing on his pipe.

The pod is coming right across our track. Unless we change course, we'll run right into the whole pack of them.

"Helmsman, come left fifteen degrees rudder,' Pike yells down the hatch, as if reading my thoughts, and cocks an eyebrow. 'Wouldn't do to run into the middle of them would it?"

"They wouldn't take too kindly to that." Waldron adds, puffing on his pipe.

That's all we need, to embroil ourselves in a fight with a pod of whales. What could an enraged whale do to the steel pressure hull of a submarine? Visions of the *Pequod* being smashed to driftwood by an enraged white whale in Melville's *Moby Dick; Ishmael* floating on the coffin, the *Samuel Enderby,* Queequeg, Elijah, the madness of Ahab....

Pike raises the glasses to his eyes once again, "Well Professor, what do you make them?"

Waldron glances at him slyly, ignoring the veiled insult. "You mean what species?"

"Yeah. You know all that useless stuff!"

Giving Pike a harder look, Waldron politely asks to borrow my glasses. He steps over and raises them to his eyes. The range has closed. Now less than a thousand yards.

The pod comes on, a sight of majestic grandeur. The hulky black shapes, one behind the other in closed ranks, part the water as they rise and drop with each passing swell. Their spouts show a brief puff of white against a broad backdrop of green. "I'm certainly no expert,' Waldron begins, still peering from behind the glasses, 'But by the way the head is shaped and how it protrudes from the water, and the angle the spout is at...I'd hazard they are sperm whales."

We watch them in silent awe; the great horizontal tails break the surface then disappear back beneath the waves. These massive gentle monsters, the behemoths of the sea moving inexorably on to some unknown destination, moved as they have a thousand times before, and will a thousand times more.

Where are they going? A lifetime of roaming the seas, traversing the endless, empty ocean for these nomads of the sea. We know so little of them.

And so little of ourselves.

The sea has picked up a bit. Once a bottle green a short while ago has now turned a darker mouse gray. A brisk wind deepens the swell, brushing the tops white, like awnings blanketed with snow. Showers of spray begin coming over the bulwark. Heavy blue-black rain clouds hang malevolently in the sky to the southeast. Barometer falling - so there's a thunderstorm coming. The balmy seventy degrees has dropped to at least the mid-fifties. The XO gives the sky a sour look. "Bound to run into some crappy weather eventually,' he declares evenly, zipping up his leather flying jacket just handed up to him through the hatch. 'We've had unusually good weather so far. Too good to last, of course."

He calls for foul weather gear, and after a few minutes it comes up to the lookouts, rain jackets and sou'wester rain hats. I exchange my windbreaker for a slicker, but retain my cap. The XO calls for extra lens paper for the binoculars, then produces a cigarette and offers me one, "Better smoke while you've got the chance. In a little while it'll probably be so wet you won't be able to get one lit.'

Lighting it, he lets it droop from his lips as he gives the menacing clouds a going-over with the glasses. He's a mid-westerner, I heard, from Missouri. An Academy man, where he played a little football. Wanted to go into battleships first, I think. That's all I know. Pretty much a quiet, introspective type. Reminds me of Gary Cooper.

Between two of the highest and blackest clouds, a thin bolt of lightning flashes, arcing in a crooked line. A moment later the sharp explosion reaches us; the dull reverberations roll over the water. We move closer to the threatening black tumor. The billows and folds that reach down toward the surface of the water seem ready to burst with rain. Titanic mounds of coal hovering in the sky pulled along by an unseen train.

"Biblical,' the XO opines, studying the baleful specter.

The air is becoming heavier. Lemert has come up for a smoke and reports the barometer taking a nosedive.

"Keep your eyes open boys,' the XO instructs us, 'anything could be hiding in a squall like this. It's perfect cover for destroyers."

Behind me, Lemert and the lookouts are all fitted out in their foul weather gear. Under the gray coats and slant-brimmed hats they all look like a bunch of Cape Cod fishermen. Lemert grins at me, "I feel like such an idiot in this get-up!"

The XO and I still have our caps on, but after another look at the foreboding sky he calls for a sou'wester. I'll keep my cap. The coming rain is a perfect chance to weather it a little.

When it begins, it starts as a pecking sound. The falling drops smack into the deck and the steel structure surrounding it. It hits the rubberized cloth of our slickers and sou'westers. Getting harder and harder. The water dimples in million places with the brief impact of the rain until the sky opens up and it becomes one massive deluge. . Later, coming down from the bridge for a cup of coffee to warm up, I'm moving past the galley when I catch snippets of conversation from some of the First Watch, who are crowded around the mess tables, carrying on in their usual vociferous manner.

"Thing is,' Cutter, the Torpedoman explains, 'it used to scare people - especially women! They would come to the track and see me doing close to a hundred miles an hour and faint dead away! Motorcycles are great - they'll scared the hell out of you!"

"You actually won a couple of races?" Machinist Schumann asks.

Cutter nods, "Fifty to a hundred bucks at a time, you know, your regular county fairs - Succotash queen, a worthless blue ribbon for whoever's got the biggest melons and pumpkins, fattest pig - stuff like that."

"Succotash queen?" Somebody repeats.

"Yeah. You know, some wholesome local wench who gets picked for reading the most books or whatever. Some local girl-next-door type that every mother in town aspires her daughter to be. Funny thing was, underneath all that innocent exterior; she could usually suck a golf ball through a garden hose!"

A cacophony of hoots, catcalls, cheers, and wolf whistles.

In the control room, an hour after midnight. In front of the plotting table, the Skipper stands next to Waldron and Pike, who has just come off watch. Pike shimmies out of his slicker, shaking like a wet Saint Bernard. A chart lies on the table, our progress marked in a thin pencil line across it. Unable to obtain a star fix for the last eight hours due to the squall that continues to rage around us, the XO has had to rely on dead reckoning to figure our position. This entails taking our speed and course and mathematically figuring our relative position from the last star bearing. The Skipper, with protractor and dividers in hand, checks the XO's trigonometry. Shifting his cap back on his head, he does his mental gymnastics, lays down the dividers, takes pencil in hand, and figures some more.

Our location is several hundred miles east of the Luzon coast. Luzon - the biggest of the Philippine Islands - is the northernmost link in an island chain that stretches for thousands of miles through the Pacific. The island group comes to an end near the same longitude as the tip of Borneo. An irregular line of islands with the largest two - Luzon in the north and Mindanao in the south - broken up and criss-crossed by a plethora of straits and channels.

A steady spattering of water comes down through the open hatch. The main hatch to the bridge is left open on account of the main induction valve. Located in the after part of the conning tower fairwater, it closes whenever a wave breaks over it. A specially designed mechanism shuts the mushroom-shaped valve before the seawater has a chance to enter the air pipes that feed to the engines. When the valve shuts, the engines draw their air through the boat, causing a noticeable and irritating change in air pressure every few moments. Your breath is drawn away and the eardrums pop. The hatches to the bridge and conning tower are oblique to one another, but this does not stop the water from finding the path of least resistance. The idea of course, is to channel it so that it drains into the boat's bilges, and pump it outboard with the bilge pumps.

Laying the pencil down, the Skipper scratches his beard thoughtfully and looks up at us.

"Gentlemen, for all intents and purposes, give or take fifteen or twenty miles by dead reckoning - we're here."

A host of blank looks announce our arrival in a war zone. Chief Schrier appears, holding his oil logbook. He shows the Skipper the figures of our diesel fuel consumption for the last twenty-four hours. The Skipper takes his pencil once again in hand and initials it absentmindedly. Then, turning back to the plotting table with a vengeance, he stares at the chart for a brief moment before smacking it. "Shipping coming down from the home islands, heading toward Luzon would filter down through this area here."

"It is the most direct route." Waldron adds, striking a match and drawing the flame into the end of his pipe. In between draws through the stem, the flame leaps up at least three inches from the bowl. "From Honshu from the north, and from the Marianas in the east."

"Heading toward the Balintang Channel and Aparri." The Skipper concurs. "Aparri is the place. I'm sure that's where Tojo is bringing in most of his supplies."

"Time for some action!" Pike chimes in, licking his lips.

"Should be a good hunting ground." Waldron agrees judiciously, his eyes not leaving the map.

The Skipper's cold steel stare bores through him. He glances once more at the blue map spread out before us. "Come right to three four eight, all ahead half!' He turns to Pike, 'Squall showing any signs of letting up?"

"Rain has let up a bit, winds about the same - out of the southeast at seven."

As if to punctuate his words, the boat rolls sharply to starboard, sending the Skipper's figuring pencil rolling across the plotting table.

The Skipper lingers a moment longer than the rest, staring at the map. His head nodding slowly. "Good hunting ground."

He speaks very quietly, as if only to himself.

A little excitement stirs up later. Lemert rolls out of his bunk in agony with a toothache. Kemper turns up - examines him - and diagnoses a complete near-abscess. Result: the tooth must come out.

"When can you do it?" The Skipper wants to know.

Kemper shrugs. "Right now?"

Lemert gasps and all color evaporates from his face.

"I'll need something to pull it with though."

"You don't have *anything*?" Lemert croaks as Kemper shakes his head sympathetically. "I've been trained to patch up bullet wounds sir, not pull teeth."

"What do you need?" The Skipper asks, with a crease in his brow.

"Can the Chief spare me a pair of pliers?"

Lemert comes straight out of the chair. It takes four strong, able-bodied men and ten exhausting minutes to put him back there again.

A commotion in the passageway - excited voices and tramping feet. I struggle to wake up, catching bits and pieces of conversation as men go by.

"When?"

"Just a little while ago, Swensen caught it -'

"From who?"

"*Tarpon.'*

Since that's one of our boats something must be up. Rubbing sleep from my eyes, I struggle to get up. Outside, the Gunner's mate stands next to Tashtego. Both stare warily down the passageway toward the control room.

"What's up?" I ask.

"The Nips!"

I turn and head into the control room. Waldron is there, his shirt wet and sticking to his chest. His beard glistening with water. Next to him is the similarly sodden Skipper. Waldron must have just come off watch - what time is it? It must be near 0400 or better. The Chief comes in with a rolled up chart, places it on the table, and unrolls it.

"Where was he?" Waldron asks, drying the bowl of his pipe with a small hand towel.

The Skipper places a cigarette between his lips and leans over the chart. In his left hand is a small piece of paper. I can see writing on it.

"One hundred twenty degrees north,' the Skipper mutters under his breath, reading from the slip of paper, 'Nineteen degrees west.... That would put them right here,' a long, lean finger juts out and stabs at a point on the map. "Course one seven five,' he continues. 'Speed eight knots,' his finger taps the chart once again, 'right here."

Waldron clears his throat. "With this squall, he wouldn't have had a chance to get a star fix in the last fifteen hours though."

The Skipper dips his head, agreeing. "It's dead reckoning, but it's all we have to go on." He glances up and notices me; a tight grin forms at the corners of his mouth, "Well Ensign, looks like it's time to bust your cherry."

"*Tarpon,*' Waldron explains, 'northwest of us, spotted an enemy convoy probably headed for Luzon. If they maintain their present course, we'll be making contact shortly."

A pang of excitement shoots up my spine. "How long?"

"Next three to four hours." The Skipper's face reads like a starving man about to eat for the first time in a month. He takes a long drag on his cigarette. A wisp of smoke escapes from between his lips and lingers in the air a moment. He looks back down at the map. "If they maintain present course, we should come in starboard of them. We'll come left to three four zero."

"Maintain present speed?" Waldron asks.

The Skipper nods abruptly. "For now. Doesn't make any sense beating ourselves to death, there's enough spray coming over the bridge anyway. How're my batteries Chief?"

The Chief grins reassuringly. "Couldn't have more juice in 'em if I'd plugged 'em in myself!"

"Good. Good,' he mumbles, rubbing his eyes and suddenly looking tired.

The steward brushes past me balancing several mugs of coffee in his hands.

"Coffee sir?"

"Johnson, you're a mind reader."

The Skipper gratefully reaches out and takes the offered cup. He hooks his leg around the little wooden stool that sits in here and drags it over. Sitting down heavily, he takes off his worn and weathered cap, lays it beside him on the chart and runs a hand through his tangled hair. It doesn't look like he's slept at all. Maybe the weather kept him up. Unlikely for an old salt like him.

"Three ship convoy?" Waldron says, seeking confirmation.

"Four, maybe five including an escort. One destroyer for sure. Class unable to determine. They positively identified a tanker, along with two or three medium-sized steamers. They didn't have time to identify them."

"Why not?" I ask.

The Skipper glances at me sideways. "Got pounced on. Destroyer found him up and started dropping ash cans. Pelted him for a good hour, then sped off."

Visions of a depth charge attack; the fifty-five gallon oil drum cans full of high explosive, spinning end over end down into the depths. Set to explode at a preset depth and crack our pressure hull wide open - it's enough to stand one's hair on end.

"The *Bullhead*'s a sturdy lass,' the Chief says confidently as if reading my mind, 'she'll take the worst the Japs can dish out." Looking at the Chief, it is strange the transformation that has come over him. The day of our departure his hair was cropped not an inch away from his head and he was clean-shaven. Now, after almost two weeks at sea, the powerful boxer's body is topped with hair that is now long enough to comb with a part. His beard the same color as his hair - jet black - is growing out full and with body. He has a strong Mediterranean look to him now.

All of us for that matter, have undergone the same metamorphosis. Our families probably wouldn't recognize us if we bumped into them on the street. I - for one - no longer even know the man that stares back at me in the mirror when I brush my teeth in the morning. When the officers sit round the wardroom, the scene is a roundtable of Civil War generals. Our families would be shocked. We're haggard and unkempt, every one of us, officer and bluejacket alike. We look like a bunch of mountain men.

So, three to four hours the Skipper says. A glance at my watch - half past four. Dawn's in about another hour from now. About seven or eight we should have contact - if the enemy doesn't change course. Therein is the crux of the matter, that one important word - *if*. *If* the enemy stays on course, *if* the weather allows the visibility to improve, *if* our lookouts spot them in time, *if* everything goes according to plan...*if...if...if*....the supreme variable.

"The "J" factor's on our side." States the Chief confidently.

"The "J" factor?" I repeat, furrowing my brow.

"The "Jesus" factor. You've heard of 'no atheists in foxholes,' well it's the same thing."

"Do you think God actually takes sides in a war?"

"I think God,' the Skipper sighs, looking at me after a moment's reflection, 'Is one day going to look down, decide this great little experiment of his has gone terribly wrong, and wipe us all off the face of the earth."

I pull back the spray soaked sleeve of my oilskin jacket to glance at my watch - 0630 hrs. For the last hour and a half I've been up here with the First Watch, staring into the gray mist that surrounds the boat. The rain has let up, but the sky is still full of black and heavy gray clouds that lie low in the sky - almost seeming to touch the water in places. There is some evidence that the front is breaking up; a few shafts of sunlight streak through a hole in the clouds here and there, but beyond that it looks no better. With the wind there is no change. It beats against our faces, bringing with it the stinging Pacific spray that fouls and gums the binoculars, causing us to reach even deeper into our reservoir of scurrilous imprecations to describe our surroundings.

"This is pointless! They could sail right past us and we'd never see them!" Pike spits, thoroughly disgusted and twirling his arm in the air in a futile gesture.

The sea is coming across the beam, from starboard to port. Figures, a beam sea is always the worst, because of its effect. The boat lolls as it rises on the crest of a wave, then rolls and skids sideways. The bow drops and hits with a sudden and unbalancing lurch the valley on the other side. You have to watch for it, maintain a low center of gravity, and be flexible enough in the knees to compensate for the abrupt shift in weight. It's kind of like swinging on a pendulum. And once the steel prow smacks into the rising water, a salvo of spray shoots across the bridge.

Pike cusses under his breath again. He wants more than anything for his watch to be the one that spots the enemy. As I understand it, it was his watch that made the first contact on the last patrol that led to the first sinking. A strong sense of competitiveness runs through the boat, so much so that all the watch officers now have three cases of beer riding on it. Whichever watch sights the enemy first, the other two are to furnish the winner with three cases of beer upon return to Pearl. Some of the bluejackets have even taken up bets on which watch it will be. My money is on Pike, because of his aggressiveness; he's always spoiling for a fight no matter what the odds.

The XO on the other hand, is more scientific. A precise calculator, he takes in all variables and contemplates them one at a time. Possibly a little slower in the attack and a bit more cautious, yet thorough. And Waldron of course, is the gentleman warrior, thoughtful, reverent, and charitable. He possesses a Robert E. Lee-like quality.

The sound of boots on the ladder. "Permission to come up?" It's the Skipper's.

"Granted!"

A sou'wester topped head appears. A pair of binoculars draped around the neck. The Skipper plants himself in front of the periscope housings, takes a deep breath - drinks in the salt air - and lets it out in a long, contented sigh. His spirits seem to have remarkably improved. The melancholia of only a few days ago seems to have vanished. Now, he no longer feels the helplessness of before. No longer does he have to sit idly by while messages come in bespeaking of misfortune for his acquaintances and friends. Now, he can strike back.

Tilting his head back, he studies the sky with curiosity. "Interesting thing about squalls,' he begins, 'is that they can come up almost out of nowhere and really give you a hell of a beating. We were out of New London once, a training cruise on one of those old "R" class boats,' he gives Pike a sly look, ' you remember those little sardine tins? Sky had an evil look to it all morning. I had the bridge watch - on a little stoop that passed for the cigarette deck. It was about noontime, the air was getting heavier and heavier - barometer dropping like a bomb - when all of a sudden it was like somebody flipped a switch. Thirty knot winds inside ten minutes, sea easily an eight on the Beaufort scale - and I'm hunkered down on this little metal stoop hanging on for dear life. Wasn't even time to get into foul-weather gear or lash in with safety belts! Fifteen and twenty foot waves smashing over the bridge! The entire foredeck just disappeared. Thought I was a goner for sure that time. Almost got washed overboard three different times. It's April right? Water temp's maybe forty degrees! Couldn't feel a thing! Totally numb! Officer of the deck starts screaming we're all going to die, and the lookout next to me starts praying to Jesus. Boat's rolling an easy fifty degrees, and I'm curled up into a ball listening to this all around me and thinking how absurd the whole thing is, and that maybe I ought to shit-can the idea of submarines altogether. God, what a mess!"

Producing his cigarettes, he hunches down under the bulwark to light one. So he's going to stay awhile. He's in his element, the hunt is on.

0745 hrs. Change of the watch. The Second Watch comes up to take over. Still no sign of the enemy. Pike's cursing a blue streak as he reluctantly goes below. His hopes of being first to sight the enemy are now effectively crushed. The XO comes up to take over, snickering the whole time.

"What's it like being under a depth charge attack?"

Both the Skipper and the XO flinch as if poked with a hot iron. Their eyes affix me with a cold, hard gaze. "Pray you never find out." The XO says brusquely, frowning at me.

"Suffice it to say,' the Skipper continues after mulling it over for a few moments, "it's like being sealed inside an empty fifty-five gallon oil drum with some idiot slamming away on the outside with a colossal sledgehammer. It's the worst thing imaginable. It's not like being in the infantry - an infantryman has places to run; a shell hole, a trench, or a building; some structure to hide behind. But with us...'

"You just have to grit your teeth and take it. ' The XO interjects, 'All we have is the boat and each other."

The Skipper flicks his cigarette butt over the side. "A bare inch of steel. And all it takes, is one little crack - no thicker than a hair on your head - and it's all over. Our survival really hangs in the most delicate of balances."

0930hrs. Still nothing but a vacant, empty sea enshrouded in a veil of gray. The wet mist and flying spray fog over everything, including my spirits. My arms ache from holding up the binoculars for the past four hours, and my eyes have been exposed to the saltwater for so long that they burn like fire. My fingers are numb. The inside of my mouth feels like it's coated with salt. This whole enterprise is not only miserable, but probably futile. The enemy is probably miles away from here. The *Tarpon* - as Waldron pointed out - couldn't have gotten an accurate star fix for their position report. If they were off by even five miles, it might as well be fifty in this weather.

1052hrs - nothing but fog, mist and salty spray. Visibility hasn't improved, and I'm beginning to think we're chasing after a white elephant. My triceps now hurt so badly they scream if I even so much as lift an arm. The rolling and pitching haven't done much to improve my omnipresent nausea. I'm becoming pretty useless as a lookout.

The Skipper really is at a loss. He doesn't see how his calculations could have missed the mark. Twice he has gone below to recheck his figures. His agitation increases. He vectored in all "x" factors he says; wind, speed, course, sea running, evasive maneuvering - everything. Just as I am going to ask for permission to go below to dry off and warm up, he orders the bridge cleared for diving.

So even he has finally given up now.

But, after leveling us off at eighty feet, he orders the sound heads rigged out. Boatswain's mate Duffy plants his soaked body on the little stool in front of the hydrophone controls, and exchanges his sou'wester for his headphones. The Skipper has our speed cut back to a crawl.

Of course - a sound search! Why didn't I think of that before? They very well could be in the vicinity, and we just can't see them. And water transmits sound at a phenomenal rate.

I watch Duffy; wet blond hair sticks to his head in uneven, curly waves. His equally blond beard glistens, silver-like, with moisture. Slowly, meticulously, he flips the lever in front of him that controls the hydrophone direction. Wincing as a drop of water runs down his smooth forehead, he swipes at it with his free hand. Eyes half-closed in concentration, furrows appear above his brow. Somebody mentioned he's from Kansas, his father's a railroader. In the crew's mess I've heard him talk of working summers for the Santa Fe Railroad. Odd - deep in the heartland of the mid-west and he winds up in submarines. And how did he get to be so good on the sonar? So far, I haven't seen any evidence that the Skipper thoroughly trusts anyone else on the sound.

Duffy's eyes are completely closed now. The lever in front of him turns ever so slowly. Next to the ex-cross-tie walker is the Skipper, hovering like a teacher over a pupil. The Skipper's bright blue eyes are riveted on him, as if willing him to pick up something.

Duffy winces slightly and opens his eyes. "Lot of surface noise,'

The Skipper frowns. "Too much to block anything else out?"

Duffy half-shrugs and closes his eyes again. I hear the XO sigh in resignation, tugging at the tying strings of his sou'wester before pulling it off. He glances over at me and gives a mocking twist of the lips.

"Right ten degrees rudder,' the Skipper orders.

"Right ten degrees rudder....aye." The hunched form of McGowan replies softly.

Another minute goes by. It's as still as death in here. Nobody dares breathe lest it interferes with Duffy's hearing.

Duffy stiffens. His eyes snap open. "Screw noises! Very faint, bearing three five five!' he leans forward as if to preserve the sound. A hand darts up and turns dials, 'Several ships with reciprocating machinery."

The Skipper yanks the second set of phones hanging next to the sonar set. He places one phone against his ear, his eyes darting all around. He begins to nod slowly.

He and Duffy exchange looks.

"Come left to three four zero,' the Skipper orders, his eyes lit up like I've never seen them before - two burning, penetrating orbs of fire. 'Surface!"

The bow smashes into a heavy dark roll, parting it as neatly as if cleaved in half by an ax. Boiling white, it lashes against our faces in retribution. Not to be undone, the sea rears back and comes at us once again, only to shatter itself anew against our knifing prow. At full speed we cut a path through the dense closed ranks of black water; bow plunging, deck tilting, men spitting, men cursing.

The chase is on.

The Skipper is up flush against the bulwark. A pair of binoculars glued to his eyes, only lowering them long enough to wipe them clear with lens paper. The XO is on his right and I on the left. The Skipper has ordered Duffy to remain in the conning tower and stand-by on the sound gear in the event of a dive. The Gunner's mate has taken his place in the periscope shears.

It is the Gunner's mate who sees them first.

Off the starboard bow, a structure - a large, seemingly gargantuan steel side with booms and cranes towering above the deck - looms out of the murk. It is unmistakably man-made. It's odd, as much as we're tossing about it looks as though the enemy ship is standing still. He looks like he's going away from us at a sharp angle. The XO is suddenly squirming in beside me, to get at the TBT. Snapping his binoculars into the cradle, he begins finding the range. "Bearing - three six zero! Range - five four double-oh! Angle on the bow - starboard twenty!"

"Battle stations torpedo!' the Skipper cries, 'Make ready all tubes fore and aft!"

With the noise of the engines, the whistling wind, and hiss of flying spray I don't even hear the bells of the alarm going off below.

"All right, here's one. Now where are the rest?" The XO demands as Waldron appears to take over. The XO disappears below to take up the plot without receiving an answer to his question.

Tarpon's report said three steamers plus a tanker and a destroyer. Where are they?

"Where the hell's that destroyer?" The Skipper bellows. "Left ten degrees rudder! New course....three three zero! We don't want to get too close or we'll be spotted. Give me a bearing Mr. Waldron!"

Waldron, with erstwhile pipe clenched in his teeth, ducks his head behind the TBT. "Target bearing.... three three five!"

"Where the hell are the others?"

"Could be a tail end Charlie,' Waldron proposes.

The Skipper cocks his head; "I need a speed plot!"

After echoing the order to the quartermaster, it comes back a few moments later - estimated at eight knots. The Skipper nods. "I thought so."

Pulling ahead of the first *maru*, a second emerges from the mist a few minutes later. I study it with my glasses; tall superstructure, overhanging booms and cranes, raised poop deck aft - another merchantman.

"Look at the waterline - they're loaded - to the Plimsoll mark!" I feel his eyes boring through me. 'Supplies meant for the Japs on Luzon!' he's savoring so much his mouth is practically watering. "Best way to have 'em!"

"Time for a little payback!" Waldron remarks acidly.

"Where's the tanker?"

The Gunner's mate cries out once again - another contact off to starboard. The Skipper snaps up his glasses almost before the Gunner's mate's last word.

"That's it - the tanker!"

Through the haze only part of it is visible. In contrast with a freighter, the tanker has a wider, fatter, and lower silhouette. A flush deck with tall derricks instead of booms and a more rounded, overhanging stern. One fat stack is visible, aft.

"Tanker bearing,' Waldron says, swiveling the TBT and aligning it with the enemy ship, 'three two eight!"

"Distance between targets?" The Skipper demands evenly, still training his glasses on the tanker.

In the conning tower, the XO takes the new bearings for the tanker and plots them on the chart, and - doing his magic with his trigonometry and algebra calculates the distance between the two. After a moment it comes back from the quartermaster. "Distance between targets.... two five double-oh!"

It is then that I notice that I'm having trouble keeping the binoculars straight, and it's because I'm shaking like a leaf with a combination of nervous excitement and terror. Even my knees quiver. That feeling I had when we encountered that Jap submarine out of Pearl has returned. Pearl - it seems like a hundred years ago - Pearl.... the *luau*.... Pike and his .45...

"My guess is that third freighter,' the Skipper asserts, 'is about the same distance ahead of the tail end Charlie."

Waldron raises up from behind the TBT, "In a line formation with the tanker to starboard?"

The Skipper grunts in agreement.

"With the escort to starboard of the tanker?"

Another grunt.

"Who to hit first?"

The Skipper lowers his glasses. Staring out over the rolling sea, creases appear in his bearded cheeks and two furrows right in the middle of his brow. He barely seems to wince as spray strikes him. He stands there like one of those bronze statues at the Academy, with water running down the brim of his sou'wester. The hundred little streams of brine then fall onto the shoulders of his slicker. Cascading down in uneven widths to find their way onto the deck, then draining out the bridge scuppers so that the whole process can begin again.

Peering through my glasses, I notice that the silhouettes of the enemy ships have changed form. They now look like they're getting thinner. Stern first, they are moving away from us.

"They're tacking!' Waldron reports, 'They're commencing a zig pattern!"

"Maintain present course and speed,' the Skipper says, 'we'll end-around, then dive for a submerged attack on the lead ship."

I can only guess at the Skipper's line of thinking; were we to attack now, we would have to race in between the enemy ships. They would surely spot us then, and probably bring a racing destroyer down on our heads. A destroyer we *still* haven't seen.

With every crash of the bow and accompanying white plume of spray, I wonder why the enemy hasn't spotted us. But the Skipper doesn't seem concerned. With the visibility so bad he must consider the risk negligible. I pray he's right.

"Still no sign of the escort!" Waldron reports, swerving the TBT from side to side.

"If he's still on the other side of the convoy,' the Skipper avers, 'we're all right. If he's not,' he stops, leaving the sentence unfinished.

"- we'll know soon enough." I declare, capping the thought for him.

The ship silhouettes become thinner and more obscure until it only one, a freighter, is barely visible. Then, it too fades into the gray gloom that surrounds us. Once again, we are alone. Alas, but for how long?

It is Lemert's voice that is screaming. "CONTACT DEAD ASTERN!"

Three sets of binoculars whirl around. Through the terrific haze I can see a tall, dark gray form cutting through the water. The outline is very slender, high superstructure. Above it, the faint crossed form of the mast just visible. Heading straight at us. It's certainly no freighter.......

"DESTROYER! HARD ASTERN!" The Skipper's words slice into me like a razor-sharp knife.

"Lookouts below! Range and a bearing Mr. Waldron!"

"Bearing one two zero! Range...five oh-double-oh!"

"*Clear the bridge!*"

I jump through the hatch, my slicker whipping up over my head and land - full force - on Seaman Anderson's leg. A groan of pain, screaming and yelling around me. I am vaguely aware of the Skipper's lean form coming through the hatch - scuffed soles of two sea boots heading straight for my face -

"Chief - *take her down!*"

"Rig for silent running! Rig for depth-charge! Right full rudder! All ahead one-third!"

I roll to one side and scramble to my feet.

"Goddamnit!' the Skipper spits, gritting his teeth, 'Of all the shitty luck!' his eyes look like they're on fire. 'Sweeps! The bastard's conducting sweeps around the convoy! Rig-out the sound heads!"

"At least we know the bastards aren't stupid!"

"That they're not!"

"Think he saw us?" Pike wonders, standing in front of the TDC.

The Skipper gives him a blank look. "We'll know for sure in a minute. Ease rudder amidships."

"Ease rudder amidships....aye sir." McGowan replies over his shoulder.

"Sir, all compartments report rigged for depth charge and silent running." The Yeoman reports. The Skipper barely nods, then let's go of an exaggerated sigh as he leans against the periscope housing next to Duffy. Duffy's right hand rests on the hydrophone lever. With his left, he presses an earpiece tight against his ear.

"High speed screws bearing one two zero.'

The Skipper keeps one eye on the bathythermograph - an instrument that records the temperature of the surrounding seawater and shows any abrupt change. A thermocline or temperature gradient registers on the paper. This is our only defense now, a layer of cold water that will cover us like a blanket, reflecting the enemy's echo-ranging sonar. Along with silent running, and a good bit of luck - it is our main defense when submerged.

"Report depth!"

"Approaching nine-zero feet sir,' Waldron replies, standing at the diving controls.

"Level off."

"High speed screws approaching. Bearing constant - one two zero."

"Estimated range?" The Skipper frowns.

Duffy turns his head slightly, cocks it this way and that, then glances up. "About three thousand yards...'

"You asking me or telling me?" The Skipper pushes contumaciously.

Duffy swallows. "Telling you sir."

"Is he echo-ranging?"

Duffy shakes his blond head, "No sir. Not yet."

I begin to hear something I've never heard before at sea. My first inclination is that we're making noise, that something aft has been knocked loose and is dragging along the stern. But, quickly and steadily it becomes louder. It sounds like a freight train, the rapid *swish-swish-swish* as the wheels roll over the rails. With a cold shudder of reality, I realize it's not us - but the Japanese destroyer.

"Destroyer approaching!' Duffy reports needlessly, since we can all hear it.

"Estimated speed?"

"Twenty knots plus."

The Skipper calmly glances around at each one of us in turn, "Relax all, there'll be no attack yet. He'd have to be doing at least thirty for an ash-can run, otherwise he'd blow his own stern off!"

Closer it comes; *swish-swish, swish-swish, swish-swish* - a steady thrumming, drumming beat. It grows in volume until it sounds like it's just outside the upper hatch. If it was possible to open the hatch and look out, I would expect to see the belly of the enemy ship within arm's reach. To be able to reach out and touch the cold, gray steel that wishes us death......

Even in my inexperience, I know the Skipper is taking a hell of a chance. Our keel is roughly at ninety feet. Our conning tower extends about twelve feet above that. The enemy destroyer draws probably about twelve to fifteen feet. So, that means about sixty-five feet between the keel of the destroyer and our deck. If the destroyer drops charges, there's not a lot of room for error - it's point-blank range. For us, it would be fatal. However, I sense a method in the Skipper's madness. He's anxious to get back near the surface as quickly as possible. He's gambling that they did not see us.

I notice that Pike and the yeoman both look upwards too, as if looking in the direction of the sound allows them to hear better. I even find myself doing it, as the thrashing screws becoming louder and louder. As for McGowan, I can see nothing as his back is to me - only the tartan tail of his cap. Only the Skipper and Duffy keep their eyes down.

The beating is a steady thunder now, a heavy roll of drums. He must be directly over us.

"Left ten degrees rudder....all ahead full!" The Skipper orders, raising his voice to be heard over the thundering crescendo. I notice his right hand grasps a pipe in the overhead. So, he's prepared for it too.

In my mind I try to picture the ship above; destroyers are long, sleek ships with a low silhouette, well primed for adverse sea conditions. Their tall, knife-edged bows can cut through the heaviest sea and are probably the most seaworthy of ships next to submarines. They pack a fearsome wallop, with large caliber guns and multitudes of depth charge racks and "Y" gun throwers. The warship recognition manual rates the Japanese destroyer as the most powerful in the world, even better than ours.

Above us, there are men coming on watch - going off - sleeping, eating, and doing every other trivial pursuit that fighting men do in their off hours. Who are they - the men that man her decks? Where are they from? What were their occupations in peacetime? Are they as afraid of us as we are of them? They would probably all be decent fellows if they didn't serve such a criminal regime.

One minute turns into five, then into ten. The heavy beating slackens. The destroyer has passed over us. We remain undetected.

Duffy twitches on his little stool, "Several heavy screw noises bearing zero one zero! Reciprocating machinery for sure!"

The Skipper grins like a Cheshire cat. "That'll be the convoy. "Control, make your depth five-five feet! Come left to three five five....all ahead two-thirds!" He glances around at us with a proud gleam in his eye, "They tacked right toward us - how's that for luck!"

Quartermaster Harmison fidgets. I notice he has a small length of rope with him that he keeps tying into different sailor's knots; one moment a bowline, then a half-hitch, then a square knot. Furrows of concern have appeared in his wide forehead. His large, brown eyes drawn tight with worry. Strange how we all deal with our nervousness in different ways.

A word from control - five-five feet. The Skipper steps over to the attack scope housing. "Up 'scope!" I reach over and hit the switch on the "pickle." With a whine the shiny exterior of the housing begins moving upward. The Skipper shifts his cap on his head and bends at the knees to meet the business end as it clears the well. Snapping down the knurled handles, he commences a sweep. I must stay in front of him at all times in order to see the proper reading for the azimuth ring at the top and the stadimeter range-finder at the bottom.

"What was the last sound bearing?"

"Zero one zero.'

The Skipper steps back and swivels the scope to the proper bearing. Absolute silence in the conning tower. My heart thumps inside my chest like the heavy double-beat of a bass drum.

"I've got visual!' the words are like the opening of a pressure valve.

'First target....bearing - mark!"

"Zero one three!' I read. *It feels so good just to be able to do something.*

"Range,' the Skipper's arm reaches down and twists the stadimeter dial, which focuses in on the target's range, showing it on the dial on my side of the periscope, 'Mark!"

"Four five double-oh!"

"Angle on the bow....starboard fifteen!"

Out of the corner of my eye I can see Pike cranking in the information into the TDC. The information transmits - electrically - to the torpedoes in the tubes.

"Medium-sized freighter,' the Skipper reports, studying the enemy ship, 'maybe eight or nine thousand GRT, well deck, middle superstructure....one stack....one, two....four masts - two high and two low.'

Out of the corner of my eye I notice that Harmison flipping through the pages of a book. The Skipper shifts the scope several degrees. "Second target....bearing-mark!"

"Zero two five!"

"Range....mark!"

"Five one double-oh!"

"Second target is a medium-sized tanker....bridge forward one-third, superstructure aft with one stack....well deck....two derricks - one forward of bridge, one aft, forward of after superstructure. Angle on the bow...starboard twenty-eight!"

With a snap the Skipper shoves the handles back into place. "Down 'scope! All ahead full! Plot - give me a solution!" In the interim Harmison has finished his search. He turns the manual toward the Skipper, who gives it a studious glance. "Yeah. That's it."

"*Kamogawa Maru*-class freighter,' the quartermaster reads. 'Nine thousand three hundred one GRT. Draft when loaded - twenty-six feet, nine feet six inches light."

"Target's course?" the Skipper snaps impatiently.

"Two four zero!"

Michaelis is up here with the ISWAS - a plastic slide rule that consists of a series of concentric compass roses of different diameters. Also included is a bearing indicator, which enables the assistant approach officer to keep track of the solution problem without having to rely on the TDC. The odd instrument got its name from the fact that you can set it up for where the target *is*, and see it from where he *was*, thereby mathematically determining his next location.

The Skipper shifts his cap back on his head and stares at Michaelis expectantly. "Distance to track?"

Michaelis lifts up the strange looking piece of plasticized paperboard and shifts the circular rule around. "Two five seven five, normal approach course....three two zero."

"Very well - helmsman, come left to three two zero!"

Harmison flips more pages in the manual, the Skipper leans over to check it and nods again. "*Manzyu Maru*-class tanker....nine thousand three thirty six GRT. Draft - twenty-six feet when loaded, nine feet light. Oil capacity - seventy-one thousand barrels."

The Skipper fixes Pike with an iron gaze. "We'll use tubes one and two on the freighter, tubes seven and eight on the tanker, set torpedo depth ten feet,' he turns to O'Toole just behind him, 'Stand by to open shutters!"

O'Toole repeats it in his high-pitched voice for the benefit of the forward and after torpedo rooms.

"All ahead one-third.'

Engine annuciators ring as we slow to a crawl. Obviously the Skipper wants to take another look. "Michaelis, what should the freighter bear?"

Michaelis brushes a comma of hair from his forehead and consults his ISWAS. "Zero zero five."

"Up 'scope!"

Both bearing and range are marked. The Skipper then completes a full circle with the scope - grunts in frustration - and snaps the handles up. "Down 'scope! All ahead full! Still no sign of the destroyer!"

Pike clears his throat. "Sweeping the starboard side of the convoy?"

The Skipper nods absentmindedly. "Possibly. If he is, he'll be back!"

A few minutes go by. I try to still my trembling body; I'm both scared and excited at the same time. If the other officers are as edgy as I am they don't show it. Pike busies himself with the TDC dials, Michaelis fiddles with the ISWAS and both look around with bored expressions. The Skipper is of course the epitome of calm as he glances at his watch. "Distance to track?"

"Just about there now sir, shoot anytime." Michaelis says, consulting his ISWAS.

The Skipper jerks up his thumb, meaning for me to raise the scope. "All ahead one-third....open outer doors, stand by for final bearing and shoot! If that destroyer's anywhere around things could get dicey, at this depth and moving at a crawl is kind of like being out in public with your pants down." His sweep begins to slow, then stops abruptly. "First target....final bearing - mark!"

I squint my eyes hard and lean up toward the azimuth ring to get as precise reading as I can.

"Zero two five."

"Set two and one half degree deflection on the spread."

"Will do sir,' cranking - sounds like a clock being wound, as Pike sets the torpedo gyros and deflection angles. "Set!" he declares, not taking his eyes off the TDC for even a second.

"Tube one - FIRE!"

Out of the corner of my eye I see Pike reach over and slam the plunger on the firing panel in with the palm of his hand. Immediately there is a brief hiss that is quickly drowned out by a loud, crashing whine - the torpedo's steam engine engaging. It screams violently as the counter-rotating propellers claw through the water to get up speed. My ears pop. The compressed air used to move the torpedo up in the tube is vented back into the boat by means of a poppet valve. This is so a string of compressed air bubbles don't jet to the surface, revealing our location. During the last war this was a constant problem. Like waving a red flag at a bull, the roving destroyers could simply chase down the mushrooming bubbles and plaster the area with depth charges.

"Tube one fired electrically sir." Pike reports unemotionally.

"Time?" the Skipper demands curtly.

"Three seconds....four,' Harmison counts from his stopwatch. It's his duty to keep the time on each of the torpedoes. 'Five seconds....six...'

"Tube two - FIRE!"

Another hiss, followed by a screeching whine and popping eardrums - already the Skipper is swerving the hairline in the periscope center onto the next target.

"Tube two fired electrically sir."

"Second target! Final bearing - mark!"

"Zero one zero!"

"Set!"

"Tube seven - FIRE! Tube eight - FIRE!"

Two more slight jolts and hissing. Up go the scope's knurled handles, "Down scope! Left ten degrees rudder! All ahead full!"

I notice Duffy adjusting the gain of his sound set. He listens a moment - hand to his earpiece - then cocks his head around, "All fish running hot, straight, and normal sir."

The Skipper lifts up his cap and scratches his head. "Time to impact on first target?"

"I make it at just over thirty-five seconds now sir."

"And the tanker?"

"About....ninety seconds sir."

"Sound - where's my destroyer?"

Duffy begins an all around sweep with his hydrophone. With his head cocked at an angle and his eyes screwed shut, he looks like someone about to be pricked with a needle. It is interesting to observe some of the various positions he assumes when concentrating. I understand a good hydrophone operator is a rare find, and actually has more in common with an artist or wine connoisseur than with the warrior caste. This talent to discern different sounds out of the dark depths is something innate. Just as a wine connoisseur can name a grape vintage just by sampling the aroma with his nose, an adroit soundman - just by his ear- can tell the difference between high-speed turbines or reciprocating machinery. He can ascertain a ship's speed simply by counting her screw beats that merge altogether for those of us who lack the God-given talent. It's kind of like singing, either you have it or you don't. Some people like Duffy, have a peculiar affinity with the sounds of the sea that keeps the rest of us in a complete quandary. As he does his magic, all the rest of us can do is look on in complete wonderment. Opening his eyes for the first time in minutes, he says, "Can't make a clear determination sir,' he says regretfully, shaking his head, 'There's too much surface clutter."

The corners of the Skipper's mouth turn downward and he looks disappointed. "It'll clear."

I try to picture what it looks like on the surface. A freighter and a tanker, weaving and tilting in the swell, with torpedoes streaking toward them. Will the enemy crews spot them in time to evade their destruction? In this deeply rolling swell, it won't be easy. And what of the destroyer? Is he hovering nearby, waiting to pounce on us with a vengeance? Will he be able to run down the bubble tracks left by our steam fish or will the swell camouflage them? More importantly, will the torpedoes make it to the targets and explode as they're supposed to? What will the fate of ours be? God willing, they'll strike home and send a few thousand tons of the Emperor's shipping to the bottom.

"Time to impact on first target?" the Skipper snaps.

"Sixteen seconds...fifteen....fourteen --'

A thunderous roar interrupts Harmison. The boat shakes from stem to stern. Immediately there is a second explosion, louder than the first. Our fish have struck home! One Nip headed for the bottom! I feel a sudden euphoria - our first success!

"Goddamnit!' A look of perplexing rage on the Skipper's face. Suddenly I'm confused - did we not hear two hits? Michaelis's face contorts as if in pain. Harmison looks like he's just been punched in the stomach with an pair of brass knuckles.

"Torpedoes one and two both prematured!"

The Skipper is sputtering with rage. He looks as though he's about to lash out. His face becomes a strong shade of scarlet as he demands a report on the second set of fish on their way to the tanker.

Duffy shrugs, hand at his earpiece, "Still hot, straight and normal....as far as I can tell sir."

The Skipper blows out a breath with both cheeks - like venting ballast tanks. "All ahead one-third. Up 'scope! Control - stand by to go deep!" He squats and catches the business end as it clears the well. Rising with it, he walks it around.

"First target....already turning away. He's got his rudder hard over...pointing his stern at us. Second target - already tacking hard to starboard - fuck! Time to impact on the tanker?"

Harmison shakes his head dejectedly, "Almost a minute sir." I catch the meaning in his tone. There now is absolutely no hope of hitting the tanker - if he's banking away this early, the fish will surely miss.

"Royally fucked!" Somebody spits.

The Skipper suddenly freezes behind the scope. At the same time Duffy lets out a yell, "High-speed screws bearing two four eight!"

"Destroyer approaching,' the Skipper reports, with more than a note of resignation. "Bearing - mark!"

"Two four eight!" I reply.

"Range - mark!"

"Four eight double- oh!"

The Skipper slams the knurled handles of the scope up in anger. "Down scope! Left full rudder, all ahead two-thirds! Control - make your depth two zero zero feet! We're gonna get shit on for nothing!" He stares at the floor plates looking disgusted. "Helmsman, meet her at one eight zero."

McGowan cocks his head slightly, "Will meet her at one eight zero....aye."

Silence in the conning tower. We're screwed - the intercept of the *Tarpon*'s message, the relentless pursuit through a heavy sea, finally making contact, and to have it all end like this. So it's true what they've been saying about the MK XIV torpedoes.

"What good can we do out here if our torpedoes are nothing but pieces of shit?' I hear Waldron pondering below. "We might as well just stay in port. This is senseless."

"Sound contact bearing two five one....high-speed screws. Reciprocating machinery noises fading." Duffy reports.

"Report depth!"

"Passing nine zero feet....nine zero five - '

"What's his estimated speed, sound?"

Duffy - whose face is now turned away from me - is all hunched over like he's taking a college exam. "Twenty-three....twenty-four knots....certainly no more than twenty-five. Closing in around two thousand yards out. Bearing steady....two five one."

"All ahead one-third." The Skipper wants us quieter now; the enemy is getting closer.

"He'll start echo-ranging in a minute." Pike observes, with a trace of agitation. But the Skipper betrays no emotion, keeping his eyes fixed on the deck plates. I wonder what wonders go on inside his head. This is our second brush with the enemy, and again he seems distracted. It's almost like he falls into some sort of trance; a type of intense concentration. Right now, the Skipper is really the only one who stands between us and death. He must call all the plays; every speed and course change, every depth fluctuation. The rest of us are his executive arm, executing his orders at his word. Our lives are literally in his hands.

"All nonessential lights and machinery off." the Skipper orders. "Amperes and wattage will be hoarded like the food of a starving man. There is no telling how long we may need it. Give me a bearing sound."

"Still steady....at two five one."

"Right five degrees rudder. Steady on one eight five."

I'm beginning to sweat. Beads of perspiration have formed on my forehead and on the back of my neck. My chest feels damp too. Next to me, Harmison is already sweating. It runs in long rivulets down his cheeks and crests just above his bearded upper lip. The temperature rise is because there is no air moving inside the boat. When we're rigged for depth charge, the boat is sealed up a tight as a bank vault. And the E-motors aft generate one hell of a lot of heat. If the water outside the pressure hull we're colder at this depth, it would keep the inside of the boat much cooler since it would draw off some of the heat. Everyone up here is beginning to break a sweat.

"He's slowing,' Duffy says, with a hint of expectation, 'speed dropping fast!"

"Now he'll start echo-ranging." The Skipper states matter-of-factly.

As if to punctuate his words, an eerie *pinging* sound comes through our steel hull. It starts out slowly, seeming to rise in crescendo, and float through the dark depths around us. There's no mistaking it. The haunting tone penetrates our thin steel pressure hull, sending icy shivers of dread up trembling spines. I wonder just how close the enemy destroyer is.

The Skipper's eyes slowly rise up and stare over at the Yeoman. "Pass the word....I want absolute quiet! You understand? No dropping tools or containers, not even a cough."

The Yeoman relays the Skipper's order over the speaker system in a hushed whisper.

His eyes continue to rove around the conning tower, taking in each man and his station. He pauses a moment when he comes to Harmison, who - leaning against the hatch guard rail - is in the process of tying a slip knot. He's so totally absorbed in what he's doing, he's completely oblivious to the Skipper's penetrating gaze. Proceeding to meticulously create two slip-ends worthy of a sailor's knot manual, he lays the knot together and pulls it tight. The Skipper's eyes go from the knot to Harmison and then down again. "Kind of a lost art, knot-tying I mean."

Harmison looks up with a start. A slightly embarrassed countenance flickers briefly over his face, then disappears. Apparently he doesn't care whether he's seen or not.

"Not much place for it in today's navy,' the Skipper continues, looking around him. 'All surrounded by steel, copper, and brass now. The golden days of the wooden clippers and schooners are over. It's a shame really, the romance is all gone."

The high-pitched chirping is getting increasingly louder.

"Bearing?" The Skipper asks, as easily as if he were asking for a breakfast roll.

Duffy cocks his head and turns his wheel ever so slightly. A brief glance up, then, "Changing to two five five...two five seven, moving toward two six zero."

"He's swinging around. Helmsman, come right ten degrees rudder. Steady on one niner five."

Inside his head the Skipper must have a mental picture of what the big picture looks like; our course versus the enemy course, degree of turn, etc. He's always trying to keep either our bow or stern pointed directly at the enemy. This presents the enemy with a smaller and thus harder silhouette to get a fix on from his echo-ranging sonar.

"Always keep them guessing, never let them box you in, and do the unexpected." He philosophizes, looking at me. That peculiar glint has returned in his eyes, now cast into even more of a supernatural aura by the shadows that fall across his face. "Earlier Ensign, the game was a queen against a knight, now it is bishop versus pawn."

Before, when we were on the surface the advantage lay with us; superior speed, lower silhouette, greater maneuverability, and the element of surprise - like a wolf stalking a flock of sheep. But now, it is we who are the pawns in the game; moving at barely a crawl, much less maneuverable now that our turning circle is widened considerably - a fox at the mercy of hounds. We - the hunter - are now the hunted.

Ten minutes pass and nothing happens. Our eerily lit dwelling emits no sound save for the beating of our hearts and the incessant *chirping* of the enemy sonar. It's probably the most unsettling and insidious thing I've ever heard in my life. Every time I hear it, it sounds like the enemy is sending us a message via every pulse; w*e're here, we will find you. No matter how long it takes. We will find you, and kill you all.*

"Hmm,' the Skipper murmurs, 'this fellow seems to be in no hurry. I'd 've bet he would've dropped a string of charges by now."

"Enemy destroyer closing,' Duffy whispers, 'range no more than two thousand."

"Right ten degrees rudder....steady on two zero five."

I see what the Skipper's trying to do. He's attempting to keep turning inside of the destroyer, in hopes that the enemy won't notice us. The only downside to this is that the enemy will continue to close the range until he'll be right above us. But, under the circumstances, it's all we can do. If we poured on the coal in an attempt to make a mad dash for freedom, the enemy would surely hear us. Then it would all be over in a few minutes.

Michaelis disappears down the hatch to help out Schumacher in the maneuvering room aft. The XO pokes his head up from the control room for the first time since making contact with the convoy. He reports Chief Schrier is going through the boat making sure everything and everyone is squared away. The Skipper only stares back at him with a puzzled expression, as if he heard the report in Mandarin.

A glance at my watch - thirty-five minutes. We have been under pursuit by the enemy destroyer for thirty-five minutes. It seems like hours.

Pike undoes the top three buttons of his shirt and tugs at it to let some air in. It strikes me as a futile act, it's impossible to get cool in here. Even the steel skin of our sides is beginning to sweat; shiny beads of condensation over everything. It's beginning to become stifling. The humidity is becoming worse.

"Closer now,' Duffy whispers, 'no more than a thousand yards....if that."

Quietly the Skipper orders us down another fifty feet and has the motors reduced yet again to sixty revolutions per minute on each shaft. This is barely enough speed to maintain control over the boat with the bow and stern planes. He's keeping a close eye on the bathythermograph.

"Bearing?" the Skipper's voice is little more than a barely audible whisper.

"Bearing now zero zero zero....speed about the same."

The Skipper winces as if he'd bitten into a cherry pit, "Left full rudder. Steady on one eight zero."

Chirp-chirp-chirp - it's all around us now. The enemy is coming up on our stern. At our present course, he will run right over top of us.

"Range closing....fast!" Duffy exclaims nervously.

The Skipper opens his mouth, but before uttering a word, a dull ringing *bong* echoes off the side of the conning tower. Fear wells up in my chest.

"Right full rudder! All ahead two thirds!"

Duffy whirls around on his little stool, with sharp creases evident in his forehead "He's shifting to short-scale! Speed increasing!"

"Ease rudder amidships."

Pike winces and grabs hold of a pipe in the overhead. "Fuck!"

"Knock it off!" The Skipper - his tone like acid.

Duffy's left hand shifts the gain dial on his set. He moves it up and then immediately twirls it all the way down. In one motion he snaps off the earphones, "DEPTH CHARGES IN THE WATER!"

"Brace for it!" the Skipper yells this time, but I guess it doesn't matter if they hear it.

With a deafening roar worthy of the earth's loudest thunder, the boat lifts up and is hurled violently sideways. A giant hand literally lifts the boat and shoves it hard over. The entire world reels to starboard. Everything and everyone reels off balance. Loose gear tosses about, the lights blink and threaten to go out. The first explosion is closely followed by another equally as severe, knocking me to the deck. Then another. Deck plates dance up and clang together. One smacks me in the face. My ears ring, from somewhere comes the sound of screaming. A few seconds to realize it's the voice of the Skipper.

"RIGHT FULL RUDDER! ALL AHEAD FULL!"

In my stupor I think I hear the Yeoman mutter something about Jesus, but his words vanish under the next cavalcade. The need to crawl away, to hide somewhere - anywhere - grips me like a vise. But where is there I can go? Trapped in here like a steer waiting for slaughter, sealed up inside this iron coffin like a can of beets. A bare inch-and-a half of steel between us and the nether regions. Dear God......

I roll on the deck, my head ringing. Voices shout all around me in pitched fervor, but I cannot make out the words. Something suddenly showers over me. Water? No - it's solid. More smashing, crashing blows. How can our pressure hull withstand this type of punishment? *Please God, make it stop! Please make it stop!*

Heavy breathing. Gasping for air. Panting like wild animals. Silence all around. A pause in the assault? A strange hissing rattle replaces the explosions. A hand reaches out, someone shakes me.

"Ensign? Sir? Are you okay?"

I find myself staring into the bearded, round face of the quartermaster, his eyes two round orbs of red. Managing a nod, I try to sit up. Something falls off of me, I look down. Funny little nibulets of brown matter, looking like rabbit droppings. Then I realize it's cork, from the electrical insulation and glass. Sometime during the pummeling a light bulb must have burst.

"Christ! Goddamn glass all over the place!" a voice curses from the control room.

"Jesus! Quiet!' the Chief hisses.

We're no longer at full speed. The vibrant humming of our electric motors has slackened. Duffy has his headphones back on and continues sweeping. The Skipper braces himself against the attack scope housing, wrapping his right arm around the shiny metal shaft. Shoulders arched, jaw set, and eyes burning; the epitome of defiance.

"All compartments report!" he snaps curtly to the Yeoman. Turning to Harmison, "What's the count Quartermaster?"

"Nine, so far sir." So the quartermaster keeps score.

The enemy's echo-ranging has stopped for the moment. But the *swish-swish-swish* of his screws is readily audible. Does he think he got us? Duffy continues flipping his hydrophone lever back and forth, "Contact moving off. Bearing zero five zero."

"He'll be back."

"Sir - all compartments report light damage. Broken light bulbs or valve glass only."

"Very well."

"Screws coming around to zero four zero....zero three five....zero three zero....sir. Sounds like he's coming around again."

The Skipper nods. "He is. Come left ten degrees rudder, all ahead two-thirds, control - level off at two eight zero feet!"

"Leveling off at two eight zero aye!" That was Waldron, I know how he's holding up. Probably like the rock of Gibraltar that he is.

"Destroyer approaching!' Duffy reports anxiously, 'bearing one eight five!"

"Range?"

"Under a thousand easy!"

The hollow, echoing pulse of the enemy's sonar splits the quiet. "Right full rudder. Steady on two one zero." So, now the Skipper is trying to turn well out of the destroyer's path. Should the Jap turn into us, he would have us cold. But the Skipper isn't banking on that, he's hoping the Jap will maintain his present course and run right by us.

"All ahead one-third!"

Silence in the conning tower. Each of us holds our breath as if the very sound of our breathing could cost us our lives. The looks on our faces bespeak our innermost thoughts; Pike's twisted grimace, Harmison's furrowed brow, the Yeoman's terrified eyes, and the Skipper's calm, thoughtful countenance. Duffy's hunched form, and the strong straight back of McGowan on the helm is all I have to go on for them as I cannot see their faces. I wonder what my own face looks like to the rest of them, for my own feelings inside - stark abject terror - shivers right down to my spine.

The pulsing beats of the enemy's echo-ranging are louder now. Behind it is the unmistakable rumble of his screws at low speed. What a strange war of sound we wage against one another. To us noise is the equivalent of death. To him the noisy electronic pulses are a way of finding us. He can make as much noise as he pleases, without concern for his safety. But we must act and move as cautiously as thieves in the night; covering our every move, emitting not a sound, stealing away into the dark depths as stealthily as a cat.

Duffy's head abruptly cocks at an angle. "He's getting a return echo."

The Skipper looks over, momentarily confused.

"Shifting to short-scale!' Duffy continues, 'Speed increasing. He's starting a run!"

"Shit!" somebody stammers.

"Right full rudder! All ahead full!" Again the Skipper is trying to turn inside of him.

Barely has Harmison clicked over the engine annunciators than there is a sudden *click* and an iron sledgehammer slams into the boat. The lights flicker, then die. Darkness envelops us like a tomb.

"Auxiliary lighting gone!" Somebody screams.

Click--Whamm! *Click*-- Whamm!

" - to emergency!" Half of the sentence was lost in the explosions.

My world shifts, the deck falls out from beneath me. I feel myself falling backward. More charges. I can't tell one explosion from another, they all degenerate into one maelstrom of ear-splitting, gut-wrenching blows. Nausea overcomes me. Gorge rises in my throat.

"Get the stern up goddamnit! Control - level her out!" The Skipper is screaming at the top of his lungs. *Click* --Whamm! *Click* - Whamm!

"*Switch to emergency lighting goddamit*! When I give an order I expect it to be carried out! Rudder amidships! All ahead flank!"

"Breach in the main induction valve!' the Yeoman screams, 'Boat making water!"

"Knock off the theatrics!' the Skipper snarls, 'If you can't make damage reports properly, you don't belong up here!" The last syllables of the Skipper's words dissolve into another series of hammer blows. I hear a light bulb shatter into a million pieces. Shards of glass spray all over like canister fire. A sudden cry of pain. The shrapnel has found a mark.

Click - Whamm! *Click* - Whamm! *Click* - Whamm!

An ugly hissing and gurgling follows.

"Twenty....twenty-one,' Harmison says softly, still keeping score.

"Pharmacist's Mate to the control room!"

"Oh Christ! -' somebody moans. I don't recognize the voice.

"I want a proper damage report from the forward engine room NOW!"

A faint glow in the tower. The lights have come back on. Swallowing hard, I'm to the point of vomiting. A sour smell wafts up through the control room - somebody else has beaten me to it.

"Who bought it?" Harmison wants to know.

"Me.' McGowan sighs, flexing a bloodied upper arm, 'Fucking glass!"

"Forward engine room reports six inches of water in the bilges, after engine room reports about half that. They report top seal of main induction was lifted up by depth charge explosions."

The Skipper steps over to the control room hatch, "Have the Chief take a look-see in the engine rooms. I want a report on immediately." He turns around, "All ahead two thirds. Helmsman, our course?"

"Two four seven sir." McGowan's voice has a tremble in it.

"Left ten degrees rudder. Steady on two three seven. All ahead one-third."

The Skipper then orders us down another fifty feet. That makes three hundred forty feet above the keel. We're now below the shipyard's recommended depth limit.

Kemper - the Pharmacist's mate - climbs up into the tower. "Who?" Harmison jerks a thumb at McGowan, 'Mac got some glass in him." Kemper immediately moves over to the Scotsman and begins tending to his wound.

"Sound - what's he doing?" The Skipper asks, moving up behind Duffy.

Duffy places a hand up to his earpiece, "He's slowing."

"Getting ready to turn about and come at us again." Pike notes with resignation, "We could try a sound bearing and shoot at him."

The Skipper dismisses the idea with a twist of his lips. "Are you really that stupid? He'd just chase down the bubble tracks....' he leaves the sentence unfinished, but it doesn't take a genius to figure out what he means.

The Yeoman reaches a hand to his earpiece. He listens a moment. I can just make out the tinny tones of a voice coming over the wire. "Sir, the Chief reports there's six and a half inches of water in the forward bilge, five and a quarter in the after bilge. He requests permission to transfer it throughout the boat."

The Skipper shakes his head. "Permission denied.' He steps over to the hatch, 'Control - flood all forward tanks!"

We're going to have to do something. The boat is out of balance. We're moving through the water dragging our stern along behind us. By shifting some of the weight around forward, the boat will be back on an even keel. But it's going to be a tricky process, because if we run our pumps the enemy above us will surely hear them.

Now Waldron has to vent some of our water weight so that we do not become too heavy. Since by laws of natural physics the deeper the boat goes, the heavier it becomes. The boat weighs more at our current depth than it would at say, one hundred feet. Our displacement increases due to the compression caused by the water pressure pushing in on us, actually making us smaller. Now, we must gain back some of that weight forward to try to even out the keel.

"Open bow buoyancy. Flood forward trim. Open main ballast tank number one, flood to full capacity." The snapping of metal levers on the vent control manifold.

"Jesus H. Christ! *Quiet!*"

"Forward planes up twenty. Aft up fifteen."

The process has begun.

In the air hangs a wet curtain. Sweat pours off of us like it was coming out of a slow running faucet. Our clothes stick to us like wet paper napkins. Harmison has already shorn himself of his sweat-soaked shirt, and Pike's shirt is undone as far as his navel. Mine sticks to me all over, but I'm hesitant to remove it. If I do, everyone will see me trembling.

"Give me a bearing sound."

"Bearing constant sir, zero one zero."

"What's he doing?"

"Sounds like he's idling....wait! He's gunning his engines, banking around for another pass!"

"Boy this guy is good!" Pike avers sarcastically.

"But I'm better Pike!' the Skipper snaps. "Left fifteen degrees rudder! All ahead full!'

Above I can hear the enemy destroyer. Once again the freight train is roaring down upon us. This is like one of those serials they used to show before running the main movie in theatres back home. A good guy, a bad guy and an innocent fair maiden, the latter of course is kidnapped and tied across railroad tracks with a speeding train looming over the next rise. The express train is bearing down upon us.

"Range?" The Skipper demands.

"A thousand yards max."

The Skipper now orders the rudder hard over, in an attempt to turn *outside* of our pursuer. He checks our speed not one knot. We're slicing through the deep almost at top speed. The Skipper's attempting to run out from under him in the opposite direction. We're making noise of course, but when the enemy commences a depth charge run he is moving so fast his hydrophone and echo-ranger are absolutely useless. He is running blind, and will drop his charges on where he thinks we ought to be.

I see Duffy shifting the gain on his set down. Moving at this speed is not without its drawbacks for us, since water flowing over the hull interferes with Duffy's hydrophone. His head turns, looking very much like a hairy skull in the dim light, his eye sockets vacant and lifeless. Through the haze I see his lips moving but his words do not reach me, they are swallowed by the massive thrumming of heavy machinery above us. As if in slow motion his hand reaches up and yanks off his headphones. "Ashcans on the way!"

The Skipper's two fiery eyes - orbs of crimson red - flicker as he glances around the conning tower, "Hang on!"

The charges explode astern - I can tell that immediately. A pressure wave slams into the stern and kicks it around. The whole boat reels sharply to port. I feel like my eardrums are going to burst. My head screams. A sudden tightening in my chest, the nausea returns. *Choke it back, don't lose control!*

Hold it down!

"Twenty-four....twenty-five...'

I suddenly want to reach out and throttle the Quartermaster; *Shut up Goddamn you! It doesn't matter how many we're getting! Just shut up for Chrissake!*

The Yeoman's eyes are wide with horror. I think he's one of the new men. But he is not an anomaly, for I'm sure my own eyes speak volumes of the terror within which grips my soul between iron jaws.

Pike on the other hand, looks as though this horrific beating is nothing more than a mild inconvenience, to be endured like a slight headache that will go away in a little while. True - he twists his face up into a tight grimace each time the destroyer lays a pattern over us, but his whole attitude is one of nonchalance. The Skipper is much the same way, except for his brief outbursts concerning damage reports and information coming from other areas of the boat. Harmison is a silent sufferer. I can see in his face and his demeanor that his nerves are stretching to the limit. But his smooth, melodious voice keeps a calm count of each explosion. And Duffy is far too involved in his sound gear to show much outward display of emotion.

The detonations are getting a bit further off now. The boat no longer shakes so much. Strangely, I do not hear that funny click before the explosions now, but the rumbling and gurgling afterward are still as loud.

"What's that sound?" I ask, trying to keep my voice even.

"What sound?"

"That gurgling and bubbling after the explosions?"

"Oh - ' Harmison responds, as if I'd just asked him his favorite flavor of ice cream, '- that's the ocean crashing back into the hole in the water created by the explosion."

I notice the Skipper look over with interest at my question. "When a charge explodes,' he begins, 'It literally blows a hole in the water - creating a vacuum. At this depth, the pressure is such that the weight of the water around immediately crushes the hole and fills it in. That's why you hear all the bubbling and rumbling." He stares at me as if waiting for some type of acknowledgment. "Did you notice that clicking sound earlier, before the detonations?"

Silently I nod.

"That's the detonator going off a split-second before the main charge. When they go off close aboard, you can hear it." A wry smile appears across his chiseled face. "Interesting, isn't it?"

Scary would be my term for it.

In the interim, Duffy has put his headphones back on and is sweeping around. "Depth clutter beginning to clear,'

"All ahead one-third!"

Duffy has his hand to an earpiece. Turned towards me, his eyes search above for some invisible object. "He's slowed again. He's idling."

"How long can he keep this up?" I ask.

"For hours." The Skipper says with sigh, leaning back against the attack scope housing and crossing his arms.

Another glance at my watch, an hour and a half we've been under attack. My thinking is a bit different now. Here I thought the navy was the better end of the deal; no slogging around muddy countryside with a rifle and a field pack or having to sleep in mud. But this gut-wrenching, skull-splitting, nausea-inducing hammering by depth charges surely equals - if not surpasses - the worst of artillery barrages. And when under attack, all we can do is sprint short distances and dive deep for cover. We no longer hold the initiative.

Another electronic pulse of energy courses through the depths. I squat down onto the deck plates and hunch over into a ball, as if by staying as small as I can maybe the enemy won't find us.

The Skipper yanks off his cap and runs a hand through his tangled hair and sighs, "Stay on him!"

Twenty minutes pass and nothing happens. The Nips must have lost us. He has only dropped one more pattern of charges well astern which the Skipper thinks was on either a thermocline or a school of fish.

"It had to be something like that, ' Duffy agrees, 'He got a return echo - I heard it."

Another ten minutes pass. Silence in the conning tower. All eyes are riveted on Duffy as he shifts his directional lever back and forth, his eyes screwed up in deep concentration.

"Contact moving off -' he whispers, '- half-speed on engines."

"Range?"

"Four thousand yards easy!"

After a quarter of an hour, the Skipper orders speed increased to two-thirds. There's a bit of nervous anticipation to see if the enemy will re-acquire us. Minutes pass in nervous anticipation, but he continues moving off in the opposite direction. Now the Skipper orders the pumps engaged to siphon off some of the water in the engine room bilges. The heavy *thump-thump-thump* reverberates through our steel hull as the Chief starts them, a sound that would have surely given us away had we did it within the enemy's earshot. Orders to the control room - the boat now assumes an up-angle as Waldron has the planesmen ease back on the bow and stern planes. Though the atmosphere in here is heavy and smothering, it is suddenly easier to breathe. A pall of death no longer hangs over our heads. Each man's eyes no longer hold the stark terror of a little while ago. I hear a few jokes and bawdy comments as each man finds himself again, shaking off our horrible ordeal and leaving it behind us.

We are alive.

The Skipper steps over to the ship's speaker system. He leans close to the slotted metal screen that acts as both speaker and mike and flicks the switch, "This is the captain....Tojo's lost contact with us and is well astern...'

A sudden wild cheer goes up in the control room. This makes it official.

'Well done gentlemen,' the Skipper declares, grinning like a proud football coach, 'we had our fillings rattled a bit for two prematures, but you did well. We'll even the score, that I promise you." Snapping the switch back down, he turns to Duffy, "Estimated range sound?"

"Screw sounds diminishing sir, range opening to about five thousand yards."

"Surface."

The three resounding blasts on the klaxon are music to my ears. We have made contact, been knocked around, and come out of it for the better. As our steel coffin is opened, my nose detects the salty aroma of the sea air.

Freedom.

On the bridge the Skipper lights a cigarette and calls for a pad of paper and a pencil. Once the quartermaster hands it up, I position myself so that I am peeking over his shoulder. He scribbles fast and almost without thought:

MADE CONTACT WITH CONVOY IN RAIN SQUALL X ONE AO THREE AKs ONE ESCORT DD X TWO PREMATURES NO HITS X TWO 1\2 HOURS DEPTH CHARGE PURSUIT X DAMAGE SLIGHT X PROCEEDING INTO PATROL AREA

                                            CO BULLHEAD

AO - that's the tanker, and AK is the designation for freighter. DD means destroyer.

He times it, then hands it to the quartermaster and orders the XO to add our position to it and then have it encoded and radioed to Pearl. I can't help wondering if the starched whites at ComSubPac will have any idea what it is like to undergo two and a half hours of depth charges.

"Damn,' the Skipper murmurs, leaning against the bulwark and staring out over the rolling sea, 'Damn!"

Later I'm moving through the crew's mess. Can't help but notice the subdued atmosphere. A few men hunch around the tables, with cups of coffee or the odd glass of fruit juice in front of them. Half-eaten pieces of fruit or sandwiches lie around. A sour smell comes from somewhere.

Daschler, Kemper, and Garnett are involved in a card game of some sort at the nearest table. E-mates' Paxton and Wagner - who sit at the table across from them - are busing themselves with a crossword puzzle they got from somewhere, and Torpedomen Hood and Reece sit looking vacantly around.

We can do nothing but stand around and be miserable.

A little while later, I'm moving toward the coffee maker in the crew's mess when - moving past the radio room - suddenly Lichty drops his book and snaps on his other earphone. Snatching up a pencil, he starts scribbling frantically across a little pad of paper.

What's this?

I stop and wait. Word travels fast, as Michaelis shows up after a moment, a half-eaten sandwich in his left hand. Still chewing, he hovers over Lichty until the radioman drops his pencil and tears off the sheet of paper from the pad. Michaelis snatches it out of his hand and without a word, turns and heads for the wardroom and the decoding machine.

Lichty - his work completed for the moment - drops the left earphone from his head and picks up his book. This strikes me as odd. I wonder if he is even the least bit curious about what the random sequence of letters and numbers he noted down mean. If he is, it certainly doesn't show.

A few minutes later I'm standing next to the Skipper as he leans over Michaelis's shoulder, reading the message as Michaelis punches it out on the decoding machine. It's from *SKIPJACK*, somewhere to the Northwest of us.

ENEMY CONVOY SIGHTED X 22 DEGREES 30' WNW 117 DEGREES 10'N X MEDIUM-SIZED AKs X THREE DDs X COURSE 140 SPEED 8 X AM ATTACKING X

CO SKIPJACK

I can tell the gears in the Skipper's mind are already turning, that particular furrow that bisects his forehead has reappeared. He calls for his charts as the XO appears, still rubbing sleep from his eyes. Michaelis clears the decoding machine off the table as the Skipper places his chart down and unrolls it. The chart is large enough that it completely covers the stained linoleum-topped table. Without being asked, the XO produces a pair of dividers and a protractor. The Skipper leans on the table, supporting himself with his elbows and gives the message another glance, "Twenty two degrees latitude....thirty minutes....west north west,' he mumbles, pursing his lips and manipulating the protractor and dividers. "Get me the oil log,' he directs over his shoulder, marking a position on the map with a penciled "X." This, apparently, is the position related to us from *SKIPJACK*.

Standing just beside the Skipper, I notice a small group of islands both north and south of our track. Cocking my head to one side, I read the names: Rabuyan Islands to the South, and the Batan Islands to the North. A thin penciled line denotes our course, which is roughly dead center of the Balintang Channel. The main island of Luzon lies just a hundred miles or so to the South.

The Chief appears with the engine oil log under his arm. In the interim the Skipper has finished calculating. "XO.' He holds up a piece of paper he has been working on. Apparently he wants the XO to check his figures. The Skipper takes the oil log from the Chief and begins thumbing through the pages. The Chief stands beside him, pointing out certain bits of pertinent information.

The XO looks up from his figuring. He nods in agreement.

"By the base course line it looks like they're heading toward the western side of Luzon, probably Lingayen Gulf....that's an even thirty hour run at top speed." He stops and looks expectantly at the Skipper, who glances back again at the oil log. Picking up his dividers, he measures the distance once more.

Our rising balloon of hope punctures when the dividers suddenly drop heavily onto the table. The Skipper stands back and sighs dejectedly.

"Too far away." Without another word he goes out.

A little while later Michaelis comes in with another message to decode. A few minutes later, he sighs despondently and pulls the piece of paper out of the machine:

CONVOY ATTACKED X ONE PREMATURE TWO DUDS ONE MISS X FOUR HOURS DEPTH CHARGE PURSUIT X FOUR BATTERY CELLS CRACKED X SCOPES WRECKED X PORT CRANKSHAFT BENT X AM RETURNING TO BASE X

CO SKIPJACK

The Skipper, followed by the XO, comes into the wardroom. He stares at the decoded message for a full minute, then his hand drops, and the paper falls to the table. Without a sound, he turns and disappears back into the passageway. The XO glances at it and exchanges a vacant look with Michaelis. The XO shakes his head with twisted lips. "What a fucking waste of time!"

Monday. Twenty-one days out of Midway. Haven't seen the Skipper all day, didn't even come out of his quarters this morning for breakfast. The XO says he's pouring over his charts, convinced the Japanese are taking a more roundabout route into Luzon. He can't fathom why we've gone seventy-two hours now without a contact. He says this area should be teeming with Jap shipping.

So far, we have added a big fat zero to the Allied war effort. We might as well be out on a leisure cruise. All we do is burn up fuel, eat, drink, snipe at one another, and smoke too much. And the worst part of it is, the war's only a month and a half old so far. We shake our heads and ask each other, "Where the hell is the enemy?"

The cloud cover has broken, bringing an end to the incessant drumming of the rain. Now, a perfectly clear quarter moon, brilliantly phosphorescent, hangs in the sky as if suspended by an artisan's picture wire. Its milky-white light peeks out from around a large hole in the clouds, turning the white puffs of water vapor around it a gothic shade of gray. The glowing sheen bounces off the water, creating a kaleidoscope of sparkling, shimmering crystals which dance before our eyes and travel on into infinity. Shafts of moonbeams search out the different size holes in the clouds, arcing across the endless sky like a thousand hunting searchlights.

It is near midnight. Waldron has the deck, Torpedomen Hood and Reece in the periscope shears. I've been up here with him the better part of the watch, nothing else to do down below. For almost three hours, we've been staring out over an empty ocean.

Waldron puffs on his pipe in silence. He has emitted barely a sentence since coming on watch. So - I think, it's getting to him too, this incredible creeping feeling of frustration. None of us are immune.

"CONTACT OFF PORT BOW!"

Like a bolt of lightning Torpedoman Hood's shout sears through me like a hot iron. Instantly awake, I make the bridge bulwark in a single stride.

"Where?" Waldron demands.

"Five points to port sir!"

Up with the glasses. The world of flickering moonlight on top of rolling swell dances before me. Goddamn these stupid binoculars! How are you supposed to be able to focus - wait! The outline of a ship! My finger reaches up and twists the screw between the two hand grips that work the focus. Of the hull, not much is easily discerned. But the bridge and superstructure along with the masts silhouette clearly against the glowing sky.

The enemy - if it weren't for the moon, we would have gone right by him.

"Left ten degrees rudder,' Waldron orders, eyeballing the angle between our bow and the enemy ship.

A body crushes up against me, pushing me out of the way. It's Michaelis getting at the TBT.

Waldron emits a pensive grunt. "Sound general quarters!"

"Only one?" The voice demands in my ear, taking me completely by surprise. It's the Skipper - right next to me! Where the hell did he come from? His face hidden behind a pair of binoculars. "Mark bearing and range!"

"Target bearing....one niner three,' Michaelis croaks, his head twisted at an obtuse angle to get in behind the TBT, 'Range...six-oh-five-oh!"

"Very well. Waldron - relieve Michaelis on the TBT."

"Aye sir." Waldron ducks around both the Skipper and me so that Michaelis can go below to his battle station.

"Course?" The Skipper demands.

"One nine zero sir."

A few moments of silence follow. Everyone on the bridge closely examines the dark shroud around us for any other ships. It would be strange for this one to be out here all by itself, what with the well-protected convoys we've come across so far. It could be some sort of a trap. After all, the Japanese must know there is an enemy submarine in the area - our foiled first attack alerted them to that. That could be why we've gone seventy-two hours without a sighting - the Nips have probably rerouted most of their inbound shipping.

"Hmm,' the Skipper mumbles. "Odd for this fellow to be plowing around out here by himself."

"A Q-ship?" Waldron queries.

A slight, grudging nod. "Possible."

"Don't suppose it's a tail-end Charlie from another convoy?"

A brief tilt of the head. "Hard to say."

"He's inbound that much is sure." Waldron declares, ducking his head again behind the TBT, 'We're looking at his starboard quarter."

"Can't tell yet if he's tacking?"

"No sir."

"We'll wait."

After a few minutes, coffee is handed up. The hot mug warms my chilled hands. Sipping the hot liquid helps to revive my body a bit. I squeeze my eyes shut - open them wide again, then stretch out my neck muscles to get the blood moving. Must stay alert. Even though my senses are alert, my body is weak from the fatigue of standing up here close to four hours. Setting my cup of coffee down on the small metal ledge that juts out of the forward bulwark, I flex my arms and silently cursing the heavy binoculars.

Waldron keeps a close eye on the enemy ship through the TBT, noting both bearings and ranges at sixty-second intervals. It soon becomes apparent that our prey is on a tack, since his bearing is not constant. Watching through the glasses, I can see the silhouette of the ship become thinner as he swings his bow around. Now all I see is the rounded protuberance of his stern with the straight stack above it, then the bow comes around and once more it looks like a ship again.

"Hmm,' the Skipper mutters, doing some of his mental figuring. He cocks his head around and calls for a time from the quartermaster in the conning tower. Earlier, the Skipper had Harmison begin timing the enemy ship to get a bearing around what intervals her changes of course are structured.

"I make it just under fifteen minutes since contact sir."

"Very well. I need a solution plot!"

The crouched figure of Waldron stands up beside me. "Sir, with the right track, we could maintain present course and speed,' he says, stabbing the bowl of his pipe into the air for effect. "If we wait for him to tack back to the Southwest, that will bring him right in front of our bow tubes!"

The Skipper's lean face glows eerily in the moonlight. "His maneuvering doesn't seem that drastic. Surely he knows there's submarines in the area. Fifteen minutes is too long to be on the straight and narrow in a war zone. He's making a one hell of a mistake.' He winces all of a sudden, as if a bad thought or memory had crossed his mind, 'Poor judgment. Either he's a Q-ship or he just doesn't know how to play this game."

In the interim the solution has come back from the plotting table. Just as Waldron thought - maintain present course and speed for the next eight minutes, then swing around ten degrees and run at full speed until we close the range. Then all that's needed is a final bearing, an opening of the outer doors and a push of compressed air, and the torpedoes should do the rest.

If they work that is.

"We'll stay on the surface for this one." The Skipper declares unemotionally.

In a way, the Skipper actually seems to regret the mistakes the Nip is making. Is it professionalism that makes him do it, or does he simply hate to see stupidity that costs lives - no matter what side they may be on? Maybe in a different way, the Skipper can see himself somehow in the same predicament. But he's too sharp for that, he would never allow himself to be so complacent. It's a waste of time to think about such things anyhow. There's no way you can figure out an enigma, and the Skipper is just that.

The Skipper glances at the moon. It hangs in the sky, a perfectly curved slice of greenish-white light. The sky is clear, little pinpricks of light that are stars show like diamonds on a field of black velvet. A few clouds lie below the glowing sliver, shining silver in the pale light. Whatever we do, I know we don't want it behind us. That would illuminate us to the enemy. We must stay in the shadows, like a cat stalking a mouse.

"Time?" The Skipper demands.

"Just a little over fifteen minutes sir." Harmison replies.

"Estimated target speed?"

A pause while Harmison consults the XO on the plot. Then it comes back; enemy speed twelve knots.

"He's turning!' Waldron exclaims, like a man witnessing the birth of his first child. 'He's swinging around this way!"

The Skipper snaps up his binoculars, "Flood tubes three and four,' he orders.

"Open outer doors!"

"Target bearing - one four zero....Range - four eight double -oh!"

"Helm - come left to one four zero. Set torpedo speed high. Depth twelve feet." The Skipper is keeping our bow pointed directly at our prey, to present the narrowest silhouette possible. My spine tingles with excitement. "Distance to track?"

"Plot makes it at just over two five three-oh sir!"

"Very well. All ahead full!"

With a responding shudder, our vibrant diesels kick over, shoving the boat through the wallowing swell at a steady fifteen knots. I glance aft, a white train of glittering foam follows along behind us.

"One stack....middle superstructure....two masts - one fore and aft....raised fo'c'sle on bow." The Skipper bellows, straining to be heard over our throbbing diesels.

Raising my glasses, I see that we're coming in on his starboard beam. It looks to be medium-sized, maybe four or five thousand GRT. The ship itself looks ghostly, all black and darkened out. Is it real? Maybe there aren't any men on board at all, maybe it's been fixed on auto-pilot for the whole journey. Through my glasses, I see the bow raise up and neatly part a large swell; sheets of foam split into two halves, then disappear. No, there are men on board. Living, breathing men, inside a darkened ship pulsating with machinery. They don't know it yet but their world is about to change for the worse.

"Bearing still steady - one four zero! Range - three eight double-oh!"

I lower the glasses and grab a hold of the bridge coaming. The metal is cold, it vibrates with every stroke of diesel pistons. The diesels make everything shake; every nut and bolt, every can of food, every bottle of juice, even the fillings in our teeth.

The enemy freighter is looming larger and larger out of the night. He comes on in his straight tack - altering course not one degree. I can see him easily with the naked eye now, the night is so clear. When will he see us? Surely there are lookouts posted. At this speed we're throwing up a sizable bow wave. And with the luminescence of the water, how close will we get until we're sighted and he throws his rudder hard over in a vain attempt to get away from us?

"All ahead half!" Our commander stands ramrod straight, looking almost as if he is made of wax; he doesn't even seem to be breathing. Not a muscle twitches, not an eye blinks. But he's an old hand at this game. He's learned the hard way. He knows what he's doing. My confidence in him knows no bounds.

"Range - two nine double-oh!"

"Permission to fire at twenty-five hundred."

Four hundred yards; that's all that stands between life and death for this enemy freighter. Will the crew get off before she goes under or will she carry them to an icy grave? The ocean is over a thousand feet deep here. That is beyond the reach of anything except the hand of God.

"Aiming point for first torpedo, just forward of forward mast. Aiming point for second torpedo, directly under bridge superstructure. Range - two seven five-oh!"

Amazing. Only two thousand seventy-five yards out and they still haven't seen us. But then again, that's what gives the submarine it's advantage on the surface, especially at night. Our silhouette is so thin and so little of the boat rises above the water that we're practically invisible unless they're right on top of us.

Minutes pass in anxious silence. I can now clearly make out the thin line of his masts with their heavy block and tackle arrangements at the top. The steel side of his starboard beam looks to be a slate-gray color. I can even make out streaks of rust along his waterline. What happens if they see us and start shooting? The Ship Recognition Manual states Japanese merchant vessels carry deck guns.

"Range - two five double-oh! Stand by for final bearing and shoot! Final bearing - steady one four zero!"

I mumble a silent prayer so that our torpedoes will run straight, true, and send the enemy to the bottom. The quartermaster's head and shoulders appear above the rim of the hatch. "Set!"

Waldron sticks behind the TBT as if glued there. "Tube two FIRE!"

The quartermaster echoes the order to Pike on the firing control panel. I wait for the jolt as the torpedo rushes out of the tube, but it doesn't come. The only motion is the boat rumbling through the swell.

"Tube three FIRE!"

Looking out over the bow, I catch a glimpse of a white trail of bubbles shooting out over the surface of the phosphorescent water. My eyes stay with it until it vanishes into the night.

"Time to impact?' The Skipper demands.

The quartermaster's head and shoulders appear again. "Twenty-seven seconds sir!"

I stare at the slowly tilting form of the enemy freighter. Any moment now it is going to disappear in a flash and an explosion. It suddenly occurs to me that this will be the first torpedo I've ever seen hit a ship - *if it explodes.*

A sudden flash and a horrendous crack seizes my breath. A deafening explosion quickly follows. An orange ball of fire leaps up from the bow of the enemy ship, rising at least a hundred or more feet in the air. For a brief moment it's as bright as day. The whole ship is illuminated from stem to stern. The shock wave and concussion press against my chest like a steel vise. A column of water sparkling like a hundred million diamonds arcs out and above the fiery ball, shimmering and flickering in the fervid spectacle.

It is then that the second torpedo strikes home.

The second detonation is right underneath the ship's middle superstructure. For a moment it looks like the entire ship lifts up out of the water. The bridge and smoke stack completely disappear in a flash and a crashing roar. Another towering geyser of water, as tall and as full as a hundred year-old oak tree. Thunderous reverberations across the surface of the water; a rolling, echoing, rumbling that continues on into infinity. Eliciting a moan like that of a wounded animal, the enemy freighter immediately slows and settles by the bow.

Awestruck silence on the bridge.

"Jesus!" Waldron mutters.

"She's had it,' the Skipper eulogizes. 'Her bow's been blown off!"

Through the glasses I can make out the jagged and burnt pieces of metal that once led to the bow. All that remains is a jagged hole vented to the sea. A rapidly spreading inferno begins to engulf the ship from the what was once the bow aft to where the bridge used to be. Moving along the beam, I can see half-naked figures running around wildly - the crew! My God, how could anything human survive that blast? I see men diving over the side, desperate to escape their doomed vessel.

"There's people on deck!' Waldron notes with alacrity.

"If they're abandoning ship,' the Skipper interrupts, 'They better do it fast! They've got maybe ten minutes!"

The freighter now lists heavily to starboard with the fire spreading further aft. The flickering flames of her fires paint an eerie kaleidoscope on the surface of the water, broken here and there by foaming spouts as frantic crewmen plunge into the sea from canting decks.

I hear their voices now; crying and shouting in frustration and terror in a language I do not understand. I silently thank God that it is them and not I cast adrift in an empty ocean.

"In a couple of minutes,' Waldron warns, 'she's going to go belly up. They had better not tarry."

Already it is impossible for the crew to launch lifeboats from the port side. The way the ship is tilting, the boats wouldn't make it to the water, they will get hung up on the steel side and break up. They can still be launched from starboard since it's clear down to the water's surface. But in a few more minutes when the ship rolls, anyone or any boat caught on that side will be crushed by the ship coming down on top of it.

We are going to pass inboard of the stricken freighter within a few hundred yards. The Skipper dryly comments that he'd like to try and get the name of the doomed vessel before she goes under. I watch him; his face is as solid as a hunk of granite, the light of the flames paint an orange-red sheen across his bearded face. He looks every inch the warrior.

Word comes up from the quartermaster; Swensen reports intercepting an *SOS* just transmitted in the clear from the enemy ship.

"They give the name?"

"Yes sir, *Tiniosan Maru*. Also included an *SSS* with the coordinates."

An *SSS* - that means attacked by a submarine. Now, somewhere in Imperial Naval Headquarters they'll stick a pin with an American flag on it in a board map and alert all shipping in the area.

"Very well. Log it Mr. Harmison." The Skipper treats it matter-of-factly, as if he'd expected it all along.

"Permission to come up?" It's the XO's excited voice.

"Granted!"

The XO steps out onto the bridge with Pike right behind him. The XO whistles through his teeth.

"Any moment now,' the Skipper nods.

"Strike a few thousand tons from the Emperor's registry!" Pike yells from below.

There are cries and shouts coming from the water.

"There's a lifeboat!" Waldron exclaims, pointing to a small white boat bobbing in the swell a few dozen yards away from the stricken vessel. I raise my glasses; shadowy figures of men with oars desperately trying to distance themselves from their doomed ship. The water around the boat is lousy with bobbing heads, like somebody released a whole crate of floating cantaloupes. Yells, shouts, and cries of hysteria float over the water.

The whole thing is surreal.

With a sudden loud metallic groan the freighter's stern comes free of the water. She is in her final death throes. Now, a loud crashing and rumbling.

"It's her cargo!' The XO stammers excitedly, 'It's shifting and busting through the bulkheads!"

Another groan, worse than the first.

"There she goes!"

As if in slow motion, the stern rises completely out of the water. Slowly, like a lumbering whale she rolls over onto her starboard side and seems to pause a moment. Screams of horror as those still too close to the ship realize their impending fate. The dying ship rolls completely over crushing a multitude of bobbing heads underneath it and one of the lifeboats. In a final act of desperate futility, the lifeboat crew hold up their oars as if this could stop the several thousand tons of burning steel coming down on top of them. One man drops his oar and jumps out of the boat, paddling madly. He disappears in a flash of rolling, hissing metal.

Blood-curdling screams, then silence. Only the swishing of foaming water as the sea rushes in to claim its newest prize. The water boils where the ship disappeared, like the newly turned earth of a fresh grave.

"Eight and a half minutes,' the Skipper says, showing his watch. 'It took her only eight and a half minutes to go under."

"Davy Jones' Locker claims yet another." Pike adds, not to be outdone.

The quiet is unsettling. But it doesn't last long. A minute later the crewmen in the lifeboats spot us and begin shouting and yelling. I don't have to understand the language to know what they're saying.

The nearest boat is no more than fifty or sixty yards from us, coming up on our starboard beam. I can see the men standing up as they spout invectives at us. The man in the bow wields an oar like a sword in one hand, and shakes his fist at us with the other.

"They'd better save their energy,' the Skipper comments with a hint of sarcasm, 'it's a long row to Luzon."

The XO scratches his bearded cheeks thoughtfully. "One of their ships might pick them up if any picked up the distress call."

"Is that likely?" I ask.

"Hard to say,' the Skipper shrugs, 'if one is headed in this direction, maybe. The Nips don't seem to put the premium on a man's life the way we do."

The angry voices are quieter now, the lifeboats are falling astern. After the XO goes below, I stay and watch them bobbing along in our foaming wake. For some inexplicable reason, they seem to captivate me. I cannot tear myself away to go below. What do they do now? What are they thinking? Will they make it to Luzon or will one of their ships pick them up? Gradually they become harder and harder to see, until they are nothing but faint little white specks on a sea of black. These too, finally vanish into the darkness and we are again alone.

Simple reality is that the men in the lifeboats are really already dead. Such is the harsh reality of life out here. No one can survive on the open sea in an open boat without food or water for long.

In a week without a saving hand, most will already be dead.

Next morning. Twenty-second day out of Midway. Our first success has vaulted everyone out of the doldrums. Our appetites have returned. Planting ourselves at the wardroom table, we make a feast on a huge breakfast of navy bacon, powdered eggs, and fried potatoes. Even the Skipper eats.

For the first time on this patrol, we feel like real fighting men. The differences are easily seen. That peculiar glint in the Skipper's eye has returned. Pike is more relaxed than uptight. Lemert no longer broods so much, and for the first time in my life I feel like a combat veteran. Waldron, Michaelis, Schumacher, and the XO are all in noticeably higher spirits.

Later, as I take a turn aft, I see that our first kill has also affected the bluejackets. The Chief is in his happy-go-lucky form again, and there are smiles and looks of contentment on otherwise previously pinched faces. Motormac's Pettigrew and Skjonsby have gotten together a poker game with others from both the Second and Third watches. The motor machinist mates are recognizable from other crewmen because they're always the most greasy, exhaust-blackened, and oil-stained of all crewmen. Hence, their nickname of "oil kings" is quite befitting.

That afternoon I'm moving through the control room when I come upon the ship's log, lying open on the plotting table. I stop to read:

2430hrs - Sighted medium-sized AK - *Soyan Maru*-class; 5600 GRT. Showing no lights. Course 190 Speed 12

2433hrs - Went to General Quarters.

2436hrs - Tubes three and four flooded and readied for firing.

2445hrs - Target tacked to port - new course 180. Slowed to allow target to come across our bow.

2455hrs - Permission to fire granted to OOD.

0105hrs - Lt. Waldron fired tubes' three and then four at target. Torpedoes observed to be hot, straight, and normal.

0106hrs - First torpedo strikes target on starboard side. Target's bow is completely blown away. Target noticeably slows. Six seconds after first explosion, second torpedo detonates underneath stack.

0103hrs - Target transmits uncoded SOS and SSS with coordinates. Identifies herself as *Tiniosan Maru*.

0107hrs - Target already listing heavily to starboard. Crew observed beginning to abandon ship. Main deck aflame, fire rapidly spreading aft.

0112hrs - Heavy rumbling heard from stricken target - thought to be cargo shifting and buckling bulkheads.

0114hrs - Target capsizes and observed to completely sink from sight.

I recognize the writing of the quartermaster, with the Skipper's approving signature beside each entry - so that's it in a nutshell. The whole process of getting into position and firing reduced to a few short sentences for the benefit of ComSubPac and posterity.

Over the radio Swensen's picked up another *SOS* from a Japanese ship that has been torpedoed.

"That should be the *S-41* - she's northwest of us." The Chief observes.

Late the next morning, still hovering over my sketches of diagrams and similar nonsense and with my umpteenth cup of coffee when a cry comes from the bridge; the port lookout has sighted something in the water. Eager to put aside my work, I head for the bridge.

A flock of seagulls hover and flutter in the crystal blue sky above the rumpled rolling swell. They stay low to the water's surface. Something there interests them. Looking through the glasses I can see some debris bobbing about. It rises up on top of the swell, vanishing as it drops into the valley created by the pointed, creamy pinnacles of the wave tops.

"Anybody make it out?" The XO asks, scrutinizing the area with his binoculars.

"I can make out some boards and one or two boxes.' Daschler comments, in the shears just above us, 'And some other debris but that's pretty much it.'

The XO adjusts our course ten degrees to port. Apparently he wants to take a closer look at the wreckage.

"Permission to come up?"

"Granted!"

The Skipper appears and steps out onto the bridge. "What's up?"

"Over there sir - ' He points with his arm, ' - two points to port."

'Probably -' the XO continues, rubbing his nose with his forefinger, '- some wreckage from the freighter torpedoed last night."

The Skipper merely grunts. "Let's take a look."

The water has a strange look to it that becomes increasingly prevalent the closer we get. The surface of the water is a jet-black color. Peculiar, as there's not a cloud in the sky. What's more, the closer we get, the darkness of the water seems to cover a larger and larger area.

"Oil slick." The XO observes without emotion. What else could it have been?

"There's something else there,' the Skipper says, raising an arm and pointing, 'Could be a wooden crate or something."

I see it too, about dead center in the field of wreckage bobbing up and down like a cork, only visible for moments at a time. Now, as we enter the wreckage our bow wave parts the plethora of broken, wooden planks and other debris that lie in our way. I notice a look of concern on the Skipper's usually quiet, relaxed face. "Wouldn't do to get any of this junk caught up in the props." He says, glancing over the side and aft with an anxious look.

The bobbing object comes closer. Scars of black show in it, crisscrossing in every direction. The object now has discernible angles; the part that rises above the water angles at the front and flares out along its sides. It is distinctively boat-shaped. Seagulls perch all over it; hooting and screeching like wild hyenas.

"It's a lifeboat!' The XO exclaims quizzically.

"Or the remnants of one."

The Skipper is correct. Coming closer until it is no more than a stone's throw away from our port saddle tank, the pointed stem is visible sticking out of the water at an obtuse angle. Lengths of rope hang over the gunwale, trailing in the water beside it, the result of a frantic and hasty abandonment. The scars of black scorched into the white wood shows that at some point this boat came through or quite close to - either a fire on deck or flaming oil. The stern of the boat is either crushed or has been ripped off somehow, as the pitiful vessel is half sunk with the deck awash.

"Mother of God!' Daschler abruptly exclaims. There's something in his voice I've not heard before.

Then a rising swell tips the boat toward us. For a split second I think the gulls have found a perch amidst these thousands of miles of open ocean. Then just as quickly the scene becomes one of horrible reality.

The seagulls have done their work well. Every head has been picked as cleanly as could be done with a flensing knife; bare skulls with toothy grins, empty eye sockets gaze vacantly with hollow stares. The charred, black gristle which in life was flesh covers the bodies like an ashen blanket. Their lifeless arms and legs, stiff and rigid, are drawn up tight and sticking in the air at weird angles. Several of the arms end in stumps as the gulls have already picked off most of the fingers. On the stomach on one corpse, a length of fire hose is coiled. A gull perched there suddenly bends over and pecks at it. It comes away with part of the hose in its beak. It hangs there limply. The gull tugs at it, causing the corpse's stomach to twitch abruptly. A moment later I realize it isn't fire hose.

The wind blows toward us, bringing with it the sickening stench of putrefying corpses. As the little boat rocks to and fro, the motion causes the corpses to nod at us; bidding a ghostly, ghastly greeting.

I turn away. My stomach heaves. I'm able to make it to the leeward side of the bulwark as I hold the vile surge down in my throat. The Skipper mutters something about "Gulls being rats of the sea," but I'm not listening. My entire world consists of horrid revulsion, shock, and painful, violent vomiting.

Saturday. The XO and Pike quiz me on my submariner's notebook, to see how I'm coming along. The rest of the day is spent wandering from the bridge to the crew's mess for coffee, and watching contests in "who can be the coarsest." Each man relates a real experience and tries to gross out everyone else. So far, Daschler, E-mate Garnett, and MotorMac Skjonsby are about the best around.

"After I got out of boot camp, I made a bee-line for the local brothel." E-mate Garnett explains, wolfing down one of Jonesy's ham sandwiches. "As I'm paying the madam there, she tosses me a couple of rubbers right? So I go in, and there she is - this medium broad bitch about two ax handles across the beam and loaded to the gunwales....just lying on the bed waiting' for me, with a bottle of gin in one hand and a cigarette in the other. Definitely a broad who's into her work. Anyway, she's waiting' for me to jump her and do my thing. So I tear off my clothes, and put on one of the rubbers the madam gives me....right? So, I start getting her ready - kissin' her and tryin' to warm her up. That bitch kissed like a wet teabag....just awful! She slobbered, and I mean really disgusting! Spit all over the place! Anyway....I'm ready to plug her now, so I start guiding my better half into her. I get a little way in and then I just stop - something is definitely not right here. So I reach down and get a couple fingers in her to see what the problem is, and guess what I pull out? A goddamn rubber! Last guy she popped left his rubber in there when he pulled out of her. I'm layin' there on top of her holding this sick looking thing that's all wet and hairy and I'm stunned! She looks down and starts screaming! Like she's having some sort of fit. I completely lost it at that point - cock went limp and it wasn't coming back up. The Madam comes in and starts yelling at me, the broad's still in hysterics mind you, and accuses me of beatin' her up and all kinds of shit! I hop back into my drawers, make momma give me my money back and I'm outta there, and that's a fact!"

It takes a few moments for anyone to respond. Everyone's doubled over in fits of laughter.

"Garnett - you are one vile human being!" Pettigrew moans.

"Who said he was human?" Copenhaver demands.

"Anybody that knows me knows I've got a real pet peeve when it comes to showering." Skjonsby says.

"Which is?" Reece - the torpedoman - asks.

"I like having my own soap. I don't like sharing soap with nobody."

"So?"

"So - the only way you can have your own soap is if - in the middle of a shower - take the soap and lather up your pecker really well so you get a good amount of pubic hair all over the bar of soap-'

Moans of disgust all around.

Skjonsby starts nodding his head, 'and that way nobody else will want to us it."

"And you consider yourself part of the human race?" Pettigrew snorts, shaking his head.

"Shit-' Daschler snaps back, 'that's nothing. At a bar in Honolulu once I had a pressing urge, so I go into the head, but all the stalls are full - right? One guy in there is puking his guts out, another's so bombed he's passed out on the commode, and the door is locked so I can't get to him. There's a guy in the last stall - and I know him - a third-class torpedoman from *Guardfish*, he's taking a shit and won't come out. Tells me to go fuck myself. Well I'm standing there, sharp pains shooting through my guts because I gotta take a dump, so I say to hell with it! I drop my drawers and squat right there on the floor, leaving this nice big brown pile of kielbasa right square in the middle. Goddamn it was beautiful! I grab some towels, wipe my ass, and then dump all those towels on top of that asshole from *Guardfish*. He starts screaming, sitting there on the pot with all these brown, shit-stained towels sticking to him, and he had on *dress whites*! One shit-loaded towel stuck to the top of his head! But what's he gonna do? Chase me around the bar with his pants down around his ankles and shit all over his clean dress whites?"

Waldron passes through at that moment. He looks at me with his pipe jutting from his mouth and merely shakes his head. "Heathens."

But his words are swallowed up in the roaring, raucous din of the event. So far, when it comes to being gross and disgusting, Daschler is by far the best.

We're lounging around in the control room early the next evening, staring at one another for the umpteenth time when a cry comes from the bridge, "Smoke on the horizon!"

As if a live hand grenade is tossed into our laps, we spring into action. In one motion I grab a pair of 7x50's off the post and take the ladder two steps at a time.

On the bridge. Waldron has the deck. The Skipper is already there. Above, the sun is just beginning its descent below the horizon in a crystal blue, cloudless sky. The sea rolls on by us easily; a crinkled light royal blue, groundswell without foamy tops. The omnipresent *hiss* as we part each one in turn. The incessant *throb* of our Detroit diesels.

"Where?"

"Five points to starboard." The Skipper replies, "Barely above the horizon."

Up go the glasses. I swerve them just about the right distance from the bow - I'm getting better and better as a lookout - but all I see are what looks like a faint cloud on the horizon. I don't see anything that resembles a smoke trail.

"You see them Ensign?" The Skipper asks, 'That little cloud there poking just above the horizon?"

Oh - so that is it. "Yes sir." I lie convincingly, as if I'd known it all along.

"There's at least two - maybe - three ships there. Too much smoke for just one. We may have another convoy on our hands." It dawns on me that this is the first time I've seen him in sunlight for a few days. A little sunburned where his beard doesn't cover his face, and maybe a bit thinner than when we left Pearl. But otherwise, still the same; cap cocked, eyes fearless, jaw set, and body poised. The movie bigwigs in Hollywood spend years pulling their hair out trying to find someone who cuts such an archetype figure.

"You have a range Mr. Waldron?" The Skipper asks calmly.

"I make it just over thirteen thousand yards sir."

"Bearing?"

"His bearing looks to be one eight five sir."

"Time of initial contact?"

Waldron glances at his watch. "Nineteen-oh two sir."

I glance at my watch - nineteen-oh six.

"We'll study them for a while." The Skipper avers, producing his cigarettes.

We observe for a good hour, like a wolf stalking sheep. Watching the flock to learn it's movements and habits before lunging in for the kill. The Skipper's taking his time, he wants the perfect solution. And when he strikes, I wouldn't give a dollar for their chances.

Night creeps up on us. Lower and lower the yellow ball gets in the western sky, until it becomes a perfect orb of crimson just before it sinks below the horizon. The blueness of the sky dims, getting darker and darker until thousands of little white diamonds appear above, sparkling with heavenly light. The moon hovers over us, a perfectly pale, glowing white crescent slice in the sky. And with it, the sea darkens until it seems we glide along a surface - not of water - but of oil.

1600 hrs. Change of the watch. Pike comes up and relieves Waldron on the bridge, Tashtego and Steele relieve Hood and Reece in the periscope shears. The Skipper remains however.

Two hours now. As the darkness approaches, so do we. The Skipper has closed the distance to the enemy to within eight thousand yards. The enemy's plot has proven difficult to figure out - he's moving faster than expected. The XO's calculations put him at about twelve knots. As for the plot, the XO is just about to the point of tearing his hair out in frustration. Every time he thinks he has a bead on the enemy's zig pattern, he makes an unexpected tack to one side or the other. The base course has been figured - one seven two - a course that will take him right into the port of Aparri.

"More supplies for Tojo's war effort,' the Skipper notes, a tight grin forming at the corners of his mouth.

I step below to grab a quick smoke since it's too dark now to smoke on the bridge. Inside the boat the tension is readily evident; nervous fingers fumble with cigarettes, incessant tapping, pacing, the beads of sweat; all signs of a boat on contact. Expectant looks greet me at every step, as if by my presence on the bridge I am privy to more information. All I can do is shake my head and shrug.

The Chief comes in, moving aft. "Stay near your battle stations' boys, it could come at anytime. Jonesy, keep plenty of coffee and sandwiches made, this could be a long one."

As the Chief moves into the after battery compartment, everyone's gaze seems to follow him. Duffy cheerily turns up, recognizable a thousand miles away with his stark blond hair and equally blond beard. He glances around expectantly. "This reminds me of an exciting time I had in a bordello in Manila once....the head madam was a hundred and fifty and her girls we're all in their eighties."

He doesn't get much response today. The spirited banter and carrying on that is usually the norm in here is conspicuously absent now. The men are turning inward again, readying themselves for what is coming.

There is a heavy air of expectation.

Back into the control room. Passing the radio shack I notice Lichty scribbling on a piece of paper. Something's coming in.

"Lt. Michaelis to the radio room."

He shows up a moment later, a half-eaten orange in one hand and juice dripping down his fingers. Wiping his hand up and down his shirt, he squeezes past me and steps into the electronic-packed little hole. "What's up?"

After taking it from Lichty and decoding it, it turns out to be an urgent request from ComSubPac to report our position. It doesn't take a genius to figure out that if we broadcast a message now, the enemy will hear it and the whole game will be up.

"That's ComSubPac, ' Copenhaver chuckles. 'Always such perfect timing."

Michaelis begins to get a little wound up about it. "What am I supposed to do?' He says, pacing around outside the radio room, 'What? I just can't *not* answer ComSubPac!"

The Skipper is more succinct and to the point. Informed of the request, he steps down from the bridge long enough to give Michaelis a quizzical look and a frown, "Ignore it." With that, disappears back up the ladder.

Copenhaver grins. "Classic, laconic Tyreen!"

The XO's hunched form at the plotting table pivots around abruptly. "Silence! I want silence in here! There's too much goddamn bullshit!"

An insubordinate Copenhaver replies by screwing up his face in a hilarious contortion of mock anger - his handlebar mustache twitching furiously. Pike starts giggling so much he has to leave the room so the XO doesn't see him.

"Plot - third ship sighted!' the quartermaster's voice booms out from above,

'Bearing one niner five. Range eight oh-double-oh!"

Our jaws drop as we all snap quick looks at one another - *three* ships!

I head for the bridge.

Muffled voices. Sounds of spray and a light wind.

"- seem to be anyway, not on either side at least." The Skipper's in the middle of a thought.

"Behind maybe?" Pike offers.

The Skipper's head cocks slightly to one side, "Certainly not out in front,'

"What are they?" I ask, practically breathless.

The Skipper's head slowly nods. "One freighter and two large transports. Big ones! An easy eight thousand tons each.."

"Escorts?"

"Haven't seen any yet." The Skipper replies, with a momentary glance in my direction.

Pike clears his throat. "Submarines maybe?"

The Skipper's head twitches abruptly, "Impractical. He'd have to run the whole time on the surface - he'd never keep up with them submerged. Anyway they're too close in shore. No aircraft protection so there's got to be a tin-can around somewhere. The Nips aren't kicking our ass by being stupid!"

It's strange. The moonlit shapes seem to be towering stationary structures. Their sheer size appears to preclude them from moving about in the sea. There must be a scientific name for this visual phenomenon.

"Plot - I need a solution!"

The Skipper leans expectantly over the open rim of the hatch. A glance below him shows nothing but blackness dotted here and there with the dim glow from the faces of the various luminous dials and gauges. The quartermaster's hoarse voice comes back a moment later. "They're still working on it sir!"

I sense - more than I hear - a grunt in exasperation from the Skipper. "Pike, you have the conn, I'm going below."

"Aye-aye sir."

I clamber in behind him. The XO and the tracking party cluster around the plotting table in the control room, a large chart before them. Pencil dots and hash marks denote ship positions, and drawn lines represent ship courses. The chart is a fairly tangled web of weaving and bisecting lines with no clear pattern to them. The XO is leaning over the table, a large frown on his face, with large ruby-sized beads of sweat dotting his wrinkled forehead. The protractor he holds in his left hand lies along a line he has just drawn, and is darkening it in with the point of his pencil. He mutters something unintelligible.

The Skipper glances at him sharply, "What?"

Before he has a chance to answer, a shout comes from the tower. "Enemy targets shifting course to southwest, bearing now two zero five!"

The XO looks as though he's going to erupt. "Goddamn -" He runs a frustrated hand through his lengthening hair. 'Look at this,' he says, moving to the side so the Skipper has a full view of the plotting chart. "About fifteen minutes after first contact, he makes a twelve degree tack to the Southeast - like he was going to run behind us. Then about twenty minutes later he tacks due north, then eight and a half minutes later he tacks again to the Southwest. It's nuts, there's no rhyme or reason to it, and he's kept it up now for over two and a half hours. Now he's tacking to the south-southwest,' the XO throws up his hands in frustration, 'He's all over the goddamn ocean!"

The Skipper looks pensive, staring blankly at the chart in front of him. "So what do you think?"

The XO shakes his black haired head. "Either it's the most ingenuous tacking maneuver ever devised or their convoy leader doesn't know what the hell he's doing! But I'll tell you this, he's burning up one hell of a lot of fuel and not making much headway. It's like he's out here steaming around in circles!"

"You still think they're headed for Aparri?"

A sharp nod. "Would have to be - if they came out of the home islands, their fuel reserves should be fairly low."

The Skipper crosses his arms and scratches his beard. "Since there are no escorts they could be waiting until first light to either rendezvous with a destroyer or aircraft."

The XO's frowning countenance nods slightly. "Possible."

The Skipper shifts his cap back on his head and sighs. "All right, stay on it. We'll increase speed, get ahead of 'em, and see if we can put ourselves at a strategic point between them and Aparri. Sooner or later they've got to come across our tubes." He turns toward the hatch to the conning tower, 'To engine room, all ahead full! New course one eight three!"

"It's weird you know,' the XO says, staring fixedly at the chart, 'It's almost like they know we're here."

"Don't be silly!' The Skipper glances at the chart again as the XO bends down and plots our new course. Just ahead of the line he draws, looms the northern coast of Luzon. "We're going to have to watch it,' the Skipper declares, a note of warning in his voice, 'that's too close to the coast for comfort." Turning, he disappears up the ladder.

An hour later another message is intercepted from ComSubPac, directing our boat to acknowledge and report our position. Again all we can do is shrug our shoulders and ignore it. Motormac Skjonsby, lounging in the crew's mess, cackles like a hyena and waves a half-eaten Danish above his head. "Another twenty-four hours and we'll all be "overdue and presumed lost! Wouldn't that be a hoot!"

Several of the others pick up his lead. They're infatuated with the idea of returning from the dead. They're at it for a good three quarters of an hour. My shipmates are proving to be masters in the macabre.

The hands of the chronometer in the wardroom read twelve minutes past the hour of three. I stare at it only half lucid. None of us can sleep since we could be in action at any moment. This game of cat and mouse goes on. Eleven hours have now passed since our initial contact. It is now clear that the enemy is not tacking in any particular pattern. If they were, the solution would have been worked out long ago. The enemy is tacking at their convoy leader's whim. It is an effective tactic, they are still alive.

For the last six hours we've stood around and stared at one another, smoked too much, told one lie after another, and watched our beards grow. There was some hope that the nightly poker game in the forward torpedo room might prove to be some relief, but even that broke up after about thirty minutes. Either no one could concentrate or everyone's tired of Daschler's perpetual bullying. The only excitement came when the steward found another cockroach in the pantry. This proves beyond a doubt that we still harbor unwanted passengers on board. Another massive cockroach hunt is underway, and the stopping up of the crew's head courtesy of Seaman Andersen. The Chief is thoroughly convinced if we run out of shells for the deck gun, we can use Andersen's refuse instead. "Had to use acid to thin the stuff out,' he says, wiping his sweaty brow, 'I'll bet the boys up at BureauOrd could fashion anti-tank shells from the stuff."

A red-faced Andersen moves through the boat while enduring a host of taunts and jeers from the rest of the crew. Copenhaver - on the other hand - is the sole voice of support. "A good, solid shit is the sign of a good, solid sailor. A man has to be in tune with his bowels. Don't listen to 'em kid! You're doin' great!"

An infernal screeching blast jolts me awake. Bolt-upright, the sound washes over me like a bucket of ice-cold seawater, it's the diving alarm! Across from me Lemert is already half out into the passageway. I catch a glimpse of the chronometer on my way out, almost 0500.

I shove my arms up through the control room hatch and fling myself up into the tower.

"Steady on one eight zero helm."

Michaelis's head and shoulders appear as he pops up from the control room, he's late. A look of irritation from the Skipper. "A bit behind our time Mike."

Michaelis fumbles with his ISWAS. "Yes sir."

Taking up my position next to the attack scope, my eyes fix on the Skipper. The enemy must be close, close enough to facilitate diving for a submerged attack. And it's getting light up top. Those transports are sure to carry deck guns.

"Passing five zero feet captain!" Waldron reports from the diving controls.

"Level her off at eight zero Waldron."

"Keep an eye on our time quartermaster, in exactly three and a half-minutes we'll take a look-see."

Harmison thumbs the stopwatch in his right hand. Already the glass face is smeared with sweat. "Yes sir."

"Coming up on six-five feet!"

"Blow negative to the mark!"

A sudden hiss turns into a roar; a fire hose under high pressure. The boat's nose begins to come up as Waldron has the planesmen ease back on the diving angle.

'Flood all forward and after tubes, set all fish for high-speed run."

Furrows crease the part of the Skipper's brow not shielded by the peak of his cap. I follow his steely gaze to the pit log - our underwater speed indicator. About four and a half knots, that means the motors are turning over at half speed. I can see the Chief now, along with the E-mates, hovering over our precious General Electric motors like mother hens, checking levels of wattage and voltage output. Not an ampere too much, nor a volt too low. Just enough. The motors - along with our batteries - are as vital as blood. The slight *hum* that emanates aft reminds me of bumblebees in the spring, buzzing and humming as they move from flower to flower.

Duffy cocks his head and turns sideways, displaying a freshly lit cigarette clenched between pearly white teeth. "Coming in loud and clear sir. Bearing zero eight three, reciprocating machinery, heavy screw sounds."

"Come on in gentlemen,' The Skipper mutters under his breath.

"Approaching two minutes sir." Harmison reports, glancing at the stopwatch.

"Very well,' the Skipper leans back toward the open hatch. "Control - make depth six zero feet. All ahead one-third."

"Sir-' O'Toole looks up, 'forward and after torpedo rooms report all tubes flooded and ready for firing."

"Very well."

"Conn, leveling off at six zero feet!"

"Very well - up 'scope!"

My right hand flicks the switch on the "pickle." With a whine the periscope rises up out of its well. The Skipper meets it as the business end clears the base of the floor plating. Snapping the handles down, he shoves his eyes into the eyepieces. "All right now Tojo,' he mumbles, walking the scope around, 'have we got a surprise for you."

I stay in step with him all the way. He stops rather suddenly, catching me in mid-stride of another step and almost causing me to stumble over my feet.

"Finally getting your sea legs Watts?" Pike grins evilly. I ignore the insult.

"Okay, first target,' the Skipper has stopped and raises his voice so that the XO - down in the control room at the plotting table - can hear him, 'a transport, starboard end of convoy....Bearing - mark!"

"Zero five two." I read.

"Range - mark!"

"Eight oh-five-five."

"Second target, transport in middle of convoy...bearing - mark!,'

"Zero seven one,'

'Range - mark!"

'Eight oh-five-two,'

"Third target...an AK furthest to port...bearing - mark!,'

'Zero niner three,'

'Range - mark!'

'Eight oh-double-oh,'

'Angle on the bow....Starboard forty-five! Down 'scope!' The Skipper takes a step back as the metal shaft drops back into its hole. 'Control....Make depth eight zero feet, all ahead two-thirds! Michaelis...I want a one twenty track on the fish. We'll take the middle transport first with the stern tubes."

Already Pike is cranking the information into the TDC.

Michaelis's face pinches as he holds up the ISWAS. He circles the slide rule around slowly, searching. "One twenty track will be just under two thousand sir."

Only our torpedoes can screw us now.

You can hear the enemy through our thin steel hull; the heavy throbbing of propellers. It is even possible to discern the different sounds they make as they beat through the water; the thunderous *thrum-thrum-thrum* of the combined ships.

"Screw sounds bearing zero one zero." Duffy reports, through a stream of gray cigarette smoke.

The Skipper's head turns ever so slightly. "Control, make your depth six zero feet. Stand by for final bearing and shoot."

Approximately twenty seconds later, the Skipper orders tube seven fired. Six seconds later the fish in tube eight is running through the sea. Then tube nine, and tube ten. Four torpedoes, with roughly a combined cost of forty thousand dollars, streak toward unsuspecting prey.

"Well, that'll ease some of the hot-bunking aft." The Chief weakly jokes from the control room.

"Right full rudder!' The Skipper exclaims, each word coming out like a gunshot. 'All ahead full! Meet her at two six zero!"

He's swinging our bow around for the freighter.

Several seconds pass before Duffy reports all fish "hot, straight, and normal." The Skipper is frowning now, in that peculiar way he has. "Time to impact?"

Harmison glances at his stopwatch. "Now about forty-five seconds sir."

The same thought is running through every man's mind in the boat; *will the fish work? Will they explode? Or will we be cheated out yet again?*

Harmison keeps an eye on his stopwatch. He begins counting down at ten seconds, going down to two. "Seven should be there about....now sir."

Nothing - only silence. *Damn it to hell!*

"Eight - three...two....about now!-'

The sound is unmistakable; a clap of gargantuan thunder reverberates through our hull. The boat shakes, and an instantaneous cheer goes up in here and down below. *A hit!*

"Ah-ha!' Pike bellows, 'Scratch one Tojo!"

Immediately we hear another deafening roar, followed by another thunderclap - *three hits out of four!*

"Not bad shooting." The Skipper admits, as he orders us to periscope depth. "Michaelis, what should the freighter bear?"

"Zero one seven sir."

"Up 'scope!"

The whine of hydraulics, followed by the *clack* of metal. "Third target in sight. His rudder's hard over to port. Looks like he's gonna try 'n make a run for it." The Skipper swivels the scope back around in the opposite direction and pauses a moment as he studies the scene. "Both transports dead in the - *Christ*!" He twists the knurled grip of the right handle, going from low to high power on the periscope. Something's wrong. "XO to the conning tower!"

Harmison turns and repeats the order but it is unnecessary. The XO's familiar form quickly comes up through the hatch. "Sir?'

"Take a look at this -"

The XO ducks behind the scope. Our eyes are riveted on the Skipper, who's drawn face betrays little. The XO grunts. "Well - what do you know!"

Pike shoots a look of exasperation over at me.

"How far are we from the coast Mr. Bainbridge?"

The XO steps back from the scope, his face a mixture of emotions. "No more than ten or twelve miles sir."

The Skipper ducks back behind the scope. "They're getting into the boats with their equipment."

"Sir -' Pike breaks in, unable to contain himself any longer, 'What is it?"

The Skipper steps back. "Take a look for yourself Lieutenant."

As if shot out of a cannon, Pike dives behind the scope. He whistles through his teeth, " Je-SUS H! Two goddamn troop ships! And they're loaded!'

The Skipper is affixing the XO with a serious stare. "Mr. Bainbridge, could those troops could make the coast of Luzon before nightfall?"

The XO weaves his head from side to side. "Might be after sunset, but about that."

The Skipper is quiet for a long moment. His eyes gaze around at each of us in turn. From somewhere comes a clicking sound.

"Gentlemen, ' the Skipper says finally, turning to all of us, 'Strategic bombing by air has already killed thousands of non-combatants in the Pacific and in Europe. What we have here are two Japanese transports loaded with troops. The transports are settling slowly. The troops are abandoning - *with their equipment* - into the lifeboats.' He pauses and stares into our eyes. 'It would be a court-martial offense to let those troops get ashore. That would be aiding and abetting the enemy. Now without the loss of one innocent life we are going to prevent those troops from getting ashore. For each one that makes it ashore means at least one more dead or maimed American or Filipino on the Bataan Peninsula. Any questions?"

"Now we have the bastards and the tables are turned." Pike is practically salivating.

"The freighter sir?" From Michaelis.

"We're going after him right now! Stand by to surface! We run him down and take care of those boats. Initially we'll try to chase them out of the lifeboats. I don't want any man shot directly unless they fire at us."

"And if they do?" Pike asks.

"Then it's open season." The Skipper replies, without a second thought.

The scene is reminiscent of a bunch of twentieth century pirates; bearded, smelly, grimy men clustered under the hatches brandishing an arsenal of weapons; belt-fed .30cal machine guns, BAR's (Browning Automatic Rifle), drum-fed .30cal Lewis guns, bolt-action Springfields, a few Thompsons, and almost all of us with a .45 strapped to our hip. The Gunner's Mate is in the conning tower with our single .50cal belt-fed machine gun to go up through the bridge hatch when we broach. He holds it almost lovingly, as if it were a woman. His biceps bulging from the weight of the heavy weapon. Seamen Andersen, Quinn and Matthews are right behind him with ammo belts draped over their chests, looking very much like turn of the century Mexican *bandidos*.

Waldron is holding the boat at about sixty-four feet, awaiting word from the Skipper to blow the safety tank. When this done, Waldron will bounce us to the surface with the bow planes.

"Deck gun crew will man through conning tower's forward door." Pike instructs the gunners assembled under the forward area hatch. "Ready ammo will be fired until shells come up through the forward hatch!"

The Chief stands by the magazine, passing out helmets. Lemert, who's gun captain, waves it aside.

"A bullet in the head is a sorry reward for pride." The Chief points out.

"I'll take my chances Chief." Lemert reassures cockily, waving the Chief aside.

The Skipper has one last periscope observation. "Looks like he's going to try a mad dash for the coast. Well, it won't do him any good. Blow main ballast!"

A sudden, violent explosion of high-pressure air and immediately the boat lurches upward.

"Passing fifty - forty-five...coming up on thirty-five...twenty,'

The boat rockets to the surface.

'Tower clear -'

"Crack hatch!"

Below me I hear Pike haranguing the deck gun crew, "Go-Go-Go-Go-! C'mon Lemert - move your ass!'

Before I'm even to the bridge bulwark I hear a deafening report. I get there just in time to see a white plume of spray well ahead and slightly to starboard of the freighter - the gun crew is already in action. All around me men are up here are frantically setting up the machine guns. The Gunner's Mate gets his .50cal set up on the mount on the cigarette deck, and the .30's go onto little welded on brackets at either side of the bridge. Copenhaver goes forward with a Lewis gun.

Whamm! A geyser of foam erupts just off the freighter's starboard bow. It usually takes a few rounds to find the range, but pray it doesn't take too long.

"Down one!" Lemert shouts, peering through the gun's range-finder.

Brass-cased shells come up. Both Daschler and Tashtego load shells for the gun, Daschler taking them as they are handed up from the forward hatch and handing them to Tashtego, who slams them angrily into the breech.

"Fire!"

Whamm! The shell slams squarely into the aft-end of the bridge superstructure, followed by a chorus of hoots and wild cheering.

"Hose down that poop deck!-' The Skipper yells, peering through his 7x50's, '- they've got a gun back there!" He whirls around, 'Give me all four engines on line! All ahead flank!"

Creaking and snapping of machine gun bolts. Next to me Wainwright locks and loads a belt into his .30cal. The Skipper reaches out and points frantically. "There - you see it?-'

Waldron lets out a yell. " *Jesus - there's Japs all over it*! They're swinging it around-'

Wainwright's .30cal explodes. With it jackhammering and kicking, he sways it back and forth. I look up at the stern of the Jap ship. It can be no more than fifteen hundred yards at the most if that. Even with the naked eye I can see bare-chested figures tumbling to the deck around it - victims of Wainwright's steady hand. The din becomes even worse, as the rest of the machine guns open up. The noise is unbearable. The water around the ship is painted with thousands of little white plumes.

Whamm! The three-inch goes off again. This time the stern of the Jap freighter erupts in a red fireball, debris flying up into the air.

The Skipper suddenly lets out a banshee squall in triumph.

Whamm! Another eruption in the after end of the bridge. With a groan of tearing metal, the ship's stack is shot away and part of it drops into the sea. Lemert slams one round after another into the stricken freighter, efficiently raking it from the stern forward, until the bridge structure is no longer recognizable and the top deck is in ruins.

A moment later, I catch the Skipper screaming something about a forward gun. A sudden orange flash and thunderous detonation almost burst my eardrums. Sounds of a freight train going overhead. I snap around; a white geyser erupts in the sea several hundred yards out. Even in a miss, it chills down to the bone. It was meant for us.

"Left ten degrees rudder - all ahead half!" The Skipper half-turns, "He's dead in the water. That first round that struck his stern must have taken out the steering linkage, he hasn't tried any maneuvering since then."

Already several fires have broken out on deck of the stricken vessel.

"Looks like the crew's heading for the lifeboats." Waldron observes.

Pike chuckles coldly. "He's definitely had it."

The Skipper leans over the bulwark, "Lemert!'"

"Sir?"

"Put a few more rounds into his waterline, then secure from firing."

"Yes sir!"

The next round is neatly placed right up the Nip's ass - his rounded stern. It opens up a good-sized hole - even from here we can hear the water rushing in. Lemert continues to blaze away, and a good dozen or so rounds later, the stern begins to settle. With that, the boat whips around and heads back from where we came. "We've unfinished business to attend to." Pike notes, fumbling with his cigarettes.

The Skipper fishes in his pocket for a cigarette and places it between his lips, lighting it from Waldron's trusty Zippo lighter. "Men, - listen up -' he says, raising his voice to be heard over our rumbling diesels and the *swish* of spray, 'If possible, we don't want to make more than one pass at these boats. One pass should do it. Remember - chase them out. Only if they start shooting do you fire directly into the boats, but once they're in the water, leave 'em alone. Understood?"

"Aye-aye sir!"

"Let's see how genteel the Jap is when the tables are turned."

Sound of a bolt being rammed home behind me. I turn - it's Pike with a BAR. He looks at me, and then at my hands. "You better either get a weapon or get below. When this starts it's going to get nasty up here."

The Skipper looks at me a moment. "Harmison!-' He shouts down the hatch, '- we got any more BAR's down there?"

"No sir."

"How 'bout a Springfield then?"

"Wait a minute -'

After a moment one is handed up. The Skipper hefts it and holds it out to me. "You know how to use it?"

The need to prove myself grips my soul in a tight fist. For the first time in my life, someone will actually be shooting *at me*. "Yes sir!" I respond, taking the rifle from him.

"Keep your head down and hit what you aim at."

"We just might bust your cherry yet Watts!" Pike taunts, slapping me on the back.

All I can do is force a grin through clenched lips. The lifeboats, never out of sight, are getting closer now. One transport has already gone under, but one is still half-afloat, with decks awash. Some of the boats are still pulling troops off it.

"Anybody see what they're doing?" Pike asks.

"Looking rather vexed, I would think." Waldron jokes, watching through his 7x50's.

I hear Pike drag heavily on a cigarette. "Well, they started the damn war so let's give them a good taste of it!"

"All right -,' the Skipper lowers his glasses, 'choose your targets and stand by,' he leans over the bulwark, 'Lemert -'

My knuckles go white as I grip the rifle stock between clenched hands. *Any minute now....*

A sudden shout in Japanese followed by report of a rifle echoes over the water. A screeching *zing* as the bullet ricochets off the conning tower.

"*Jesus Christ!*'

"COMMENCE FIRING - FIRE AT WILL!" The Skipper barks, and an entire ship's complement of weaponry opens up in an ear-splitting fusillade.

The three wooden launches closest to us are chewed into pieces in a matter of seconds, their high gunwales seeming to evaporate under the hail of five machine guns. A host of khaki-clad bodies spills out into the sea; arms still holding weapons, legs flailing, mouths open and screaming. The water around them is pocked by hundreds of impacting bullets as the guns sweep over them yet again. The forward three-inch starts working over the boats ahead of us. I watch - in a mixture of fascination and horror - as one of the shells splashes just in front of the boat and then ricochets right through it. The boat buckles in the center, folding up just like a man's wallet. Arms, legs, and pieces of torso are flung dozens of feet into the air. My ears begin to numb from the screams, yells - cries for ammo - amidst the cacophony of weapons.

The Japanese are firing back; frantic men in tightly packed boats furiously working rifle bolts. Objects are flung at us - strange looking shapes that arc end over end....

"The bastards! - they're throwing grenades!' Pike screams, slamming a fresh clip into his BAR. Flipping it over, he snaps back the bolt and looses off a burst at the nearest lifeboat, only several dozen yards away. A man - probably an officer by the looks of him - who stands up in the forward section of the boat, catches the burst squarely in the head. His head suddenly vaporizes in a burst of crimson, showering the men around him with blood and other cranial contents, and then the body - eerily - freezes in place. The torso - without the head - and arm still outstretched, poises like some gruesome figure in a wax museum. Strange figures aim rifles at me, I hear bullets *cracking* around me, all my doubts evaporate as I slam back the bolt of the Springfield - draw a round - then ram it home. Wrapping my arm through the sling and bringing the rifle to my shoulder, I sight down on squirming khaki figures and squeeze the trigger.

At times it seems to almost go in slow motion. Working the bolt of my Springfield, I see horrific scenes played out almost like in a movie. The Gunner's Mate cutting wide swaths with his .50cal, and the resulting explosion -

sudden, violent bursts of splintered wood, blood and bone - as the large slugs slice into the boats. And the way a man disintegrates when hit by a .50cal round is astounding. The body literally explodes. If one strikes the chest it usually seems to take off an arm.

A sudden cry of pain. The Skipper whirls around. Looking past him I can see Copenhaver spread-eagled on the platform. A puddle of blood has formed near his right leg.

"Pharmacist's mate to the bridge!' The Skipper yells and turns to me. "Watts - take over the gun!"

Without a word I scramble over the bulwark and slide the butt-end of the .30cal Lewis into my right shoulder. I am numb, not only from the noise around me but for what I must do. I must become hard - like iron - harder than I have ever been in my life. There is no room for softness or pity here. This is kill or be killed. This is *real*. Every Jap that I can kill will mean I have saved an American life. If the drums of ammunition keep coming, I will kill them all.

*   *   *

The guns are silent now. The barrels red-hot and wisping smoke. Around the boat is a vast field of debris. Broken and shattered planks, large pieces of lifeboats still intact, shot-up life preservers, torn pieces of clothing, all kinds of assorted junk. We have reaped a mighty - if grisly - harvest. The bumper crop is in corpses. They float in every position imaginable; face up and down, curled up or spread out, draped over smashed, half-sunk lifeboat gunwales, or like most of them, in pieces. Solitary arms, legs, and viscera intertwine in a horrid spectacle of movement as they are buoyed up and down by rippling swells. Corpses sway and bob in a ghastly water dance of the dead. At each dip of our prow, flotsam and corpses are flung out at every turn. Now and then a corpse will twitch and jerk. At first I thought it might be men still alive, but then I see dorsal fins scything through the water and splash as the creatures below fight over the choicest pieces. Nature has already returned to claim her bounty.

The Skipper orders the guns struck below and heads us back out to sea. He wants to clear the area quickly. The boat's prow swings around, our diesels rumble as their load is increased, and we leave this foul water behind us. I stay up on the bridge for a while, not really knowing why. But the direction in which I train my eyes is *forward*, not aft. The Skipper and Pike are there.

A cigarette is thrust into my midst by a weathered hand. I look over to see the Skipper beside me. With unsteady hands I place it between my lips.

"You did well Ensign." He says comfortingly, handing me his lighter and looking at me.

"Thank you sir." The sound of my own voice shocks me; it is uneven and hoarse.

"When you came aboard, didn't you tell me that you'd been reading about war since you were a kid, that right?'

I nod.

'Well Watts, you've just seen it."

Copenhaver was lucky - a clean flesh wound through the thigh. The

Skipper's given up his private bunk, and had Copenhaver moved in here right after they carried him off the bridge. Kemper says without any complications he should be up and moving around in a week or so. Sitting propped up in a bunk he beams proudly, declaring that getting shot is the best thing that's ever happened to him. He even has his own bunk, in itself a windfall worthy of the most intense jealousy. He pulls no watches, his chow is brought to him at regular intervals, and - if he's hungry enough - Jonesy will cook up something extra special for him. Rumor has it a chocolate cake is on the way already. After a shot of morphine and with his plugs of chewing tobacco, accompanying spittoon, and magazines - he's as happy as a clam.

"Hell,' the Chief growls, after looking in on the stricken fellow petty officer, 'if I would've known what a man gets for getting shot around here, I'd 've taken that bullet!"

The Skipper's in the control room, perched over the plotting table reviewing a message he's composing for ComSubPac. He's very tidy about this process. It always seems like he wants to say exactly the right thing. He crosses out words, adds others, and continues to stare at the pad of lined paper with his characteristic frown. The final version before encoding reads:

ATTACKED SMALL CONVOY AFTER TWELVE HOUR PURSUIT XX SANK ONE AK IN RUNNING GUN BATTLE XX ALSO TWO AP'S LOADED WITH TROOPS DESTROYING THEIR BOATS XX FOUR TORPEDOES EXPENDED XX AM PROCEEDING NORTHWEST INTO

PATROL AREA

CO BULLHEAD

It turns out the rumor is true - the chocolate cake materializes. It appears; quite large and thick with fudge frosting. Jonesy proudly places it on the galley's counter and has the steward take it forward. It almost doesn't get there. Poor Johnson is almost mugged moving through the control room by sweet-tooth crazed fanatics who will stop at nothing to get hold of it. I smell a real riot brewing. Copenhaver - in all his supposed misery - is instantly deluged with half the crew trying to get in to get a piece of it. The Chief mischievously considers stationing a man outside the entrance with a BAR with orders to shoot to kill. It's complete madness.

The Skipper's jaw drops when he sees it. "Where'd you get the eggs Jonesy? I thought we used them all up."

Jonesy merely blushes and replies he had a few stashed away, 'for a special occasion."

It is all the Skipper can do to shake his head in disbelief and smile. "You've outdone yourself this time Jonesy. It's a round of beers on us when we get back."

Jonesy beams like a man whose wife has just delivered their first born. He's clearly the hero of the hour.

That night, as I lie in my bunk staring at the craggy pipes above my head, visions of the day's events come up to me. Again I see bobbing heads swimming toward me. Their faces contorted in masks of hate. How is it that today became? How is it that those men came to follow leaders who decided to step away from civilization and wage war upon other nations?

This generation has not had an easy time of it. At every turn, the world seems to be coming apart. First the Depression; everyone out of work with little hope of obtaining any. No money, no food, no nothing. People reduced to selling the clothes off their backs as not to let their children starve. Just as things became a little better, we turn around and get kicked in the face with a world war. Is God angry with us? Has he decided to punish this generation for the sins of man? How many of us struggled through the Depression only to find our lives now hanging by a thread in this war? We have nothing to offer anyone. Some of us might have a job if we're lucky, waiting for us if we make it home alive, and maybe a little money for a year or two of college. We have at most a girl, but few of us are married. But the final factor that figures into this equation is our lives, and these are expendable. We know that full well going in. Our fathers did their duty before us, like their fathers before them. Now it is time to do ours. Not so much because of tradition, but because we must fight to preserve what they were able to attain and accomplish. We fight for the preservation of the world we know; our way of life. We fight totalitarian giants who - well prepared with an abundance of men and materiel - are clearly winning the war. We - completely unprepared and short of everything - to date are losing. The only thing we have that no one can take away is our honor.

The Skipper, Waldron and Michaelis all sit at the wardroom table with exhaustion written on their faces. Now that the Skipper has given up his quarters, he's bunking in here for the duration. Waldron and Michaelis have the next watch, so they're just killing time until they relieve Lemert and the XO on the bridge. The Skipper grins when he sees me. "Can't sleep Watts?"

"Just a little restless sir."

Waldron's kneading tobacco into the bowl of his pipe. "After today I'm not surprised."

"Lot of excitement." The Skipper agrees.

Michaelis chuckles, "Watts got his cherry busted today."

Waldron scowls as if he'd just smelled a rotten potato. "You've been hanging around Pike too long!" He says with a frown, placing the pipe stem between his teeth.

Michaelis shakes his head. "Our moral compass."

Waldron merely responds with a shrug and a raised eyebrow. "Every zoo has its animal tamer, and this one's surrounded by uncaged apes."

Michaelis starts grunting like a gorilla. Waldron's pipe makes a stab in the air. "See what I mean?"

The Skipper looks on this exchange with a tired, but bemused expression. His face is a mirror reflection of exhaustion. His movements are slow, and a little clumsy. How long has he been awake? I can't remember when he last slept.

The Skipper's head begins to slide down onto his chest, but just as it dips he catches himself - and sits up straight. After stirring himself awake, he instructs Michaelis to "put that record on,' he says with unfocused eyes, 'the one about England."

Michaelis sets his pictures aside for a moment and turns around to the little phonograph sitting on the shelf. Going through the pile of records next to it, he finds the one and places it on the turntable. After turning it on and lowering the arm, metallic crackling comes out of the speaker. Sudden fatigue overwhelms me. I lean down on the linoleum-topped table, and nestle my head in my arms. Metallic sounds beckon me toward slumber as the compartment rolls and creaks from side to side.

They'll be blue birds o-ver....

the White Cliffs of Do-ver....

Tomorrow, just you wait and see.......

*   *   *

A major development during the night. Sometime after 0300 Radioman Lichty picked up a transmission from Pearl - new orders for the boat. Instead of maintaining our vigil in our assigned patrol area, new orders send us into Corregidor, that isolated and embattled bastion of the Philippines. After reprovisioning and rearmament we are to put to sea and proceed to AREA

SEVEN, just off the coast of the island of Honshu, the Japanese mainland.

Is it a blessing or a death sentence? ComSubPac was very clear in the orders, they want us in and out of Corregidor in one night - and *only* at night. There will be no sailing into Corregidor in the middle of the day. The risk of being chewed up by enemy aircraft is too great. Darkness - and more than a little luck - will hopefully afford us a protective shroud.

Still, it won't be easy, the Skipper warned at breakfast, even at night. The Japanese Navy is all over these waters, and the ever present danger of destroyers and patrol boats, hugging the coastline shelling inland positions for their army, is immediate. And once we get into shallower waters we lose our ability to maneuver at depth, and thus discovery is tantamount to death.

"I've got him sir,' Duffy says with a hand to his ear. 'Coming in clear, bearing one niner three."

Thirty-five minutes after midnight. Leveling off at one hundred feet now. A few minutes ago Torpedoman Hood spotted a small ship off to starboard in the darkness and pulled the plug. We're not at periscope depth, but well below. I don't believe the Skipper wants to create too much mayhem on our way into Corregidor. The more we expose ourselves, the more the Nips will know where we are. The art of submarine warfare is after all, being the hunt*er* and not the hunt*ed*.

"Anything else moving around?"

Duffy listens for almost a minute, turning his wheel in a full arc. Slowly, he begins shaking his head. "Don't hear anybody else. I think this guy's a lone duck."

We listen for a good three-quarters of an hour. Nothing. The patrol boat went on by us none the wiser.

The Skipper chuckles. "You know all this reminds me of playing hide and go-seek like when we were kids. A little more lethal though perhaps."

"Just a bit." Waldron confirms, maintaining a straight face.

"AIRCRAFT OFF PORT QUARTER!"

The diving alarm sounds and immediately the forward section of the boat drops away. The whole room slants sharply forward, sending mugs and plates careening off the table to smash on the deck plates below. The shift in weight almost throws me off the seat, and I have to grab hold of the table post to keep my balance.

"Shhhiiitttt!' Lemert groans, losing both his book and the battle of physics as he slides off the seat bench to tumble into a twisted pile of arms and legs - turned crosswise - on the deck. "Hang on!" The Skipper instructs lightheartedly, "Never be caught unprepared!" He is of course, a stanchion of immobility.

Shouts of both surprise and invectives come from the bow compartment. I can picture the torpedomen in there, ducking out of the way of the lengths of chain that hang down from the overhead. A surprisingly loud crash just outside in the passageway - followed by a moan.

"What was that?"

"One steward down!" The XO yells as if he were at a football game, "One to go!"

Lemert attempts to struggle to his feet. But it's impossible, the angle is getting steadily worse, it's like trying to climb uphill. More debris flies about, everything loose tumbles toward the forward bulkhead. Pieces of crockery lunge out and try to take our heads off. And I'm losing my grip on the table. The boat is easily on a forty-five degree angle already.

"Jesus -" I gasp.

Cabinets now fly open on their own accord; a tumbling maelstrom of books, papers and assorted junk. I lose my struggle and join Lemert on the floor. "I think Pike's getting a little overzealous with the bow planes." The XO observes dryly, keeping a tight grip on his coffee cup lest it becomes a lethal object.

I notice the XO shaking his head in disgust. "Of all the nerve! Doesn't he realize we've got a chess game on here?"

The Skipper makes a dismissing motion with his right hand. "What do you expect of Academy types? It's your move."

I feel like I'm in a vaudeville routine; Lemert and me doing slapstick and the Skipper along with the XO providing the appropriate humorous commentary. The boat begins to come back a little, the angle is now lessening. Pike's bringing the keel up. Getting to my feet, I look around. The wardroom is a complete shambles, the contents of the shelves and cabinets lie scattered everywhere. Shattered crockery litters the deck and crunches noisily at every step.

The phone buzzes. The Skipper picks it up listens a moment, then drops it back into its cradle. "Schumacher spotted a couple of Nakijima's."

"Think they saw us?"

"If they did we'll know soon enough."

*   *   *

"All right we go! Steer one one zero. All ahead two-thirds!"

The Skipper slaps the periscope's handles back into place. For the last six hours we've waited submerged for the cover of darkness to creep in and cover our movements. Darkness has come, but has not brought with it a blanket of security. The surface is crawling with Jap patrol boats. The Skipper even reported seeing several destroyers shelling inland positions. Shelling *our inland positions that is*, those people on Bataan are not faceless.

Pike - as usual - was busting for some action a little while ago. Wanted to pick a fight with one of the DD's. "One fish - just one -right in the guts!' He bellowed with gleaming eyes, thoroughly enamored with the idea, 'It'd be so easy with them sitting there dead in the water!"

"Pike - ' Waldron calmly notes, 'has a death wish!"

The Skipper is unyielding. To get in and out of Corregidor without detection is our goal. So, we are to continue submerged which has its own inherent dangers. The XO knows that the entrance to the channel is mined. He has the minefield's classified plot in his hand - but what if ol' Jap has decided to plant a few of his own? Our forces here no longer have the ability to sweep them.

Everything that even attempts to come out of Corregidor is pounded by air and by sea beneath the waves.

The Skipper's keeping a close eye on the charts. Duffy echo-ranges off the bottom at regular intervals to make sure we don't plunge our bow into a mud bank. The depth in here varies, and navigating into Corregidor submerged is not something on the curriculum at New London.

We rig for silent running. The Skipper's worried enough about the noise we're making pinging with the sonar. "If any oriental ears are on a hydrophone,' he observes, standing over the plotting table and pulling a cigarette from a rumpled pack. "The game is up."

The XO's bending over the table, squinting at the charts like a mad scientist. "According to this, there's heavy minefields to the northeast and southwest, and a single picket line just east of us."

The Skipper hunches down to examine the papers more closely, studying them for a full minute. "What do you want to bet they're not there anymore."

A mixed look comes over the XO's face. "What d'you mean?"

"How long have the Nips been in charge around here - almost a month? It's my guess a good number have been swept by now. After the first ship French-kissed one they'd bring in minesweepers."

E-mate Garnett is standing next to the Chief as he pulls his shirt over his head. The Chief recoils as if pricked with a hot iron.

"Sweet Jesus Garnett! That aroma isn't even human! When was the last time you had a bath?"

Garnett thinks a moment. "You know Chief, honestly I don't remember. Back in Pearl at some point."

"For God's sake man - do something! No wonder it smells like a goddamn hog pen in here!"

The Skipper anxiously looks fore and aft as the lookouts climb quietly into the shears. We are dead in the water, the Skipper wanted to get a good look around before the diesels were turned over. The channel water slaps against our saddletanks and superstructure, producing little booms that sound hollow and dull - like drumsticks on slack drumheads.

Blackness. A light wind comes across the still-dripping bridge bulwark, bringing with it the heavy aroma of sweet smelling vegetation. In the clear sky above us an irregularly cut three-quarter moon hangs in the sky, comfortably nestled in between two large, billowy clouds glowing incandescent from the silvery illumination. The water, smooth and black, seems to move about as the moonlight flickers, dances and shimmers about on the surface. All is eerily peaceful.

"Looks clear enough.' the Skipper mumbles.

"Uh-huh,' the XO, next to him agrees.

"Lookouts?"

"All clear starboard sir."

"All clear port sir."

"Aft - all clear sir."

"Very well.' He steps back to the open hatch, 'Bridge to engine room -' his voice barely above a whisper, 'Kick over number one and number two main engines. All ahead half."

A moment later a heavy rumble splits the stillness as the diesels turn over, followed by a roar as the first cylinder explodes. It's so loud I jump - every Jap within a hundred miles must have heard it.

"To the helm, steer three four eight!"

We slice through the water, alert for anything. What would spell our doom now would be a patrol boat or one of their shallow-draft destroyers. There is not enough depth beneath us for escape, and a gunfight could hardly come out in our favor. For better or worse, from this point onward we will remain on the surface.

From somewhere I hear the sound of thunder. Rain! That would be perfect cover for us! I look skyward but see only broken, fragmentary pieces of clouds.

A chuckle beside me. "You're looking in the wrong direction Watts,' the Skipper declares, 'look landward. What you hear is artillery fire."

"Artillery?"

"Welcome to the Philippine front." He says through a bitter smile, his teeth flashing white in the inky blackness.

After a few moments of listening it makes sense. The angry bursts are far too frequent to be a creation of nature. Now and then you can hear the whistle before the shell explodes. You can even detect the report of the gun, the sound is flatter than the explosions, which are more piercing.

"Wonder who's those are?" The XO mulls to no one in particular.

Each blast conjures up visions of embattled and beleaguered American and Philippine defenders hunkered down in shell-torn trenches and foxholes; enduring the ceaseless pounding with gritted teeth underneath mud-spattered helmets and white knuckles gripping rifles with fixed bayonets.

Forty-five minutes pass when the outline of the *Canopus* hoves into view. In the dark and with us so close to the water, it seems gargantuan. About the same size as the tender *Sperry* - back at Midway. The Skipper cuts our speed, stations the maneuvering watch and begins swinging the boat around the nestle against the small barge next to it. In doing so, on the tender's port side a large gash reveals itself, just aft of the tender's clipped bow. Even in the darkness grotesquely twisted metal stands out. Ripped up and curled back over itself, like a giant attacked the ship with an enormous can opener.

"Good God!" The XO exclaims, examining the damage, 'they must have taken a bomb right down the funnel!"

Amidships is where the stack was. No stack now to speak of, just grossly flared pieces of steel looking like some malevolent blooming flower. The Skipper grunts. "Either somebody's been playing with explosives or the neighbors aren't all that friendly."

Mooring lines arc through the air to the barge. The heavy bass beat of our diesels comes to a rest. I look around; already the tender's crew is feeding over fuel hoses and boxes of provisions have appeared. The torpedo crane on the barge is ready with a shiny new Mk XIV fish hoisted in the air. A few men on the barge slide a gangplank over to our deck. A figure steps over the gangplank and pauses.

"Lieutenant Commander Tyreen - permission to come aboard sir?"

The Skipper leans over the bulwark. "Granted!"

The figure rounds the conning tower. With a slow and belabored gait, the figure steps up to the cigarette deck and extends his hand. "I'm the Captain of the USS *Canopus*,' the figure whispers. "Gentlemen, welcome to hell."

Book III:

Typhoon.....

"Christ!' Waldron spits, tossing the sheet of paper onto the table thoroughly disgusted.

The abrupt shift of his personality is stunning. Michaelis blinks and looks at him in surprise - as if unsure of the transformation he has just witnessed. "Yeah - you're right. Not too good, I guess."

Waldron stares straight through him like a man witnessing the passing of a soul. "All of them are done for - you know that! And what the hell can any of us do about it?" He fishes in his pocket for his pipe - but not in his usual calm, methodical manner. His movements are jerky and abrupt, the process of filling his pipe leaves flecks of tobacco sprinkled all over the tabletop. I've never seen him this way before.

The Skipper however, doesn't say a word. He sits, with hands clenched round his coffee cup, like some great all-knowing Sphinx. Michaelis turns to him. "Sir?"

The question hangs in the air. Before we cast off from the *Canopus*, a young seaman came aboard wanting to know we could mail a letter for him to his folks back home. He produced a few sheets of paper, apologizing that no one had envelopes anymore and handed them to the XO, pointing out his parent's address at the top of the page. Now every soldier's letter is normally censored by his commanding officer - as some information is classified and is not for public consumption. Not sure whether this had taken place, the XO gave it a few cursory glances. I did not understand his consternation until he handed it to me. The filthy paper has obviously has been wet at some point and the hastily scrawled writing is barely legible. He wrote: *When we try to sleep, we lie quivering in our foxholes while the Japanese shout taunts at us through the night. Last night our Filipino runner disappeared and the next morning we found him hanging disemboweled from a tree in front of our positions. Oh Mother, why has our country forsaken us? Where is President Roosevelt? Where is the Navy? Why do they not help us? Do they know what goes on here? Do they know that each day is spent with death and the putrid smell of death as corpses rot in the shell-blasted jungle? You may never read this but know dear Mother, that I love you and Dad with all my heart. I have acted as a man throughout this and I promise you when my time comes I will die like a man. Tell Marisa...well, just tell her.*

Your loving son,

Ricky

The Skipper looks up, and for a moment his roughhewn face is but a blank. Then just as quickly lowers his eyes. "They're all going to be sacrificed, simply because we have nothing to get to them. It's a tragedy of circumstance. The Japs have been itching for this fight for a long time; they had it planned and thought out. They knew it was coming and our stupid politicians didn't. The Japs hold the aces in the deck. All we can do is react to them until we gain the initiative. Our best hope right now is that in mainland waters their guard should be down."

*   *   *

We sprint across the South China Sea on three engines, leaving a boiling white ribbon along behind us. It's been eight hours since we hauled in our last line from *Canopus*, and bid the trapped crewmen a melancholy farewell. Their cheer all but a facade. Waldron characteristically remarks that condemned men rarely resign themselves to their fate until the last minute. But whatever hope of salvation is gone, incredibly their fighting spirit remains. We heard many stories of Japanese atrocities among the Filipinos civilians, rape and murder, beatings and a particularly loathsome tactic peculiar to Japs - beheading. There are Filipino villages where every man has been beheaded with a *samurai* sword for refusing to renounce the United States and the Philippine government. Sometimes Jap troops amuse themselves by smashing infants heads into stone walls.

"We know two words Captain Tyreen,' we overheard the captain of the *Canopus* say, '*Kill Japs!* We'll kill them with guns until the ammunition runs out, and then we'll kill them with knives and bayonets. Then with our bare hands if we have to, but we'll kill them! Every one of us wants to exist for that sole purpose. Three quarters of my crew are now up on the line pulling duty as infantry. We know we're not getting out, I know it and most of the men do. Nobody talks about it much; it's just the way the cards fall."

This is the stuff legends are made of. It's a modern-day Alamo.

Word spreads fast among the crew about the Japanese atrocities. Moving through the boat I hear clusters of men hunched together talking in semi-hushed whispers. That night, as I'm lying in my bunk, it is the topic of conversation in the bow compartment.

"Can ya' believe that?' Howe spits. 'Stinkin' Japs running around cuttin' people's heads off?"

"I wouldn't put anything past the fuckers.' Tashtego snorts.

"What gets me is what they're doing to those little kids!' Cutter exclaims icily.

"Pretty fuckin' sick!" Somebody comments.

"Hey, we got some licks in,' Howe notes proudly. 'Remember those troop transports?"

"I say we start doing that to all Jap ships we sink, turn machine guns on all the lifeboats!"

A pause. I hear some creaking sounds, like somebody shifting about on a bunk.

"No, that wouldn't do." Tashtego states flatly.

"What d'ya' mean?' Cutter bellows, his voice laden with sarcasm. 'Hell - it may not be totally kosher but look at what they're doin'!"

"Because, then you bring yourself down to their level,' Tashtego points out. "And then who is right and who is wrong? We shoot up those lifeboats because they had Jap troops in them - *combatants* and by killing them we saved our men and Filipinos too. If we start shooting everybody full of holes then we're just as bad as they are. And we are supposed to stand for something higher, am I right?"

A few mumbles and grunts of agreement.

More creaking and a few coughs followed by a sneeze.

"Lose your brains?" Garn wants to know.

"Fuck you!" Unmistakably Steele's thick New York accent.

"Does your mother know ya' talk that way?' Cutters snipes, 'I'll bet she took ya' to church every Sunday."

"And I was tryin' to pop the girl sittin' next to me every time!"

A few whistles and a low, animal-like growl. "You're a sick man Steele!"

"So I've heard. You know most of the parents back in Schenectady would never let their daughters go out with me."

"Can you blame them?' Howe chides; 'I wouldn't let my daughter go out with you!"

A sound akin to someone ventilating his backside. "You don't even have a daughter asshole! Besides - any offspring you might have would come with both sets of equipment!"

Cackling laughter and ape-like grunts. It's a regular circus up there.

Next morning. After getting a cup of coffee in the crew's mess, I'm moving into the control room when the XO comes down from the bridge with a concerned look on his face. He's clutching his sextant in his right hand.

"What's up?"

He shakes his head as he sets the delicate instrument back into its box. "Heavy red sky to the Northwest - blood red.' He says, sneering with derision. 'I don't like it."

"And that means?" I prod, trying to get a little more out of him.

He cocks an eyebrow, producing a crease that bisects his brow. "We'll know soon enough.' Immediately he gets busy with his trigonometry and algebra to plot our position. "Soon enough."

That afternoon I notice the boat is rolling and pitching more. The dips are sharper too. You'll be moving along in a compartment and suddenly the deck will drop right out from underneath you. After this comes the sharp blow as the falling prow reaches the wall of water beneath it. The boat yawls, shudders, groans and creaks. You'd think it had arthritis in its joints.

Copenhaver, who's up and moving around now - albeit with a limp - plants himself in the crew's mess and sways easily with the increasing motion. "It's going to get a little bumpy I'll bet." He observes, munching on one of Jonesy's Danishes.

Garnett stares at him. "Okay Confucius, what are you talkin' 'bout?"

"We're runnin' into a storm."

"You're full of shit!" Torpedoman Garn admonishes.

"Really? Well then we'll see, won't we?"

For a few moments only munching can be heard. Then a belch.

"Not bad. I'll give you a five on that one."

"What makes you think we're headed into a storm?" Garnett presses.

"Seaman's instinct. Remember I learned the hard way - on the Great Lakes. There storms blow up with the sun still shining."

'Enough already!" Garnett admonishes.

'And then the Pacific, ' Copenhaver continues, ' - which in no way lives up to its name."

"I don't think so." Garn disagrees.

"Want to lay some money on it?"

"Bet as much as you can lose fuzz-face!"

"You makin' fun of my mustache boy? Them's fightin' words! I'll lay an even twenty you've got shit for brains!"

"You're on!"

A little while later Radioman Lichty comes bobbing out from the radio room with a report of numerous transmissions from enemy ships. Didn't think there was anything to it until Michaelis looks at it a few moments and frowns. "That's odd." Taking it to the Skipper in the wardroom, who studies it and then sits back with a puzzled look. "What do you make of this?"

Michaelis shrugs. "Normally nothing, but look at it, some of the transmissions were encoded and some were not. Why would they do that? It could be pure laziness - but I can't believe the Japs are getting that complacent."

The Skipper lights a cigarette and stares into the overhead. "Why would the Nips send messages encoded and in the clear about sailing courses and departure dates?"

Michaelis shrugs again and walks away, leaving the Skipper fingering the paper and looking puzzled.

A field of deep blue-black covers the western quadrant of the sky, which gradually lightens to a lighter powder blue to the East. Stars show like needle points on a dark shroud - but only in the East. Before us an empty - yet angrier - sea. The swell is long and deeper; the boat lurches up and down, cants sideways and shudders as the bow buries itself in deep breakers. In just a few minutes where the sun will dip below the horizon, the water already shimmers with bouncing orange light. Pike has already ordered slickers to the bridge since there's a lot of spray coming over the bulwark already. In between rolls we throw them over our heads and squirm into them.

Pike coughs and spits as he replaces his cap just in time to catch a burst of spray in the face. "I've got a feeling there's more to this than anybody thinks!"

The wind increases. A steadily blowing force earlier now whips at us at every turn. It seems to be everywhere and blowing in all directions; first over the bridge, then it abruptly shifts and takes us from the rear, and then the side. The sea is being whipped into an angry froth.

I can't get to my wristwatch but it should be about time for the First Watch to be relieved. *Please let it be time.* Fatigue gnaws at me. Even standing still you use all the muscles in your body just to maintain your balance. A movement behind me - a sou'wester-topped head is poking out of the main hatch - *praise God!* Here comes the Second Watch!

Michaelis and Lemert come up, followed by Daschler and Duffy, all decked out in oilskins. I stand beside the hatch dumbly while Pike shouts the vitals to Michaelis - course, speed, and - comically - the sea and weather conditions. He could use just one word - shitty. That would sum it up.

I lower myself gingerly into the tower and then the control room. Dangling on a ladder with the boat bouncing around like this can be dangerous if not lethal. Finally planting myself on the deck in the control room, just as the boat rolls heavily to port. Caught in the middle of the room - with the ladder behind me - I fall toward the jutting edge of the plotting table, take it deeply in the thigh and cry out.

"Pick yourself up.... Dust yourself off.... Start all over again!" The Skipper sings teasingly, amused at my plight, as the boat begins coming back on an even keel.

"What was that from?" Somebody asks.

"The movie *Top Hat* - Fred Astaire and Ginger Rogers. We have that record around here someplace, don't we?' He muses, as if suddenly remembering a fortune stashed someplace he'd forgotten, 'Chief - where is that?"

The Chief - lounging by the air manifold - scratches his head and disappears in the direction of the wardroom.

I get up. Pike has steadied himself against the ladder and is shaking out of his slicker. He and the Skipper exchange a glance. "It's going to get worse, isn't it?" Pike asks, looking comical with his wet hair standing straight up on end.

The Skipper nods through a smirk. "We've figured out why the Nips are rerouting shipping, there's a hell of a storm coming our way - possibly typhoon-strength." He holds up a sheet of paper in his hand. "Lichty and Swensen have been intercepting these the whole time you two were topside."

"So what do we do?" I ask.

The Skipper grins like a Cheshire cat. "Eat light and hang on."

Oh lovely. My stomach knots.

Pike runs a wet hand through his soaked hair. "Typhoon strength huh?'

The Skipper nods blankly. "It's gonna be a regular Coney Island Roller coaster ride."

"Well, I always liked carnival rides!" Pike says with a grin. He's thoroughly enamored with the idea. To him it sounds like fun. He doesn't notice me staring at him as he takes his slicker back to the engine room to lay it out to dry. *That is a man with a sick mind.*

Overhead the loudspeaker crackles. Apparently the Chief has found the record.

Please teacher, Teach me something......

Nice teacher, teach me something....

I'm as awkward as a ca-mel....

That's not the worst....

As I move aft to put my slicker in the engine room, the Skipper's drumming his fingers on the plotting table to the beat of the music. A cry comes from above; Michaelis is already calling for a cut in speed. Must be a lot of water coming over the bridge.

Few storm preparations are underway. We're not like a surface ship; the only hatch that isn't secured is the main hatch to the bridge. This must remain open so the diesels can draw air when the main induction valve closes. We have no topside gear, no major guns to secure - our single three-inch is locked down - and no large superstructure to worry about. About the only thing worth noting are several seamen - Matthew's, Andersen, and Quinn - going through the boat stretching line along the middle of each compartment. Apparently it's the Chief's idea. This is so that anyone caught by an unexpected pitch or roll will not go crashing into the exposed sharp metalwork ringing the sides of the boat. At least that's the theory.

The Chief's trying to calm some of the apprehensive looks coming at him from some of the more inexperienced crewmen. "This is nothing at all,' he says, doing his best to sound reassuring, 'No big deal -really. The submarine is the most seaworthy ship there is - nothing can happen to us. We're safer here than in a battleship. Those big battlewagons weave like the Empire State Building and can easily capsize. That can't happen to us at all. The storm can't smash us and we can't sink, so just relax."

Tottering back toward the crew's mess for a cup of coffee. I've probably moved ten feet in ten minutes. The boat is in a constant state of movement. It falls, slams into what feels like a concrete wall, breaks free, and maintains equilibrium for a brief moment before the bow drops out again. It is during these times that I try to move. The most dangerous part is slipping through the hatch coamings in the bulkheads. If you lose your balance here - mid-way through - you come down squarely on thick steel with your crotch. Visions of being a soprano in a boy's choir in my later years.

Into the control room. The Skipper's over at the plotting table with Lemert - who's just come down from the bridge. Still in his oilskins and sou'wester he looks like a half-drowned animal. Whatever their exchange was it appears to be over, as Lemert moves back to the ladder.

"How goes it?" I call to him.

He stops and regards me a moment with a sarcastic expression. "You always ask such inane questions?" Without another word disappears up into the tower.

"Barometer's dropping like a stone.' The Skipper comments with a bemused look, bracing himself against the gyrocompass repeater and balancing a cup of coffee in hand. "Hope you've got an iron stomach." He leans over to the table and slides the log toward me. Placing both hands on the edge of the table, I look down at it. Under the heading 15 February 1942, I follow the column down until I reach the time for the last entry:

2120hrs: Wind west-northwest, 5 to 6. Sea 5, approaching 6. Accumulating clouds but visibility very good. Barometer 750.5 and falling. Squall-like conditions.

I stand back up. As if to punctuate the log entry, the boat shudders and heaves sharply to starboard. If it weren't for the Chief's anti-roll line, I would have careened full force into the high-pressure blow manifold. Maybe his idea works after all.

I nod toward the log. "Guess I won't be eating much in the next few days." It comes out as more of a question than a statement.

The Skipper cocks his head to one side. "Sometimes that boomerangs on people. Better to have something for your stomach to get rid of than nothing at all."

Stumbling on through the control room. Swensen sits calmly in the radio room, one foot propped up against a lubricating oil pipe, with a magazine in hand. His posture speaks volumes; relaxed yet attentive, poised but not stiff. He might as well be back home sitting behind a counter jerking sodas and relaxing between customers.

Another carefully negotiated crossing of a hatch coaming. Now, toward the coffeepot. I take the last mug from the tray beside it and hold it under the spigot. It strikes me that the designers had enough foresight to bolt this contraption into the wall, this way it can stand even the heaviest of seas.

The Chief's perusing his oil logs again - a fetish with him lately. Seems like every time I pass through the control room he's hunched over the plotting table with one of those canvas-bound ledgers spread open on the table. "Incredible,' he says after a moment, tracing an oil-stained index finger over a smudged yellow page. 'Do you realize that by the end of this patrol we'll have covered over half the Pacific Ocean! From Oahu to Corregidor, from Corregidor to Japan, and back to Oahu. Can you believe it?' He looks at me proudly. 'You know we're following in the steps of Magellan!"

I can only look at him with a pained expression.

He looks at me confused for a moment, then chuckles and makes a dismissing motion with his hand. "What this? Hah! This is nothing! A little squall that's all. Ensign, I could tell you horror stories about real storms - stuff that would really make your hair stand on end!"

Hearing them now, I can honestly say, does not interest me in the slightest.

'But this is nothing at all - ' he continues, 'now - winter of 'thirty-eight, that was something! Really separated the men from the boys. I was on the *S-29,* just coming out of Cavite. Hell of a storm blew up, full-scale typhoon it was; sky as black as coal, a driving rain that felt like it was coming out of a machine gun barrel. Sea easily a nine on the Beaufort Scale, and we've got to run on the surface because the 'Old Man' depleted the 'can with training dives.' He pauses to take a breath, his eyes getting bigger as he tells the story. He's totally into it.

"So we're stuck on the surface, right? A wave smashes over the bridge completely swamping it. Seawater comes down the open bridge hatch in torrents. Shorts out every piece of electric gear in the conning tower causing electrical fires. So we've got to shut the main hatch and the tower hatch to the control room don escape gear and have fire extinguishers handed up to us so we can put 'em out. Lost a diesel on that cruise too, seawater got into the main induction and swamped the port diesel. There was seawater in the goddamned pistons! Yard shop likened to kill us all!"

A movement behind us. The Chief is needed. I take the window of opportunity to break away and carefully head for my bunk. Then a new contest arises. The deck plates play games with me - I'm never sure where they're going to go, up, down, sideways - or all three in the space of seconds. Then they jump as the bow drops off a large wave and rattle around in their framework. Again, the bulkhead to the forward battery compartment is the clincher - it's a game of chance. Which way is it going to go? Should I lay money on it dropping down or bouncing up - or doing both? Do I wait until the bow shudders or on the long rise of the next wave? Who's to know?

There. Standing below my bunk. Now, how to get up? Someone comes in behind me.

"Hop up on the reverse roll.' Lemert instructs, coming in from the passageway, 'Otherwise you might get tossed out."

I look at him. He's just come off watch and is sopping wet; red face and bloodshot eyes, droplets of water hanging in his beard, shirt sticking to him like glued paper. Looks like he had a bad night with the bottle.

"How is it up top?"

Lemert regards me with a sarcastic expression as he attempts to dry his wet hair. The boat bucks violently to port. Caught off balance he slams into the side lockers with a heavy crash.

"Goddamnit!"

I scramble into my bunk. Lemert gets up and looks up at me. "Is this your first storm?"

After I grumble in the affirmative, Lemert turns round and half-disappears behind the curtain that divides us from the passageway. When he reappears, he's holding a tin pail in his right hand.

"What's that for?" I ask, more for confirmation than anything else.

He smiles through bearded, wet lips. "For you - who'd you think? If your stomach decides to have a fit, I just don't want it coming down on me."

"Not going to happen." I lie.

Lemert wedges the pail at the foot of my bunk between two bundles of thick cable that stick out from the bulkhead. "If you say so,' with that he rolls into his bunk and falls silent.

A sound stirs me. Harsh, naked light peeks in from around the curtain. There's a figure there clad in heavy weather gear, with a sou'wester over the head. A curved object protrudes from the mouth - Waldron. That means it's about 0400. The curtain abruptly slides back into place as he steps into the middle of the room. Half out of interest and half out of boredom, I watch him.

Planting his feet well apart to maintain a low center of gravity, he begins stripping out of his gear. First thing to go is the slicker. He pauses several times as the boat rolls, and steadies himself a few times with a grip on a steel pipe rising from the floor. All buckles undone, the slicker slides off him and crumples to the floor. Then the sou'wester - he doesn't bother untying the strap underneath, just whips it over his head. It joins the slicker in the crumpled pile. Then he moves over and sits down in the wooden chair positioned against the lockers and begins untying his boots. The process continues until he's down to his shorts. He's very meticulous about each item. Then, he reaches into the jumbled pile of clothing and retrieves something. Sitting back in the chair he removes the pipe from his mouth. Sound of a zipper - the tobacco pouch. Filling his pipe takes three sharp rolls and two hard shudders. Time wise, probably somewhere near ten seconds; I'm learning to count time in movement of the boat.

Striking a match against the steel pipe where he braces his bare right foot, he settles back and draws the flame down into the bowl of his pipe. A moment later I detect the familiar aroma of his tobacco.

Amazing. After all the punishment topside any other man would probably have stripped and dove straight into his bunk. But not Waldron, he has to relax with a bowl first. I watch him intently; completely composed, the only sound that comes from him is the hissing of air as he draws through the stem. His head cocked, as if deep in thought. What could he be thinking of? Does he have a girl back home? Strange, but I can't remember him ever mentioning any. He's quiet and Sphinxian - like the Skipper. Neither ever boast of their sexual exploits. In reality they're both probably big-time swingers.

I'll bet he's due for his own command soon. The Skipper I'm sure would hate to lose him. He has that air of a commander. He'd be a good one too, careful yet still aggressive. He would be a completely different commander than Pike would be, for example. Pike is more of a loose cannon - full speed into everything.

The figure remains this way for some time. Silent and still, only moving whenever the motion of the boat demands it. After awhile he stands up, knocks out his pipe in the metal sink across from him, and rolls into his bunk. A little while later his snoring begins to mix with Lemert's.

So that's that.

Getting down from a tossing bunk can be much harder than getting in. The anti-roll rails aren't much help in this respect either. They're more like bars on a cage. They rise up above the bunk a good four inches so I can't go over them. I'm going to have to pull one of them out. And how much leverage can one get lying down? I grit my teeth and flex my right arm, grasp the lower bar nearest my waist with my right hand and lift with all my might, but it won't budge. The metal prongs are rusty on the ends, so they don't move about smoothly. I'm trapped like a cornered animal. This means I'm either going to have to go out head first - but that's not feasible either. If I do that, I'll land on my head. The upside to it would be that maybe it would put me out of my misery altogether. All right, so I'll have to sit up. No big deal except that in my current state, it's possibly a fatal maneuver. But I past the point of caring long ago.

Sitting up, I yank the bar out of its holes and toss it behind me. The whole compartment suddenly shifts to starboard. Caught half-turned and unbalanced, my world slips out from under me as I crash to the deck below.

I lay there for a few moments, my hip and shoulder lanced with pain. Lifting my head, I notice Lemert's sleepy gaze regarding me curiously.

"You really know how to make an entrance. Ever consider vaudeville?" He asks in all seriousness, leaning his head back down.

I crawl over to the ventilation pipe and use it to steady myself as I get up. It's a good thing I'm still in my clothes. Getting dressed would be impossible. I stagger out into the passageway.

"Watts - ' a voice calls out from the wardroom just as I'm passing the open doorway. I look - it's Michaelis, motioning with his arm. 'Come on in, we've got breakfast already."

Mumbling morning salutations I shuffle in and ease myself onto the bench seat. Michaelis - flanked by the Skipper and the XO - sit before mounds of bacon, sausage, powdered eggs, and toast. The sight of it alone causes my stomach to lurch.

"Jesus!' Michaelis exclaims, looking at my face, 'Louisiana swamp water isn't as green as you!"

"Bad night?" The Skipper inquires from behind his omnipresent coffee cup. I only nod my head silently in reply. A knowing look comes across his face. "Something like this your first time out is pretty rough. You'd better eat something, and I don't mean *just* toast. This might be your last chance for hot food for awhile, Jonesy's already having trouble keeping his pots on the burners and we're still pretty much at the edge of the storm. That's why he served up breakfast early."

"Cold cuts and Danishes from here on out,' the XO pointedly observes, piling another hefty portion of sausage on his plate. 'Eat up while you can Ensign."

I know they're right but in reality I have not the slightest inclination to touch the stuff. Any other morning all this would be a regular feast. My stomach - empty as it is - still feels like there's a ten-pound lead weight square in the middle.

Michaelis takes up an extra plate sitting on the table and scoops up a few slices of bacon, two links of sausage, and some eggs. Then, taking a towel from behind him pours water on it and places the tray squarely on top of it. "There,' the communications officer says, sitting back, 'now it won't wind up in your lap."

As I begin to nibble - cautiously - the XO clears his throat, then takes a swig of coffee. Anyway...number three diesel was running a bit hot last night,'

"Oh?" The Skipper's eyebrows arch in surprise.

The XO nods. "Nothing too bad, only about thirty degrees above normal. The Chief and Schumacher checked it out. They seem to think it might be the bearing cams not getting enough lubrication. The Chief had them increase the lube oil flow and that seemed to help, but before we do any high-speed running, we ought to go in and have a look-see."

The Skipper nods, still chewing as he shoves his plate in front of him. Reaching into his pocket he produces his cigarettes and places one between his lips. "We'll want to do that before we get into our patrol area. See that it's done today. Can't make much speed in this sea anyway."

The XO nods eagerly. "That's what I was thinking sir."

Michaelis cackles like a hyena. "Engineers aren't happy unless they've got something torn apart and are elbow deep in grease."

"What's the only difference between men and boys?' The XO poses through a grin. He swallows the last of his coffee and starts to get up. "I'll let the boys know and get everything ready." He disappears into the passageway.

A few moments of silence follow. I pick at my food as if each bite could contain high explosive.

"Any idea of the storm's track?" Michaelis asks through a mouthful of sausage.

The Skipper merely shrugs. "Not a clear one. These Pacific typhoons are unpredictable. Just when you think they're going in one direction then they switch around and head someplace entirely opposite. Normally they seem to take a roughly east-southeast tack, but the things can run north to south, east to west, just about any way you can imagine. We'd be lucky if this one would stay bottled up in the South China Sea, but the odds are against it. The way it's moving now, it'll shoot straight out into the Pacific, then probably blow itself out there.' He falls silent as he stabs out his cigarette in the ashtray. "How you doing Watts? Food helping?"

"Bit early to tell sir." I lie convincingly.

"What you need Ensign is some fresh air. Why don't you take the next watch on the bridge with Michaelis here? Might air you out some and do you some good."

The statement is not phrased as a suggestion, but as an order. Well - sick or not - it's up top I go.

Michaelis emits an amused grunt. "Air out? Wet down would be more the term for it." He grins at me like a hunter sizing up prey for the kill.

0725hrs. Twenty minutes before I go up onto the bridge. I'm standing in the control room with Daschler, Duffy, and Lemert - all of us bundled up in slickers, foul-weather pants and sou'westers; like a gathering of a Cape Cod fishing fleet. Michaelis is roving about attending to last minute pre-watch business. It all seems strangely serene somehow - except for the violent motion of the boat. The calm before the storm.

I'm more that a little apprehensive. Will I finally lose the breakfast I've struggled to keep down? I study my fellow actors in the scene; Daschler seems not the slightest bit concerned, he cusses and gripes about the slicker being too tight on his powerful upper body but not much else. Duffy calmly puffs on a cigarette and looks bored, fingering the strap of the binoculars round his neck with his free hand. Lemert's munching on a Danish and swaying easily with the boat's perpetual motion. Totally free spirits, one and all.

A gush of water shoots down the control room hatch. Directly underneath the hatch opening, a major rainstorm is in progress. I try not to notice - I have to be as smooth as everyone else.

"Bumpy." Duffy observes.

"Yeah."

"Might want to get a last cigarette in sir,' Daschler suggests to me, still tugging at his slicker, 'Might be kind of tough to get one lit topside."

As I go through a series of wild contortions to get at my cigarettes inside my slicker, Copenhaver comes in from the crew's mess. Near total recovery from his wound, he's well enough now to stand watches. He looks at us with mock seriousness and surprise. "Kind of early for Halloween, isn't it?"

"Look who's talking? You're the one still in costume." Daschler shoots back.

Duffy's eyes flash mischievously. "You'd never know it though with that double-tailed mouse under his nose."

"Hey - hey, that's hitting below the belt! I don't make fun of your face."

"Your face invites ridicule.' Duffy persists. 'It would be impolite not to accept it."

The petty officer stares at us in shock. "Here I stand - a wounded man in the service of his country - a hero really - '

Daschler and Duffy snort simultaneously.

' - Having to deal with the insubordination of two whore-mongering Neanderthals."

"*Whore-mongering Neanderthals?*" Daschler repeats, incredulous. "You've been sneaking behind our backs and reading Webster!"

Duffy's shaking his arm. "Hey - three prostitutes I've personally swung from tree limbs with would be very upset with that last crack!"

The petty officer raises his head and stares into the overhead. "Heavenly Father, I stand vindicated!"

"Hah!"

At that moment Michaelis turns up and checks his watch. "Second Watch - stand by!" He glances over at me. "Don't get washed overboard -' he commands, '- the Skipper would never let me hear the end of it!"

We straighten up and suck in our breath. I double-check my slicker to make sure all the buckles are fastened properly. Let's see - buckles tight, glasses around my neck, lens paper stuffed into every available orifice, boots well laced-up. Everything checks - except my stomach. Maybe breakfast wasn't such a hot idea after all.

"Second Watch - let's go!"

We follow the watch officer up the ladder one after the other, like worker ants marching in single file. Negotiating the ladder's rungs while so clumsily dressed is not an easy task. I have to feel for each wet rung - put my foot down hard on it, then grasp the next with my hand - all the while the ladder's bobbing and weaving. This is a high part of the boat after all. A shower of water shoots down and over us - without looking up I can tell we're near the hatch. It is then that I hear a whistling sound. Whistling? It takes a moment to fathom -

My God - it's the wind!

Michaelis is up and out - I'm right behind him. To the right Tashtego and Buckley are already waiting to go below, water dripping from their sou'wester brims. Pike's yelling something into Michaelis's ear. Impossible to hear anything. Shrieking wind and smashing waves.

Quick - get out of the way of the hatch! Move over to your station and sector - starboard side!

As I look out over the bow, my amazement is total - nothing but white water. It doesn't look so much like a sea anymore but a never-ending mountain range of white-topped peaks. Our deck is entirely awash - the golden teakwood isn't visible. Only the foam-capped slats expose themselves for brief moments at a time. The top of the three-inch gun is just visible, but not the barrel.

The sky is no longer clear. Heavy blue-black lumps of coal protrude from the sky, surrounded by swirling masses of a dull and foreboding grayish hue. The wind is strong - thirty to thirty-five knots already. It whips spray off the white wave tops and hurls it into our exposed faces like buckshot - a stinging, biting, maelstrom of salty bullets.

A slap on the arm. Michaelis is trying to tell me something. I lean closer. "WHAT?"

He bends down raises his voice until it's almost a scream. "WHEN YOU SEE ONE THAT'S GOING TO BREAK OVER THE BRIDGE SING OUT!"

I reply "Yes sir,' but the words are carried away with the wind. The bridge suddenly drops and heels hard to port. Caught without a firm grip - I lose my balance and crash onto the steel deck. My nose barely misses smashing into one of the bayonet locking rings on the open hatch. Doesn't hurt much, thank God, because I'm wrapped up like a mummy in all this foul weather gear.

"HEY!'

I look up to find Michaelis staring down at me with a crooked grin. "FIRST THING YOU GOTTA LEARN OUT HERE IS TO HANG ON!' Immediately he starts laughing and shakes his head, 'STILL GOTTA BUST YOUR CHERRY!"

I struggle to get up. After two false starts I finally get to my feet. A shower shoots across the bridge, catching me right in the face. I come up sputtering and spitting. More laughing beside me.

"YOU ALSO GOTTA LEARN HOW TO DUCK!" Michaelis cackles. My inexperience is a boon for his amusement.

Trying to forget my torment, I wedge myself in between the TBT and the periscope housing. There - that should steady me a bit. I take a deep gulp of air and look up.

The scene unfolding itself in front of the boat is both fascinating and horrifying at the same time. The bow will rise up on top of a crest, throwing out giant sheets of white, before plunging deeply through the reverse slope. If another breaker is upon us before the bow rises again, the falling action will cause the bow to bury itself deep in the bottom of the wave. When this happens, the breaker launches up onto the deck and careens down the entire length of the foreship before smashing into our tower with a roar. Columns of water cascade over the bulwark. From port, from starboard, bucketfuls come from the open cigarette deck aft - everywhere veritable crashing torrents of angry water.

I fumble with my binoculars. But even before I can get them to my eyes the ship rolls one way or the other and almost throws them out of my hands. A sudden lurch as the bow plunges into a wave trough, causing my head to smack into the sharp eyelets of the TBT. In pain I cry out, only to receive a mouthful of Pacific brine for parting my lips.

I cough, choke, and spit; I'm standing here having the living shit beat out of me. Salt stings my eyes.

"STAND BY! DANGER AHEAD!" Michaelis yells.

I look up. Through stinging eyes I see a rolling, hissing breaker tearing in from port. It's headed directly for the bridge.

"HANG O - '

The last syllables of Michaelis's words are swallowed by a rushing sound, almost like the sound a strong wind makes as it slices through thick branches with leaves. Curling foam - spattered like frosting on a hastily iced cake. The thick cream arcs out and reaches toward us, like a boxer lunging in for the kill. All we can do is grit our teeth and duck our heads.

The blow is stunning in power and couldn't have been better placed by Joe Louis. A hard fist comes down squarely on the bridge of my nose, then tries to burst through my eyelids. The follow up is the leaded punch to my stomach that drives the breath from me. I open my eyes. There's water in the bridge up to our knees, swirling and sucking as it tries to tear us out the open back. I can't help thinking if one goes overboard now; there's no hope. No way could a man be fished out of this madness. You probably wouldn't survive more than a minute anyway. And even if the boat could halt in time - which is impossible - how in God's name could you ever see a solitary bobbing head amidst all these mountain peaks? The very idea makes my blood run cold.

Michaelis lets go with a rebel yell. He looks over at me, grinning evilly from ear to ear. He appears to be having the time of his life. "JUST LIKE CONEY ISLAND WATTS! LOVE A ROUGH RIDE!"

I feign a smile through closed lips, as if I'm enjoying it too. Personal honor dictates that I must be - or at least seem to be - as tough as he is. Feeling bile rising in my throat I swallow hard. No! - Don't lose control!

However bodily functions are stronger than willpower. My stomach violently constricts and I double over, vomiting up all of my breakfast onto the deck plates. Opening my eyes, I witness a grotesque pool of the vile gruel coagulated between two weld seams.

I rise up. Michaelis is staring at me.

"YOU ALL RIGHT?"

I nod in embarrassment wiping my mouth with the back of my sleeve.

"THIS'LL TURN YOU INTO A SEAMAN YET!' He yells, emitting another high-pitched cackle as the bow dips sharply into another wave. For him, this entire affair is one of abject amusement - like a child playing in the snow. For me, it's like being trapped inside a boxing ring with some sadistic maniac. Every second another jolt, every minute another punch - no matter how many times I duck or otherwise try to evade the merciless blows, the water searches out and finds windows of opportunity to strike me. If I duck my head, it merely comes up from under my chest and slaps me in the face. If I hold up an arm to protect my face, it simply goes around the limb as if it weren't there at all. If I turn completely around and expose my back to one coming over the bridge, one comes in from aft and I wind up getting creamed from both sides.

The binoculars hang round my neck completely useless. There's no way I can use them. I have to devote all my energies to simply hanging on. They really ought to provide some kind of safety belts for us up here. It's an oversight that could cause somebody his life.

There is no concept of time. I don't know how long we've been up here and the movements that would necessitate checking my watch are out of the question. But one thing is quite clear; the storm is getting steadily worse. The wind is stronger now than before. Probably getting upwards or forty knots or better. The only good thing to say about that is that my nausea has abated slightly - due more to the exertions needed in hanging on than anything else.

The hissing waves quickly meld into deafening explosions of a sea borne madness. White water rumbles all around us. My sou'wester brim is totally useless. The wind is so strong is flattens it back against my head thus leaving my face completely exposed. My eyes have become mere slits. I can only keep my eyes half-open for seconds at a time as torrents of spray shoot across the bridge coaming. Not that I could see much anyway. These white-capped peaks are so high already I doubt whether visibility is a couple of hundred yards at any given moment. The troughs of the waves could hide all kinds of secrets from us, but were we to run into an enemy ship about all we could do would be to shake our fists at it. In this weather our weapons are useless. Even to a green submariner like me that is obvious. Our unreliable torpedoes would certainly never make it to the target. In this sea a premature explosion would be understandable. And the three-inch deck gun might as well be on the moon.

A sudden bellow of alarm from Daschler. My head whips around to port. Through stinging eyes I see an angry gray cetacean charging for the aft end of the conning tower like a bull gone mad. Instantly my whole body goes rigid and I grab a hold of the TBT with all my might. Michaelis's staring upward - openmouthed - with a look of surprise.

"WHOA!"

The instant before the gray mammoth breaks, the boat heaves sharply to starboard. My steadfast grip on the TBT is torn away and I'm hurled into the steel of the bridge bulwark. Behind me comes a scream of pain - Duffy slams against the single steel rail that is the only thing standing between him and death. A heavy blow to my face, then ripping sensations like someone tearing at it with sandpaper. A hydraulic press crushes my chest. All at once I'm in water up to my neck. Is the boat sinking? Instinct for self-preservation causes me to crane my head up to stay above the level of rising white foam. More yells, screams and curses. Somebody moans. My back screams with pain, like somebody's just taken a sledgehammer to my spine. Coughing and sputtering. The world begins to come back to an even keel.

I open my eyes; the deck is still fresh with sizzling foam. Michaelis - in a half-kneel and two feet from me - looks around with a bewildered grimace. I hear more moaning and notice a doubled over figure in the periscope shears. It's Daschler. Another curse from the shears tells me that Duffy is still among the living. Someone's shouting from the conning tower. The boat rolls again, a white sheet shoots over the coaming and peppers us with dime-size drops.

I struggle to my feet.

"EVERYBODY OKAY?' Michaelis yells, getting up and moving over to the open bridge hatch. The answer to his question does not come in the form of words, but rather a chorus of coughs, spits, and curses. Satisfied for the moment, Michaelis engages in a yelling contest with the quartermaster in the tower. Then he turns round and shuffles back to the bridge coaming.

"LISTEN - ' he yells, not out of vexation but to make himself heard - 'FROM NOW ON, WHEN A HEAVY ONE ROLLS IN AND LOOKS AS IF IT'LL BREAK INSIDE THE BRIDGE, WE CLOSE THE HATCH - GOT IT?"

Wearily I nod. I've heard stories about other boats who've taken too much seawater down the main hatch, usually resulting in a nasty electrical fire as the seawater comes into contact with exposed electrical cables, immediately shorting them out. These are very difficult to put out. The moment you snuff it out in one place, it smolders and bursts into flame somewhere else. It's Like fighting a multi-headed serpent.

"STARBOARD SIDE.... ON THE WAY!"

Duffy's yell snaps my head around. A greenish-gray mass tears toward us. Buckling and hissing, it overlaps with other waves, building upon itself until it's a solid wall of water that's easily thirty feet high. Like some stalking monster, it rolls inexorably toward the conning tower as if shrewdly aimed by Neptune himself. I stare in awe; never in my life have I seen waves such as this. The size and raw power a wave harnesses can't be imagined unless experienced.

"SHUT THE HATCH!.... HANG ONNNN!'

The leviathan strikes, smashing itself into a million pieces against the steel side of the bulwark. The world goes black. My eyes are shut tight. A choking cough. Huddling underneath the bridge coaming, violently vibrating metal above me - like somebody's on the other side trying to punch through it with a jackhammer. The roaring in my ears turns into a hissing. A centrifugal force tries to wrench me away from my tenuous foothold. Water laps at my neck. I'm gripping the TBT so hard I can hardly feel my hands any longer. They must still be there; gripped round the welded steel brace or else I'd 've been swept out the cigarette deck by now. Sound of fat frying. Dare I open my eyes? Could I have been swept overboard by this titan and not know it? Could I already be in the water and not know it? How long would I survive?

"JESUS motherLOVIN CHRIST!" It's Michaelis. So if I'm in the water, we've both been swept overboard.

I open my eyes. Gray steel dripping with seawater is inches from my face. So, I've made it after all. A metallic *slam* behind me. Someone's opened the hatch.

"GODDAMNED MOTHER OF 'EM ALL!"

I stand up and spit out Pacific brine. But what's the use? The boat's dipping down into another breaker already. Sheets of spray flail my face. My eyes burn like red-hot coals from the salt water. In spite of the misery, I can't help a slight grin from forming at the corners of my salt-caked lips. There was a poem I read once:

And woe to you men....

Who go down to the sea in ships....

How long can something like this go on? Days? Weeks? Months? It's only been a little over twenty-four hours so far and I'm thoroughly done with it. Silently I pray for deliverance to calmer waters, with gently rolling swell without foamy tops. To blue skies and light breezes, not Force Seven gales. Sunshine and sweet air, no angry waves just wrinkled creases formed by the tides and easy breeze.

It's becoming hard to imagine such things ever existed.

This is a match of physical strength between man and the sea. The sea has all the advantage and it is one she always wins. We are but mere mortals and tire easily. But the waters grow even more and more vexed and furious. Strength is not a problem for them. The waves are now over thirty feet *and rising!* It's total madness.

It is with indescribable joy that I notice a sou'wester-topped head poking out of the hatch. Out of the figure's mouth juts a pipe - Waldron! The Third Watch is coming up!

We - of the Second Watch - are reprieved.

I scramble below right behind Michaelis. Yet even off the bridge the waves reach us. Three times during our descent down the ladder into the control room, we are deluged under gushes of water shooting through the hatch. The boat weaves and wobbles. On the ladder it's like swinging from a circus trapeze.

The Skipper's familiar form greets us in the control room. He's standing with feet well apart over the plotting table, a cup of coffee in hand. "How is it?"

Michaelis pulls off his sou'wester and shakes his head. It takes him a moment to get the breath to say anything. He tugs at his slicker, panting like a blown horse. "Sea's a seven, approaching eight. Wind out of the west-northwest as eight, moving to nine,' he pauses for breath, 'Visibility two - maybe three hundred yards, but not constant. Pretty soon the bottom will drop out."

The Skipper runs a hand through his tangled mop of hair. "We're secured from evasive maneuvering, no need for it in this sea." As if to punctuate his statement, a shower shoots down from the bridge, splatters all over the deck plates and gurgles and foams as it finds its way into the bilge. Our Ahab jerks his head toward the crew's mess. "Go get yourself a cup of coffee and get dry."

*   *   *

There's a group at the tables in the crew's mess, playing cards. They seem indifferent to the wild contortions of the boat, which is now heeling a good thirty-five to forty-five degrees. Copenhaver's one of them of course. Nothing fazes him, not even getting shot. If the boat was sinking and he was in the middle of a hand, he'd probably don his Momsen Lung and go on with the game.

Now, through the crew's mess and into the control room. A glance to my left;

Radioman Sharpe sits in the radio room tilted back in his chair with his feet wedged firmly against the wall. I also notice his face isn't the healthiest color I've ever seen either.

The waves pummeling against the buoyancy tanks produce one heavy, unbroken vibrato that numbs the ears. It's like a hundred men were standing outside the boat hitting it with sledgehammers.

I have to wait for the reverse roll before scrambling into my bunk. Fatigue consumes me like some insidious disease; my entire body is sore. A glance in the small square mirror in here above the sink leaves me speechless. My entire face is the color of steamed lobster. My eyes are bloodshot and swollen, and there are flecks of white in my beard. It isn't premature age, but salt. My lips even have white highlights to them. My hair is matted to my scalp, and thick with the salt and impurities in seawater. I look like the pitiful wretch that I am.

But I don't care. All I need is to get into my bunk and become unconscious for about a hundred years. Sleep - a peaceful, blissful slumber - I would give my life savings for. A grab a hold of the side rails, wait for the roll - and then the dip - and put all the force in my weak legs that I can muster and push off. The resulting screams from my leg and arm muscles almost cause me to cry out. By the time my chest is flat on the bunk, I'm gritting my teeth because of the pain.

After a few minutes I realize that rest is a figment of the imagination. The boat - in its constant movement - won't allow me to find the right position in which to lie. When the bow drops, my head jumps off the small pillow. When it rises, my feet rise up into the air and press my head into the steel wall behind me. My whole weight rests for one long moment on my head. Add to this that I have to hang onto the rails beside me - a futile attempt at immobility. The fluctuating change in pressure every few moments when the main hatch is closed and the diesels draw their air from inside the boat sucks my eardrums in and out. It feels like your inner ear is about to be sucked out of your head. Then, when the hatch opens, the pressure just as quickly drops and your ears pop; in-out...in-out....out-in. A vicious cycle of pain. How the hell can anyone sleep under these conditions?

The sea continues reaching for new heights in violence. Why doesn't the Skipper pull the plug and dive? We could drop to a quiet depth and have peace again. I already know the answer; the batteries - we need to maintain as high a charged level as possible. This storm's not going to blow itself out very quickly. No, however distasteful - we'll have to ride it out on the surface. Unfortunately, there's no other way.

My time in my bunk does not last long. The bouncing around is simply too much. Up, down, sideways, another quick jolt up, a shudder down, the bunk cants at forty-five degree angles and the whole process starts over. I have to get out of here.

Letting myself down easy is impossible. So I just swing a leg over the bar, then an arm and let myself crash to the floor on the next roll.

"What the hell are you doing?" Lemert demands in surprise, rolling over onto his side and looking at me.

The last thing I need now is to have to explain myself. I mumble something incoherent and stagger to my feet to grab the tin 'vomit' pail I had wedged between my legs. Lowering myself back down to the deck plates, I curl up into a ball in the corner with one arm crooked round the pail. A few minutes go by when Lemert must notice I haven't gotten back up into my bunk. I hear him roll back over.

"Watts?"

I grunt.

"You on the floor? - What the hell are you doing on the floor?"

"Trying to survive." It's the first honest thing I've said all day.

"You sick?"

The question doesn't even justify a response. Maybe death really isn't that bad. It would put an end to the suffering at least.

*   *   *

Next morning. In the wardroom. Even though there's no hot food, the breakfast ritual in here goes on. We nibble at Jonesy's Danishes, some fruit, and wash it all down with buckets of coffee. I sit next to Michaelis, with the XO and Lemert across from us. Waldron and Schumacher are still sacked out in their bunks - they had the last watch. The Skipper of course is in his usual place, at the end of the table. He sits there looking like a shepherd keeping a close eye over his flock.

Just sitting requires strenuous effort. The compartment cants and dips to forty-five plus degrees, then shudders and shakes. Even with anti-roll rails, you've got to hold onto your coffee cup at all times lest it slide off the table and smash onto the floor.

For the last thirty minutes I have been the main object of amusement since Lemert spilled the beans about my sleeping arrangements last night. Everyone's flabbergasted; they've never heard of such a thing. I defensively point out it was a last resort, and that my stomach couldn't take all the bouncing around up in my bunk.

The XO's shaking his head and grinning like a hyena. "Now I've heard it all."

And Michaelis is practically in hysterics.

The Skipper motions to a plate of sliced pineapple. "Try a little of this. You've got to eat something or you'll really be in a bad way."

What nobody seems to understand though is, *I'm already in a bad way*. Quietly acquiescing, I slide a slice over onto a plate and begin to chop at it with my fork.

The Skipper, the XO, Michaelis, and Lemert soon engage in a conversation regarding the storm. It would seem the Skipper has that unique Englishman's gift for understatement. He describes the current sea conditions as "rather sloppy." I can't believe my ears. *Rather sloppy?* I can think of a thousand adjectives and invectives to use to describe our present environment, but those would not be among them. How much worse can it get before he pulls out all the stops? Does every officer and bluejacket have to be a particular shade of green or do we have to be knee-deep in water in here before he takes notice? We'd probably have to have three compartments fully flooded before he pushes the panic button. Once again, he defies description.

What is strange is that each of the officers seems to take this storm as the most routine thing in the world. Nor do they bear the slightest signs of discomfiture. Is it all an act or are they really this tough? I believe the Skipper is. I can't imagine anything getting him out of sorts. He sits there like some legendary seafarer, calmly smoking a cigarette and sipping his coffee whenever the motion of the boat allows. He's even talking of coming up to the bridge for the next watch. The way he acts, you'd think he'd gone round Cape Horn half a dozen times and actually become bored with it.

The XO's not far behind. His eccentricities are born out of his logarithms and algebraic equations. For him, the storm is a minor hindrance since it blocks his view of the stars - that's all he lives for. I've never once heard a complaint from him concerning the rough seas. Only grumbles about missing his star fixes and getting us off course.

For Michaelis, one watch with him on the bridge explained everything. The crashing waves, flying spray and pitching deck - is his element. He's a kid in a candy store. I'm fully convinced he's half-mad.

The Second Watch officer elbows me in the ribs. "Better get dressed. We're topside in forty-five minutes."

I cringe - *we?*

I notice the Skipper's head nodding in agreement. "Best thing for you is activity Ensign. The more you stay active, the less time you have to dwell on being sick. In fact, I'll be going up with you."

"An extra pair of eyes is always good." Michaelis adds with a sickening note of good cheer.

Now I know they're both mad.

"STAND BY.... DANGER AHEAD!"

A foam-topped monster roars in from starboard. From the trough to the crest it's an easy forty-five feet high. Forty-five feet of immense power. Liquid muscle that might as well be steel. A crown of white rings the top. Nature at its most terrifying.

It slams squarely into the middle of the tower superstructure. An explosion follows - as loud as the sharp report from our three-inch. The wave dies a self-inflicted death as it disembowels itself on our starboard saddletank. But the crest - as well as most of its punch - makes one final lunge over the bridge coaming to lance us with liquid bayonets.

Only three of us - Michaelis, the Skipper, and myself - remain on the bridge. The Skipper ordered Daschler and Duffy below; the seas are too high to risk them being in the periscope shears. The possibility of being washed out is very real. Besides, visibility is practically zero anyway. You can't see over the next mountain peak.

It's no longer possible to be up here without being lashed in. Safety belts have been fashioned from lengths of rope that we loop around our waists and secure to the metal braces jutting out from the steel coaming in front of us. Without them we would be swept overboard in a matter of seconds.

The Skipper's right. I'm so busy trying to maintain equilibrium and keep myself upright that my severe nausea seems to diminish somewhat. I wouldn't give a dollar for what I'll be like when I go below later, though.

"PORT SIDE.... AFFFFTTTT!' Michaelis screams at the top of his lungs.

"SHUT THE HAAAAATTTCH!" The Skipper bellows simultaneously, and the hatch bangs shut as the quartermaster in the tower yanks hard on the lanyard.

I snatch a glance to port. What meets my eyes makes my blood run cold, a bulging giant of grayish-greenish white looms out of the surrounding mountain range. An angry tower ringed in foam - sputtering and hissing - barrels hell-for-leather right for the superstructure. The great fold of water moves at high speed, getting larger and larger by the moment. This titan is easily fifty feet high and becoming taller and taller by the second. The sea and sky behind it completely disappear under its mushrooming bulk. Its hue deepens as it grows upon itself, sucking up great amounts of surrounding water for its own aggrandizement. It is no more than forty yards away.

My eardrums compress. The boiling mass is such that it actually increases the air pressure in front of it.

The boat swivels violently to starboard as the leviathan sucks the water out from under us. The deck cants at an obscene angle, an easy fifty-five degrees. Closer now, no more than twenty yards.

A guttural sound comes from the Skipper's throat; the mass bearing down on us impresses even him. Michaelis is staring upward, mouth open. "JEEE-SUS HCCHHH!'

I want to turn around - turn my back to it and hide my head - but for some inexplicable reason I can't. As if hypnotized, I watch fascinated as the watery creature draws ever closer. Building and building, growing and growing, metastasizing like some great cancer - the mother of all tumors.

"HA-A-A-NG ONNNN!"

I whip my head around and throw my arms round the TBT, linking my prune-like hands. My eyes catch a brief glimpse of the starboard side. I suddenly realize the water I'm looking into is almost level with the bridge coaming.

A huge anvil crushes our backs. My grip on the TBT is torn away and - in the blink of an eye - I'm pressed flat to the bridge deck. The loud express train of a moment ago is totally muffled, replaced by a wild gurgling and rushing - I'm underwater. I open my eyes - nothing but pale green all around. Then something lifts me off the deck. I'm completely suspended in space. Totally weightless - it lasts only a second. Then the cold, wet steel of the bridge deck punches me in the face yet again.

Something is holding me under. I can't breathe or move. Like lightning it flashes through my mind: *there have been cases of men being drowned up here.*

The leviathan must have totally submerged the boat. We should have come up by now. In spite of its inherent seaworthiness, submarines have foundered in this way: an avalanche of seawater overwhelms the bilge pumps, grounds out all the electrical circuits - starting electrical fires - then floods the bilge. With electrical power gone and the batteries shorted out, there's nothing left to do but pray.

Still underwater - my lungs are nigh bursting. Another moment more and it'll all be over. Panic is beginning to set in. Can I claw my way up? There could be air just inches above my head...

A force yanks at my shoulder - am I now to be torn apart?

Whirling, sizzling foam on my face. A blast of wind - air! Through burning eyes I stare into a chiseled face - the Skipper. His mouth is wide open. Is he yelling? - I can't hear. Water drips from his prominent nose and glistens in his beard.

Fresh air streams into me like cold water. Immediately I'm dizzy. The Skipper shakes me. I hear another shout from Michaelis. The Skipper shifts his gaze and looks past me - his jaw tightens. With his left arm he slams me between the TBT and the periscope housing so hard I cry out. But the infernal roar around me drowns it out so efficiently that even I don't hear it. The Skipper grabs hold of the TBT and ducks his head just as another hammer of white fury descends upon us. The entire bridge fills. The water rises up to my solar plexus.

A glance over the coaming: the entire foreship has disappeared beneath the waves. Nothing before us but angry water. Yet slowly and heavily, the bow lumbers up out of the water and attempts to shake off its tormentors, only to have the struggle begin anew.

Our bow - locked in constant, close combat with the sea - paves the way - smashing, battering, tearing, squashing, and clawing its way relentlessly forward.

An eerie sound fills the air whenever the forward part of the boat rips free of the raging sea. The boat's flexible radio antenna - stretching from the top of the bridge to the bow - bounces so hard in the wind that it takes on a musical pitch. The high pitched shrilling can be heard until the foreship buries itself in the next breaker.

The water and the sky are joining. The wind has become so heavy that it's almost impossible to open the naked eye to it. You can only look forward through barely opened slits, and even then your eyes are tearing and burning so severely from the spindrift and sea salt that everything is fuzzy.

What we need are eyes that can peer into saltwater, like a fish's.

The sky remains slate-gray, low hanging and ominous, morphing the sea from a greenish-gray to a malevolent black. Intercut in these are great swaths of white, hurling and tumbling upon one another, building each moment, each one bigger and more powerful than the one before. Each raging at us with a vengeance to kill. These creatures of gray, green, and white wreak a torture on us hitherto unknown. Who could fathom that water, revered in paintings, poems, and lore since time immemorial, could hound us to the very edge of despair? Who could perceive the beating we would suffer at its whim? Who fully realizes the powers these waters harness?

Ask any man who's spent time at sea and he will tell you.

Just before noon - change of the watch. That I make it down into the control room in one piece is nothing short of a miracle. Battered, beaten, and bruised as if I'd gone ten rounds with Max Schmeling, I drop like a sack onto the floor plates and make a feeble attempt to struggle out of my oilskins. Countless times I have to grab hold of a lubricating oil pipe jutting up from the pump room so as not to be smashed headfirst into the planesmen's controls at the diving station.

Every article of clothing on me is completely soaked through. I strip and stagger aft to place the sodden bundle in the engine room.

Moving through the boat, I notice that I am not the only one affected by the storm. Vacant eyes greet me as I pass by, even the crew's mess is subdued. Fireman Henley, Motormac's Schumann, Pettigrew and Skjonsby sit at the tables in apathetic silence. McGowan, Swensen, and a few other men cluster in the after battery compartment staring at the floor. Even in the engine room, Motormac's Hartmann and McClusky stare around with drawn faces and barely look up when I come through the watertight door.

Due to the bucking and rolling, I have to pull myself along by gripping pipes in the overhead to maintain balance. And thanks to the hammering diesels, it is warmer in here than in the other compartments. In spite of the dank atmosphere - heavy with the smell of diesel oil - and the infernal noise, it is surprisingly comforting.

As I spread out my clothes on top the blower, I realize my fatigue is quickly turning to total exhaustion. I need to rest, if just for a moment. Feeble and weak, I sit on the squat wooden stool that's in each of the engine rooms. Out of the corner of my eye, I notice the wiry figure of Hartmann approaching. He stops a few steps from me as I look up at him. He winces as if just pricked with a pin. My face must look as raw as it feels. Digging in a greasy shirt pocket, he produces a pack of cigarettes and holds them out to me with an equally soiled hand. Gladly accepting and lighting it from his Zippo, I lean back. A crooked smile emanates from his exhaust-blackened face.

He turns away and goes back to his engines. I'm little more than halfway through my cigarette when the urge to drop my head on my chest and close my eyes is overwhelming. I should get up, and go back forward to my bunk. But the strength just isn't there. I need to rest a moment, until I get my strength back. Looping my arm through one of the oil pipes that juts out from the engine just inches from my head.........

Sometime later, my eyes snap open. How long have I been out? There's a blanket lying around me - how did that get there? A little stunned, I look around. Motormac's Skjonsby and Pettigrew are on duty in here now - I must have slept through the change of the watch! Pettigrew's studying a series of gauges on the port engine as he notices me. He mouths what looks like a "good morning" even though it must be near dusk.

Slowly I get up. Clad only in my skivvies - dry now but stiff with salt - I wrap the blanket round me like a shawl and stumble forward through the bulkhead, plodding along like an old woman.

In the control room I see the bent form of the XO hunched over the plotting table. Charts lay out in front of him. He's shaking his head as he fiddles with a compass. A protractor lies next to his left hand.

"It's no good,' he says bitterly, the corners of his mouth downturned, 'I haven't had a star fix in almost a week! We could be miles off course by now!"

A week? I didn't know we'd been enduring this pounding for that long. In my pathetic state, I've lost complete track of time.

'There's no way - ' he continues, seeming pleased to have an audience, 'That we're going to reach our patrol area on schedule. Even with dead-reckoning it's a complete impossibility! And who the hell knows when this storm's going to blow over!"

A great gush of water shoots down through the hatch just behind me. Cursing can be heard up in the tower. The compartment shudders and shakes, then the floor drops away. A loud clattering from above - somebody's coming down from the conning tower.

"Look out below!"

A rustling followed by a heavy thump - the sound of someone sliding down the ladder. I turn around. It's the Skipper - his oilskins shiny and glistening wet. Water drips from his sou'wester and his face is the color of boiled beets. Another torrent pours through the hatch and washes over him. For a moment, he's completely invisible under a shroud of green and white. Then, he comes up shaking himself and angrily wrenches off his sou'wester. "Damn this stinking weather!" Then he spits, running a prune-like hand through his soaked hair and thrusting out his jaw and cackles sarcastically as he tosses his sou'wester on the floor and begins to unbuckle his foul-weather jacket. He calls for a pad of paper. The XO tosses him a towel from one of the several hung around the room and - wrestling out of his jacket - proceeds to dry his upper body. Yeoman O'Toole shows up with some paper and a pencil. Still grumbling, the Skipper begins to compose a message.

"In this sea,' the XO begins, staring vacantly in front of him, 'We can't make any headway because we have to run at such low speed. Higher speed would be dangerous and probably lethal. Not only would we be beating ourselves and the boat to death, but higher rpms on the shafts could drive the boat deep into a wave and in effect involuntarily submerge the boat. That could drown the bridge watch."

The control room abruptly cants to port at a disgusting angle. The plotting table gouges into my lower stomach. The XO has to grab hold of his charts so that they don't slide onto the wet deck. "Goddamnittt!"

"Welcome to the Rodeo Pacific of nineteen forty-two." Schumacher comments dryly, stumbling through the after bulkhead.

The XO turns round and regards him acidly. "I fail to see any humor in this."

Schumacher looks around slyly grinning like a school kid but refrains from saying anything more.

The Skipper finishes scribbling, tears off the sheet of paper and hands it to me. "Give this to Michaelis for encoding and transmission."

"Aye-aye sir."

Heading forward, I glance at the yellow piece of paper in my hands:

WEATHER CONDITIONS WORSENING X

WIND 8-9 SEA 8 - APPROACHING 9 X

IMPOSSIBLE TO MAKE PATROL AREA ON SCHEDULE X

COURSE 010 X SPEED 5 X

CO BULLHEAD

So we sail at a measly five knots. At this rate we'll get to our patrol area this time next year. In the wardroom, Michaelis takes it without a word and immediately goes to work. I watch him as he crouches over the encrypting machine. The strain is even beginning to show on him too. The deep shadows beneath his eyes testify to the fact that he hasn't had a decent night's sleep in over a week. His eyes have that glazed look of too much coffee, too many cigarettes, and not enough solid food.

This storm is whittling away at each one of us. How much longer can it go on and how much worse can it get?

The irony of that very question hits me in the face a few hours later. I'm in my bunk hanging on for dear life when the boat begins a sickening series of wild acrobatics that threaten to fling me out of my little berth. First the bow drops sharply, and I wait for the shudder as it strikes into the sea below - but it doesn't come. The bow continues to fall, propelling me up in my bunk so that I have to grab a hold of the pipes above me so that my head doesn't slam into them. Then, the whole compartment shudders and quivers as the bow finds the sea below it. For what seems like an eternity - the boat freezes in this position. We just hang there - like laundry on a line - until the frenzied sea hammers the stern down. The boat pancakes heavily, the steel groaning and creaking under the enormous stress.

A sharp blow propels me forward - then a shudder. The entire boat quivers like an arrow shot into a hard wooden plank. It's the bow, buried in - and trying to break free of - a wave. Then a sudden release from the clinch as the prow finally smashes through the oceanic wall.

The resulting relieved feeling lasts only a moment. The bow dips evil and shudders as it again buries itself. The boat clumsily attempts to cartwheel - first from the front, then from the side. Loose gear spills out and rattles over the floor plates in a wild ride of the sea. Wild cursing up in the bow compartment, accompanied by a few moans. Below me, even Lemert and Waldron start spouting obscene invectives.

The First Watch is on duty. How the hell Pike and the rest can hang on topside in this weather is a complete mystery. The bridge watches though have been cut in half, two hours instead of four. To withstand any more is simply beyond the realm of human endurance.

We lay in our bunks like corpses stiff with rigor mortis. Every muscle in our bodies bulges and strains to keep us immobile. I grit my teeth and try to make myself as heavy as possible, but it's all a desperate act of futility. The sea batters us around like some little toy doll or marionette. It's a perfect analogy! The sea is our master, it pulls our strings and makes us move in the way *it* desires. We play the role of Pinnochio to a Stromboli-like sea.

I chuckle bitterly. Pinocchio - cartoons before the afternoon matinee. Nickel bag of popcorn wedged between your knees; all happy, peaceful recollections of an earlier time now gone forever. We weren't marked by war then; will we still be able to enjoy such things? Or are we doomed to stumble through the rest of life forever haunted and cursed by the war. But such trivialities are important in life. Will we be able to resume our lives? If we lose this war, certainly not. The world we knew will go right out the window if we're conquered by the Germans or enslaved by the Japs.

The blasting klaxon brings me back to reality - we're diving!

The bow noses down. We seem to hang there, the surface tension is such that it's hard for the boat to leave the surface. Commotion in the control room - Copenhaver's ordering the man on the vent manifold to open the vents to the safety tank. A series of crashing roars as waves slam into the tower. The foreship must be submerged; the sea is breaking into the outer superstructure. Another crash - then silence.

Over the next twenty minutes the jarring begins to subside until - incredibly - there is nothing more. The boat levels off. A collective sigh of relief comes up from all quarters - peace has finally come!

I give a silent prayer of thanks to whoever pulled the plug. At last, peaceful slumber awaits. I don't need to hang on any more. My God - is this real?

A little while later I get up to make a trip to the head. It's as still as death in the boat. Everyone off duty is sacked out. Not a sound to be heard. Total exhaustion has overtaken us all.

However, in me the storm has left deep etchings. In spite of the tranquility and sereneness, my body still feels like it's being battered around. I'm still in the habit of hanging on to things too.

Next morning I awake to find the boat still silent and running on an even keel. I prick up my ears and listen for a moment, hearing the humming of our electric motors. Alas, we're still submerged!

Thank God!

I lay back down, intending to enjoy the peace for as long as possible. Sometime later, my nose detects the aroma of cooking odors. My stomach rumbles with hunger. Just as I'm about to clamber down from my bunk to investigate, the XO sticks his head in to inform us that hot breakfast is served in the wardroom. As if of one body - Waldron, Lemert, and I all vault out of our bunks for our first real meal in a week.

The word 'breakfast' turns out to be a misnomer. 'Smorgasbord' would be a better term for the feast Jonesy has lain out for us. Not only eggs, navy bacon, and sausage, but also fried potatoes, pancakes with syrup, chicken fried steaks, baked potatoes, and plenty of toast - a real feast!

We tear into the food like a pack of voracious wolves. Who knows when we may have the chance again? And a week is a long time without something solid in your stomach.

As it turns out, we stay down the entire day. The Skipper has decided to give the men a break and let them catch up on some rest. God knows we need it, for tomorrow - the Skipper informs us - we're back to the surface.

Several times I wake up in my bunk, and lie there in the darkness listening to my surroundings. It's amazing, there's not a sound; no card playing, no drinking stories, no boasting of exploits in the whorehouses - nothing. It's like everyone is dead. It's as quiet as a grave, like a ghost ship plowing through an empty sea.

That afternoon, still dozing in my bunk, my ears detect faint notes of music coming from somewhere. I hop down from my bunk to investigate and stick my head out into the passageway - it's coming from the wardroom. The curtain is parted. Moving a little closer, the Skipper's hunched form rests at the end of the table. A record is on the phonograph. The music is clearer now too......

Night and day, you were the one......

Only you beneath the moon and under the sun....

In the roaring traffic's boom, In the silence of my lonely room....

I think of you, night and day......

Hat off, and eyes closed, his left arm leans on the table. A faint smile on his lips. It would seem criminal to disturb his peace. Abruptly the song ends, leaving in the air only the crackling of the needle spinning round and round on the record. Then slowly, he opens his eyes and sighs. He seems far away, deep in thought. Just as I'm about to make my retreat he notices me.

"Watts - come in." He says, motioning to me.

"I'm sorry to disturb you sir, I heard music - '

He shakes his head. "Sorry if I woke you. Can't very well play it on the surface in this sea." He pulls a cigarette from a rumpled pack lying on the table and places it between his lips. "You get enough to eat?" He asks, pushing the pack over to me and motioning me to take one.

I nod, pulling a cigarette out. "Stuffed myself like a pig sir."

"Better?"

"Yes sir, now that we're submerged."

He nods. "Enjoy it while it lasts and eat all you can. I've ordered the galley to stay open for the next twenty hours."

"How much longer will we be in the soup, Sir?"

"A few more days at least. At most a week."

My heart sinks. That means we have to endure more of this relentless pounding. How much more can I - we - stand? Doesn't it come to a point beyond the realm of human endurance? If only we could stay *submerged*, then all our problems would be over. But we can't. We're wholly dependent upon the atmosphere. It's our mother, it nurses us and gives us the key element necessary in submarining: air. Air for our diesels to run so that they can turn generators to charge our batteries, air that is mechanically shrunk and stored in special steel flasks as compressed air. Air to breathe, air for the blowers to circulate and cool the heavy lead batteries in the battery rooms. *Air....air....air.......*there's no getting away from it. Maybe someday naval engineers will come up with new technology that will allow submarines greater endurance, speed and range underwater. All part of the ongoing conflict of men trying to conquer the sea.

"Are you doing all right?" He asks, implying a certain importance.

I sense - more than I know - what he might be getting at. "I think so sir."

"All of this-' he motions with his hand toward the boat and the existing elements, '-is a bit much your first time out. I want it to work for you Ensign. I think you've got what it takes."

His candidness stuns me. "Thank you sir."

The Skipper leans over and sticks an arm in a cabinet. Withdrawing it, he clutches a new record in his left hand. He looks at my slyly as he puts it on the phonograph. "Sometimes a man's only saving grace is music."

Before the new record ends, his head has dropped onto his chest and he is deep in sleep.

Our holiday passes too quickly. We are just beginning to become something like human beings again when after breakfast the next morning the Skipper gives the order, "Prepare to surface!"

Immediately my whole body tightens like a coiled spring.

The presentiment is not unfounded, as the boat passes one hundred fifty feet you can already detect motion. It begins in earnest; first, the movement comes at the bow, rising and falling in the groundswell. This carries aft to the stern. The boat tips and tilts as if on a pendulum. It's fantastic! Here - this deep beneath the waves the storm is still able to transmit its violence.

The First Watch is all suited up ready to go topside the moment the tower clears. Pike, bundled up in his oilskins, stands under the tower hatch looking threatening. Tashtego looks totally unconcerned, and I pretend to put on as stalwart an air as I can, but knowing what I'm about to endure keeps my face tight and drawn. And the closer we get to the surface, the more wild the yawing becomes. Now, the boat teeters from side to side, bounces once, twice, then three times, and rolls a sharp thirty degrees.

"Better keep the brass monkeys lashed in tonight!" Somebody moans.

"Better to hang onto 'em,' somebody yells back, 'that way you always know where they are!"

The banter continues, but I'm not paying much attention. In my right hand, I finger a little device rigged up by the Chief. It's a brass clip, connected to a length of hemp rope that runs around my waist. A safety belt, but with one important difference. Before, you had to burst through the hatch and hang on for dear life while you looped the loose end of the rope around something. Now, all you have to do is pop out of the hatch and snap yourself in, or at least that's the theory.

"Passing two-five feet. Tower clear!"

"First Watch - let's go!" Pike bellows, taking the ladder rungs two at a time. I follow right behind him sans his enthusiasm.

As the quartermaster cracks the hatch a great deluge cascades down over him and into the control room. Through this inundation men must move. We claw our way up and onto the bridge. We must get onto the bridge and snap in before we're washed overboard.

In one motion I hook my brass clip round a supporting metal bar that runs around the lower inside of the metal breakwater. A movement engulfs my vision; a great mountain of water passes down the starboard side, it's crest easily topping out at sixty feet high. The air is oddly still; we're in the trough formed by two gigantic waves. Like tall buildings on land, these liquid wind breaks shield us momentarily from the wind, but it's there. I can hear it, it's above us sweeping across the peaks of the waves. The boat bends and shoots upward as we scale an approaching leviathan, climbing higher and higher like a cable car to a mountain top. Then the bow breaks free of the water, and hangs for a moment, suspended in midair, before dropping like the blade of an ax down the other side. Great plumes of white foam shoot out from the forward section on either side as the bow bites deep into the wave. Now like a runaway freight train we careen toward the trough at the bottom at lightning speed.

The boat jerks on the upswing as it bottoms out in the trough. My stomach drops. The boat weaves from side to side, shudders, buckles, and quivers. The analogy the Skipper made some time ago to a rollercoaster ride was quite befitting.

Through a series of shouts and hand signals, Pike instructs us that the main hatch is to remain closed. Our diesels must have air, so they're going to try opening the main induction valve. How long it will remain so is anybody's guess.

Within the first ten minutes on the bridge, my face feels like it has been rubbed raw with sand, my eyes burn like fire and my hands go numb. The violent jerking and pitching of the boat causes the rope around my waist to tighten painfully. Soon the region burns like fire - the rope's sawing motion is tearing into my skin. Like some guileful blood-sucking insect, the seawater finds this wound too. All I can do is grit my teeth and take it. The safety belt is life. Wedging myself against the periscope shears I stare out over where our stern should be. I hardly ever see it, continuously buried as it is beneath blankets of foam. It's almost like we've gone to sea only in this blackish gray conning tower, you hardly ever see the rest of the boat. Countless times I scream out "BRACE!" As a heavy breaker rolls in over the stern to smash into the open cigarette deck and flood the bridge.

I'm becoming convinced that the sea itself has gone insane. A full-scale typhoon it may be, but it's as if the ocean itself rages.

About halfway through the watch Pike lets out a howl.

"DID YOU SEE THAT?" He yells, pointing off the starboard bow, stabbing his arm in the air. "A SHIP! A SHIP IS THERE!"

Straining with all my might, I stare until my eyes feel like they're going to pop out but can see nothing but foaming wave tops. For a moment I wonder whether he couldn't be hallucinating, sometimes violent seas can do that to people. But he jabs his arm in the direction yet again. "THERE! THERE IT IS!" He whirls around and yanks open the hatch. "CAPTAIN TO THE BRIDGE! CONTACT OFF STARBOARD BOW!"

After a minute or two I do finally spot something, Something is there among the heavy peaks, visible for only seconds at a time. I can make out a dark hulk, but that's it.

Pike has a pair of binoculars handed up. He alternates between staring out over the mountain range and steadying himself against the wild pitching. "A SHIP!' He exclaims, with such zeal you'd think he'd just won a million dollars, 'DEFINITELY A SHIP!" He ducks behind the TBT and takes a bearing.

The main hatch suddenly bangs open, and the Skipper emerges, a stooped figure in oilskins. A pair of glasses bouncing round his neck. When he's clear the hatch bangs shut again. "WHERE?"

Pike points. "THREE POINTS TO STARBOARD SIR!"

"BEARING?"

"ZERO TWO-TWO!"

"RIGHT TWELVE DEGREES RUDDER - STEER ZERO TWO TWO!"

Pike lifts the hatch to shout the course change to the helmsman in the tower as the Skipper raises his glasses to his eyes. But the sea conspires against him, as waves continually break over the bridge coaming, dousing all of us and fogging his binoculars.

"PORT SIDE - BRACE!" Tashtego hollers, as all four of us simultaneously duck behind the steel coaming. A roar - followed by thick lips of foam - and again sizzling water swirls and sucks at our legs. Then it's up again, to stare into the maelstrom and be beaten some more.

Time passes, it takes a little while to get a bead on this contact. The Skipper remains poised against the coaming, desperately trying to figure out what we have in front of us. It's certainly a freighter, the mast-goalpost-mast structure is clearly recognizable. We dare not get too close. In this weather weapons are useless. About the only thing he could do would be to try to ram us. But he could report our position. A welcoming committee interests no one where we're going.

After lowering his glasses for the hundredth time, the Skipper finally comes to a verdict.

"IT'S RUSSIAN! HE'S FLYING A SOVIET FLAG!"

A Russian freighter - he's as mad as we are.

Pike mutters something about having the signal lamp handed up, but the Skipper shakes his head - it's too risky. "RESUME PREVIOUS COURSE!" Are our Commander's last words as he disappears below.

A chance encounter at sea with a Russian freighter in a storm, otherwise nothing has changed.

Most of the faces of the crewmen in the control room have a wan and tightened look. Their pallid countenances are as gray as the surrounding metal itself. Nothing to do except suck it in and try to hold it down.

Apathy is becoming our constant companion.

The Chief comes in from aft. A clipboard in hand, and smiles silently at me as he goes about checking over his list. Like a shopkeeper-taking inventory, he wanders around checking this and that before going over and lifting up the metal grating over the pump room. After a few minutes, he reappears, mumbling and scribbling something on his clipboard. He approaches the Skipper and requests permission to halt the drain pump discharge for a short time, so that the bilge strainers can be cleaned. Even though we're taking a lot of water through the main hatch, water is not the only thing to find its way into the bilge. The bilge pumps suck up a miscellany of solid material; the strainer traps flakes of paint, small pieces of metal, as well as vomit and other gruel. Should this crap get into the lines of the drain systems, it would screw up the delicate workings of the drain pump. And since the drain pump has been working at full capacity ever since we entered the storm, the strainers are just about clogged.

I don't envy the poor devils that'll have to clean off those strainers.

The Skipper assents, exhorting the Chief to do it quickly.   Almost every second there's a torrent coming through the hatch, and at this rate the water rises quickly in the bilges.

The condensate level is building up. While the boat's air-conditioning system keeps this irritant from becoming too severe, the system is only working at half capacity, since one of the York-Navy Freon 12 compressors has been having a cylinder problem.

The storm is thrashing the mechanics of the boat as thoroughly as its human complement.

Doing even the simplest of things requires concentrated effort. Trying to maintain a cup underneath the coffeemaker spout in the crew's mess necessitates every ounce of strength and focus I can muster. Even holding the cup so that the hot contents do not splash over you is a game of chance.

Over at the mess tables, some of the crew cluster in an impassive cast. There's Seaman Grayson, Lichty, Schumann, and Steele, Garn, Hood, Reece, with a few others from the First and Third Watch. Barely a murmur of conversation comes from them. The only expressions on their faces are winces now and then when the boat makes a sharp roll to one side or the other. Their eyes stare vacantly around or remain fixed on the table in front of them. Quite a few of them - Grayson especially - are particularly green around the gills. Now I notice a few tin pails nearby along with the sour smell of vomit. This sea is even making the veterans queasy.

If it keeps up like it is, soon there won't be anyone left well enough to run the boat.

The after battery compartment - the crew's quarters - is as silent as a tomb. From where I'm standing all I can see is a twisted configuration of limbs stretched out in every conceivable direction. There's nothing even remotely human about it; a pile of amputated limbs and severed heads, coldly cast aside by some sinister, modern-day Dr. Frankenstein.

But wait! One of the corpses is coming to life! Stirring from its grave, it drops one leg on the deck - twists it's body - then the other leg, and rises to walk the earth one final time. It lumbers out of the compartment, cold arms steadying it against faltering in a bouncing world. It moves toward me, eyes hollow and unseeing. The corpse yawns. Is it angry because of being woken up from eternal sleep? Will it go berserk and wreck the galley? No, instead the corpse opens its arms wide - yawns again - then scratches its blond beard. The corpse is Duffy - the Boatswain's mate.

"What schmuck didn't pay the calm weather bill?" He cracks, staring at the compartment tilting around him.

Mild grunts and a few groans - nobody's in the mood.

"You know what sounds good - a slice of cheesecake,' he presses evilly, 'with lots of gooey cherries on top."

Grayson winces and turns noticeably greener. Somebody growls that they're going to pound Duffy into gooey cherries if he doesn't shut up.

"Whatsamatter? Can't stand a little bumping around? ComSubPac ought to transfer the lot of you to rowing skiffs on the St. Lawrence River."

A few more evil looks accompanied by sounds not even remotely human. Duffy's clearly enjoying himself. Wearing a sinister grin he swaggers past me for a cup of coffee, then notices one of the tin pails strategically placed at the end of the benches. "Split-pea soup or pork and beans? Can't decide which!" He asks, staring down into it.

A chorus of moans and half-retches. My stomach does a double somersault before I can choke it back down. Time for me to get the hell out of here.

I'm heading forward when the Chief steps back into the control room and reports to the Skipper - all bilge strainers cleaned and ready to resume outboard pumping.

And not a moment too soon, as there's already thirteen inches of water in the control room bilges.

*   *   *

I wonder if I will ever be able to watch one of those Hollywood sea movies again and believe in what I'm seeing? The ones that they shoot on sound stages with a mock-up of a ship's bridge fitted on rockers. Stagehands then throw buckets of water into the actors' faces as the film rolls. Invariably, their ship is torn to shreds beneath them, with somebody always being swept overboard and saved just in time by the hero who just happens to have a long rope conveniently nearby. Naturally the sea accommodates them by calming down just long enough while the hapless victim is fished out. Roaring back with even greater ferocity as everyone stands around congratulating themselves on how lucky they are. What nonsense.

But what you never see are the real things; the bloodshot, swollen eyes with green highlights. The endless bruises accumulated from slamming into steel countless times. Grim pinched faces, the pale skin, drawn mouths, thin and gaunt bodies stooped over in exhaustion. You never experience the retching smells of vomit and men unwashed for weeks at a time, of musty mold and thick diesel oil. You never hear the endless complaints and cursing, nor the sound of men doubled-over is spasms of vomiting. If it ever was accurately portrayed the audience would probably be revolted by it. It's actual hand-to-hand combat, this man versus the sea. And man never wins, he only endures.

The bow compartment has come back to life. I catch snippets of conversation whenever the noise level allows:

"I haven't been banged around this bad since my girlfriend caught me in bed with that salesgirl from Macy's."

"You pig! Whatever happened to good taste?"

"I never thought I'd hear that question from you!"

"What did she do?"

"She slapped me! Right across the face! Had a bruise for a week. Walked around like I had a birthmark or something."

"Well, it was your own fault then."

"Hey Steele - you're Jewish right?"

"Yeah - what's it to ya?"

"Is it true what they say about Jewish guys having small peckers?"

"That's bullshit! We're just a very clean people. When you've got a foreskin, it's like walking around with half a limburger cheese."

Moans and grunts of disbelief. "Now that was revolting!"

It quiets down as the boat does a sharp barrel roll and comes up kicking and bucking like an unbroken bronco. Chainfalls bounce around. A few coughs followed by as many moans.

"You know what this is like? A trapeze - a damned circus trapeze - and we're the idiots doing the stunts."

"Well I'm ready for the intermission."

"Well - I think my crabs are gone."

"Hood - you better be kidding or the Chief's gonna have your ass!"

"*Crabs!*' Steele exclaims in panic, 'who's got crabs?"

"Why worry, we've already been at sea so long that we'd all have 'em anyway. Besides, weren't you ever taught to share?"

Steele starts moaning. "Aahhh--Crabs! Crabs! Crabs! My innocence is lost!"

Hyena-like laughter and wild cackling. They're at it like this for the rest of the night.

An entire night of gritted teeth and clenched fists. Three times during the night Waldron gets up from his bunk and wedges himself in the chair with his feet up against the small sink. He sits there shaking his head as he lights his pipe, describing the current sea conditions as nothing short of insufferable. "I've seen my share of squalls and heavy gales.' He notes with quiet reserve. 'But this takes the cake." He then informs me that the boat has begun to roll to sixty-five degree angles within the last five hours.

"A real rarity,' he avers, slashing in the air with the stem of his pipe, 'something you'll be able to tell your grandchildren about someday. If we were on a conventional surface ship, we'd be in serious trouble. Storms like these will tear them apart. I wouldn't give a dollar for the chances of that Russian freighter we ran into." The room suddenly cants at an evil angle. Waldron looks pointedly at me. "Sixty-five degrees easy." He reaches up with his free hand and adjusts the pipe in his mouth. Below me Lemert groans like a wounded animal. It's a full thirty seconds before the boat even attempts to right itself.

But it doesn't happen. Instead, the boat is slammed hard over to port. More shaking and groaning - by both man and vessel. Then the bow drops, and one of the lockers by my head bangs open, disgorging its contents in a violent clatter.

Waldron's pipe is poised in his hand as he looks down at the pile of accumulated junk with a curious expression. "Sea shrapnel." He remarks, totally serious. "Wasn't that your locker Watts?"

At this point I couldn't care less. I don't give a damn if the stuff winds up in the bilge. I stare at the glowing, naked light bulb protruding from the overhead and try to imagine myself somewhere else. A movement below me - Waldron's picking up my things. Standing up, he attempts to put them back in my locker - but the sea has other ideas. Twice he's flung against the side of my bunk hard enough to make him cry out.

"Why don't you cut the play-acting?" He says painfully, looking at me.

"Huh?"

"You're sick. It is no shame to admit, you know."

I mumble incoherently about not being sick, but obviously I'm not as good a thespian as I thought. But this has been a role I've been attempting to play twenty-four hours a day for over a week now. It's not my fault I can't stay in character for that long. It's impossible under these conditions. Not even Barrymore or Olivier could deal with this one.

"Remember Watts,' Waldron continues, propping himself back in his chair. 'Nobody's the Rock of Gibraltar."

"Except the Skipper and Pike." Lemert interjects.

"Those two are another subject entirely."

A little while later we have something to really get pissed off about. An unexpectedly heavy deluge floods the ship's air-conditioning system, pouring through the ship's supply hull valve. Then, it is scooped up in the air ducts and shoots through the whole system. As the system resembles a spider's web of pipes and ducts all over the boat, seawater cascades into every compartment. The blowers and condensers short out - both going up in flurry of sparks. The Chief and a party of bluejackets scamper aft with fire extinguishers.

The Chief's sputtering with rage. I've never seen him like this before. With glaring eyes he assembles a group of E-mates in the control room, and they split up to check the damage.

The only thing readily apparent is that the air-conditioning system is going to be on the fritz for a while.

About an hour later Michaelis turns up grim-faced and a message in hand. "Look what Swensen's picked up."

Turns out it's a *SOS* from the Russian freighter. "Cargo hatches stove in. Bulkheads giving way. Steering lost. Abandoning ship." The message continues, giving the coordinates but what's the use? We're too far away. And even if we could make it to them the chances of pulling the survivors from these insane waves would be next to impossible.

"In this sea they won't last ten minutes,' Michaelis winces, 'the waves will turn those lifeboats into flotsam in no time." Shaking his head he disappears aft without another word.

Even Pike is empathetic. "Poor bastards!"

So, Waldron's gloomy prediction was right after all.

Next morning. The calendar says Sunday, a day of peace - only not for us. I go up onto the bridge with the Skipper and the First Watch. Complete mayhem greets me. Waves towering at fifty and sixty foot heights. Visibility zero. The boat is pummeled from all sides. You never see the deck - before it can climb out from under the great monsters, yet more wait in ranks behind to push it back down again.

Yet, the sea shall not have us. We will beat her by enduring her. As she lashes out with icy fists of foam, we will laugh in her face and openly show contempt - she will not break us down. We will live and we will breathe the precious air that ekes through the salty mists that leap toward us. We will spit in her, and throw up a balled fist when the liquid lances arc over the bridge. We will keep a keen watch despite our pitiful, burning eyes, and hang on with our wretched, prune-like hands. We will pull our salt-encrusted legs from the sucking vortex inside the flooded bridge. We will lean forward and take all the force she has to throw. We will become maniacs and learn to love every minute spent on the bridge. A powerful - yet damning - love that no one but a seaman understands. We will take all she has to give, and lunge back at her with our steel, knife-edged prow...

No, the sea shall not have us.

Later, both Pike and I are crumpled on the control room floor trying to regain our breath from a stint topside when a string of invectives comes down from the tower. McGowan - on the helm - is having a vile time trying to hold the boat on course. We're taking the sea across the beam, which in these savage waves is impossible to steer against.

"Which way?"

"To starboard sir!"

The Skipper comes up with a solution. "Alter course ten degrees to port! Steer three five-five!"

"Aye-aye sir!"

Turning into the waves and taking them head on can counter the swinging action. But unfortunately, it doesn't affect our violent pitching in the slightest. So, we're heading three five-five instead of zero one zero; it's the biggest excitement of the day.

Schumacher appears, sauntering through nonchalantly and making a crack about the "garbage being left on the control room floor." It doesn't take a genius to figure out whom he's talking about. Ignoring the thinly veiled insult, I wearily stagger to my feet. I have to go back aft now and to lie out my wet things. I move haltingly, like a drunken man.

"You know, it's funny,' the Skipper comments, leaning against the gyrocompass repeater with his ever-present cup of coffee in hand. "I've noticed it in every storm I've ever been in. When a boat starts to roll - really roll - every man reverts back to toddler hood in the way they move around. Really strange."

Thanks to our drowned air-conditioning unit, mold and mildew are fast becoming public enemy number one. It's amazing how fast it goes to work when there's no air circulating and the walls drip with condensation. The vile fungus has already taken hold on my leather shaving kit that I keep stashed in my locker. Large, widening swaths of it sully the cowhide in half-dozen different places. It eats into our boots, even as we wear them. Jonesy has to keep all the provisions locked safely away in the hold lest they become soiled and rotten. One of Waldron's shirts has been eaten clean through. We are powerless against it.

The deck plates though, are the real danger, as condensate not only forms on them but also runs down from the walls and collects in slippery pools. The floor in the control room is like an ice-skating rink. It's a lethal weapon. The bilge pumps have to run non-stop just to keep up with it.

Soon the slick deck plates claim their first casualty. Duffy, in the process of going on watch, slips and almost puts an eye out smacking into the 225lb-blow manifold. Gives him one hell of a black eye, a real shiner. Again Kemper has to come forward to have a look. "From now on, hang on!" He remonstrates, tosses him an ice pack as he disappears aft. Copenhaver cracks Duffy 'looks like he's run afoul of the complaint department in a bawdyhouse." An undaunted Duffy merely flashes his omnipresent smirk and disappears up into the tower.

A little while later its Reece's turn. Caught in between the bulkheads during a sharp roll, he loses his footing and goes down - straddling the coaming. By the time Kemper gets to him Reece is curled up in a ball on the floor, legs drawn up and hands folded over his crotch. His face looks like he's just bitten into a sour lemon. Copenhaver of course, makes hay with this one too. He plants himself in the control room and announces that once Reece finds his voice he'll be a soprano and a little less well endowed.

Silence follows. Nobody takes up the banter. Everyone's too exhausted, too sick, too worn out, to care.

"PERMISSION TO COME UP!"

I scream so loud that my lungs nearly burst. An oilskin-clad figure hunched under the bulwark glances in my direction. The figure moves. It's so dark - can't tell who it is. Can't hear anything - howling wind, crashing waves. Sounds like we're next to a mammoth waterfall. The figure's movement becomes more violent - finally I recognize an arm frantically pumping up and down. Hoarse strains of a voice: "SHUT THE HATCH!"

I struggle upward, but the slick ladder rungs and ankle-deep water in the bridge make it impossible to get a firm grip on anything. Instead I squirm out like a worm - on all fours - pushing off with my legs. A shout above me - what?

"AFT! HANG ONNNNN!"

Since I'm not belted in! I panic and scramble for a handhold. The water in front of my nose begins to recede. I hear a roaring sound; it's getting louder. A stooped figure above me with clenched teeth. A hand reaches out and latches onto my wrist. The roaring is all around me now. Then I'm hurled violently into the bulwark, taking full force of the blow on my left side. All at once I'm on my back, staring upward into ghostly figures without faces. More screaming, some of it not human. Darkness all around.

Where am I - in the sea? My open eyes see tall steel stalks that vanish into the mist. They weave this way and then that - the periscope shears. The blow drives the wind from me. Something grabs me by the neck and yanks hard. Am I now to be choked to death? The force is pulling me, away from the dripping steel skirt that surrounds the scopes.

Another surge rushes in and everything goes quiet - I'm underwater. *Push yourself up!* My left arm won't work - it's numb. Is it still there? Then push up with your right. Push! That's it damnit! Push! A force yanks my head up - into the air. I gulp the salty mists as deeply as my lungs will allow. Something grabs at my waist and pulls hard - the safety belt - they're after the safety belt. Then I'm being pulled to my feet. A body leans close - it's Michaelis.

" WHAT THE HELL ARE YOU DOING?"

I cough and gag. I can't speak. My stomach constricts violently; I've swallowed a lot of seawater. Draping my right arm over the bulwark, I expunge the foreign contents into the swirling foam that pulls at our ankles. The bridge now climbs skyward, water pouring out of the scuppers and open back like the gates on an open dam. It rises - like a runaway elevator gone berserk - seemingly hundreds of feet in the air until it remains poised for a brief second. Then, the deck cants obscenely forward and we shoot downward into the trough. The boat pancakes, shudders and groans, then repeats the entire process for the thousandth time.

A slap on the shoulder - Michaelis's yelling something. Even though he's six inches from my face I still can't hear him.

"WHAT?"

"YOU OKAY?"

I hastily nod and give a 'thumbs-up.' And I'm halfway telling the truth this time. As long as I can keep my vomiting under control, it's not so bad. Is it possible that I'm becoming used to this? The severe beating all of us are taking up here is horrific, but I bear the sea no malice. For the very reason I came up here was to get my mind off the morbid thoughts of a little while ago. And it has worked, albeit with a few bumps and bruises. I devote all my energies to hanging on, ducking at the appropriate moments, and singing out when heavy ones roll in. I'm learning that this - just like anything else - can be borne.

The secret, I believe, is hardening yourself so that you refuse to be beaten. No matter how many times a breaker punches you in the face. No matter how many times the sucking vortex tries to wrench you into the sea. No matter how painful the bruises on your body or the salt searing your eyes. "I WILL BEAT YOU GODDAMNIT! YOU CAN'T BREAK ME!"

I feel Michaelis staring at me. "WHAT?"

I shake my head, still grinning like a madman.

There is one important change in the last twenty-four hours. The cloud cover is beginning to break up. Instead of one long, unbroken, low-hanging plain of blackish-gray, now patches of blue can be seen. Nor are the clouds as dark anymore. And the wind no longer feels like it comes out of a high-pressure air manifold. It's still strong - but intermittent - and froths the tops of the waves when it gusts, but the overall meaning is that there is light at the end of the tunnel. Though no weather expert, I know enough that it signals the end of the front. At some point within the next few days, we should be coming out of this.

Each time the foreship smashes through one of these gray-green titans, an ear-splitting explosion follows. The wave, gouged open by the fourteen hundred and fifty tons of black steel plowing through it, continues moving forward to close up its wound. Then the width of the deck causes the whole wave to collapse, and the deafening blast that results sounds like an artillery shell cooking off. It's enough to make you want to cover your ears.

This cruel sea invades everything: our feelings, our bodies, our minds, even our senses.

My skin has been rubbed raw by the stiff oilskins, and exposed to the flailing seawater for so long that large, painful pustules have erupted underneath my arms, on the back of my neck, and on the inside of my thighs - everywhere the oilskins chafed my flesh raw. The side of my face is sore where I smashed into the deck with it the other day, my eyes burn so bad they water constantly, and the inside of my mouth feels like it's caked with salt. And on my hands, a kind of eczema has begun. The skin is cracked and peeling, it comes off in strips. Kemper had a look and gave me a kind of ointment for it, explaining that sometimes flesh - when exposed to saltwater for long periods - will react this way. He says it usually doesn't last long and to keep the salve on it at all times. I hope he's right, as the 'molting' jokes have already begun. I'm not the only one affected though; most of the men who have a bridge watch have come down with similar skin inflammations.

Like some parasitic bacteria, the sea continues to eat away at us.

A little while later my stomach's rumbling with hunger, so I get up to see what I can scrounge in the galley. I come upon the XO's form bent over a chart laid out on the control room plotting table. It's grids, lines, and markings are not unlike those on his other charts, but yet this one is different. Much different. At the top right-hand corner a coastline juts deeply out into the sea. Across the landmass, in curving bold and black letters is printed: **Honshu - Southern Japan**.

His brow creased in concentration, and alternately clenching a pencil in his teeth as he moves his dividers, protractor, and straight edge around atop the chart. It's fascinating to watch him, he's so into it: his body goes taut, a deep "V" appears in the middle of his forehead, his eyes become mere slits, and little beads of sweat break out on his brow. The thought power is astounding. Somebody said the Skipper's convinced he's a mathematical genius. I wouldn't doubt it for a minute.

The XO picks up his compass, and settles it on one of the pencil lines he has drawn. With a frown, he flips the adjusting screw a few turns until the angle between the legs widens. Now a blank look comes over his face as he pencils in a small curving line with the penciled end of the compass. Finished, he sets the compass aside and takes up his protractor. He measures a moment, then picks up his straight edge and connects the lines with a pencil.

"Where are we sir?" I venture after what seems like an appropriate pause.

The XO remains quiet for almost a full minute. He doesn't look like he's heard me at all. His chart is the epitome of distraction for him. Then slowly he raises his head and straightens his bent frame. He taps his pencil on the marking he placed on the chart. "We're just less than three hundred nautical miles from the Japanese coast."

"How close are we going in?"

"That's up to Tyreen.' He states without looking at me. Bending down over the chart he is once again in another world.

Anyone who speaks of the 'silent sea' should sit for a mere hour on a hydrophone. This would cure them quickly of such ill-conceived notions. Duffy's in the conning tower fiddling with his sound gear. "It's really fascinating what you hear sometimes.' He tells me. "It's a lot like being out in the country."

"What do you hear?"

He shrugs while cocking his head to keep his earpiece balanced over his ear. "Well, you hear whales whenever they're around. It's kind of a lonely moaning sound. Sometimes a clicking, really depends upon what type of whales they are. Sometimes you pick up real eerie stuff you can't make heads or tails out of. Right now, since the sea's running so high, you hear a sound like steaks barbecuing on a grill - that's what a heavy sea sounds like down here. Here,' he turns back to the hydrophone controls and flicks a switch. The small speaker at the bottom of the unit crackles and suddenly the conning tower if filled with a peculiar *sizzling* sound.

I grunt. "Who would think something sounding so innocent could beat the living hell out of you?"

Duffy grins. "Uh-huh."

The Boatswain's mate turns a few dials, then fiddles with the gain. The sizzling sound immediately fades into the background, and a *swishing* sound can be heard. Duffy looks a little surprised and grins.

"What's that?"

"Probably a school of fish, swimming over the foredeck."

The sound abruptly fades.

For a full hour we play with the set. Duffy instructs me in the uses, advantages, and limitations of the hydrophone. But mostly we sit quietly and listen to the sea around us. I can't help but think what sort of creatures make these intonations that come to us out of the dark depths. Do we know every creature that inhabits this cold, still world? Or are there great leviathans yet undiscovered? The sea is as alive as the countryside on land. You just have to listen, and entire new worlds open up.

Submariners are fortunate. We sail into a different world. Even the hydrophone operator on a destroyer cannot hear everything that we do since he's riveted to the surface. The thermoclines that shroud and shelter us like a protective blanket from a prowling destroyer's echo ranging filter out and mask sound that he can't hear. These cold, still depths afford us peace when sixty-foot seas rage on the surface. What a shame we couldn't have a porthole to look out and see this world as it travels by. Yet all is not wonderful and safe, the sea is notoriously unforgiving.

Duffy suddenly stiffens and plays with the hydrophone's gain. He twists it this way, then that. A strange, rapid, clicking sound becomes louder and louder. He stares into space a moment, his lips parted. The clicking is becoming faster. He looks at me as his mouth breaks into a smile.

"Shrimp."

BOOK IV:

Above us, Hell.....

A canting bridge. Foaming and swirling water. Roar of waves. Waldron - the epitome of a seaman - easily discernible by his pipe jutting out from under his sou'wester-capped head. Move out of the way so Hood and Reece can get by. After they disappear down the hatch, Waldron remains, briefing Pike by shouting into his ear. They might as well be whispering - can't hear a word of it. Quick now! Belt yourself in! A forty foot mastodon will tear you out of here as easily as any sixty-footer could.

The horizon has blown itself clear. The sky is the most brilliant robin's egg blue. Not a cloud to be seen. However, the sunshine is harsh and blinding. Our eyes have become accustomed to our dark cavern-like dwelling. Like a group of perpetual nocturnal vampires, we're not prepared for such natural light.

The wind blows in strong gusts - the remnant of the Herculean gale-force that blew at the height of the typhoon. It blows across our starboard beam, causing the boat to loll, waggle, and pitch wildly as it dips down into the deep troughs of the waves. The damned stiff oilskins are already chafing away at the scabs on the back of my neck. Pretty soon the skin back there will be rubbed raw again, and all the time spent applying Kemper's salve will have been in vain. The area tingles already. Shortly it will begin to burn like fire as the salt finds its way into the wound.

The sea - a dark, dingy gray during the storm - now reflects a greenish blue under the dazzling sun. In places where the sun catches it just right, the frenzied water sparkles like glittering jewels upon a field of green felt. Pretty as it is, it isn't easy to look at because the brightness feels like it's burning your retinas.

Pike thumps me on the arm to get my attention and motions toward our plunging bow. I detect a grin on his face through his fuzzy beard. It takes a moment to figure out what he's pointing at. Then the bow rises up over a large wave and I see it - a bright, thick rainbow arcing over our prow. The variegated band is bursting with a plethora of colors. It hangs in the air, moving with the prow as if bolted to the steel plating. It seems to wink at us, vanishing every time the bow bites deep into a wave and reappearing as it struggles back up into the waterlogged air. Inwardly I smile - rainbows, one of the lost wonders of childhood innocence.

"PORT SIDE ABEAM!" Pike yells, ducking at the same time.

Dripping heads bowed. Burning eyes shut tight. Salt-caked lips firmly closed. Breath held. Aching muscles flexed and rigid. Queasy stomachs rumbling - this eternal combat with the sea is becoming a way of life for us.

I'm finding it harder to believe that I was ever a creature of the land.

The sound of the klaxon bolts me fully awake. Frantic yelling from the control room. "Dive! Take her down for Christ's sake!' Michaelis frantically yells, '*Take her deep*!'

Slamming of vent levers. The main hatch clangs shut. Squeal of valves being closed. More grunts and curses.

"Rig for silent running! Rig for depth charge!'

I hit floor right behind Waldron. Just as we're coming out into the passageway, the Skipper's curtain is ripped back as he bolts into the passage, his open shirt fluttering as he moves. "What -?' but then is cut off in mid-sentence by a tremendous explosion. The angling floor tremors violently as the three of us are flung around in the passageway like rag dolls: I smash into the petty officer's partition with such force it knocks the wind from me.

Waldron lets out a surprised-sounding groan, and I look over at him to see him groping for his pipe, which has been knocked out of his mouth and lies on the floor. The angle of the floor is getting steeper and steeper by the second.

"Jesus,' the Skipper hisses, trying to pull himself to his feet, '- what the hell are they doing?"

Crack - Whamm! Crack - Whamm!

The Skipper's up and twirling the sealing handle of the watertight door that leads to the control room. He gets it open, but now the angle of the dive is so bad that we have to climb uphill to get over the hatch coaming.

"Get her nose up!' the Skipper bellows frantically, staggering to gain footing, 'Fifteen degree up-angle on bow planes NOW!"

More detonations - a rolling cavalcade of giant sledgehammers. The lights flicker, and for a fleeting instant it's as still as death in the boat. Suddenly I feel all alone, the only man alive in this three hundred-foot long sewer pipe. It is as if everyone else has vanished without a trace. Then somebody utters a vulgar oath, and the specter is shattered with all the force of a brick through a plate-glass window.

"I said get her nose up goddamnit!" The Skipper snarls as I snake over the hatch coaming and into the control room. I'm the last one. Wainwright pulls the hatch shut behind me and dogs it down. It's dark in here, only a few naked light bulbs to cut through the darkness. The Skipper's moving deliberately toward Duffy at the planesmen's station. Duffy's standing up, holding the control wheel in both hands and hauling back on it - like he's trying to pull it free of the wall. "Bow planes are jammed sir!" Duffy cries.

"Boat out of control!" Lemert shrieks, standing there in his dripping oilskins.

In the blink of an eye the Skipper has his hands on the planes' wheel. Duffy jumps back out of the way. The Skipper throws his whole body into it - but it's no use, the bow planes don't move an inch. Then burly Daschler gets into the act, but even his gorilla-like strength isn't enough to budge them.

"All stop!' the Skipper roars, 'All back full!" He's staring at the depth gauge in the middle of the console. The needle rapidly approaches four hundred feet.

"Three hundred fifty.... Sixty.... Three hundred seventy,' Lemert, standing behind Duffy and Daschler reports frenziedly, his voice climbing a few octaves, 'Approaching four hundred!"

The viscid fluid in my veins freezes: *we've got a problem.*

The Skipper half-turns toward me. The look of alarm on his face is the same one that grips my insides in a steel vise. Instinct takes over; we must cut the boat's speed and get the bow up. Otherwise, we'll dive too deep eventually implode.

Another explosion kicks our stern is kicked violently over to port. Thirty-degree roll at least. The Skipper is flung into the diving controls with a heavy crash. "Blow negative!' He croaks through a face heavily contorted in pain, 'Blow!"

Wild hissing of high-pressure air; *they're going to hear that.*

And they do - three more gut-wrenching detonations in a span of mere seconds. In front of me Lemert pants like a wild animal, the knuckles of his left hand - clutched around the ladder leading into the tower - have gone white. His shoulders rise and fall with a rhythmic constancy.

Daschler grunts, groans, and sputters curses, trying to bring the bow plane wheel back around: teeth gritted and eyes bulging - looks like he's having some sort of seizure. His groans turn into an animalistic roar.

We stare at the depth gauge between the plane controls as if it held the key to everlasting life. The needle passes the four hundred fifty-foot mark and is coming up on five hundred. We're like a runaway freight train - no brakes, we can't stop. Even if the boat were light overall the simple kinetic energy of our downward motion is enough to keep us sinking like a stone.

The needle passes five hundred. Lemert's breathing heavier now. His lips quiver briefly. "Boat out of control! We can't stop her! BLOW ALL TANKS!"

The Skipper's head swivels around a full ninety degrees. "Belay that! Lemert you're relieved! Waldron take over!"

"Aye sir." Waldron says, stepping up to the controls.

"Blow bow buoyancy!' the Skipper roars, his eyes back on the depth gauge, 'All back emergency! Secure from depth charge! Every other man to the aft torpedo room, *now* - move!' Turning away to head aft I note the needle of the depth gauge is already moving toward six hundred feet. As if on cue a hair-raising shudder runs through the length of the boat. From somewhere comes creaking and groaning. Then a metallic popping noise followed by a sudden shriek - like fingernails on a chalkboard. An icy hand runs down my spine: *Electric Boat guarantees only three hundred feet.*

Like Damocles' sword it hangs over our heads.

Garnett's twirling his U-wrench on the high-pressure air manifold like a mad baker whipping cake batter, admitting high-pressure air into the bow buoyancy tank. If any air escapes it will rise and create a giant mushroom-like bubble as it expands on its way to the surface. Our tormentor will easily see the immense globule on the surface. And into this boiling spume he will lay his pattern of charges. It can't be helped. Unless we halt our descent the sea will surely kill us. The pressure hull is voicing its protest. We can take our chances with the depth charges, but not with the sea; with the sea there is no margin for error.

A few alarmed reports: some flanges, packings, and valves giving way to the outside pressure. Bluejackets scramble about with wrenches and ratchets to make things fast and try to stem the flow of water. The hull continues to moan in pain.

The Chief stands at the bulkhead which leads into the crew's mess, his face contorted in a grimace - frantically hustling everyone aft. "C'mon boys -' he snaps is a gruff whisper, 'move! Pick up the pace! Let's go!"

Getting aft isn't easy. It's an uphill climb. The deck is canted at a slippery forty-five to fifty degrees. Everything loose tumbles forward. Men slip, fall, and curse. We must be as quiet as mice.

A terrific roar shoves the boat hard over to starboard. Lemert winds up on the deck and I'm flung into the metal door of the crew's head with a resounding crash.

"For the love of God,' the Chief spits hoarsely, 'Q*uiet*!"

Two more blasts followed by a third. Tojo must have spotted the froth from the venting bow buoyancy tank.

Two exhausting hours later we've managed to give Tojo the slip. You don't have to be an expert to figure out it was by a slim margin. The Skipper's livid; now the Japanese are fully alerted to our presence. There's a real scene in the control room as the Skipper hauls Michaelis up before him demanding an explanation. He grills the communications officer with a vengeance, but it apparently it wasn't Michaelis's fault. The Japanese destroyer "Came steaming straight out of a fog bank with a bone in his teeth.' Michaelis explains wide-eyed, trying to placate the Skipper. "We couldn't see it over the wave tops - at least not until he was almost right on top of us."

The understanding Skipper dismisses him still grumbling. "Of all the shitty luck! Every Jap with access to a *sampan* is going to be out looking for us now! This is going to bring every destroyer in the Bungo Suido area down on our necks!"

But it is Lemert however, who must explain his loss of nerve.

My heart goes out to him; the downcast aura on his face, the knowledge that his error could have been fatal, his inability to look the Skipper in the eye reminds me of a kicked puppy.

The Skipper orders Lemert to the wardroom. So whatever's going to happen will happen in private. Waldron attempts to head the Skipper off. "Sir - if I may - it isn't the worst thing -' he says under his breath, trying to maintain a quiet urgency as the Skipper head forward for his *tete a' tete*, '- it's a mistake any of us could have made."

"Waldron, we are on very dangerous ground here. Everything we do is by the slimmest of margins. You know we must control ourselves. We must master our fears, not the other way around. If you can't control your nerve, what good is a man like that to have aboard? I won't have any of my boys making this boat their tomb. If he can't handle the stress, he doesn't belong here. You do understand that?"

"Of course sir."

"Lemert, you doing all right?" I ask, sitting down on the edge of his bunk.

He barely glances at me. "Leave me alone."

"You don't -'

"Something wrong with your hearing?"

At that moment Waldron comes in and looks at us. "Well?"

I shrug helplessly. Waldron takes the cue, and - pulling his little wooden chair over - sits down next to Lemert's bunk. He takes his cap off and holds his pipe nimbly in his right hand. "Lemert, I'm going to talk and you're going to listen. I'm talking to you now not as your superior officer but as your friend. Okay, you screwed up! But are you going to be a baby about this and let it ruin you or are you going to take it and learn from it. Do you want to cave in, throw away everything you've learned - waste it all - over a momentary loss of nerve? It isn't good - but it is understandable. Enduring a rain of high explosive isn't easy for any man. Every man has his breaking point. It isn't easy for me either. You don't think my knuckles turn white and my teeth chatter? I think about running sometimes. It's human. We're not machines. This is your second patrol. I've had more time in the boats than you. I've seen many come and go. Now if you'll get your head out of your ass and quit getting in your own way, you have the makings of a fine submarine officer. But that's up to you. You make the decision either to let this ruin you, or learn from it and become better for it. If you walk away, you let us all down. And that's being yellow. I know you pretty well now Billy, and one thing I don't think you are is yellow. You think about that." He gets up, puts his cap on - reinserts his pipe between his teeth - and goes out.

I fish a pack of cigarettes out of my pocket. Placing one between my lips, I then hold the pack out to Lemert. Glancing at it, slowly his right hand comes up to take one; it's a good omen.

Another round goes to the Imperial Japanese. Thanks to our unreliable torpedoes, a large factory ship is able to stay in service of Emperor Hirohito. Early this morning, a three-hour tracking party plots a faultless solution only to have one torpedo explode prematurely and the engine simply quit on another. This is a hair-raising experience as the sinking torpedo is now lethal only to us; it literally becomes a depth charge as it falls into the depths, as the surrounding water pressure will crush the warhead.

"BureauOrd's gonna blame it on us!" The XO points out later during a roundtable in the control room with the officers. "They'll just say we don't know how to shoot!"

"Bullshit!" The Skipper fires back. "Pike; go back over them again."

"Yes sir."

An hour later he's back, sweating like a pig and covered in grease.

"Well?" Our Ahab asks expectantly over his omnipresent cup of coffee.

The Torpedo & Gunnery Officer wipes a grimy hand across his forehead. "According to the manuals and my own practical experience, everything checks out. I can't find any mechanical reason why these fish aren't performing. It's the screwiest thing I've ever seen."

Schumacher clears his throat. "This is smart - go charging into the Bungo Strait with dud torpedoes? By anybody's measure that comes real close to committing suicide."

"Sir - ' the XO begins, ' - we should question whether it's an intelligent idea going into the Straits at all. We'll be putting ourselves at great risk without any means of attack or self-defense."

'We've still got the deck gun!" Pike protests.

The XO looks like he's just bitten into a sour lemon. "Don't tell me you're that stupid!"

"Sir, ' Pike fumbles with his greasy fingers for a cigarette, 'I may have a way out of this." He stands there blinking at the Skipper.

"Anytime Pike, I'm in for the duration."

"With your permission, I will disconnect the Mark VI magnetic exploder and reset all exploders for contact detonation."

The XO guffaws. "That's a court-martial offense. BureauOrd will put all our asses in a sling!"

Pike nods. "Maybe, but if you have a better idea Mr. Bainbridge, my ears are wide open."

"I'd say it's worth a try." Waldron pipes in.

"What else is there?" Schumacher adds.

The Skipper shakes his head. "I don't see any other alternative. I will log it that it was done on my authority. Proceed Pike."

"Yes sir."

       *   *   *

Running submerged for the past three hours. The surface is lousy with little Japanese fishing smacks called *sampans*. Hardly more than fifty feet in length, these small, wooden Chinese Junk-style vessels act as picket boats for the Japanese Navy. The Skipper gives them a wide berth, for they would sound the alarm to the nearest military authorities if we allowed ourselves to be seen.

Thoroughly bored, I hang around the control room with little to do. Despite the monotony my stomach flutters with excitement: by the XO's last calculations we are no more than a dozen miles outside the Bungo Strait. Even though the Japs must know that there is an enemy submarine operating in the area, they don't know where we are now. And the Skipper said he wants to be well inside the Strait before making any more attacks.

After a while of staring mindlessly at the diving controls and the backs of the planesmen, I notice our speed has been cut considerably, until we're barely moving at a crawl.

"What gives?" I ask Waldron, pointing to the speed indicator over the heads of the planesmen.

"Have to wait for an escort." He says simply, shifting his pipe to one corner of his mouth.

"What d'you mean - escort?"

"Into the Strait. Minefields."

Christ! It never even occurred to me.

"Any good sized ship will do,' he continues, ' just has to have a deeper draft than one of these damn fishing smacks."

"How long do we wait?"

"As long as we need to."

Three and a half-hours, innumerable cups of coffee and cigarettes later, Duffy picks up heavy screw beats over the hydrophone. "Single screw. Reciprocating machinery,' he reports, ' bearing two nine six."

"Shit!' I hear the XO spit, 'He's going the wrong way!"

At two nine six - which puts him coming out of the Strait instead of going in - just the opposite of what we need. A movement behind me - the Skipper's already at the ladder climbing up into the tower. Beside me, Waldron sighs. "This could take awhile."

It's the understatement of the year.

Above I hear the whining periscope motor. A moment of silence, then "It's an ocean going tug,' the Skipper reports, 'Heading north, shit! Down scope!"

"Can't these lousy Japs just make it easy for once?' Pike sighs.

"What d'you think?" The XO wants to know.

"It'll be dark in a few hours,' the Skipper declares, ' if nothing else comes along we'll get on the tail of one of these fishing smacks."

"At the front door without a key!" The Gunner's mate snorts sarcastically.

"The whore's lying down, all spread and ready and we're still at half-mast!" Copenhaver chimes in, looking uncharacteristically grim.

"Gentlemen,' Waldron instructs, grinning like a Cheshire cat, 'we've got to put on our raincoat before the fun begins!"

We all stare at him stunned.

Loud clatter in front of me - I'm jolted awake. Rumbling of diesels aft. Diesels! - *We must be on the surface!* I shake myself; I fell asleep here under the ladder. I struggle to my feet. Schumacher's standing beside me - where did he come from? He's usually aft. He's absolutely filthy- drenched in sweat, grease all over him and his face is blackened with diesel exhaust. He looks at me blankly a moment, as if seeing me for the first time. Abruptly he swivels his head toward the tower. "Yes sir!" Then without another word disappears aft.

I look around in a daze.

"Hey Watts - break out your Michelin guide, we're in!' Michaelis says to me from in front of the diving station. "That tug circled around and came back. We fell in right behind him. Welcome to the Bungo Strait." He's grinning from ear to ear.

I blink. "We're in?"

He nods. "About an hour - square on that tug's ass!"

I shake the last bits of sleep from my eyes and grab a pair of 7x50's off the hook. "Permission to come up?"

"Granted!"

I stumble out into pitch-blackness and bump into the periscope shears. Only when my eyes adjust can the faint pinpricks of starlight be discerned. There's not much moonlight; high broken clouds shroud it like an enormous mantilla. Only a dull, eerie glow pokes brokenly out from around the vapor masses. The sea is equally black, looking like a vast pelt of wrinkled shale, with lips and curls of white where the water has been disturbed by steel vessels.

Straight ahead, about dead center of the bow, is a triangular formation of lights - the Japanese tug. Using the glasses, I can just make out his squat shape and rounded stern where there is Japanese writing. A light up in his superstructure fades in and out from time to time, probably from someone walking around in front of it. The plume of smoke emanating out of his fat funnel is even blacker than the night. A heavy oil-soot smell; he's a coal-burner. Distance between us probably no more than twenty-five hundred yards.

Minutes pass drenched in silence. Nobody seems to feel the need to talk. Anything said comes in clipped whispers, as if our naked voices alone could give us away hemmed in as we are by the enemy's mainland. It's an eerie feeling, different than anything I've felt before. The enemy now surrounds us on three sides. There's only one way out. No entire ocean to maneuver in. Here we are boxed in, not an unknown sensation for submariners but now different. Once the enemy knows we're here, all they would have to do is blockade the mouth of the Strait with destroyers, and it doesn't take a genius to figure out what happens then.

"How far is it back to Pearl?"

"Hmm?" Waldron seems startled a moment by my question. Lowering his glasses he takes his pipe out of his mouth and stares at me. "Over two thousand miles. Why?"

I shrug. "Curious."

"Getting spooked?"

"Yeah." My candor surprises even me.

"Relax Watts, nobody dies on this boat without Tyreen's permission, and that's *very* hard to get."

"I just hope *the Japs* know that sir."

Waldron smiles reassuringly and pats my shoulder.

A while later, as I'm going below to purloin some coffee and a Danish, Lichty lets out a yell from the radio room. "Hey - we made the big time!"

By the time I get there, already a half-dozen other crewmen have crowded around. Sticking my head through the nearest opening, I catch the melodious, seductive voice of Tokyo Rose:

"...Of the crimes they now commit against the peace loving people of Japan. The imperialistic war mongering American administration led by the Jew Franklin Roosevelt has sent this submarine to our home waters, and yesterday it made an unprovoked attack on a defenseless merchant ship, belonging to our beloved Emperor Hirohito. The attack I'm happy to report, was an abysmal failure. Americans come to sink ships in Japan with faulty torpedoes. Americans only play at war. They should at least make sure their weapons are up to the task of waging war on the world. The Emperor's Naval Forces at this time are running down the American submarine and it will be sunk shortly. And if his Majesty's forces capture any of these sick Americans, I can assure you they will publicly be hanged as pirates."

"Pirates?' Copenhaver, just behind me, exclaims with a broad grin, 'Hey - I like that!"

"Stow it!' Pike scolds, 'I'm trying to listen!"

She goes on to talk of "the Japanese people rising to this fight with our swords sharp, our teeth bared, and our hearts without pity" and making innuendoes about both blacks and Jews, but I'm no longer listening.

"Jesus Christ!' the XO snorts, 'I'm gonna puke!"

Lichty flicks a switch on one of his radio sets killing the broadcast. He sits back in his chair and picks up a paperback book he has been reading. "You listen to her too much and you'll wind up with the shits!" He declares, fishing a cigarette out of his pocket and inserting it between his lips.

Heading on back into the crew's mess, I pass by the Chief, who's shaking his head from side to side, "How can an entire nation be taken in by that garbage?"

"Aww relax Chief!' Copenhaver advises. 'That's for the psychologists to figure out after we kick their ass! Isn't the first casualty of war the truth?"

For once the petty officer is making sense.

The Skipper nearly comes unglued when he finds out about the 'pirate' crack and our one way ticket to the gallows. "So we're pirates? And they're gonna hang us? I wonder if they know that those little bastards that piloted that midget sub into Pearl during the attack are sitting safe and smug back in the States, eating *American* food, sleeping on an *American* cot, smoking *American* cigarettes, reading *American* magazines, and getting off looking at *American* pin-up girls? Hell, the war's over for them and they'll have a better life as prisoners of war than we do on the line! Are we mistreating them?" He's shaking his head in disbelief.

*　　　　　　　　　　　　　*　　　　　　　　　　　　　*

Waldron suddenly lets out a yell; a shape materializing out of the gloom. In one motion he snaps his binoculars into the TBT. "Four points off the starboard bow!"

"Right twelve degrees rudder, new course three five zero. All ahead full! Station the tracking party! This guy gets the idiot award of the year!"

"Running lights!' Waldron grunts.

"They're complacent in their own backyard.' The Skipper avers 'The Nips have got to know we're in the area. Probably don't think we have the balls to enter the Strait."

"Target steady on three five zero. No signs of evasive maneuvering."

"Ship's time?"

"Zero three three four hours Sir!"

"Very well. Quartermaster, make notes for the log: at zero three thirty two hours, sighted ship of as yet undetermined size and class, though appears to be merchant. Got that?'

"Yes sir!"

"Any escorts in sight Mr. Waldron?"

"No sir."

The ship looming just over our prow keeps me spellbound. Totally incognizant of its fate, moves inexorably on to its death. Like some semi-paralyzed leviathan it remains on course with lights blazing from the masts, completely oblivious to its appointment with destiny.

"Range three two double-oh!"

The Skipper noisily clears his throat. "We shoot under twenty-five hundred."

"Target speed twelve knots Captain!' the quartermaster hollers 'Target course one four zero!"

"Very well!"

"If everything remains the way it is -' Waldron meditates, 'this should be pretty cut-and-dried."

"Don't get complacent!" The Skipper shoots back pointedly.

We close the range. The outlines of the ship ahead become clearer, bulbous bow, tall derricks, and superstructure aft - it's a tanker. She's low in the water and that couldn't be better. The ships are not half as valuable as the cargoes. It's the cargoes we're after, especially war materiel. Since Japan has to import all of her oil, a tanker makes a nice target.

A moment later the first torpedo is on its way.

The ship in front of us shows nothing that would give us the indication that we have been detected. I can now make out the deep 'V' of foam curling away from the tanker's bow as he ploughs ahead. Sometimes ignorance really is bliss.

"Time?'

'Five seconds....six - '

"Tube two - fire!"

Silently I tick off the seconds. *Three seconds.... Four.... Five seconds.... Six....*

"Tube three - fire! Time to impact on first torpedo?"

"I make it just over a minute ten seconds sir."

"Sir, sound reports all fish hot, straight, and normal!"

"Very well Mr. Harmison.' the Skipper shoots a glance over at Waldron, 'We'll see about that won't we?"

I'd look at my watch, but it's impossible to see the face in the dark. All I can do is silently pray that the fish will work. It's really strange, after the fish are shot an odd feeling of helplessness settles over you. Once all the math is done and they're sent on their way, there's nothing more we can do. It's all up to the technical wizardry inside them to do the job. Dependency upon mechanical machines; is that what war is coming to? But of course there will always have to be men behind them.

"First torpedo should be there about now sir!"

Nothing - just the stillness of the night, lapping waves and a whispering breeze. The Skipper snorts. "Time to impact on number two?"

"Ten seconds sir.... Nine.... Eight.... Seven,'

What's the use in counting? It'll probably be the same story with -

A bright red-orange flash suddenly leaps from the water into the air; brightly illuminating the tanker and the sea around it. The sound comes a split-second later, a shattering detonation with such pressure every inch of my skull feels like it's compressed inward. The giant tongue of flame does not recede, but grows even larger and begins to travel the length of the ship, setting off a chain reaction of titanic explosions in its wake. By the time the last torpedo strikes home aft, near the bridge superstructure - the ship is ablaze from stem to stern and literally disintegrates itself with every internal blast. The ship's sides actually appear to buckle outward and bend weirdly at an obscene angle. A horrendous screeching and rendering of steel.

The heat is such that sweat streams down my face. The entire area is lit up as bright as a sunny day. Voices yell - its coming from inside the conning tower. Yells, cheers - exhortations of victory. In the intense light I catch a glimpse of Waldron's face, eyes wide with horror, lips parted, face chalk white.

"JESUS H. -' the Skipper gasps, 'SHE MUST BE CARRYING GASOLINE!"

More explosions; a rain of debris begins smashing into the sea around us.

"RIGHT FULL RUDDER!' the Skipper orders frantically, 'ALL AHEAD FULL!"

The boat heels over and away from the blazing holocaust. My initial observation of the buckling hull is correct; the bent sides are blown outward with such violence that shrapnel ricochets of the sides of the bridge superstructure. So stunned am I by the scene before me, I ignore the reflex to duck. A moment later it's all over - absolutely nothing remains of the vessel, as if the Great Houdini has plucked it from view. Only a few patches of fuel floating on the water remain ablaze, their tongues licking skyward in a vain attempt to reach oxygen. But the flames' own insatiable greed is its own demise, as the fire devours what fuel there is left and the pall of smoke hanging above suffocates whatever is below. With a flicker worthy of a dying match, the flames vanish almost as quickly as they came.

Off our starboard beam, there is now nothing. Only a quiet sea.

The Skipper has really put on the speed in these last few remaining hours of darkness. He wants to get us a far away from the site of the last attack as possible before dawn, because then we will have to submerge. We are 'going into reversa', in other words turning night into day. We will sleep during the day while we stay submerged and surface at night to secure our battery charge. The Skipper detests this type of tactic since it limits our effectiveness, but due to our location it is a necessary evil. The XO's in full agreement, hastily adding that "if there's a big dog running loose in the yard, you don't try to go barreling through the front door."

Once the enemy finds out we're inside the Strait, the Skipper observes, they're going to come after us with a vengeance.

The dawn is just beginning to emerge: the horizon in the west glows a faint rouge-red, lightening the sky in that quadrant of the heavens, ironically like the Japanese "rising sun" flag. Inside the vortex, the fuzzy outlines of clouds can be seen, lazy and ill-defined set against the contrasting firmament. The sea rolls on by us, easy in its gentleness and showing a sparkle here and there where the blossoming light caresses.

Pike contorts himself into an exaggerated stretch and yawns widely. "Nothing quite like the dawn you know. It's a shame most people sleep through it.'

I nod drunkenly, surprised by his sudden candor. Pike really is totally unpredictable.

'Especially at sea,' he laments with a look toward the brightening horizon, 'Majestic and peaceful. It's all those things and more. Well,' he says through a sigh, 'I guess it's about time to pull the plug." Leaning over to the hatch, he shouts "prepare to dive!" Just as he is about to order the lookouts below, Tashtego lets out a yell: "Mastheads off port bow!"

Pike whirls around - snapping the binoculars to his eyes in one motion. "Secure the dive! Captain to the bridge!" He yells, 'Watts, give me a TBT bearing and a range!"

"Sir?" I stammer. I've never done that before.

His head snaps around. "You *heard* me Ensign! Start earning your keep! You've seen it done enough! Do it!"

"Yes sir!' Still entirely unsure of myself, I step behind the TBT - snap my binoculars into the cradle - and sight down on the little row of crosses.

The thumping of booted feet followed by the Skipper's deep voice.

Using the hash marks on the inner rim of the dial of the TBT, I rattle off the coordinates, "Targets bearing two nine zero. Range nine five three five!" I look up - Pike's pointing out over the bow with his arm. "There,' he says, 'about four and a half points to port sir."

The Skipper's glasses remain poised in the air. "Uh-huh,' is the only sound that escapes from him. I duck my head behind the TBT again, anticipating the Skipper's call for yet another marking of the coordinates.

The masts are higher now. There's no mistaking it. They are definitely higher.

"They're coming right over the hill." Pike avers a trifle surprised. 'Really pouring on the coal!"

The Skipper lowers his binoculars for the first time. "Notice anything funny about the masts Pike?"

Pike makes a face - squints - and up go the binoculars again. "Triangular shape."

The Skipper grunts. "Warships. Merchant vessels don't have that sort of rigging."

"Destroyers!"

The binoculars come down one final time. "Clear the bridge."

Duffy sits at the hydrophone controls, twisting and turning his lever and fiddling with the controls. "Heavy screw sounds bearing two nine seven,' he blinks, then moistens his thin lips with his tongue, 'Turbines - turn count twenty-five knots easy sir!"

The Skipper grunts knowingly. "See? What'd I tell you? Only warships make that kind of speed."

Two nine seven - that means he's tacking.

Harmison coughs and digs one finger in his ear. There's a book clutched in his hand, the warship recognition manual. He's staying one step ahead of the Skipper. No doubt he'll be calling for that soon.

"Screw sounds moving, now bearing three one zero." Duffy reports unemotionally.

The Skipper steps away from the scope. "Right ten degrees rudder. Steady on three zero. All ahead one-third. Up scope!"

I thumb the switch. The oily shaft rises up out of the well and the Skipper catches the business end just as it clears the deck. Rising up with it, he completes a total three hundred and sixty-degree sweep before settling on the surface contacts. He hesitates; excitement and anticipation tingle at the base of my spine.

"Stand by to go deep! Looks like two Fubuki-class destroyers up here - one stack, one turret aft, one forward,' he suddenly snaps the handles back up, 'Turning this way. Down scope! Take her deep! All ahead full!"

The deck inclines forward and a sharp increase comes in the eerie humming aft. The Skipper steps back and shifts his cap back on his head, ordering all compartments rigged for depth charge.

"They see us?" Pike asks anxiously.

The Skipper shakes his head. "Doubt it, too far away. But they're tacking again, toward us."

A few minutes tick by. Then my ears detect the first heavy propeller beats, pounding and pulsating like kettledrums. With each passing moment they grow louder. They aren't echo ranging, that's impossible at their current speed. But what if they should suddenly slow down to listen?

"Where do you suppose they're going in such a hurry?' Pike asks of no one in particular, 'You suppose the cats out of the bag?"

The Skipper looks at him in disbelief and cocks his head. "What would you think after our little fireworks show last night?"

Pike purses his lips and remains quiet. The Skipper's right; why else would the destroyers above us be pounding around?

"You see,' the Skipper continues suddenly, and I see that he means to filibuster. "What we have to do is become a sort of seagoing Nathan Bedford Forrest or John Mosby, the enemy can know we're there, we just have to stay three steps ahead of him. Like now,' he lifts his eyes upward toward the surface, 'this was an attempt at an ambush, the Nips are probably hoping we'll pick a fight with the DD's. But we're not that stupid. We'll let them sail on their merry way and wait for more vulnerable pickings later. Savvy?" Flashing a sly grin, he looks round to each one of us in turn.

I smile inwardly. Once again the Skipper puts it all in perspective. Is it any mistake that he seems to do this at the moments when nerves are stretched the tightest?

The heavy screws above begin to recede. I exhale and let every muscle in my body go slack.

"Save your strength Ensign,' the Skipper entreats, studying me with his penetrating gaze. "The real storm is yet to begin."

*   *   *

"Convoy speed?"

"Plot puts them at ten knots sir."

"That should suffice."

On the bridge. Near midnight or better. For the past two hours we've been on the surface tracking a large convoy coming down the Strait. At least eight ships by the count so far. However, there's a down side - on our flank of the convoy, the unmistakable silhouette of an escort can be discerned through the inky blackness. Moreover, there is one on the far side of the convoy; we can hear them echo ranging. Duffy's finely honed ear has picked up two different pulsating beams. And at a mere ten knots, their sets will be highly effective.

However, now that we're on the surface their sonar is not a threat to us. But they still have lookouts, and despite our low silhouette and freeboard, we're not invisible. The naked eye now becomes our worse enemy, helped as it is by the shimmering three-quarter moon hanging in the black sky. The glowing orb follows us around everywhere, like a miniature spotlight suspended from a wire at the stern. There's even a large, bulbous formation of clouds just beneath it, which reflect the moon's light and make it even brighter. If it wasn't so unnerving, it would actually be enjoyable: pastoral formations of vapor, nestled up against a glistening heavenly body, surrounded by a glittering sky dotted here and there with minute accumulations of quartz; all shining and twinkling. Romantically it's heaven sent, for two starry-eyed lovers alone together in a field or on a beach somewhere - only not here. Not now. Here we need complete darkness for our concealment, nothing less will do. Our very lives are dependent upon a dearth of light.

The Skipper though shows no signs of suffering from any unease. Unshakable and stoic, his mind concentrates instead on figures, torpedo tracks, and speeds. Despite the heavy protection, he's going in to attack.

"Plot has their tacking system worked out for sure?" The Skipper wants to know, and Waldron dips down toward the hatch, relaying the question in a hushed whisper to the quartermaster. It's funny, we're still well over a mile away from the nearest ship, yet everyone feels the need to whisper like we're creeping up to an enemy foxhole. There's no explaining it.

"Yes sir,' Waldron hisses under his breath while standing back up. "Base course is one three seven, fifteen degree tacks to starboard every thirteen and a half minutes, one five two and a half held for seventeen minutes. Then they increase speed to twelve and a half knots with a thirty-degree shift back to port to hold one two two and a half for another thirteen and a half minutes."

"When are they due for their next tack?"

"Another eight and three quarters minutes sir."

"All right. Maintain present course and speed. I'm going below to check the plot; you have the conn Mr. Waldron. Under no circumstances are you to let those ships get closer than they are right now. Clear?"

"Aye-aye sir."

The enemy column is off our port quarter. If the enemy stays on the same tacking system, and never deviates from it; i.e. never making an abrupt shift in course, increasing or reducing speed, and tacking at regular intervals, it's basically cut and dried.

"What do you think?" I ask Waldron after the Skipper has disappeared into the hatch.

He turns and grins crookedly around the stem of his unlit pipe, his white teeth showing brightly in the moonlight. "Watts take a powder! You're trigger-happy! Be patient, we'll have plenty of fireworks here in a little while."

"Aren't you worried about those destroyers?" I press.

The Lieutenant fixes me with an irritated look. "I'm concerned about them, yes, but what good's *worrying* going to do?"

A few minutes later the column of ships begins to shift; they're coming about. "Coming about", one of those antiquated sailing expressions not really fit for use on a vessel under engine power, but for some inexplicable reason, used anyway whenever a ship is tacking. Now, the hulls seem to shorten, then we stare at them bows on, and then they begin to lengthen as the maneuver to starboard is completed. Now they will begin marching across our wake.

Waldron curses under his breath. "Damn! Look at the phosphorescence of the water! We might as well be painted pink!"

It's the plankton that does it - tiny, microscopic organisms in the water that lie deep during the day and blanket the surface at night as they come up to feed. Our foaming wake is like an amalgam of seltzer water and condensed milk. How can they miss that?

"Bridge to Captain.... Convoy commencing tacking maneuver to starboard!"

I stiffen. As the column of ships comes around the other escort reveals itself; long, wide, and low-lying - it's a single stacker. Destroyers: floating platforms of death, complete with torpedoes, five-inch guns, numerous AA mounts, and of course - depth charges. Whatever maniac invented those things is a real sadist.

A guttural grumble escapes from Waldron's throat. "This might be a new experience."

"Meaning?" I press, wondering in the back of my mind whether or not ignorance really is bliss.

"*Asashio*-class. I'd bet my life on it."

Asashio-class.... Asashio-class.... I've read the manuals enough times, what did it say about them?

The Skipper reappears. Emerging out of the hatch like some suddenly uncaged animal, he quickly steps over to the bulwark and raises his binoculars. "They'll be tacking again in ten minutes,' he announces unemotionally - as if perusing a dinner menu. "That's when we'll hit them. We'll stay off their track and race in behind the starboard DD. That'll really mix it up!"

Only the sound of our thrumming diesels and breeze whisking over the bulwark disturbs the placid night. Abruptly the Skipper turns around and looks aft. "Where are the colors?"

"You mean the flag? - I had it struck sir." Waldron replies with uncharacteristic meekness.

"Why?"

"I thought the Japs might be able to spot it, so I had Harmison take it below."

"Bullshit! Get it back up here! I want these bastards to know *who's* coming at them!"

"Yes sir!"

A moment later Harmison appears on deck with the enormous flag cuddled in his arms. Affixing the flag to the hemp lanyard around the jack staff on the cigarette deck, he runs it out and steps back. As soon as he does, the strong breeze catches it and 'Old Glory' snaps out smartly and begins waving majestically in the breeze.

"Right full rudder! All ahead full! Meet her at zero zero zero!"

Our prow tears into the black water with such vehemence it feels like we might actually be lifted free from it. Ripples of white fan out from our sides in even lengths carved with mathematical precision. The zephyr coming over the bulwark blows strong and cool against the face, pungent as it is with the smell of burning coal, combusted diesel fuel, and ocean salt.

We bore in for the attack.

The Skipper stands as stalwart as a thick, wooden mast and with his binoculars fixed to his eyes. All I can see of his face is a bit of his forehead just below the brim of his worn cap. He emits not a sound, instead ceding the scene to Waldron as he calls out continuous bearings for the targets ahead from behind the TBT. This is important, the Skipper just announced that we are no longer than two minutes away from the firing point.

Three ships loom ahead of us like a single, colossal, overlapping structure, two large freighters and a transport. The Skipper wants to unleash four fish at this target alone, with the last two forward fish going after the two freighters just off to starboard. There's only one destroyer on this side of the column, and we're behind him. Luck is with us - will it hold?

The Skipper has deftly maneuvered us right into the midst of the convoy. Slowly and methodically, he has stolen up to them like a thief in the night. The convoy's ten knots being akin to a slow crawl, our surface speed is the ace-in-the-hole. On all sides of us now there are enemy ships. Before us our targets, off to starboard an enemy destroyer, somewhere out ahead of us the other destroyer.

How we stole into the convoy without being seen is a total mystery. It's a bizarre thought, but the Skipper could probably become a very successful jewel thief in civilian life. He has all the requirements - dash, daring, good looks, and savoir-faire. Does he have it in him?

"All ahead half!' the Skipper bellows, 'Stand by for final bearing and shoot!" The Skipper whirls around and bends over the hatch. "Pike! Three and a half-degrees between each fish! Understood?"

"Aye-aye sir!"

"Final bearing Mr. Waldron!" The Skipper snaps, turning back to the bridge.

"Final bearing.... One seven zero!"

Harmison pops up out of the hatch and reports, "Set!"

"Let them go!"

Waldron has just ordered tube two fired when it happens: "CONTACT OFF PORT BEAM!' Torpedoman Hood screams from the periscope shears, 'COMIN' RIGHT AT US!"

A loud roar - the guttural spine-wrenching, gut-heaving crash. A freight train screeches overhead, giant fingernails scraping an enormous chalkboard. Searing wind rips my cap off. The ocean just off to starboard erupts in an avalanche of white foam that comes cascading down onto the bridge like a sudden cloudburst.

"DESTROYER!' the Skipper bawls out, 'SECURE THE TUBES! CLEAR THE

BRIDGE! TAKE HER DOWN FAST!"

More detonations. Someone's behind me.

"MOVE IT!'

A boot kicks me in the ass so hard I almost go headfirst through the hatch. I bounce off the ladder and skid down it, the friction rubbing my forearms raw. Around me figures dash about yelling wildly and cursing. The Skipper shouts orders for the helm and the engine room. Harmison screams and somebody slams the control room hatch shut.

"What the hell happened?' Pike demands angrily and in shock.

"Tail-end Charlie!' the Skipper rages. "I should've seen it coming! Should've known it was way too easy to penetrate the screen!"

A freight train riding the rails above, each of us knows what this means. My forearms are numb with pain. I need something to hold on to. I'm lying on my back. I better roll over before...

ThrummthrishThrummthrishThrummthrishThrummthrishThrummthrish...

"Depth charges - ' Duffy spits with rising inflection - it's all he has time to get out. An iron sledgehammer smashes the boat, quickly followed by several more, meshing into an unending avalanche of rolling thunder. Both light bulbs at either end of the compartment explode, and something digs into my cheek. Harmison is thrown off his feet and slams into the attack scope housing with a sickening *crunch*, then tumbles doll-like to the floor plates. The Skipper attempts to get to the fallen quartermaster, but another string of charges catches him in mid-stride and hurls him sideways into Pike and the TDC. Curses. Moans. Sound of crunching glass. "Pharmacist's mate to the conning tower!"

I reach my hand to left cheek. It's moist and wet; could only be blood. A shard of glass must have sliced into it during the last explosions. Digging a soiled handkerchief out of my trouser pocket, I alternate between dabbing at it and holding pressure on the wound to stem the flow. It doesn't hurt yet, but sometimes wounds don't hurt until later.

"Sir,' O'Toole cries, 'Forward torpedo room reports number five torpedo running hot in the tube!"

"Shit!' the Skipper hisses.

A runaway torpedo; it's the heavy explosions that do it, jarring the boat around so severely that the torpedo's motor gets tripped and the torpedo just lays there in the tube with the engine going full blast and the screws clawing through the air. In another minute the entire bow compartment will be filled with smoke and the men in there will barely be able to breathe.

Pike's already on his feet. "Sir, going forward to assess situation!"

"Sir -' O'Toole stammers breathlessly, 'Forward engine room reports -'

The sentence is carried away in the next deluge of explosions. Like giant firecrackers, the devices go off with a ripping and mind-numbing ferocity. The boat teeters hard over to port and makes an abortive attempt to lay on its side. Papers, cigarette packs, pencils, assorted gear, and human bodies are flung around as if in the eye of a hurricane. Then - it stops as quickly as it came. Now: the horrible hissing and gurgling as the ocean pours back into the chasms created by the violent explosions.

Total darkness. A flashlight comes on and the beam searches for something above my head - the depth gauge. We must watch our depth. How far have the explosions forced us down?

"Situation forward?" The Skipper demands brusquely. Barely has the last word left his lips when there's another crack of thunder outside. Suddenly before my eyes there are a greenish-blue cascades of water shooting down from above, splattering across the floor plates. Terror seizes hold - *is this it? Has the pressure hull finally given way?* More detonations slam away close aboard, each one emitting a gush of seawater from above. I'm sitting in it now, in the span of seconds it's become several inches deep. Seawater's coming in the main hatch. It is sealed and dogged down, but the violence of the five hundred or so pounds of amatol in each charge is enough to lift it off the seat. Not only are the charges lifting up a tightly sealed hatch that weighs well over a hundred pounds by itself, but - more importantly - they are lifting up against the several hundred pounds of sea pressure pressing in on *every square inch* of that hatch.

It's enough to make your skin crawl.

Another string of high explosive close aboard. The "click" of the detonator clearly audible before the whole thing goes off. It must be a full twenty or thirty seconds before things quiet down again. Twenty seconds, thirty seconds - mere slivers of infinity, but to us a lifetime.

"Sir,' it's O'Toole again, 'Forward and after engine rooms report large amounts of water taken from main induction valve, after torpedo room reports loss of a sea-valve casting on the port side. Boat making water!"

The Skipper draws a deep breath and holds it. I can only guess at what's whirling through his mind; not only does he have to try and stay one step ahead of the destroyer's commander, but also deal with every disaster here in the boat. The pressure on him in immense. Lesser men would panic and become quivering, babbling balls of frazzled nerves. I do not envy his position.

The Skipper stumbles into something and curses. "If Pike doesn't get a lasso around that "hot" fish and hog-tie it; we've had it!"

Even here we can hear the torpedo's screws screaming in the tube. They resound through the boat, in essence turning the boat into one giant tuning fork. We all might as well just start banging away with hammers; the destroyer will pick up on it and come barreling in like a bull seeing red. And that damn main induction - is it poorly designed or some structural flaw that causes it to keep jumping from its seat every time a depth charge goes off nearby?

"Get the Chief aft to take a look,' the Skipper says methodically, pausing at every word, 'I want a damage report within the next five minutes. Lemert runs the bilge pumps only when something's cooking off. Make sure he understands this." He struggles over - splashing through the several inches deep water on the floor - to Duffy a mere half-yard away from me as somebody flicks on the emergency light. Can't see his face, the light is behind him. His cap is gone - it lasts only a moment. His right arm comes up with it clutched in his hand and shoves it back on his head. That's a good sign, he doesn't look complete without it. It's reassuring, like he's silently saying, "I am in command."

A squeaking noise. Whatever it is I want to jump on it and make it stop! *Christ - don't they realize the Japs are listening? Shut up for God's sake!* Next a metallic *clank* and I'm ready to scream. *We've got to be quiet!*

More squeaking, something on the floor begins to lift up - it's the hatch to the control room. A dark mass then emerges over the coaming - a human head. The Skipper turns away and stares at it a moment, then snaps, "Kemper - get up here! And leave that goddamned hatch open!"

"Yes sir." First his bag appears, and then the Pharmacist's mate goes through a series of weird acrobatics to get up over the hatch without making too much noise, then finally struggles free and raises himself to a kneeling position. "What happened?"

"It's Harmison - he smashed his head into the attack scope housing. He's out cold." As Kemper moves toward the prone figure lying on the deck, the Skipper turns back around. "Talk to me Duffy!"

It is only then that I notice the eerie chirping of the enemy sonar. Why did I not hear it before? It's as if the Japs knew we were there all along. He just came right up on us and started unloading his charges like he had a sixth sense.

"He's circling,' Duffy whispers warily, 'Right on top of us." A sharp, sudden intake of breath, "Speed increasing.... He's starting a run!"

"Left full rudder,' the Skipper commands, 'All ahead full!"

Out of the corner of my eye I see Duffy messing with the gain dial on his sound set. Bad sign. That means it's not long to...

An iron fist smashes me in the stomach. Then two quick simultaneous blows to the face and neck. This time the thrashing is sustained a half-minute and probably more. Every second a detonation, every moment a gut-wrenching blow to some tender part of the body. A runaway roller coaster at its worst, designed by some sadistic escapee from a lunatic asylum. Everything quivers, bends, and groans.

A pause in the storm. Heavy breathing and muffled moans - like in a bawdyhouse. But how would I know that? - I've never been in one. With a pang of amusement I realize this is what I get for listening to Daschler, Hood, Tashtego and the like spin their tales of whorehouses past.

"Christ!' the Skipper sighs with a turn of the head, 'Must be *Asashio*-class. He's using "Y"- throwers!"

"Y'-throwers" are those despicable double-barreled cannons that hurl depth charges away from a destroyer on both sides of its hull. The idea is relatively simple, yet deadly; the depth charge itself is affixed to a plate, which is in turn bolted to a shaft that is loaded into one end of the gun - one branch of the "Y" in this case. An identically set-up charge is loaded into the other branch of the "Y" and when the senior mate up there pulls the lanyard, he's got two airborne depth charges sailing into the water for the price of one firing charge. Shot high into the air, they splash into the sea at least sixty yards or more away from the mother ship. It's a seagoing mortar. Then, they act just like any regular depth charge, sinking to a pre-set depth and then exploding. The advantage herein is that the destroyer can have as many as half a dozen of these things on one side *alone*, and can idle around all day shooting these things off with impunity, creating saturation patterns like drumfire. There's no getting away from them if you're anywhere in the vicinity that these are dropped.

"Sir,' O'Toole whispers, 'Chief Schrier reports breach in sea-valve casting stemmed but not stopped. He's afraid that if he tightens it too much it might break from the stress. Thinks the bilge pumps can keep up with what's coming in."

The Skipper vents like a blast of high-pressure air. "He *thinks*? He better well goddamn know!"

I notice Kemper - hovering over Harmison - fiddling with a syringe and rolling up the unconscious man's sleeve. Squishing sounds; the Skipper's moving through the already draining water. It drains off through vents in the deck to find its way into the bilge below. He comes to a halt right next to the prone body of the quartermaster and the crouching figure of the Pharmacist's mate. "Well?"

Kemper glances up and half shrugs. "I think he might've broke his jaw -'

"Christ!"

"He's definitely out of the game for a while, and he's gonna be a real hurt pup when he comes to. We'll have to get him into his bunk."

"Sir,' O'Toole interrupts anxiously, 'Forward torpedo room reports runaway torpedo engine secured, but last depth charge explosions bounced the fish right outta' the tube."

"Anybody hurt?"

"Yes sir, part of the propeller caught Steele in the leg as the fish came out. Got a good size gash-they need Kemper up there!"

As the Skipper turns to the Pharmacist's mate, Kemper's already getting to his feet. "On my way sir,' he says, lowering himself into the open hatch, 'It's a good thing I make house calls,' he adds on a lighter note before disappearing below.

The Skipper details a few men to come up and carry Harmison below. Sadly he watches them lower the unconscious quartermaster through the hatch.

The metallic snapping of Duffy's control lever splits the quiet. I can hear his breathing too; short gasps that come in spurts - like he's hyperventilating. His head is cocked to the side, allowing me to have a glimpse of the left side of his face, upon which I can just make out the drawn wrinkles in his forehead. His chest suddenly heaves in a spasmodic motion. "Second contact bearing two one zero!"

The Skipper nods absentmindedly - almost expectantly. "That didn't take long."

So now there's *two* destroyers to worry about? Another to torment us? The Skipper's innate repose and steel-buttressed nerves defy the imagination. "Right ten degrees rudder,' he orders calmly, 'Steer three three five. All ahead slow."

I struggle to get up. Crouching here being terrified isn't going to accomplish anything. "Permission to go help Lt. Pike forward sir?"

The Skipper is fixated on the sound set and Duffy. His head seems to turn a mere eighth of an inch in my direction. "Permitted."

I'm on the tower ladder when the next salvo hits. One moment my hands feel the clammy rungs that are just beginning to moisten with condensation, then they're completely wrenched free - my body is poised for a brief second in space until I come down hard, smashing into the plotting table. My left side sears with pain, blood spurts from my cheek. The detonations continue, not in neat separate concussions, but in one long, endless howl.

Hoarse shouts around me. I snatch a quick glance to my left and see Lemert hovering over the open grate that leads to the pump room. His mouth is wide open and his face is contorted in anger. He's kept a real low profile since his attack of panic. What will happen this time - will he crack? Will I? Will any of us?

I have to move to the side to get around the XO, who's cursing a blue streak and is down on all fours picking up papers and charts that have scattered across the floor. One end of a chart has become lodged in between two deck plates. He tugs at it and it subsequently rips. Screwing up his face in a look of disgust, he tosses the chart to one side and continues laboring to get at this little corner of paper. I gape at him; with all this going on around us and he's worried about this little piece of paper? If we sink it'll rot away just like us, turning a fluid green and peeling off layer by layer like putrefying flesh? We all have our modes of distraction but this seems ludicrous.

To my right Copenhaver's minding the high-pressure air manifold. His stance is that of a catcher in a baseball game. The only thing he's missing is a glove, facemask, and cap turned back-to-front. He has one arm crooked around the shiny brass pipes and in his hand he holds his tobacco pouch. With the other he kneads a plug of chew. He appears thoroughly in control; maybe a little irritated from the massive frown on his face. His fancily waxed mustache and goatee glow weirdly in the faint light. He catches my eyes and narrows his own.

"Fuckin' Japs!' is his solitary observation.

The bow compartment has that hideous air of a medieval dungeon. The smoke from the runaway torpedo engine is so heavy it is nigh impossible to breathe. The thick, choking fog hangs in the air like an asphyxiating cloud. Lit only by the emergency lamps that resemble Gothic torches protruding rudely from a castle wall, a gang of half-naked men stand around clutching heavy-link chains with long shadows cast across greasy faces; faces with bared teeth and angry looks. Heavy smell of burnt rubber, alcohol, grease and body odor.

The object of all this indignation is the body of a Mk XIV torpedo hanging out of the inner door with its tail-end on the deck plates, the whole thing twisted at an obscene angle. This isn't going to be easy to put right. A huge body on the outer side of it, between the torpedo and the starboard side of the pressure hull, is attempting to take up the slack in a chainfall - a block-and-tackle-type arrangement used for lifting and loading torpedoes. I look closer; it's Daschler, his back gleaming with sweat. My eyes begin to recognize the 'torpedo gang' through their costumes of petroleum and perspiration. Just in front of me is Hood, looking at me through narrowly defined slits. Next to him Cutter is attempting to wipe the black from his hands with an equally blackened rag. A half-dozen others have their backs to me, but Torpedoman Howe is over on my left with the Pharmacist's mate who's attempting to put a dressing Steele's nasty leg wound. Apparently a propeller edge has sliced deeply into Steele's leg. He's practically unconscious.

"Damn!' Pike spits, moving toward the stricken fish and lowering himself to his knees. The torpedo and gunnery officer has gone through a transformation since he has left the conning tower. Now, his hat is gone and his shirt - streaked with long streams of sweat - is unbuttoned down as far as his belt, and his hands and face are as grimy as the rest of the torpedomen. It's as if simply walking through the bulkhead results in an instantaneous metamorphosis.

"It's gotta come up,' he continues, through a hoarse whisper while his hand disappears below the torpedo, 'About five and a half inches before it'll clear the bottom of the loading rack!"

"Christ!' Hood hisses.

A head pokes out from beneath the torpedo - Tashtego. A quick glance to either side reveals the deck plates pulled up - he's down in the lower one-fourth of the compartment. "Sir,' he stammers - panting for breath - 'Could we get a chain around the screws, shove it forward and then lift it up?"

It takes a moment for me to piece together what happened: the torpedo - bucked out of the tube like an unbroken stallion by the depth charge explosions - has slid underneath the starboard loading rack in such a way that it cannot be lifted straight up. It must first be shoved forward the aforementioned distance before it can be raised. No small feat when you consider that the fish is resting its full three thousand-pound weight on it's after body. What we need now in here are giants.

Pike nods his greasy head. "There's no other way. But we're going to have to rig up some sort of pulley system so that we can get some leverage,' He looks out at the surrounding throng of torpedomen and blinks. 'I don't suppose the esteemed gentlemen upstairs would humor us with a tea break?"

A few nervous chuckles. The enemy sonar continues pinging away. And those damn propellers are never far off.

"Come to join the fun?" Pike cracks, noticing me.

I shrug. "Needed something to do."

His eyebrows arch upward. "That will not be a problem. Why don't you get down here with Tash?"

"What do I do?"

Pike points an oily finger toward the torpedo. "Throw your whole weight behind it on cue. Howe - Cutter, get down here with Tash and Watts."

The screw sounds above suddenly quicken and mesh together into a symphony of heavy bronze. My heart dips into my stomach.

A loud roar slams me into a body standing beside me and I tumble into the open deck - striking something hard and fleshy, followed by a metallic blow to the head. Involuntarily I cry out. Wild cursing above me. The metal next to me resonates with a type of singsong vibrato, humming and shrilling until drowned out by the next crack of thunder. I'm lifted up and bounced up and down on the hard metal like a rubber ball. My arms flail out to grasp something - anything.

Wild groaning; can't tell whether it's men or steel. I gulp for air just as the next string hits. Holding my breath, I grasp a hold of a pipe in front of me and hang on. The pipe angles downward, which means it leads to the poppet valve drain tank just below which is for bleeding off the air used to fire the torpedoes. Why am I thinking of that? It has no significance now. The deck below and in front of me bucks, kicks, shudders, creaks, and supplicates. Every muscle in my body goes rigid. I can't relax - not even for a hundredth of a second. The consequences are too severe. If someone put a piece of coal between my lower cheeks, they'd have a flawless diamond inside thirty minutes.

Put your mind elsewhere, think of anything but of the reality right now. Think of home - happiness. Easter dinners after church. The sweet aroma of honeysuckle vines as they are borne anew in the spring, lofting through the open windows. A deep blue sky with maybe a few puffs of whipped cream for clouds. Girls in pretty Easter dresses with hats to match.

Loud cracks like rifle shots - wild hissing of high-pressure air. I open my eyes - frantic movement above me. Pike shouts for something in a frenzied ire. The explosions must have ruptured a valve in the air salvage line, emitting high-pressure air into the compartment. If Pike doesn't get it tightened down; soon we won't be able to open the watertight door to the forward battery compartment. The higher pressure in here would literally blow us through the hatch and echo through the surrounding water like the popping of a champagne cork.

As Tashtego scrambles up onto the main deck, Pike is already leaning over the offending valve with a large monkey wrench. His expression contorts as the blast of air hits him in the face and he hauls down on the large nut on the end of the pipe. Barely has he made one turn that a crack of thunder hurls the boat sideways. Knocked into the air, both wrench and officer crash back onto the deck plates in a great clatter. More blows. Glass shatters somewhere. Curses and vulgar invectives. A few groans. Then a heavy scraping - the torpedo is moving!

"TAKE IN THE STRAIN! HAUL UP ON THE GODDAMNED CHAIN!"

Rapid clinking of thick links like machine gun fire. Moans of men hauling up on an enormous weight. Metal screeches somewhere. I get out of the hole and squeeze myself in between two torpedo mates for a space at the chain. In spite of the heat, the chain is strangely cool and clammy, like a snake's body. In the interim the flood of high-pressure air has stopped. Pike has succeeded in making the valve fast. From somewhere Daschler has retrieved a wooden beam. What use could a steel ship such as this have for wood? The question is answered as he uses the beam as a wedge and shoves it under the aft end of the torpedo, and with a few well-placed whacks of a mall, immobilizes it. Now panting like a spent Olympic runner, Daschler drifts back until he comes to rest against the port loading rack.

We stand around red in the face, exhausted, and dripping sweat.

"Now,' Pike wheezes grasping the length of the chain closest to the pulley, 'Comes the easy part! Let's get this baby back in its hole! All right boys - heave! Put your backs into it!"

My hands have been rubbed raw. Exacerbated by the salt in my sweat, they burn with that eerie scorched sensation of a friction wound and my cheek throbs. We're only halfway there, the itinerant fish has been moved up about three and a quarter inches so far. The distance is important, three thousand pounds takes one hell of a lot of energy and it doesn't seem like we're getting enough air in here.

As though we didn't already have enough on our hands, now we're taking water in the compartment. Depth charges, still coming down like sinister drops of rain, have knocked out the seal in a trim line hose connection, admitting a steady flow of seawater into the compartment. Tashtego attacked it with a vengeance but was only able to reduce the amount coming in, not stop it completely. To do that would require taking the thing apart and we can't do that now - we'd flood the entire compartment. That can only be done on the surface. We'll just have to rely on the bilge pumps being able to handle what comes in.

Heavy screw noises hover perpetually above. The Jap destroyers dash in, drop a pattern, then lay off idling and ping away with their echo-rangers. The bursts of energy seem to come at us from all sides. Are we boxed in? Impossible for us to know in here, only in the conning tower could we be privy to such information. When the boat is sealed up like it is now, only the most infinitesimal bits of information can get through - and that comes from whoever's on the battle phones as he eavesdrops on the damage reports from other compartments. Therein lies a real problem, since nearly all the information we do get is universally bad, and therefore colors our outlook on the situation. But what else is there to be had? In the heat of battle the Skipper's concentrating on getting us clear of our pursuers, so he can't be bothered with giving a running commentary on enemy positions, speeds, and attack runs. We simply have to grit our teeth and bear it.

From what Cutter can hear over the battle phones, we're taking a real pounding; forward engine room reports several valves, valve couplings, and an exhaust flange lost. After engine room is taking water below in the motor room - those damn propeller packings again! Maneuvering room has had a circuit board shorted out and reports another heating up. We hear nothing of the control room since the Skipper's opened the hatch between the former and the conning tower and can communicate without use of the intercompartmental phones.

A flashlight beam cuts through sooty darkness. It settles on the depth gauges affixed on the starboard side. "A little over three hundred feet,' Howe whispers anxiously. "Why doesn't the Skipper take us deeper?"

"Because the Bungo Strait isn't all that deep,' Pike replies, lowering himself wearily to his knees and then kicking his legs out in front of him to sit on the deck plates. "We don't have all that much room for maneuver.' He fishes a cigarette out of his soiled pocket and inserts it neatly in the corner of his mouth. 'Smoking lamp's lit by the way."

I fumble for my cigarettes. There is a constant need to be doing something - anything - to keep the hands busy. Not knowing what's going on is driving me mad. Sealed up inside this steel vault that might as well be a million miles away from the conning tower.

Pike looks over toward the port side where a lone bunk is in the folded-down position. "How's Steele doing?"

"He's out now,' Kemper responds quietly. "I gave him a shot of morphine. I should move him though; the air's really bad in here."

"For Chrissake Kemper!' Garn remonstrates. "Go easy with that stuff or you're gonna turn us all into a bunch of addicts!"

Kemper looks over and - for a brief moment - seems like he might come back with something but instead shakes his head and looks at the floor.

Pike takes a long drag on his cigarette and blows smoke into the overhead. It hangs like a haze, a blue-gray pall suspended in near a hundred percent humidity. "Cutter, ask the Skipper permission to move Steele aft."

"Yes sir,' he immediately begins mumbling quietly into the phone. A few seconds later he looks up. "Go to it."

Kemper gets to his feet, "I'll need - '

"Howe, Hood, and Garn help Kemper get Steele back to his bunk.' Pike orders, tossing the spent butt of his cigarette into a rusty can and starting to get up. "The rest of you, let's get back to work!"

We've moved the torpedo three and quarter inches. All at once it makes me seethe with rage: why couldn't it have been three and a half or even four inches? Why not a nice, round even number? But no, three and a quarter, the elements conspire against us. We're living proof of Murphy's Law. I can't get it out of my head.... Three and a quarter.... Three and a quarter.... It seems so insignificant.

How long will it take to move it three and a quarter more?

The Nip destroyers continue to swarm around above us like a swarm of angry hornets. Their sonar pulses ring out steadily in measured tones from either side of the boat. With increasing frequency the intonation fills you with a particular sense of doom. It is a creeping sensation that literally makes your skin crawl and break out into large welts of gooseflesh - that echo made when the pulses smack against the sides of our steel hull: *Chirp.... PONG! Chirp.... PONG! Chirp.... PONG!* - Like the clapping of a church bell at a funeral. Then the screws get louder as they gun their engines. The depth charges follow close behind. They're doing a bang-up job these Japs, almost before every explosion we hear the detonator go off right before the main charge.

"Boy these guys are good." Pike says in admiration.

"Lousy scum!" Garn snarls, lying prostrate under the port loading rack and gripping the metal base with both hands. All we can do is lie here and curse them. That and silence is our only defense.

Manhandling the nomadic torpedo back into the tube was a gift from heaven. It kept us totally occupied for a few hours. Now we have nothing to do except lie around and envisage what sort of ghastly fate awaits us from above. All around me the bodies look the same; pale skin drenched and glistening with sweat. Clenched mouths with white teeth showing through dark beards. Trembling hands. Terror-filled eyes that unceasingly scan sights unseen in the darkness overhead.

We cease to be men and become wild animals bent on survival.

*   *   *

Parched throat. Swollen tongue. Mouth sticky and dry. It must be well over a hundred degrees in the boat by now. My head throbs with every beat of my heart, feels like it could split in two. The air is becoming so humid, condensate drip from everything

- metal, brass, and flesh. Soon there will be a point where the air can no longer absorb the heavy moisture rolling down our saturated bodies. Already Kemper is going through the boat dispensing salt tablets by the handful; we've got to maintain a level of moisture in ourselves to keep from passing out and burning up from dehydration.

The boat is taking a real beating, we've got about a dozen or so leaks so far in just about every part of the boat, so we must run the bilge pumps as frequently as possible. But they make so much noise that we have to wait until the Japs make a run over us so that will mask the sound. Now this puts us in the unenviable position of actually *needing* the rain of depth charges so that we can run the pumps - and every sweating, wearied crewman knows it. We mutter silent prayers for explosives, not close, but just close enough to give us a chance to pump an extra few hundred pounds outboard until the sea's relentless hissing, gurgling, and crying quiets down again. The irony of it all is sickening.

Half-crazed with thirst and stumbling through the control room toward the crew's mess when I hear Duffy exclaim in a hoarse whisper, "Third contact echo ranging! Bearing.... One four zero. Range twenty-five hundred max!'

The Chief off to one side of the plotting table slowly lowers his head and closes his eyes. There is a fatalism in his body language.

"I'd say we were becoming right popular,' the Skipper comments dryly.

Bile rises in my throat.

"God Almighty - three of them!' Waldron says slowly, his voice almost cracking.

At that moment a head pokes out from the pump room - it's Lemert. He gazes around with a look of complete shock - he has overheard. Our eyes lock and he stares at me with a vacant expression. He remains silent, but his eyes speak volumes.

So now there's three destroyers hunting us - no bells, no announcements, no bulletins. Duffy's matter-of-factness is almost anti-climatic. We're outgunned, outnumbered even worse than before, have given up our element of surprise, and forced to remain on the defensive. How long will it take to play out the final act?

Dear God, why must men do this to one another?

"They're certainly making it interesting." The Skipper observes, taking up the challenge, 'Three destroyers. Never run into three of them at once. This ought to make the game a little more challenging."

How long has it been? One destroyer's charges are enough to shake your fillings loose, two is enough to drive you mad - but three? How can we fight against three of them? We're not even really fighting, simply attempting to steal away without any of them being the wiser. Fighting would be much easier; it is a vent, a release. But all this creeping around and attempting to hide from the enemy's echo-ranging tests the very sanity of each one of us.

The Chief hovers under the conning tower ladder with a pinched look on his square face. What's he doing? He must have been aft by the looks of him. His clothes are drenched, smeared with petroleum, and torn. Through his open shirt a large bloody gash can be seen just above his left pectoral muscle. A trickle of blood runs from it in an irregular line until disappearing into the dark splotch of grease and hair right below it. What could have happened to him? He looks like a cross between a drunken vagrant and a war refugee.

"How long have we been under attack?" I ask him quietly. He gives me a searching stare for a long moment before answering, "About twelve hours now." twelve hours - the number rolls off his lips as easily as a telephone exchange. Is it possible? Do the Nips have enough depth charges to last that long? *Oh God, why do you punish us so?*

I must have something to drink. I cannot swallow anymore, there isn't enough saliva in my mouth for me to do so. Instead the muscle contractions necessary feel more like two scabrous blocks of hard rubber chafing against one another. As I step by the open hatch that leads up into the conning tower, I catch sight of the Skipper's form: slightly bent, shirt open, left arm gripping something in the overhead. But the most comforting and reassuring sight of all, is that worn and beaten cap, still jauntily cocked on his head. *No....I must believe.... We'll make it.... Just believe...*

Another unfortunate occurrence. During our rendezvous with the *Canopus*, I learn the Skipper handed over a large amount of provisions to them as they were near starving. Several dozen cans of fruit juice and tins of food were given over to them. An act of admirable largesse, it has however turned around to hurt us. We now are in desperate need of the canned juice because we can no longer drink the water in the boat. It is now well over a hundred degrees and to drink it causes immediate and involuntary vomiting. Trapped in blistering heat with nothing to drink. No way the Chief can fix this one.

The Skipper's face is drawn and gaunt. He seems to have aged five years in the ten and three-quarters hours since I was last up here. He sits on a wooden stool just behind Duffy, perspiration dribbles off him in little rivulets - miniature rivers of sweat. His khaki shirt is soaked through to the skin and open, with the tail hanging out of his trousers. His cap is still on, but tilted back on his head so that a wet shock of hair is exposed, poking out at obtuse angles like stringy seaweed washed up on a beach. And his unblinking gaze made even more penetrating by the glassy reflection in his eyes.

Duffy snaps his control lever back and forth so much the hollow *thumping* sound it makes blends into the background just like everything else. The heat is getting to him too; bare to the waist, on his lower half he now only wears his olive-drab boxers. His feet are shoved into sea boots only half-laced and untied, and his sodden clothing - shirt, trousers, and socks - lie in a putrid pile next to the sound set. A cloth towel is draped over his right thigh that he uses to wipe his dripping brow from time to time.

The only sound that isn't blending is that of the Jap sonar, hammering away relentlessly through the depths. At two-second intervals the sound bursts through the hull, but coming though from different directions.

"Any change?"

Duffy shakes his dripping head and whispers, "No sir. Constant one five zero, one eight zero, and two five nine."

"Helm, come left ten degrees rudder - steady on two three zero."

Out of the corner of my eye McGowan's form sags a bit, then just as quickly come back up. The Skipper stiffens. "Mac - you all right?"

"Of course,' the helmsman replies in his Scottish tone, 'Never been in finer shape sir!"

"Mac, you've been on that helm for the past four hours, why don't you rest a spell.' The Skipper leans over to the open hatch to the control room, 'Mr. Bainbridge - '

"Sir -' McGowan interrupts hastily, 'there's not a thing wrong with me. I'd feel kindly if you'd let me remain at my post sir."

The Skipper eyes him warily a moment, then takes a breath and sighs. "Five hours is the limit Mac, understood? Another hour and you're going to get some rest."

"Yes sir. Thank you sir."

The Skipper keeps his gaze fixed on him for a moment, then turns to me. "We'll have to make out the best we can with what we have,' he explains wide-eyed. "I know I was probably overly generous to the *Canopus*, but it was the only human thing to do." He pauses, and stares into my eyes. "They were practically starving you know."

Duffy's back stiffens. "Contacts at one eight zero and two five nine increasing speed,'

The Skipper's eyes are still locked in mine. "I mean what if that'd been us in there, and we we're having to cinch in our belts? Wouldn't we want some other boat's crew to be generous with us?"

"One eight zero and two five nine starting a run!" Duffy practically shouts this time.

"Right full rudder,' the Skipper orders quietly without even turning around. "All ahead full. Lemert to engage outboard pumps."

The racing freight train is just above us now, hissing and panting as if pulling a heavy load up the side of a steep mountain. The first blow feels like it comes from the port side - and a little bit aft. The boat heels over a good thirty-five to forty degrees. Then there's a bit of a lull just before the entire ocean around us erupts - a waterborne version of Dante's Inferno. Countless times I'm smashed into the back of the hand railing around the hatch leading to the control room, and as my mouth opens to cry out, it is immediately - and involuntarily - slammed shut by the next detonation. I keep my eyes shut; the violence of the blows is so barbarous I'm afraid they might actually be bounced from their sockets. I don't dare breath - to do so would require opening my mouth. *Just stay shut and closed up, that way nothing can hurt you.*

"LEFT FULL RUDDER! ALL AHEAD FLANK!'

More blows, impossible to count. Moreover, why should I even bother? That's Harmison's - or rather Donnelly's job now. Harmison's out of it, the poor bastard - broken jaw and everything. But now Donnelly's up here to take his place. I heard Donnelly's brother was on the *Arizona, was* it just an accident or fate that his brother happened to be on her when she blew up and sank? Was his death quick and merciful or did he linger on in a sealed compartment waiting for help that never came? How strange it all is, the element of chance. Is it the hand of God or of fate or both?

What will he decree for us?

A tentative silence. From somewhere comes the sound of water: trickling and hissing like a half-open valve on a faucet.

"Damn it!' the Skipper swears, staring across the room into space, 'Get an open-end up here!" A stream of water runs down the search scope housing. Apparently the depth charge explosions must have ruptured the scope sealing. A second later a wrench is handed up, and Donnelly puts it to the packing gland and starts tightening it down.

"Screws are slowing." Duffy reports.

"All ahead one-third!' the Skipper barks, agitated. 'Secure outboard pumping!"

Lemert's thumping bilge pumps abruptly cease.

Donnelly steps away from the scope with a pained expression. "She's as tight as she'll go sir."

The flow has been stemmed but not staunched. A trickle of seawater yet cascades over the shiny metal housing. While no great deluge, we must surely already have a dozen or so of these types of leaks throughout the boat. All combine to make us heavier. The added weight is the same as if a torrent were let into the boat; all have the same result. The boat can sink slowly as well as fast. We're living proof of that.

After studying it a brief moment with a look of disgust, the Skipper merely nods and looks away.

I'm beginning to fantasize: cool swimming pools, iced drinks, snow, frost, a chilly breeze, anything to take my mind off the heat. The thermometer in here reads one hundred and nine degrees Fahrenheit. One hundred and nine degrees of steaming, blistering hell with no end in sight. The Nips show no inclination of giving up the hunt. Why would they? Those bastards up there are doing the same job we would. Still, whenever someone's lobbing high explosive at you, circumstance alone gives you the right to call him a son of a bitch.

Fourteen hours of pursuit now. That's eight hundred and forty minutes, fifty thousand four hundred seconds, and still the eerie pings of the echo-rangers rattle off our hull.

The Skipper's concerned about the air level in the boat: all men not at battle stations have been ordered to lie in their bunks unless ordered otherwise. Less movement means less air used. If it goes on much longer we'll have to break out the CO2 absorbent so that we won't suffocate in our own accumulated exhalation.

It is sobering to realize just how many ways there are to get killed down here.

I'm in the conning tower when Schumacher's sweaty head pokes up from the control room. He stares at me strangely a moment, as if either not recognizing me or seeing me for the first time. I look back at him. His eyes trace over me as if I was a pile of sand in his way.

"Schumacher,' the Skipper glances over at him. The engineering officer steps over to the dripping search scope housing and bends forward. "Sir, the propeller packings,' at that instant Schumacher lowers his voice to such a pitch and talks so close to the Skipper's ear that I can't hear what he is saying. It is no mistake; he doesn't want anyone else to hear his report. What could he be saying? And what's the use in hiding it anyway? If it is crucial to our survival we'll find out soon enough anyway. I can't use the Skipper's face as a gauge since it is turned away from me.

As Schumacher steps back, the Skipper looks at him and nods. It is an absentminded; almost half-hearted gesture seemingly more to appease than to convey any real meaning. I exchange an alarmed look with Donnelly, whose narrow eyes have become as big as saucers. Duffy glances back once or twice but then no more. Even O'Toole begins shifting nervously from his perch behind me. Schumacher then turns and begins lowering himself down into the control room. "Keep an eye on it!' is the Skipper's final observation.

Obviously the propeller packings are leaking heavily, we knew that some time ago.

But how bad? It couldn't be a torrent yet or Schumacher would've pushed the panic button. But something's up and it must be fairly serious to warrant a silent conversation. My eyes fixate on the Skipper; I watch every square inch of his sweating face for a good hour or better. His actions and expressions will impart everything I need to know. But as time passes, I realize it won't work as the Skipper's Sphinx-like countenance is but a mask, I can glean nothing from it. Soon I find myself cursing at his prowess in masking his thoughts. Like those masks used in ancient Greek theatre, he's all subliminal - everything's underneath.

Duffy jerks up. "Contact at one seven seven increasing speed!"

The eerie, surrealistic quiet doesn't last. A second later the *click* of a detonator begins the next cavalcade.

The Skipper looks irritated even before O'Toole finishes his report: propeller packings are making water at a rate impossible for the pumps to handle at irregular intervals. The propeller packings are located in the motor room. If the water level gets up even with our electric motors and shorts them out, it's over. Without our motors we've had it.

The Skipper stares into nothingness. Large beads of sweat dot his chiseled face like misshapen balls of paraffin. For a moment I don't wonder if all of him isn't wax, he looks so poised, perfect, and rigid. "Form a bucket brigade,' he instructs, his voice slightly hoarse, "Transfer the water into the control room bilge. It's stopgap, but right now it's the best we can do. Any man drops a bucket and I'll have his head."

I get up. I can wield a bucket as well as the next man.

In the maneuvering room the floor plates lift up to reveal a small ladder that leads down into the bowels of the boat. It is into this void that men disappear. Due to a number of shorted-out switchboards next door in the maneuvering room, the light in here is extremely dim and sparse. Every third man wields a flashlight, so that the line is home to half-dozen miniature suns.

Schumacher kneels over the opening to the motor room just a foot away, a flashlight grasped in his right hand. His hawk-like face is cast a sickening green by the weak illumination. His chest moves up and down in a deep rhythm. Perspiration glistens on him like heavy oil.

"Far....go...sir,' drifts up from the motor room, 'Any tighter the shafts will bind!" Schumacher dips his head and winces. "Take 'em as far as you can,' he hisses, 'Then back off the nuts about a quarter turn until the squealing stops. Then go forward about an eighth of an inch or so got it? I'm sending the buckets down." He looks up at us, and I see a face wracked with fatigue; eyes red, bloodshot, and sunken, sallow skin, and hollow cheeks. It's as if death is already working its way through him.

Chief Schrier pokes his head up at that moment from the motor room muttering something about needing certain tools. A tin bucket hangs in front of his face. "Not yet,' he mutters, waving it away and struggling up onto the deck plates. Hustling aft, he disappears into the after torpedo room as we stand around avoiding one another's eyes. A few seconds later he reappears with the top cradle of a tool box clutched in his right hand, and proceeds to lower it down into the uncovered opening that leads to the motor room, "Hey - look alive down there!' he hisses hoarsely, 'Somebody take this!' He then dunks his body down into the hole and disappears. E-mate Garnett leans over the hatch and wants to know when we're going to start bailing. "When *I say*!' the disembodied voice of the Chief snaps back. Silence follows, then a *clinking sound* down in the motor room - they're working on something. A *sloshing* sound, then a heavy *thud*, followed by muted cursing.

"All right - send the buckets down!" A moment later the first one comes back up, with Garnett hoisting it out of the hole with his big paws and handing it to me. The thin metal handle is warm and greasy to the touch. A look down into the bucket reveals its contents look more like oil than water, jet black with a slight sheen on the surface. In passing the bucket back to Hood. Some of the liquid sloshes over onto my chest. A slight, yet pleasantly refreshing shiver. The water is cool, which means we must be underneath a thermal layer. Of course - a blanket of cooler water to protect us! If we were trapped in warmer water, surely we would not have survived this long. I grab a hold of the thin bucket handles with a renewed fervor, for every one means less weight in our stern. I am a cog in a long, living limb that stretches from the forward torpedo room to here in the maneuvering room, all slaving to save us from a watery Valhalla.

Once again Providence and fortune remain on our side. But for how long?

The rain of depth charges is unceasing. The pack of wild dogs on the hunt above have yet to give up the scent. They circle, sniff around - detect something - roar in for the pounce, then lay off and sniff around some more. A vicious cycle of terror; punctuated by reverberating explosions, screaming and falling men, clanging buckets, and wild curses. I have become an automaton, lifting each bucket like the last and slinging it behind me to be taken by the next man while trying to turn off my mind in this blistering heat. Nauseated, punchy and slightly drunk, I stopped counting the buckets after three hundred and sixty-seven, and that was some time ago. How much water still to go? How much continues to steal its way in?

Schumacher hovers around us like a mother hen, sweating and swearing as he constantly interrupts the chain to duck down into the motor room and check things out for himself. For some reason he doesn't trust the Chief to keep him accurately appraised of the situation - which is driving the Chief mad. At one point the Chief came up the ladder so incensed his eyes bugged out of his head and - despite the darkness - you could tell he was red in the face. Schumacher seems totally oblivious, and continues to prod him about infinitesimal things, using the tone as if he was dealing with a seaman recruit. "Easy now Chief, keep an eye on those reduction gears. You sure you can handle things down there Chief? Wait a minute - better let me check." I don't ever remember Schumacher patronizing the Chief in this way before. I wouldn't be surprised if the Chief lit out and decked him.

The Chief though, bears it stoically and goes on silently with his tasks.

Sometime later, Hood collapses. His bucket upsets and clangs loudly across the deck, sending oily water in all directions.

"Jesus H. Christ! Quiet!' Schumacher demands angrily as he steps over to us, upset that his human chain has been interrupted.

"Hood's had it!'

Schumacher's eyes dart around menacingly in their sockets. "Get him forward into his bunk. Keep going - all of you! Keep going!' He whirls around and disappears below as a few bluejackets come up to drag away the hapless Torpedoman. As soon as the prostrate body has been moved, the process continues.

So, a man has succumbed to the blistering heat. The boat continues to flood, and we are still under severe attack.

Situation normal.

A little while later it happens. One of the new fellows has a fit. The combined weight of sheer terror and claustrophobia crushes unseasoned resolve and sanity. A once-normal individual is completely transformed in front of my eyes. I stare at him numbly for innumerable hours, passing each bucket of oily water to him as it is handed to me. At first he was quiet, and bore his suffering stoically. As each hour passed I could detect changes in him, nervously mumbling rosaries in a hoarse whisper that grew louder and more agitated until some of the other men began hushing him. Then suddenly, he became quiet. Nothing. I thought maybe he'd finally risen over the worst of it. In reality however, inwardly he collapsed like a stump of a rotten tree. Emitting a sudden animal like growl he bolts toward the after escape trunk. The growl becomes an uncontrollable scream as he attempts to open the hatch of our steel sarcophagus. The consequences are both unmerciful and without pity. Hartmann quickly dispatches him with utmost savagery, since a raving man now puts us all at risk. A few moments later several tired forms shuffle forward with Myers' limp, blood-spattered form in their arms. If anyone else shows signs of cracking, hopefully this dissuades them.

After Myers disappears, work continues as if nothing had happened.

*   *   *

The Skipper looks grim. His appearance is shocking; head hung low, eyes half-closed. His movements are slow and belabored. He's got to be exhausted; he's been up here in the conning tower now almost twenty hours straight, with his mind going full-tilt. A mind-numbing exercise of mental gymnastics; our course, three different enemy courses, routes of escape, depth, our speed, their speed, direction of attack runs, damage reports, orders to the crew; attempting to outguess the enemy. It's an impossible task.

"Myers is in his bunk?"

I nod, thankful that this great Sphinx has finally spoken at last.

The Skipper nods absentmindedly. "Good.... Good." He turns back around and stares at the floor plates. I can hear him breathing; it comes in short gasps that seem to quicken at infrequent intervals. The way he looks you'd think he was a boxer after a ten-round fight. The pounding we're taking surpasses anything a mere human could meter out. How long can he withstand being in the eye of the hurricane? When will he lose his edge? It would be only human, but we must believe he is more than that and larger than life with secrets unbeknownst to the rest of us. To us, the Skipper is an instrument of God - our savior, the only man who can deliver us from this blistering hell. We look up to him as if he had supernatural powers - a sorcerer who conjures up vision after vision to inspire his flock. He is our father and mother and scold us along the path to salvation, shooing us back into line whenever we waver. Does he realize this? Does he know of the crushing pressure that is brought on him by other men's minds? In other vessels it's different. Surface ships make war in groups, not so the submarine. It is a lone wolf that must be commanded by an even more remote personality.

The sound of boots scraping on the deck plates - somebody's just underneath the hatch.

"Sir?' it's the XO's voice, in a hushed, urgent whisper.

The Skipper turns his head and takes a step over to the hatch. "Yeah?"

"Latest CO2 reading shows a level approaching two percent sir."

Yet another enemy - CO2 - carbon dioxide - the end result of normal and healthy human respiration, a deadly gas if permitted to aggrandize in sealed compartments. The acceptable level of carbon dioxide is anything below three percent. Three percent is tolerable, but not for long. There is increased difficulty in breathing even at rest and any sort of physical exertion nigh impossible. Severe headaches, nausea, and sickness are common. If the level reaches four percent, it becomes lethal. Hallucinations, apathy, severe vomiting, coma and death will not far behind. This corresponds with the necessary level of oxygen in the boat, which must not be allowed to fall below seventeen percent. Below that death by asphyxiation is imminent. To maintain purity of the air level, the CO2 level must be kept at a certain point. This is the job of the thirty-seven canisters of CO2 absorbent that we carry. It usually takes twice as long as this for the carbon dioxide level to reach what it is now, but all the physical work with the bucket brigade and the hot-run torpedo forward have bitten into our reserve.

Out of the corner of my eye I notice a movement from O'Toole - a hand is reaching up to his earphones.

"Break out the CO2 absorbent Mr. Bainbridge; see to it that it's placed properly."

"Yes sir."

"Sir -' O'Toole cuts in, 'Chief Schrier reports three battery cells cracked forward and two cracked aft."

The Skipper winces as if pricked with a needle. "Leakage?"

A pause while O'Toole relays the question over the battle phone. After a second he looks up, "trying to ascertain that now sir."

"Tell him I want a report on it within the next five minutes."

"Yes sir."

"Contacts bearing two two zero.... zero one zero.... and one eight two degrees sir,' Duffy reports, '..making slow speed....all echo-ranging.'

"We're completely surrounded.' The Skipper whispers to himself. "We can't make a move anywhere."

Will the pack ever tire of the chase?

The Skipper moves back over to the hatch. "Mr. Bainbridge -'

Shuffling of feet below. "Sir?"

"What depth does the charts show for this area of the Strait?'

"Alternates between three hundred and three hundred eighty sir."

After a moment of silent reflection, the Skipper turns to Duffy. "During the next pattern, bounce the bottom with an echo; let's find out just exactly how much room we've got. The charts could be wrong since most of them were drawn up after the turn of the century."

"Contact at one eight two and closing!' Duffy reports breathlessly.

The Skipper moves over to the sound set. "Rig out the QC, bounce an echo just as soon as he lets fly.'

"Sir,' O'Toole reports, 'Chief Schrier reports seepage from cells three and five forward sir."

"Check for chlorine gas!"

"Yes sir!"

"QC rigged out sir,' Duffy sighs. "Screws picking up speed, he's starting a run!"

"Good." The Skipper notes without the slightest trace of agitation. "Get ready.'

Duffy sets his hand on the instrument that will send out the pulse of energy from our sonar heads located forward. "Here he comes -'

He's right over us now. No separately distinct beats, only the heavy roaring and hissing as though some wild beast of prey was swooping down on us. I close my eyes, clench my teeth, and tighten my grip around the coil of steel pipe just behind me. *Hold tight - keep cool - hold tight*. Take a breath now, and hold that. Make every muscle in your body as rigid as the bones that support them. It won't last too long, a pattern never does. Just a short, quick trip into hell and then everything will be all right.

For some reason I open my eyes just a mere sliver and catch Duffy nodding to the Skipper, who reaches up and grabs a hold of a pipe in the overhead. That means...

A giant hammer hits the boat. Bad - but not horrible. The next ones though, are worse; four, five, six blows in quick succession, followed by another string equally as violent.

The beating screws sounds are receding now. Quiet descends upon us. Instantly my ears detect the sound of running water. Donnelly is up and cursing - it's the search scope housing again. Water shoots down it like a miniature sculpted waterfall. Withdrawing a long open-end wrench from his back pocket, the quartermaster assaults the packing gland with it once again. The search scope has probably had it. The depth charges must have blown out all the sealing gaskets and O-rings. No way it can be used now. With the packing gland made fast as it is, the shaft is effectively immobilized, so there's no way the hydraulic motor could budge it. If this happens to the attack scope, we'll be totally blind.

"Sir!' O'Toole reports frantically, 'after engine room reports breach in a vent riser - engine room making water fast!'

"*Get those emergency valves closed!* I want the Chief in there! Where's Michaelis?'

"With Schumacher sir -'

"Get him in there!' the Skipper takes a step toward the hapless yeoman - now, for the first time, I see anxiety in his face. The loss of a vent riser - a metal pipe that extends from the top of the tank to the superstructure on the ship's centerline - is critical. With direct access to the sea, it's almost as if the pressure hull itself has been breached. Until the emergency vent valves at the tank top can be closed by hand - not an easy thing to do because you're fighting against the outside water pressure - it's like a dam has been unleashed.

"Chief reports a negative on the chlorine gas sir!"

The deck is already starting to list - aft.

"Conn!' Waldron - on the diving controls - cries "Boat gaining depth!"

A look of alarm seizes hold of the Skipper's face. "Rig in the QC! Rig in the sound heads! Blow fifteen hundred pounds of main ballast!'

High-pressure air begins roaring into the tanks. He's only going to bring the destroyers down on our necks - for this what price will we pay?

"Where's the bottom sound?"

"QC reading gives us just over three hundred eighty feet sir!"

The hiss of air into the tanks begins to slacken then stops. "Still losing depth sir,' Waldron replies with escalating dismay, 'Unable to maintain proper trim! More speed imperative!'

"All ahead full!' the Skipper barks, 'Every second man to the forward torpedo room.... now.... *move it*! What's happening aft?' He snaps at O'Toole, who relays the question, then immediately - totally exasperated - repeats it. He looks up, his face a mask of terror. "After engine room not responding sir!'

"Shiiiitttt!'

I can hear the thumping of booted feet tearing through the control room below. A total stampede, the only thing missing is the baying of the steers. What *is* going on in the after engine room? Is the compartment entirely flooded? Visions of twisted bodies suspended lifeless in a watery tomb; arms outstretched, mouths open, faces locked in a eternal look of surprise...

"Conn,' Waldron cries, 'Boat out of control! *Stern's dropping fast*!'

The Skipper whirls around to the depth gauge on the wall. The needle is poised just a hair under three hundred and fifty. Half a second later it is passed that and still moving - too fast. The Skipper erupts like a volcano. "Blow all tanks! Blow! Blow! Blow!'

Wild hissing of high-pressure air.

The Skipper's jaw juts out and his teeth form a snarl. "She's moving too fast - never arrest it - sound collision!"

Donnelly smacks the alarm with the palm of his hand. We're on a collision course with the seabed. What did the sounding read? Three hundred eighty - or three hundred ninety? The destroyers be damned, we must check our fall or...

Suddenly a sickening crunch and screech aft - the boat quivers, shakes and bucks with a howl of protesting metal. I sprawl onto the deck plates and crash into Duffy's stool. The world is inverted for a long moment, before the bow begins to drop, crashing into the ocean floor like a felled oak tree. More screeching and groaning followed by a deafening silence.

A chorus of tormented moans and curses waft up through the control room.

"Damage reports!' the Skipper is still on his feet; grim-faced and wild-eyed, 'All compartments report in!"

O'Toole begins going down the list as each compartment reports in. There's no mistaking it - the bottom has succeeded where so far the Japanese have failed. Almost every compartment reports some type of seepage, with the after compartments suffering the worst of it. He rattles on like he's reading a shopping list, 'flanges, valves, packing glands, exhaust ports, air pressure lines, gaskets,' there seems no end to it. How much more of this beating can the boat withstand? It's like being in a condemned dwelling while it collapses down around you. How much can the boat take? All machinery has its limit.

What will break first, flesh or steel?

The Skipper's steadying himself against the leaking search scope housing, his eyes glazed and glassy. I stare at him, silently imploring - pleading - that he figures out some way of getting us out of this. *He must know. He must have a way!*

"Sir-' O'Toole exclaims again, '-after engine room reports emergency vent valves closed! Flooding secured!"

For a moment the Skipper's eyes seem to come back into focus. His head swivels slowly toward the yeoman, and asks without emotion, "How much did we take inboard?"

"Michaelis reports about thirty-five inches in the after engine room space, sir."

The Skipper snorts loudly through his nose, then blows out in a long, slow, drawn-out hiss - like a serpent drawing back before it strikes. Thirty-five inches - that's over three feet of water. "That means the auxiliary diesel and generator are a total write-off. Damn! Form another bucket brigade,' he sighs, 'We'll have to transfer it to the forward torpedo room. Every man that can be spared."

Duffy stiffens. "Contact at one four zero closing fast!"

"Those bastards!' Donnelly croaks. 'Those fucking bastards! Haven't they had enough?"

The Skipper's gaze drifts over to him. "Don't worry Donnelly, they can't break us We're just too Bull-headed." He smiles broadly, proud of his own witticism.

thrumm-thrisshh-thrumm-thrisshh-thruMM-THRISSHH-THRUMM-THRISSHH...

The Skipper inclines his head and stares upward. Duffy flicks his control lever back and forth, then wrenches his earphones angrily off. His eyes begin to redden and glisten with moisture.

"It's okay Duffy,' the Skipper whispers softly, consoling him. "We can hear them. There's nothing you can do."

"*They're all around us!*" Duffy's voice cracks.

The Skipper's hand goes to Duffy's shoulder. "It's okay I said.'

Chirp....Pong!....Chirp....Pong!....Chirp....PONG!....CHIRP....PONG!

An evil grin forms on the Skipper's face. "Come on - hurry it up! We've got work to do!"

In my peripheral view I see a tear seep out of Duffy's left eye and careen down his face before disappearing into his beard.

A cockroach scurries out from somewhere and abruptly stops on the checkered metal of the deck. Incredible! I had thought we had killed them all. Yet we missed this one. I can barely see it in the faint light, but there it is. A disgustingly familiar shape creeping about on the wet deck. What can it be looking for here? There is nothing for it to eat. It will have to wait; we are not dead yet. No, not yet. This nefarious insect, if the boat floods and we all drown will it live, feeding off our putrefying flesh and growing bigger and bigger as it slips from compartment to compartment? Can the things survive underwater, getting the necessary oxygen from trapped air pockets in here? Or will it drown and rot along with the rest of us? It wiggles, and moves from side to side, it's antennae searching - probing - for God knows what. I should lunge out and stomp on it, squishing it into vile paste. But I move not a muscle, not a sixteenth of an inch - I can't. I'm frozen solid - as rigid as a corpse. Even if the order to 'abandon ship' was given I couldn't move. What is happening to me?

A skull-splitting blast of granite from above - the boat groans, yawns, and screeches in protest. Next an entire avalanche of colossal boulders - the boat is straddled port and starboard, stem to stern. It seems to last an eternity. Images real and unreal dance before my eyes. Everything is in double. The smell of smoke, acrid and pungent. The Skipper roars out something in total fury - can't understand it.

"Hail Mary.... Full of Grace.... Hail Mary.... Full of Grace.... The Lord is with thee....' somebody's praying.

"He leadeth me beside still waters, he restoreth my soul. Yea.... Though I walk through the valley of the shadow of death.... I will fear no evil...'

*   *   *

"How much work do you have ahead of you?" The XO wants to know, plopping down on an upturned floor plate next to me to catch his breath.

Michaelis scratches his sweat-soaked beard with greasy fingers. "Six.... seven hours."

The XO winces. "Kemper says the men will just keep dropping out between the exhaustion, dehydration, and lack of oxygen. We'll be lucky if we have enough left to keep the line going."

Michaelis' eyes narrow. "How much air have we got?"

"Not much. The Skipper's stretching what we've got now by bleeding air into the boat. But we've got to watch it; every ounce of compressed air is worth its weight in gold. All the canisters of CO_2 absorbent are broken out, but the stuff's expanding and getting hot fast."

"But I need all these men.' Michaelis protests, 'Without them it'll take us twice as long!"

The XO shakes his head sympathetically, but his voice remains firm. "Sorry Mike. We're just using too much air, if we don't cut it somewhere, you know what's going to happen."

Michaelis nods and sits back. Without another word, the XO turns and orders every third man to step out of line and head for any vacant bunk. Less men working means less air used, a very simple equation.

Michaelis gets up; he's a haggard wreck, hardly the cut of the fine officer I first met on Oahu. What war does to people. Glancing around with an acidic look, he takes a step toward the opened grate which leads down into the engine room space. "All right - back to it!"

Hammering away for the last ten hours at the flooded after engine room space. We will now proceed as before but with a third fewer men.

Such are the fortunes of war.

Kemper comes down the line several times an hour, clucking over us like a mother hen, distributing salt pills so we retain as much body moisture as possible, and aspirin. Severe headaches afflict all of us to a man. It is a mind-anesthetizing pain, worse than anything experienced before. The head literally throbs with each beat of the heart. Vision blurs, and fits of vomiting overcome many. Men are becoming so insensate that they take the aspirin from Kemper and chew them before swallowing. The Skipper pow-wows with Kemper about the men's condition. As each hour passes more and more drop out.

"Sir -' I hear the pharmacist's mate whisper to our commander, "what is happening is the low level of oxygen content of the air in the boat. It just keeps dropping. The only way we can stagger it is by bleeding air from the compressed air banks forward and aft. That's just stopgap - like sticking your finger in a hole in a dike. All it does is juggle the figures so the picture looks rosier than it is. If we don't get to the surface soon sir, we'll start losing people. They can't hack this much longer."

The Skipper stares at him in silence several moments before turning and walking away. There is something in his face I've never ever seen before - it is fear.

"What do I do?' our Commander asks, staring at the floor plates in the wardroom. "Keep my men down here and let them die of asphyxiation or surface and have them murdered by the Japs at the end of a rope?"

We stare back at him in helpless frustration. None of us can answer this question. Neither solution offers any real hope for us; we'll probably die one way or another.

"If -' Michaelis begins, 'we can get the water distributed and run the pumps to get it outboard...'

"If...if...if...' the Skipper repeats sarcastically without looking up, "I don't like that word anymore."

Footsteps outside. Schumacher stumbles in and collapses onto one of the benches. His skin the most horrendous shade of red I've ever seen. "Sir,' he stammers - his voice slow, belabored and halting. 'Temperature reading in the maneuvering room is now at one hundred fourteen degrees Fahrenheit. We're losing a man at the rate of one every ten minutes."

Screw sounds above, punctuated by bursts of sonar.

"The pack has the fox wounded and in the hole,' Waldron observes under his breath, cradling his head in his hands, 'all that's left is to see him dead."

"Isn't it enough for them to sink us?' Lemert openly wonders. "Or must we be spread all over the bottom in little pieces?" His sereneness is eerie, yet his calmness is thoroughly convincing.

Michaelis sighs with more than a note of resignation. "I'd say they're chances then are pretty good."

"How long has it been?" Pike croaks through a hoarse whisper.

"Almost forty hours now." The XO turns his attention back to the Skipper who - still staring at the floor plates - seems to be in another world.

"Sir, whatever you decide -'

'- we're behind you." Waldron interjects.

Finally, the great Sphinx lifts his head and looks at each one of us in turn. Straight and deep into our souls he peers, his gaze as penetrating as a beam of light cutting a swathe through darkness. Is it into our souls that he probes, a quest for the truthfulness deep in our psyche? What about him? What does he really think deep down and would he ever truly admit it to us? What does a commander do in these situations? What do the books tell them to do? Honestly tell their men that they are about to die so make peace with the Heavenly Father or do they keep it from us till the bitter end, so that we go on - and go down - fighting?

Is this really it? Is this all I am going to know of life before I've even experienced it? I've never even really fallen in love. My eyes moisten. Thankfully it's pretty dark in here.

Suddenly a hand is upon my shoulder. The Skipper's characteristic voice speaks directly to me. "We're not finished yet. No - not yet. Michaelis, how much more time do you need?"

"Four or five hours at least sir. Could be more. At this pace and so few men...'

"Keep them rotating, every hour, half-hour, or quarter-hour - whatever it takes! Understand?"

"Yes sir."

"Schumacher?"

"Auxiliary diesel and generator both drowned. We've got plugs in at least three dozen or so outboard valves and those are still leaking. Propeller packings are underwater. Port compressors completely on the fritz. Hydraulic ram pump's blown several gaskets but that can be put right. Main engine sump number four and clean fuel oil tank number one I'm pretty certain are both cracked, otherwise the gauges are toast. Busted connector rod on the engine induction hull valve, and the hydrogen detectors down. The cherry on top of it all is that the pressure hull's been dished in the after battery compartment."

"Get that hydrogen detector back up - first priority."

Schumacher struggles to stay upright. "I've got men on it now sir, but the maneuvering room main control panel is still down, half the circuits are fried out. For all I know there may be damage to one or both shafts and we may not even have a rudder. When the stern hit I know I heard tearing metal, that's a sound you don't forget. It could've been prop guards or a tube shutter, but it could have been the rudder ripping off."

"If the rudder's gone, it's over." Pike notes calmly.

"Theoretically,' Michaelis says quickly, challenging him, 'we can steer the boat with the screws."

For the first time humor enters the Skipper's face. "In enemy waters twenty-five hundred miles from home with three destroyers overhead?"

The XO leans back and closes his eyes. "The boat is becoming a pile of junk around us."

"First things first,' our Commander notes, 'we clear the water out of the boat."

Forty-four hours now. The thermometer reads a hundred and twenty degrees. There is no air; only a dense, dank, choking fog of humidity that steals the last ounces of fluid from our tormented bodies and soaks it up like some insidious moisture-gorging monster. My abdomen screams with pain. For the last thirty minutes I've been vomiting non-stop due to dehydration. My body though won't accept the hot, viscous water that we're forced to drink. Heat permeates everything; in some of the spaces where the pressure hull is exposed from the normal tangle of cables, wires, and pipes, men can be found clustered and pressed up against it. They seek what little relief there is from the cool thermocline outside. Kemper says men are actually ceasing to sweat. Result: impending heatstroke.

More of us are beginning to lose our grip on reality; some of the men talk of just opening everything up and flooding the boat in one fell swoop - in effect committing mass suicide. Others fantasize about releasing a kind of acid from the torpedo tubes that would eat through the hulls of the Nip destroyers. Some want to charge up their Momsen lungs, slip out a flooded torpedo tube, and swim back to Pearl. The most clear-headed among us want to get to the surface simply to fight it out face-to-face with the Japs. Better to go down fighting than suffer a slow death from asphyxiation.

The Chief shuffled by a moment ago; telling me that the count of the depth charges dropped on us is near three hundred. If every charge weighs five hundred pounds, that's *one hundred fifty thousand pounds of high explosive* - and yet our wretched, heat rash afflicted bodies still function!

Pulses of sonar still quiver through the depths. The dogs have not yet given up the hunt.

Forty-six hours now. Inside the boat it is still as death. One of the strongest of us has gone down, Daschler has suffered a heatstroke. Kemper isn't confident he'll make it. In his arms Tashtego carried him to his bunk and now watches over him like a mother hen.

The Chief suddenly appears from nowhere. Standing above me he stares down through two glistening orbs of St. Elmo's Fire. He wants to know if I'm Catholic.

"No - Protestant. Why?"

He looks at me with a strange glint in his eyes and smiles. Reaching down he presses my arm. "We'll be taken care of - my boy is sure of it." Then without another word he ducks into the adjoining compartment as Michaelis comes in. "Five minutes people! Five minutes and back to stations!"

Skjonsby shuffles up. "Sir, did the Chief tell you?"

I stare at his fuzzy image.

"I saw it too...she was there."

"Huh?"

"It was during one of those heavy strings we took, just after the vent riser on number three went that she appeared."

Something's wrong with my eyes, I can't seem to focus. "Who?"

"Mary - the Mother of Christ! Both the Chief and McClusky can back me up. We'd lost the vent riser; we're shipping water fast. Depth charges cooking off all over the place, then something caused us to turn around and there she was - standing with her hands held out palms up. She was so beautiful, so incredibly beautiful, with a look of incredible peace. And it was like she spoke but we heard her inside our heads, not with our ears. She said "everything will be all right, you will be saved, this is not your time to come." And we just stood there, everything seemed to stop. No seawater rushing in anymore, no more exploding depth charges, and then she was gone as quickly as she'd come.' He leans closer to me, "It wasn't a hallucination sir, I know what I saw. We'll make it out of this sir. I'd bet my life on it."

Nearing fifty hours now. Chief Schrier reports specific gravity of forward and after batteries barely above one point zero, imperative to surface. Atmosphere inside the boat cannot be expected to sustain life much longer. CO2 level approaching three and a half percent. Oxygen and compressed air reserves exhausted. Inside temperature one hundred twenty-two degrees. Sound watch can still hear enemy destroyers overhead. Regular patterns dropped every twenty minutes, very close. Boat has sustained heavy damage from enemy countermeasures. Every man aboard barely functioning due to dehydration and heat sickness. Can't see how -

The rest of the paragraph is hidden by the Skipper's folded right arm, his head cradled by the nook of his elbow. In the process of making a notation in the log he must have been overwhelmed with exhaustion, falling asleep here over the logbook on the wardroom table. How long has he been up? Not only fifty hours but also two days before that. He passed his limit ages ago. If it weren't for the heavy beard, tousled hair, and drawn lines round his eyes he might resemble a child sleeping over schoolbooks. His silent lips parted, deep breaths that come out in a kind of sigh, and a chewed pencil still clutched in the thumb and first two fingers of his right hand. *"Come unto me, all ye that labor and are heavy laden, and I will give you rest."* Matthew 11:28 - why did I think of that now?

I look around the wardroom; how it seems to have changed since we left port. Then it was strange to me, new and unnatural. Now I can't imagine ever not have knowing it. This worn linoleum topped table, already etched with cracks and stains that I could draw in my sleep. The scuffed up floor with its hodgepodge of boot skids, coffee and juice stains, streaks of grease, oil marks and sea salt. The now-glassless and dented framed photo of the boat's christening on the starboard wall, looking fresh and resplendent as it slides down the ways at Electric Boat Co. The shelves, which once held numerous books and magazines, as well as the Chief's ingenious little chess set, are now dirty, grimy, and bare. All the laughter is now gone too - along with the swaggering, self-assured voices of young warriors sailing out to do battle with the forces of evil. Our noble leader, normally so cocked, poised, and ready for action now lies sprawled out over the log, unconscious and beaten. The rest of the officers lie slumped throughout the boat, at their various battle stations, waiting and as apathetic as condemned men awaiting their executioner.

The mark of war has indelibly imprinted itself upon everything, human and machine.

Swish-swish.... Swish-swish.... Swish-swish....

The screws of the enemy are never far away. Pinging sonar - eerie dream-like echoes inside a tomb. There are several different reverberations, meaning several destroyers. *They are still looking.* I close my eyes and grind my teeth in anger. *Will it never end?*

"They just can't stand not knowing." The Skipper declares bitterly, lifting his head up and gazing vacantly into the overhead. He attempts to rub the fatigue from his eyes, then, leaning forward; he cradles his head in his hands as if trying to hold it together. "I've got such a damned headache." He crinkles his mouth into a wry smile. "You know what I miss? Birds - the sound of birds singing in the trees, -you know like in the springtime? Dogwoods in blossom - God I miss that." His glazed-over eyes stare into another world.

"Simple, mundane pleasures that everyone else takes for granted - at least people who've never been shot at. I'd give anything - ' his voice trails off as he gazes down at the mess on the table. As I study him his face goes mask-like, as if he's descended into some sort of trance. What forces battle inside him? Has he turned away from the hope of our salvation? Is he resigned to our death? I desperately need his guidance - to know all - so I know where to go in my own mind - do I prepare for life or death. But I cannot speak. Try as I might, I open my mouth but nothing will come out.

What is happening to me?

The Skipper closes his eyes and sighs. His mouth hangs open like a vacant hole, it's outline indiscernible behind his beard. "It's all so fleeting,' he whispers without opening his eyes, 'Do you think that in fifty years anyone will care what we did here? Or what happened here? Or how much tonnage we sunk? Will anyone give a shit? God - I feel so old. I feel like I've lived a hundred years." The corners of his open mouth then draw back and his teeth come forward. The whole movement forms a sort of snarl. 'This war's just three months old,' he growls, still maintaining the threatening mask, 'This will go on for years - with or without us."

From somewhere comes a hollow thumping sound, then a gurgling and spitting - very close by. No idea what it is. It's just too dark in here - there's only one light bulb burning, and that has surely been a most recent replacement as the floor and the table are littered with shards of broken glass. A moment later it is drowned by a sudden increased of screw sounds, *Thrishthrush-Thrishthrush-Thrishthrush-Thrishthrush* - a destroyer running at high rpm's. Ten seconds later comes the shudder, shock, and roar of exploding depth charges. The Skipper shakes his head and inclines his icy gaze up into the overhead, "Missed again you stupid bastards! You're shitting in the wrong hole - idiots!" Rivers of sweat cascade down the Skipper's now contorted mask, giving the appearance that his face is melting away. A rage boils up inside of him. A rage of helplessness - of madness - or remorse? Guilt? A rage for his men and their sanity?

Then it disappears as quickly as it came. In the blink of an eye the expression returns to the usual visage of composed and calm. But his eyes - his eyes still rage with the fire of a blistering inferno and his body begins to follow their lead until the metamorphosis is complete; now he is cocked and coiled - as if ready to strike. Has he gone mad or is it yet another dimension of his perplexing allure?

The Skipper - our Mars - the perfect God of War.

Footsteps out in the passageway. Movement past the open curtain; I catch a glimpse of the Chief's frame bending down to lift off the deck plate that leads to the battery compartment. He's holding a tubular instrument in his hand - a hydrometer. So he's going to check the specific gravity of the cells again. God, can there be anything left?

The XO appears in the entranceway. In the light his face looks completely ashen and devoid of all color. Is this the way impending death leaves its mark? 'Sir,' he reports through narrow slits, 'Schumacher reports bucket brigade on stand down, water has been sufficiently distributed from after engine room space,' he pauses and seems to be struggling for breath, 'We should be able to pump outboard now."

The Skipper's staring at him with a strange glint in his eye; a wet, glossy kind of gleam. "Thank you Mr. Bainbridge,' he says it with difficulty, 'it will commence on my order."

The XO blinks slowly, falters, then rallies himself and forces a smile. "Yes sir."

"Go get some rest Bainbridge."

The XO blinks again, then attempts a clumsy smirk as if the Skipper had just regaled him with a dirty joke. "Thank you sir, I'd rather stay at my post. There's too - too many men out already." Without another word, he turns and shuffles drunkenly back to the control room.

The Skipper stares after him. The glossiness of his eyes has turned moist. Light in them sparkles and dances about. His eyes blink several time in quick succession. "They don't make men like this just anywhere,' he stammers, droppings his eyes to the tabletop. "How fortunate I am to be blessed with them!"

The Chief sticks his head in from the passageway, his face blanched and filthy. "Sir, we're ready."

The Skipper nods as the Chief disappears. He leans forward, steadies himself on the table, and uses it to help him get up.

The huddled mass of stinking, sweat-drenched bodies circle round the open pump room grating like mourners at an open grave. Two stooped, sweat-drenched forms - Schumacher and Lemert - squat in the hole like gravediggers, giving the pumps a good going over to make sure they will work when the Chief flicks the switch. This is important; the batteries are in such a state that we cannot afford to waste one ampere of current.

"Three.... Five.... both sides clear.... seven,' the Chief mumbles - half-incoherent - at the high-pressure manifold, checking over the state of our ballast tanks. They must be empty if we are to claw our way to the surface. There's too much water in the boat already.

The Skipper stands at the plotting table - a queen bee in the center of the hive. The royal figure supervises our mission to get our girl buoyant again - to get her back out of the sand and restore her to previous health - like the paralytic touched by the hand of Jesus.

"Ship's time?' the Skipper snaps curtly.

"Zero two twenty-five sir." Donnelly mumbles from the tower.

That means it's dark up top. Was that part of the Skipper's plan, waiting it out another twelve hours until darkness closed in? If we had tried to surface in daylight we wouldn't have lasted long. But in the darkness we may have a fighting chance.

"Sir,' Waldron asks weakly from his position behind the diving controls, a position he's held non-stop for the last fifty hours. "What about propulsion and steerage?"

"Let's get her out of the sand first,' the Skipper avers sharply. "If we can get the boat to the surface, the crew survives - or has a better chance of it despite what the Japs say.

"That is my sole concern - all of you. If we can get under way and have control over the boat, that's icing on the cake. But now we *must* get to the surface or else."

A clinking sound followed by footsteps. A perspiring form emerges out of the pump room - it's Lemert. He staggers a few steps, then collapses onto the deck plates. "Water - water....' he moans in agony, '- something to drink....please."

Waldron bends down and cradles Lemert's head in his hands and reaches for a jug of water next to the tower ladder. "Drink this slow - real slow! Don't gulp it!' Uncapping the jug, he lifts it to Lemert's lips, who's staring at him through unfocused eyes. "Why's it so cold in here?"

The jug halts mid-air. "What are you mean - cold?"

"It's cold.' Lemert whimpers.

Waldron looks over at the Skipper. "Sir - he's shivering -'

The Skipper's looks over with alarm. "He's going into heatstroke -'

Lemert grasps the jug with his right hand and up-ends it - gulping down large amounts of water. Waldron immediately tries to wrestle it from him, "Don't - !'

Not a second later, Lemert shoves the bottle away from his mouth and spasmodically vomits, all over himself and the Third Watch officer. In a flash the Skipper is beside him, with his arm wrapping protectively around Lemert's heaving shoulders. It lasts a good half-minute, until Lemert has expended all the water out of his system. Wiping the gruel from his mouth, he looks up at Waldron, who's attempting to clean off the worst of it with a sweat-drenched towel. "I'm sorry sir."

"Forget it,' the Skipper says soothingly, laying his hand on Lemert's shoulder almost like a father to a sick son. "I've done worse on many an occasion. I want you to go get some rest now. Okay?' Lemert screws up his face and mumbles the first syllables of protest, but the Skipper cuts him off gently. "Consider it an order."

Lemert stares at him a moment, then drunkenly nods through a pinched, pallid face contorted in pain. "The pumps are...ready sir."

The Skipper nods quietly. He quickly blinks twice. "You go rest now,' he says, nodding again. "You must - we need you. You're our diving officer, remember?' Lemert manages to raise his head high enough to look back at the Skipper. "Thank you sir. I really am sorry."

"Enough.' The Skipper looks up, 'Copenhaver, help Lieutenant Lemert to his bunk."

"Yes sir." The petty officer steps forward, helping Lemert to his feet. Arm in arm they stumble forward over a canted deck. The Skipper watches them, his face back to the usual unreadable mask. "Contacts sound?"

"Closest contact four.... Maybe five thousand yards max."

"Very well. Schumacher - ' the Skipper has to take a pause for breath, 'commence outboard pumping!"

"Sir." Schumacher hits the starting switch. Will there be enough juice in the batteries to run the pumps? Nothing is happening. He hits the switch again: with a heavy *thunk,* the pumps engage.

Praise God!

It is the melody of our existence - our carillon of being. Without it we would soon be no more. Suddenly there is life in these pale, stooped, wretched figures of men that previously lumbered about like primitive apes. Whatever that outcome now, at least it has been preordained that we will not die here on the bottom like victims of some pagan suttee ritual.

Schumacher's completely animated with glee. With a grin as wide as his face will allow, he bounces up and down from the pump room like a jack-in-the-box gone berserk. His mission accomplished - getting the pumps working - his exhilaration is total. The Chief squats on the floor plates and starts chuckling like some nervous maniac, dropping his head into his hands and shaking. Can't tell now whether he's laughing or crying. Waldron braces himself at the diving controls by clenching a manifold pipe just above his head and looks around with his pipe jutting from his mouth as if he knew what would happen all along. His eyes betray an inner release, shutting tight for moments at a time then opening and staring up into the overhead. The compartment explodes with joy; Lichty stands beside me, blinking away tears and giggling like a drunken man. Next to him Wainwright looks completely stunned as he stares around with eyes as big as saucers. The XO too, perched over by the gyrocompass repeater clenches his greasy, bloodstained fists in defiance. There's probably not a square inch of skin that isn't torn and bleeding. It is the brand of working deep in the bowels of the aft engine room space.

A hand touches my shoulder; it's Michaelis grinning at me through a filthy face. "We're gonna make it! My God - we're gonna make it!" Brushing by me, he passes the broad, sweating back of Tashtego - who's head is bowed as if in prayer - still at the diving controls after nearly *fifty* hours.

"*Gaudeamus igitur juvenes dum sumus*,' the Skipper chants, 'Latin for "Let us live then, and be glad."

"Fifteen hundred pounds transferred out sir!" Schumacher reports, crowing like a rooster as his head pokes up from the pump room for the hundredth time. "Another five hundred or so and she should lift out of the sand!" Without another word he drops back down into the pump room. Even without his report we would notice that our list to starboard has lessened. Now we no longer have to scale the deck plates when we want to move around.

"When we get to the surface there can't be any screwing around, we've got to make a course straight for Pearl Harbor - the boat's condition demands it." The Skipper declares, rooted next to the plotting table as the XO lays out a chart for him with his bloody hands. The Skipper recoils at the sight. "Jesus Bainbridge!'

"Sorry sir. Bolt heads, nuts, and C-clamps aren't real kind on the skin."

"Better have Kemper take a look at them." The Skipper notes without humor, 'What woman is going to want to dance with a mummy when we get home?"

"When I get a minute I will."

The Skipper fixes him with a steely gaze. "You have a minute *now*. Get Kemper in here!"

The only way it is possible to breathe now is to let our mouths hang open and draw in whatever we can. We actually have to suck for breath. A shudder suddenly runs through the boat - *she's moving*! If it weren't for that lingering destroyer up top, the entire control room would go wild again. But to live we must be quiet. The bilge pumps are bad enough, their noise raises the hair on the back of my neck.

Groaning metal. The boat shivers again. The hull creaks and pops - veritable sounds of life! I exchange smiles with Michaelis. "She's righting herself!' he stammers euphorically. It's almost as if the boat has an innate knowledge of her rightful condition.

"You keep pumping you hear?' Michaelis jabbers - still excitedly staring at the depth gauge - 'You just keep pumping you beautiful old girl, and we'll get you out of this! Don't you even think about stopping! We'll protect you! We'll get you back to the barn - don't you worry!"

Let every sound pierce me to the soul! Let it wash over me with all the force of a waterfall! Let it all be cold and crystal clear to each of my senses! For everything I see, touch, hear, and smell, means that I am alive.

"She's clearing!'

"Bow planes on full rise!' Waldron orders excitedly, 'Stern up twenty!"

Beneath us the deck plates rumble and shake - a minor earthquake is in progress.

"C'mon old girl,' Waldron coaxes, his face flushed, stroking a sweating patch of the pressure hull - 'You can do it! Easy now, just lift up right out of the sand and we'll all be born again."

"Talk to me sound!"

"Closest audible contact.... at least.... four thousand yards sir!"

"Type of machinery?"

"Turbine sir!" Shit - that's a destroyer for sure.

"Fuck!' somebody spits.

"Quartermaster, inform maneuvering room to stand by to answer bells!"

"Aye-aye sir!"

The Skipper draws a breath and flexes his cheek muscles. "It's now or nothing!

Everything we've been able to accomplish over the past fifty hours can be completely fouled up by one wrong move. We won't have a second chance. We have neither the battery power nor the oxygen to survive any longer. If anyone carries any weight with the chairman of the board, collect it now!"

"Here she comes!' Waldron exclaims, staring into the large depth gauge in front of him. The glassless gauge's face shows the quivering needle. I draw a breath and close my eyes, praying silently for it to move faster. *Dear God, grant us deliverance. Grant us life over an impending asphyxiating death.*

"It's moving!' the XO shouts with rising glee, almost wrenching his hands away from Kemper. "It's moving!"

My eyes snap open: the needle *is* groping its way back over the hash mark for three hundred and eighty-foot mark toward three hundred and seventy! The bow is first to break free of the bottom; sluggish and uncertain like a baby whale in its first movements of life in the water. Then, it reaches a point where the stern must come with it. It too - feebly - begins to ascend.

The entire boat shakes, quivers, shudders, and pops: we are resurrected from the grave.

Tashtego and Howe grab a hold of each other's arms and raise them together in a clenched fist while keeping one hand on the control wheel. Waldron slaps both of them on the back and literally shakes with joy. Schumacher's torso has popped up out of the pump room and he's grunting like a frat boy, the XO's wiping tears from his eyes, and the Skipper remains the proud, calculating father. "All right! All right -' he exhorts, 'keep it down! We've still got company remember! Pass the word Mr. Bainbridge, everybody keep quiet until we're on the surface. We're still not out of this thing yet. And well done Schumacher, now get your ass aft - we're turning the motors over."

"Aye-aye sir." Schumacher replies, beaming like a virgin who's just busted his first cherry.

The Skipper slowly moves over to the ladder leading up into the conning tower. "Donnelly, ring up one-third speed. Course is one seven zero."

"Aye sir."

The Skipper turns to us. "Now the moment of truth. Let's find out if we have any screws."

If we have lost our propellers, our escape from the bottom will be but a pyrrhic victory. Have we come this far to lose it all now?

Tense moments while the maneuvering room engages the motors. Will there be enough juice in the batteries to turn the screws? Could the water have shorted them out? The Chief's last hydrometer reading barely registered - then what? Without propulsion we've had it.

An eerie, humming sound suddenly splits the quiet, the motors are turning *but are the screws are still there?*

"Pit log shows two knots sir,' Donnelly reports, his voice choking with emotion, 'making way of the seabed!"

Salvation! Faces around me beam like suns.

The Skipper forestalls the impending cheering by ordering everyone to remain quiet. "Now,' he says flatly, 'let's see if we've still got a rudder. Helm, come left to one five five!"

"Coming left to one five five-aye sir!"

My heart thumps loudly in my chest. Every vein, every nerve, every muscle is coiled tight. Even my backside is puckered.

"Present course,' the helmsman reports, 'one six eight...one six seven...one six six...*moving toward one five five*!"

Venting like a blast of high pressure air, I let it all fall away; the gnawing fear in the pit of my empty stomach, the horrendous pain that threatens to burst my skull, the suffocating claustrophobia, and the blistering heat which prickles our spent flesh into chicken skin. Let it all pass away into some dark unknown corner of the mind and be forgotten. Or better yet, let it lie here where it all took place, at the bottom of the Bungo Strait almost four hundred feet below the ocean's surface.

"Chief -' I hear the Skipper say softly under his breath, 'thank your lady friend for me."

Chief Schrier nods his bearded, sweat-drenched head. "I already have sir."

The Skipper grins like a high school senior on his prom night. "Let's head for the barn. We take her up in five minutes."

A message comes in from the after engine room: Schumacher reports the port crankshaft bent about five-eighths of an inch. Bad, but not horrible, it could be a lot worse. Still, it's going to make noise, but after what we've been through I can't imagine anything holding us back now.

Duffy explodes: "*Sir - screw sounds right above us*!"

It all happens in slow motion; the Skipper's face is a mask of disbelief. His eyes flicker and he looks at me, but his face has changed somehow. It takes a second for me to realize that I'm now staring into the face of an old man - as old as myself.

The mark of war has burned into both of us like acid.

Duffy is screaming now at the top of his lungs, what is he saying? I can't quite comprehend. Depth charges in the water? No, that can't be, not after -

Then I hear the explosions...

        *   *   *

"Well, it's about that time."

"You sure he can make it?"

"I don't know - but he might want to try after all this. He's earned it."

"Haven't we all?"

"How bad is he?"

"Kemper says he's well enough now. And besides, these boys haven't seen the sun in months. It just isn't healthy."

"Well, let's give it a try - where's Kemper?"

"On his way."

"Alvin? Alvin? Can you hear me?"

Warmth on my shoulder and a soothing, familiar voice. I open my eyes to see a bearded, chiseled face inches from my own. The expression is calm, a hint of a smile on the carved lips. The eyes sparkle. For a brief moment, the face is strange to me. Why? It's clean - no filth, dirt, grease, or sweat. Even the hair is combed.

I try to sit up.

A restraining arm. "Easy now."

Where am I? The place is familiar - yet oddly strange. There are other faces too; there's the Chief, Michaelis, Schumacher, Waldron - erstwhile pipe clenched in his teeth - and Lemert. They are poised around me like a host of receiving angels.

"Where am I?'

The Skipper smiles. "My bunk. Where'd you think - a Japanese prison camp? You've been out for some time."

Michaelis bends forward. "You were out the whole way back; those Jap ash cans really did a number on you."

"Severe concussion would be the medical term for it." Kemper states, drawing back the curtain and coming into the room.

Schumacher clears his throat, "We thought you might want to come up to the bridge, if you're up to it. We're here. "

"Here?"

"Pearl.' The Skipper grins laconically. 'Would you prefer Tokyo?"

I try to nod, but there's something wrong with my head. I raise my hand and feel something soft.

"Bandages.' The Skipper explains. "That last string knocked you headfirst into the high-pressure air manifold. Damn Jap bastard was just hanging over us with his engines off, must have dropped his last charges because then he sped off at full speed. You got one hell of a crack on the skull. It was real touch and go for awhile. You had Kemper and me real worried."

"Think you're up for a trip to the bridge?" Waldron asks, chewing his pipe stem.

"Yeah. I...would."

The Skipper turns to Kemper. "It's okay with the doc?" Kemper shrugs, "It's okay with me if it's okay with him,' he says pointing to me. "Just take it slow all right?"

The Skipper rises. "You're the boss doc!"

I worm my way carefully through the passageway into the control room. Familiar and friendly faces greet me at every turn; there's Copenhaver - ready to clamber up onto the deck to head up the maneuvering watch - his cheek misshapen and bulging from a wad of chew. The recovered Daschler and Tashtego stand just behind him, staring at me with mixed looks of pleasure and surprise. Our redheaded Yeoman, who nods and smiles as I pass by. Figures I have come to know, all standing about chattering aimlessly about who's going to score the biggest tonight at the Forbidden City.

Beneath and around me, the boat throbs with life; pulsating with every compression stroke of her diesels. And from somewhere comes the wailing notes of a bagpipe.

Climbing out of the tower hatch, the brilliant sun is suspended in the sky like a great and precious jewel, beating down and warming my hands and face as I steady them on the hatch rim. The deep blue sky radiates warmth and illuminates a world I despaired of ever seeing again. Fresh air, brilliant sunlight, sweet smell of vegetation, birds singing; the auspices of life.

The bagpipe is louder now. A figure above me turns around, "Well look who it is!"

As I stand up I find myself staring into the bearded, grinning face of Pike, with the XO right next to him. "You made it after all!" I move to the bulwark and rest on it. Yes, that's McGowan down on deck, standing just starboard of the three-inch gun. Over half the teak decking is missing, and something's odd about the three-inch gun.

"How do you like that?" The XO asks, gesturing at the deck gun, 'Took one hell of an explosion to warp that barrel!"

"To hell with that!' Pike exclaims, 'Look what they did to our deck! Fucking bastards!"

I stare at the misshapen barrel of our gun canted sickeningly to one side. A fluttering movement catches my eye; along our radio antenna that stretches from the bow to the top of the periscope shears there are about a dozen or so little Japanese flags.

"We have something for you,' the XO says, reaching under the bulwark and producing a cap - my cap. I thought I'd lost it. "Here,' Pike takes it from him and places it gingerly on my head, then steps back and studies it a moment. "No - too straight, needs more of an angle,' he reaches up and cocks it to one side and then grins, 'There! You're a combat officer now; combat officers always wear cocked caps! Now you're free to get killed on the next patrol."

"Isn't he just precious!" Waldron cracks with sarcasm.

There is a presence at my side - the Skipper. He winks at me. "You passed the test Watts. You made it.' He turns and cries out to the maneuvering watch already milling about on deck, 'Stand by all lines!"

"Well,' Waldron observes, cupping the bowl of his pipe in his hands to shelter it from the strong breeze coming over the bulwark. The wind caresses my face, carrying with it the aroma of fragrant tobacco, 'What's on the menu tonight at the Royal Hawaiian?"

Pike guffaws. "A thirty ounce steak, ten beers, then off to the Forbidden City for me!"

"How about you Waldron?' The Skipper wants to know.

Waldron looks thoughtful a moment, then half-smiles. "Keeping a few promises I made."

"And you Sir?" I pose.

The Skipper's eyes look skyward. "Enjoy being alive."

There's a navy band on the floating platform to starboard of us. The bandleader drops his arm and immediately "Anchors Aweigh" bursts brassily out over the water.

"Dammit!' the Skipper curses, 'Now I can't hear my bagpipes!'

'C'est la guerre!" Waldron winks.

"STAND BY FOR NUMBER ONE!"

Our hammering diesels push our bullnose closer and closer to the pier, until Tashtego - on the bow - is close enough to receive our first line.

"Whatever you do boys,' the Skipper adds, staring at the rows of dress uniforms, 'pull out all the stops - we cast off again in three weeks."

How awful we must look to them; dirty and bearded, gaunt and wan, mere ghosts of what once used to be men. How long has it been since we went out? How long ago was it that we cast off from this very harbor to sail out into mortal combat with the enemies that dared attack our country? The answer is in months, but in reality it was a lifetime ago. There are things in me - and all of us - that did not exist then. Things that will take me years to fathom. Things that only men who have looked death straight in the face and walked away could ever understand. I am no longer the inexperienced boy that stepped onto this deck a mere four months ago. I - along with every man aboard - has been smelted and reformed under the anvil of a brutal war and a raging sea. Our bodies and our wills forged and hardened, rolled and pounded and steeled to iron. It is that iron will that takes us back out in three weeks, to again be thrust into the conflagration of war. It's going to take all the iron in us to endure what we must, but there are things in this world bigger than ourselves. We are brothers in a common cause. And while there is a higher cause above all, the most basic is that we do it for each other.

"TAKE IN NUMBER ONE!" The Skipper's deep voice booms out, echoing off the water as the waiting bluejacket heaves the line out to us.

Tashtego hunches over like a shortstop as the line's weighted end lands neatly with a heavy *thunk* on the bow. As he grabs it and makes it fast to the bow cleat, the rest of the lines arc through the air, all landing heavily on deck. The maneuvering watch scrambles madly around, taking them in. With a shudder, the bullnose eases against the pier.

Sailor...rest your oar.

To find out more about Robert E. Wilhelm III or **QuarterDeck** Production Corp, visit us at www.quarterdeckent.co. See also our Facebook pages @ www.facebook.com/mastersofwarseries & www.facebook.com/marscherlordsfilm

Other titles brought to you by **QuarterDeck** Production Corp: ***Compendium of Navigational Techniques;***, *Wilhelm's School of Navigation: United States Coast Guard Approved Curriculum for Licensed Candidates by Bob Wilhelm, Master Ocean.*

www.ingramcontent.com/pod-product-compliance
Lightning Source LLC
Chambersburg PA
CBHW080432110426
42743CB00016B/3140